Alternative Religions

Alternative religions attract great public, academic and government interest in our apparently post-Christian society. Yet how did all the 'alternatives' develop, what are their beliefs and practices and how significant is their impact in terms of the world's religions and society?

This book presents a comprehensive introduction to the major forms of alternative religions: Cults, Sects, New Religious Movements, the New Age, Fundamentalism, Pentecostalism, Ethnic Religions and Quasi-religions. Stephen Hunt presents sociological insights into the rise of alternative religions, their beliefs and practices, their impact, who joins them and why, and how they are being classified and could be re-classified in the future. Public and legal controversies surrounding some alternative religions, such as the so-called 'dangerous cults', are also explored. Offering a broad introduction to alternative religions, this book offers students added insights into contemporary themes such as secularisation, post-modernity, links between religion, healing and human potential, and changes in our global culture.

For Jonathon and Oliver who know what it is to have an 'alternative' father.

Alternative Religions

A Sociological Introduction

Stephen J. Hunt

University of the West of England, Bristol, UK

ASHGATE

Published by
Ashgate Publishing Limited
Gower House
Croft Road
Aldershot
Hampshire GU11 3HR
England

Ashgate Publishing Company
Suite 420
101 Cherry Street
Burlington
VT 05401-4405
USA

Ashgate website: http://www.ashgate.com

British Library Cataloguing in Publication Data
Hunt, Stephen, 1954-
   Alternative religions : a sociological introduction
   1. Cults 2. Sects 3. Religion and sociology 4. Religions
   I. Title
   306.6'91

Library of Congress Cataloging-in-Publication Data
Hunt, Stephen, 1954-
   Alternative religions : a sociological introduction / Stephen Hunt.
      p. cm.
   Includes bibliographical references and index.
   ISBN 0-7546-3410-8 (pbk. : alk. paper) -- ISBN 0-7546-3409-4 (hardback : alk. paper)
      1. Cults. 2. Sects. 3. Religions. 4. Religion and sociology. 5. Christianity and other religions. I. Title.

   BP603 .H87 2003
   306.6--dc21   2002027695

ISBN 0 7546 3409 4 (Hbk)
ISBN 0 7546 3410 8 (Pbk)

Typeset in Minion by Bookcraft Ltd, Stroud, Gloucestershire
Printed and bound in Great Britain by MPG Books Ltd, Bodmin, Cornwall.

Contents

Figures

Tables

Acknowledgements

I would like to thank the following authors whose work has provided material for tables and illustrations: P. Brierley, D. Gerard, R. Gill *et al*, S. Harding *et al*, R. Hutton, R. Robertson, U. Sjodin, and R. Wallis. Permissions have been obtained wherever possible.

Every effort has been made to trace all the copyright holders, but if any have been inadvertently overlooked the publishers will be pleased to make the necessary arrangements at the first opportunity.

Acronyms

3HO	Healthy Happy Holy Organization
CLCOC	The Central London Church of Christ
COG	Children of God
DLM	Divine Light Mission
ISKCON	The International Society for Krishna Consciousness
NCCC	New Creation Christian Community
NCR	New Christian Right
NLP	Neuro-Linguistic Programme
NRM/s	New Religious Movement/s
SDA	Seventh-day Adventists
TM	Transcendental Meditation
WWCG	Worldwide Church of God

Introduction

'Alternative religion', as sociologists have broadly designated the range of religious expressions outside the remit of traditional Christianity, appears to be enjoying an increasing popularity along with a heightened public profile over the last four decades or so. There are several reasons why this is the case. Perhaps the most obvious is that in what is frequently assumed to be the largely secular societies of the West, any form of religiosity stands out in clear relief and offers itself as something of a curiosity. This is even more evident when a good number of alternative religions are perceived as displaying a variety of beliefs and practices which are unfamiliar, perhaps bizarre, and at times seem distinctly alien and exotic since they may originate outside the Western cultural environment.

A related explanation as to why alternative religions are of growing interest is because many are seen as controversial. In fact, even in a secular society where all indications point to the decline of the Christian churches, forms of religiosity designated 'alternative' suggest not just a minority lifestyle choice, but adherence to spiritualities with less than respectable attributes. Thus, it is probably fair to say that any mention of alternative religion is likely to conjure up images of so-called 'cults' and 'sects', and those which are designated in this way have inevitably come to be ascribed a certain notoriety. Some may be appraised as explicitly harmful, with the common assumption that they 'brainwash' their followers who are under the destructive control of unscrupulous charismatic leaders or manipulating gurus teaching all manner of curious doctrines. As far as the teachings are concerned, negative public perceptions infer a fair amount of ignorance and tend to focus upon a narrow set of beliefs of even the better-known alternative religions. This leads to generalized and often broad assumptions, for example that Mormons have many wives or Jehovah's Witnesses will not permit their followers to have blood transfusions. More often than not, these oversimplified, often false, popular accounts lead to stereotyping and a social marginalization of individual members.

A primary objective of this volume is to endeavour to explain what the alternative religions actually amount to and who believes and practises what. It thus seeks to inform by considering a wide range of 'alternatives'. Some are old, some new. Some demand austere and dedicated lifestyles, others perhaps offer something akin to a leisure time activity, so that they might appear to amount to little more than a titillating novelty. Some have beliefs that are fairly familiar, others are more obscure. A number of the alternatives are home-grown, some imported. A few are enjoying considerable growth, while others are experiencing a steady decline. Considering such a variety is, of course, no easy task. The vast expressions of alternative religions that now exist display a wide divergence of beliefs, practices, and orientations. There is, for instance, a great deal of difference between the teachings, ethos, and organizational structure of Scientology, Mormonism, and the New Age movement. Therefore, each needs to be considered in its own right.

This book also has a number of other overlapping objectives. Since it largely adopts a sociological approach, it seeks to account for the apparent rise to popularity of many of the alternative religions. Here, an examination of central theoretical frameworks is imperative. Among them are those that have been advanced, particularly over the last forty years, with the rise of so-called New Religious Movements (NRMs). In the 1960s and 1970s, an entire plethora of theories was developed to explain the proliferation of those such as the Unification Church, the Jesus movement, and an assortment of movements based on eastern mysticism. However, more innovating forms of religion have emerged, epitomized by the New Age movement, and these require new theoretical frameworks by which to understand and account for them. To the fore are those that focus on aspects of a 'spiritual marketplace'. Where consumerism is the dominant aspect of life in Western societies, there is a strong element of choice in many personal realms and this includes religiosity. Free from the pressures of conformity and tradition, those who seek religious belief in the contemporary age endeavour to discover a form of faith which is deemed personally suitable and is consistent with their lifestyles preferences.

If there is an increasing element of choice in religious allegiance then it follows that another of the key aims of this book is to answer the question of what do the 'alternatives' have to offer that mainstream Christianity does not? This is a theme explored in Chapter 1. Given that the former have discernibly become more popular at the expense of the latter, it also suggests that we do not live in an entirely faithless society. However, by no means is this a simple and straightforward issue to address and it is one which relates to several others that throw a light on the significance of alternative religion. This includes the matter of how 'alternative' religion, and 'mainline' religion for that matter, might be perceived and defined. Some of these themes are again engaged in the concluding chapter, which also raises the question as to whether the apparent proliferation of alternative religions heralds a religious revival in Western societies. In doing so it engages with some of the major debates in sociology regarding the decline or resurgence of religion and accompanying public discourse as to the social consequences of recent trends.

The subsequent chapters follow a logical progression and there is a certain continuity between them. Chapters 2 and 3 are concerned with categorizing religious organizations. Hence, these chapters begin to tackle the questions already raised: how do we classify the vast range of alternative religions? What criteria should we use? Chapter 2 develops the typology of 'cults' and, likewise, Chapter 3 considers what is meant by the term 'sect'. These are popularly conceived categories, as well as sociological terms, and are frequently misunderstood. To be sure, not all of the 'alternatives' fit neatly into these classifications. However, such typologies do offer a framework by which to discuss the range of religions to be considered throughout this volume and this allows an appreciation of quite how varied the 'alternatives' are. It will become clear in these chapters that integral to these typologies is the matter of their relationship with the outside world and traditional organized religion . In short, do alternative religions mark a hostile reaction to them or, by contrast, reflect the cultural attributes of wider society and perhaps have much in common with established religions? Clearly, these are important areas of research for sociology that dovetail with wider debates concerning secularization, by which we mean the decline of religion.

Another theme discussed in Chapters 2 and 3, and in subsequent chapters, is why certain types of people are attracted to alternative religions irrespective of whether they are adherents to highly organized movements or follow their faiths in less stringent and obvious ways. This is an interesting area because, according to numerous surveys, different types of religion appeal to different types of people. This brings us on to a further theme: the processes by which individuals come to subscribe to their faiths in the first place and (apparently more the case with full-blown religious movements) the experience of 'conversion', however that is defined. Although comprehensively investigated in these early chapters, this is a subject further considered in later ones with particular expressions of religiosity ranging from the New Age to older occultist movements.

The designation 'alternative' religion can apply to groups related to the Christian faith or to those which express one form or another of quasi-Christianity. In short, the classification can be applied to those movements which constitute some derivative of the faith, such as Mormonism or the Jehovah's Witnesses. These more sectarian forms of alternative religion are overviewed in Chapter 3 and, with specific examples, there is a consideration of the social functions of sects, as well as who constitutes the membership, and why some are more successful in terms of growth than others. Again, in relation to Christianity, Chapters 4 and 5 examine the movements which, to some extent at least, overlap with orthodox, if not mainstream Christianity. These are movements of fundamentalism and renewal, respectively. The former examines the contrasting definitions of fundamentalism, ponders the impact of fundamentalist political activism, and questions who joins fundamentalist movements – providing examples within both Protestant and Roman Catholic traditions. Chapter 5 surveys the related subject of contemporary renewal movements and considers its most prolific expression, that is, Pentecostalism, exploring its growth and fragmentation, and its principal teachings and orientations. It is a movement that provides a fine example of an 'alternative' religion which has grown to have a global relevance both inside and outside the established church structures. Sociologically speaking, Pentecostalism tells us a great deal about profound changes within Christianity and the impact of wider culture. Hence, there is some essential overlap in the origins and essential features of both the Christian and non-Christian 'alternatives'.

Chapters 6, 7, and 8 focus on the more recent and overwhelmingly non-Christian expressions of alternative religion. Chapter 6 overviews the so-called NRMs. Like earlier chapters, it commences with the necessary definitions and classifications. It also attempts to explain their attractions, who joins and why, and grapples with some of the controversies surrounding them. Chapter 7 overviews the beliefs and practices of a number of major NRMs according to their origins and dispositions – whether derived from the world religions or amounting to entirely new forms. This includes those derived from Islam, Hinduism, and Sikhism, as well as a mixture of more than one. There is the recognition, however, that these distinctions between new expressions of religion are not entirely satisfactory. This is exemplified with the New Age, the theme of Chapter 8. The New Age movement has features of both the old and new and complex overlapping strands that need to be considered in their own right. What its major attractions appear to be, who subscribes to the movement, and how it impacts on wider society, are among the other major issues discussed.

The term 'neo-pagan' also suggests both the old and the new. Paganism is usually identified with ancient pre-Christian types of religion. Many have been embraced in recent years by people seeking a unique articulation of spirituality. Hence, very ancient expressions of religion are rediscovered but frequently given a very modern veneer. Although overlapping with the New Age, not all pagans claim to be New Agers. This 'alternative' is therefore treated separately in Chapter 9. Among the areas considered are the different strands of paganism, the major organizations that represent them, and invariably who joins and why. This chapter also considers the related theme of esoteric modes of religion and major occultist expressions. The overlapping area of popular types of occultism and mysticism is the subject of Chapter 10. This chapter looks at the growth of less organized and discernible beliefs and practices embraced by the population at large. Included here are the observances of superstition, astrology, and various other forms of divination. There is also scope to consider expressions of oriental occultism that have recently grown in popularity.

Chapter 11 surveys the very contemporary cultural preoccupation with health, healing, and techniques of human potential, and how these dovetail with alternative religions of sometimes apparently very different traditions or cultural trajectories. Sociologically speaking, the relationship between religion and healing is particularly interesting because it tells us a great deal about wider social change. Hence, this chapter explains why these themes have been adapted by religions both old and new and considers the wider significance of health and healing. There is an overview of types of healing strategies endorsed and how these link with specific belief systems.

Another very contemporary area is detailed in Chapter 12, which examines the world religions. The major concerns are with the significance of their impact in Western societies, the relationship with ethnic minorities in the West, and how they add to the growing pool of alternatives. This is obviously a broad subject. While some attention is given to the beliefs and practices of such faiths as Islam, Hinduism, and Judaism, the chapter primarily revolves around the implication of these beliefs in the West in relation to the global context and issues concerned with the assimilation of ethnic minorities. These too are extremely complex themes and are discussed with reference to the major religions in specific global contexts.

Chapter 13, the penultimate chapter, focuses on the so-called 'implicit' religions. For some sociologists religious belief and practice are implicit in a wide range of social phenomena, such as sporting activities, or 'cults' surrounding popular music or film personalities, if they are meaningful and discernibly 'spiritual' to those who take part. It is evident, then, in a discussion of 'implicit' or 'quasi' religions that just about the entire gambit of 'alternatives' is embraced by this book. It might be argued that some of the forms included stretch definitions of religion about as far as they can go. This is, of course, ultimately a matter of opinion. After all, one person's 'alternative' is another's indisputable 'truth'. The final chapter, as already stipulated, pulls many of the threads together and considers the possibilities of a post-Christian society where the 'alternatives' may become the 'mainstream'.

1 Alternative religion in perspective

This opening chapter is primarily concerned with setting an agenda by which a discussion of alternative religions can proceed and with establishing some simple theoretical and conceptual frameworks by which they might be approached. Broadly speaking, this entails exploring a number of principal themes. Firstly, there is the matter of definition. In short, this amounts to answering the question as to what exactly is meant by an 'alternative religion'. Secondly, this chapter seeks to explain the apparent rise of alternative religions in what is often designated as the post-Christian society. In short, what is it about contemporary Western society that has spawned so many 'alternatives'? Thirdly, there is the related issue as to whether such religion is, for the most part, responding to a demand that appears to have been generated for an earnest spirituality outside traditional Christianity. Fourthly, there is the discussion of the possibility that a number of the alternatives have become popular because of observable social and cultural changes and that this includes developments within an increasingly secular and pluralistic society. Finally, this chapter concludes with a brief but imperative overview of several of the pitfalls associated with studying the 'alternatives'.

Problems of definition

In seeking to describe, analyse, and explain the rise of the alternative religions there are two overlapping immediate problems that are closely associated with the matter of definition. One is in regard to what can be designated 'alternative' religion as compared to 'mainstream' religion. The second is a more general issue related to what constitutes 'religion' per se, whether alternative or mainstream. This is important because it has considerable bearing on what is legitimately included in or excluded from our discussion.

As far as the latter issue is concerned, assumptions related to the growth of alternative religion engage with the wider conceptual difficulty of what does or does not amount to a religion in the general use of the term. Indeed, the task of reaching a broad definition of religion has preoccupied sociologists in the field, as well as anthropologists, for a considerable period of time. Much of the debate has centred on the core question as to what should be included in a definition from a wide range of social phenomena. In its unique approach to the subject, the sociology of religion has tended to polarize around two theoretical positions. The first, the *substantive definition*, constitutes a 'minimum definition', that is, religion amounts to a 'belief in spiritual beings' (Tylor 1903, 424). At its simplest, religion is the belief in the supernatural: God, gods, and other spiritual entities. Substantive definitions, in addition, are inclined to correspond more closely to common-sense notions of religion and are primarily influenced by the cultural legacy of Christianity with its monotheistic beliefs and a fairly well articulated system of morality. However, globally, some major faiths such as Buddhism, formally at least, make no reference to a God or gods (although most forms, including the most widespread, entertain beliefs in spirits or supernatural beings). Buddhism is, nonetheless, generally included in any list of notable religions and it is one that has, in one way or another, impacted on some alternative religions in Western societies.

It is also possible to range a good deal wider in attempting a definition of religion by including expressions of faith that may not be obviously religious in a traditional and restrictive sense. Thus, in contrast to substantive definitions, *functional definitions* are primarily concerned with what religion *does*. This is usually held to be in a positive and 'functional' way for the well-being, stability, and integration of society, and in providing a meaningful belief system for individuals. Any social phenomena which does this can be called a 'religion', although it may be void of references to the supernatural. This definition embraces so-called 'quasi' or 'implicit' religions – a number of which at least are recognizable as 'alternative' religions and will be considered in this volume. In simple terms, they amount to aspects of social life that have at least some qualities in common, although often hidden or ambiguous, with more traditional forms of religion.

By applying a substantive definition and thus a broad criterion, it is possible to group a great variety of activities and beliefs together as being 'like religion'. Religion, so defined, is broadened in scope and is inclined to refute theories of inevitable religious decline. Such definitions can also be taken to what may seem extraordinary lengths. Hence, in a definition of religion it might be possible to include, at a stretch, the numerous 'cults' of film, rock music, or sports personalities, as well as UFO cults, and human potential movements. While these social phenomena take definitions of religion to its extreme periphery, the inherent considerable diversity displayed obviously makes it difficult for us to construct categorical statements concerning the nature and rise of the 'alternatives', since definitions of religion are practically endless.

Between the substantive and functional approach to religion are numerous others that establish a definition by drawing on aspects of both. Although it is impossible to generalize, many such approaches define religion according to the characteristic forms it takes. Exemplifying this approach are Ninian Smart's six 'dimensions' of most forms of religion: the experiential, the mythic, the ethical, the doctrinal, the ritual, and its social and institutional expressions (Smart 1995, 7).

Defining religion

As a guide to a broad definition we might consider the following as the principal characteristics of religion. These characteristics do not amount to a universally applicable definition so much as certain features and functions that are frequently found in most forms of religion:

- A belief in an agency (or agencies) which transcend(s) normal sense perception and which may even include details of a different order of (usually spiritual) existence.
- A belief that such an agency affects the natural world and the social world. This agency operates directly and may have created these worlds.
- The belief that at some times in the past supernatural intervention in human affairs has occurred.
- The belief that human fortune in this life and in afterlife (lives) depends on relationships established with, or in accordance with, these transcendental agencies.
- It is frequently believed that while transcendent agencies may arbitrarily dictate an individual's destiny, the individual may, by behaving in prescribed ways, influence his/her experience either in this life or in future life (lives) or both.
- There are prescribed actions for individual, collective, or representative performances that can be recognized as rituals or ceremonies.
- Elements of placatory actions persist by which individuals or collectives may supplicate for special assistance from supernatural sources.
- Expressions of devotion, gratitude, obedience are offered by and often required by believers, usually in the presence of symbolic representations of the supernatural agency(ies).
- Language, objects, places, or seasons of the year that are particularly identified with the supernatural become sacrilized and may themselves become objects of reverence.
- There are regular performances of ritual or exposition, expressions of devotion, celebration, fasting, collective penance, pilgrimage, and re-enactments or commemoration of episodes in the life of deities who have lived in this world, as well as prophets or great teachers of the faith.

- Occasions of worship and exposition of teachings produce the sense of community and relationship of goodwill, fellowship, and common identity.
- Moral rules are often imposed upon believers, although the area of their concern varies: they may be couched in legalistic and ritualistic terms, or they may be canvassed more as conformity with the spirit of a less specific, higher ethic.
- Seriousness of purpose, sustained commitment, and life-long devotion are normally requirements for believers.
- According to their performance, believers accumulate merit or demerit to which a moral economy of reward and punishment is attached. The connection between action and reward/punishment may be influenced by devotional and ritual acts, by confession and repentance, or by special intercession from supernatural agents.
- There is usually a special class of religious functionaries who serve as custodians (a priesthood) of sacred objects, scriptures, and places; specialists in doctrine, ritual, and pastoral guidance. Such specialists are usually rewarded for their services, frequently by tribute or status.
- These specialists systematize doctrine which amounts to a body of knowledge that provides solutions to all problems, and explains the meaning and purpose of life, the functioning of the cosmos, and the human psyche.
- Legitimacy is claimed for religious knowledge and institutions by reference to revelation and tradition: innovation is regularly justified as restoration.
- Claims to the truth and efficacy of ritual are not subjected to scientific teaching, since goals are ultimately transcendent and faith is demanded both for goals and the means of their obtainment.

Defining the 'alternatives'

Our second dilemma is in defining precisely what constitutes or does not constitute an alternative religion. To make conceptualization straightforward it is possible to simply designate alternative religion as that which is not 'mainstream'. In short, it constitutes forms of religiosity that are to be discovered on the fringe of social life (the term 'fringe religions' sometimes being preferred). Hence, they are regularly understood as forming subcultures with very different values and ways of life, and therefore have little in common with either wider culture or traditional religious belief and practice, namely Christianity.

There are two principal difficulties with this simple categorization. Firstly, to speak of the 'alternatives' and make reference to their popularity is to deny the vastly different expressions of those described in this way. Many have no more in common with each other in respect of beliefs, practices, origins, organization, tradition, and the kinds of people that they attract, than they do with established Christianity. Of the NRMs, by way of illustration, some like the International Society for Krishna Consciousness (ISKCON) trace their origins to older religions, in this case Hinduism. Others, such as the Unification Church, appear to be a mixture of traditions. More recently, by contrast, the New Age movement has brought together aspects of the ancient and the very modern. Others still are completely new and innovating in their teachings and constitute very unique forms of spirituality. As far as the latter is concerned, quite a few seem preoccupied with human potential and one type or another of healing. They are perhaps better designated as quasi-religions, since it is very difficult to pin down what is specifically 'religious' about at least some of them according to conventional definitions.

At the same time, problems of definition related to what exactly amounts to mainstream or alternative religion is compounded by further developments within the broad field of religious life. It is clear that some of the boundaries between traditional Christianity and a number of the 'alternatives' are breaking down. For one thing, there is a notable convergence of interests and issues embraced. This should not necessarily surprise us since the social forces and trends that give birth to, or at least influence, some alternative religion also impact upon mainstream Christianity. For example, many Christian denominations have increasingly become more progressive and socially aware in their attitudes, endorsing such causes as ethnic relations, interfaith dialogue, and gender themes, and are committed to overcoming social problems including poverty and unemployment. These are typically some of the areas advanced, in their distinctive ways, by a fair number of the new religions.

To a degree, all this is indicative of the fact that contemporary mainstream Christianity seems to have become more secular – orientated towards the needs of human beings in this world, and increasingly losing sight of the next. Simultaneously, it marks a recognition that non-Christian religions have embraced these popular themes and there is a felt need for Christianity likewise to respond positively to these issues. Like some of the newer alternatives, typified by the increasingly popular New Age movement, there are branches of liberal Christianity, in particular, that advance a concern for the global causes that include those of inequality, environmentalism, and Third World development. Moreover, some expressions of Christianity, not limited to the liberal wing, have endorsed themes reflecting popular culture or culled from the alternative religions (this suggests, of course, that not all the 'alternatives' constitute 'alternative' subcultures). Much is exemplified by contemporary forms of Pentecostalism, which have developed, in no uncertain way, the areas of healing, holism, and human potential perhaps more obviously associated with the New Age movement.

Added to this complexity is another tendency to be found in contemporary religion: its increasingly syncretic nature. Religion is discernibly becoming more and more characterized by its mix 'n' match consistency. Doctrines and practices may be borrowed, integrated, and transformed within any given religion, be it old or new. Some commentators attribute this development to the growth of a religious 'market-place'. Religion is 'bought' and 'sold', supplied and consumed. It follows that what-ever is appealing will be legitimated, incorporated, and grafted on to a faith in order to attract new converts and to keep present ones happy and engaged. Religion, then, becomes increasingly syncretic in an ever-expanding spiritual marketplace where market forces have produced, in the words of Stark and Bainbridge (1985, 437), 'a supermarket of faiths; received, jazzed-up, home spun, restored, imported and exotic'.

Some alternative religions add to this syncretic trend by embracing aspects of reli-giosity from other cultures outside of the Western context. Many of the NRMs, arising from the 1960s, have enriched the mix 'n' match nature of contemporary reli-gion as a result of the dynamics of globalization or the development of what McLuhan (1962) first referred to as the 'global village'. Globalization implies that the world is now a smaller place and that national, political, and cultural boundaries are breaking down. This has significance for the sphere of religion. Indeed, as Roland Robertson (1992) has shown, countries across the world are increasingly influenced by other cultures and traditions as the economic and power structures of these societies become interrelated and interdependent at a global level. This is true of religious culture and tradition as much as any other aspect of social life.

In the past, Western Christianity was exported across the world and accompanied trade and colonialism. Today, it is by no means all one-way traffic. The West is now influenced by the global ebbs and flows of various expressions of religiosity emanating from other cultures. These may be in pure form, such as the various strands of Buddhism, or new and innovating ones. Adaptation has occurred through a process which has come to be known as *glocalization* – the accommodation of global influences to localized conditions (Featherstone 1990). This is perhaps more obvi-ously the case with a number of the new alternative religions. Thus, among the most distinctive features of the New Age movement are teachings which, while clearly orig-inating in Western forms of occultism, are merged with eastern mysticism, paganism, and animism (Heelas 1996). Syncretic trends and globalizing influences are also observable within at least some expressions of Christianity to the extent of confusing the boundaries between mainline and alternative religion. The contemporary church 'scene', or at least certain aspects of it, have been impacted by expressions of the Christian faith originating from such diverse parts of the world as Africa and Korea. This means that traces of mysticism and shamanism have begun to encroach on tradi-tional Christian beliefs and practices – at least partially bringing them into line with what the more esoteric new religions have to offer.

The post-Christian society

While established Christian churches and organizations may still be designated 'mainstream religion', it is more and more arduous to argue that they have a monopoly of religious life. Historically, the West has been dominated by the Christian faith in all its various forms, whether the numerous strands of Protestantism, or the Roman Catholic and Orthodox traditions. Over previous centuries Christianity provided important political, educational, and social functions and claimed, nominally at least, the allegiance of the great mass of the population. Indeed, so dominant has the faith proved to be that the West has historically been referred to as *the* Christian civilization or *Christendom*. However, it is virtually impossible to maintain that this is now the case. Christianity in most Western societies has suffered and continues to suffer a long-term demise, to the extent that when many sociologists speak of 'the decline of religion' they are frequently limiting their appraisal to the declining social repercussions of the faith.

There are good grounds for arguing that in the early twenty-first century the post-Christian society has arrived in earnest. This development is linked with what sociologists are increasingly coming to perceive as the advent of post-modernity. While the term is itself very much disputed and open to interpretation, it does however present, for an increasing number of sociologists, a framework by which to understand recent socio-cultural transformations in the West and, relatedly, changes within the realm of religious belief and observance.

If we wish to have a starting point in a discussion of the relevance of post-modernity to religion then perhaps there is none better than the work of the French writer Lyotard (1984). He argues that the post-industrial society and accompanying post-modern culture are essentially associated with a number of important technological, scientific, and broad economic changes. Yet, Lyotard suggests that the most significant transformations are related to the undermining of meta-narratives, especially those which stress certainty in the world, human emancipation, and social progress. According to Lyotard, the post-modern condition is one where everything becomes relative. There is, therefore, a prevailing willingness to abandon the quest for overarching or victorious myths, narratives, or frameworks of knowledge. This invariably implies the decline of at least some forms of religion: those which tend to be all-embracing in their scope and which historically have demanded an allegiance from all sections of society. There is now a predominant pessimism about the future. There is much less willingness to believe that the truth can be found in grand theories and ideologies, whether they are related to the secular conviction of the inevitability of progress, or the power of science to solve all human predicaments. Even less, perhaps, is there an acceptance of traditional and dominant forms of religiosity.

Don Cupitt (1998) argues along similar lines. He maintains that Western culture is no longer identified by the conviction that progress is inevitable, and that the optimistic view of history that once characterized modernity has ceased to prevail. Such ideas once offered people hope for the future and filled the world with a divine significance and purpose. They justified human behaviour, underpinned civil authority, and helped to make life tolerable under the most intolerable conditions. Now, the Christian dream of the heavenly kingdom to come, and its secular counterpart displayed in the faith of man's inevitable progress, has receded. For Cupitt, this sudden erosion of the belief in a better future has also meant the decline of the perception of a legitimate past. The Christian heritage is no more, the faith has lost its historical authority, and the undergirding of social institutions by divine legitimization and a dogmatic set of beliefs has suffered a rapid demise. The Christian way of seeing the cosmos, history, and reality as a taken-for-granted 'truth' has practically disappeared. The consequence is that, in terms of sustaining a meaning to human existence, there now exists a large vacuum.

Whether one wishes to subscribe fully to theories of post-modernity, the view that traditional Christianity is now in terminal decline is a convincing one. There exists plenty of testimony that it is experiencing a long-term dissolution. One indication of this demise might be the increasing fragmentation of the faith. The 'Church', as the official institutional expression of Christianity, has constituted a particular type of religious organization. According to Troeltsch's (1931) account, the historical Church has attempted to be universal in its embrace and has assumed that it enjoyed the fealty of the entire population. This has indeed been the case for many centuries in Europe. People were often 'born into' those religions such as the Roman Catholic or Orthodox variants of Christianity. This was a time in which the Church jealously guarded its monopoly of religious truth and refused to tolerate challenges to its ecclesiastical power either by other faiths or secular authorities. For this reason it often attempted to influence or even become part of the social and political establishment.

Especially from the nineteenth-century, Christianity has increasingly become fragmented in its institutional expressions. This has proved to be especially so within Protestantism, which articulated itself in denominational form and is most evident in the USA where, in the absence of a state Church, denominations have formed the backbone of religious life. The sociological explanation for this expansion of denominationalism is that it often seems designed to dovetail with the pluralist nature of contemporary society and give expression to the religious needs of particular social groups (Wilson 1976). Baptist, Methodist, Congregational, and many more besides, have increasingly come to represent the mainstream of Christianity today and are characterized by free and voluntary membership, a less centralized hierarchy of the church, and are void of a claim to embrace a monopoly of the 'truth' (Roof & McKinney 1987). This slow transformation of Christianity from Church to denomination in most Western societies, however, marks more than a response to the growth of cultural pluralism. It also indicates the decline of the social power of Christianity, at least in relation to the separation of Church and state, even if the process has varied considerably in tempo from one country to another.

Today, the Western world appears less and less to embrace Christian values. The faith no longer directly dictates public morality and is frequently at odds with the emerging secular society. At the same time, a good deal of statistical evidence concerning religious practice also points towards decline. This is despite the complexities associated with the validity and reliability of available data. An obvious focus of such data is the level of acceptance of Christian doctrines. Statistics produced by the European Values Survey show that, in Europe at least, belief in traditional Christianity has been undermined over a number of decades (Harding *et al* 1985, 46–7). There is now a low percentage of the general European population who believe in a personal God in the Christian sense, and there is a declining segment who believe in an absolute morality or in the existence of hell as taught by historical Christianity.

Church membership and attendance figures also provide measurement of decline, as do the rates of the performance of traditional Christian rituals such as baptism and marriage. In England and Wales, in 1990, only 12 per cent of the population were members of a church (see Table 1). In 2000, the figure was closer to 7 per cent, with the projection for 2020 approximating a mere 1 per cent (Brierley 2000). There is, of course, considerable variation of church membership in Western societies. Decline appears greater in the historically Protestant countries of Northern Europe than in the Catholic nations of the Mediterranean region, although they are now fast catching up. Church attendance is also a good deal higher in the USA for particular historical reasons. The *Yearbook of American Churches* produces evidence that today over 40 per cent of the population of the USA attend church on average once a week. However, research findings suggest that these statistics are misleading because of the way they are calculated. As a result of the 'massaging' of figures among Roman Catholic and Protestant churches, the attendance figures in the USA may be only half what they are commonly believed to be (Hadaway *et al* 1993).

Table 1   Christian Church membership in Britain

Year	All Protestant total (m)	Roman Catholic total (m)	Total (m)	Ratio	% of adult population
1900	5.4	2.0	7.4	100	30
1930	7.1	2.8	9.9	133	29
1950	6.1	3.5	9.6	129	25
1970	5.2	2.7	7.9	107	19
1990	3.4	2.2	5.6	76	12

Source: Adapted from Brierley, P. (1989) *A Century of British Christianity: Historical Statistics 1900–1985*, London: Research Monograph, MARC Europe.

Note: m = millions

The alternatives: the religions of the gaps?

As Christianity declines, alternative, minority religions would seem to have become more significant and at least achieved a higher profile. This may be simply because the demise of Christianity reveals other forms of religion which have always existed, but hitherto were largely hidden from view. On the other hand, it could plausibly mean that the 'alternatives' are filling some kind of spiritual 'gap' and fulfil a latent demand in contemporary Western society. In fact, this may have been their historical role.

Such religions, especially observable in a considerable range of pagan and 'folk' beliefs, have endured despite the dominance of Christianity. The more esoteric and occultist types, in particular, have long constituted counter-cultural currents and vied with the official and institutionalized forms for the allegiance of ordinary people throughout the centuries (Tiryakian 1974, 272–3). Certainly, the historical evidence shows that it is these expressions of religion which have tended to come to the fore when Christianity has been relatively weak and have struggled for legitimacy, especially among rural populations (Thomas 1974). Although in much more varied forms, it is possible that today's alternative religions are providing a similar function in satisfying spiritual requirements, as the current relative popularity of belief in occultist practices would seem to suggest (Table 2).

Table 2 Belief in occultist practices in Britain, 1970–90

	% of British population		
Belief in	**1970s**	**1980s**	**1990s**
Reincarnation	24	26	26
Horoscopes	23	26	23
Fortune telling	48	54	23
Lucky charms	17	19	18
Black magic	11	13	10
Spiritualism	11	14	14
Ghosts	19	28	31

Source: Adapted from Gill, R. *et al* (1998) 'Is Religious Belief Declining in Britain?', *Journal for the Scientific Study of Religion*, **37** (3), p. 513.

To argue that a demand, or at least potential demand, for fulfilling spiritual needs now exists is to refute the major thrust of the 'hard' interpretation of secularization which, while accepting that religious decline is no straightforward or simple process, identifies the demise of *all* forms of religiosity. This type of approach was advanced by the early 'classical' sociological works including those of Comte, Durkheim, and Weber who, in their own unique accounts, prophesied the inevitable erosion of religion in whatever guise it came, Christian or otherwise, and the emergence of the secular society. Each offered different reasons as to how and why religion would eventually become an antiquated curiosity and each included themes subsequently developed by other sociologists. These have encompassed, firstly, the advance of rational-causal explanations of the world, which undermined its sacred character. This means that a belief in the supernatural, a God-given system of morality, and references to an afterlife invariably decline, as do occultism, superstition, and metaphysical ways of seeing, negotiating, and attempting to manipulate the world. Secondly, secularization means the disengagement of society from religion so that the latter becomes marginalized and primarily of private and voluntary concern. Thirdly, there would occur an increasing worldliness at the expense of belief in the supernatural, even by forms of traditional religiosity. From these perspectives Christianity is not only on the decline but is unlikely to be replaced by any other significant form of religion, and that which does emerge is scarcely recognizable as religion at all.

A contrasting approach to the theme of secularization has focused on the *transformation* of religious faith into many private and individual practices in contemporary society outside organized, traditional religious institutions. Hence, religion does not decline, or is of no less importance in the contemporary world; it only changes its expression. Thomas Luckmann (1967), for instance, denies that modern man should be viewed as in essence secular, materialistic, rational, and fundamentally areligious. Rather, religion has undergone a process of *individuation* whereby people work out their own salvation and follow their own road to 'ultimate meaning'. Moreover, the continuance of religion results from the *limits* of rationalism. To put it succinctly, rationalism fails to provide for all human emotional and intellectual needs and, above all, the search for meaning in the world. Religion therefore continues many of its erstwhile functions, albeit in different forms. New religions emerge, while those historically on the fringe come more to the fore. If this speculation is correct, then today's alternative religions are truly the 'religions of the gaps'.

If people are indeed now free to choose the religion which suits them, this has been enhanced by what can be called the 'new voluntarism'. This term implies that the basis of joining any sphere of social activity is purely a voluntary choice on the part of individuals. In turn, this is a consequence of relentless social and geographical mobility which has resulted in the breakdown of communities and primary group belonging, especially that of the family. Religious activity is particularly challenged by contemporary developments since both social and geographical mobility have undermined the religious culture and the community where it was historically entrenched (Warner 1993). Away from institutional and social pressures, people are now at liberty to follow a personal quest for meaning rather than embrace a collective act of religious involvement that has typified traditional Christianity. The outcome is that there is little or no social pressure on the individual to embrace a faith through the coercion of the community since, in the last assessment, the momentum originates with the religious 'seeker' (Wuthnow 1993, 39–40).

From this kind of approach, which emphasizes allegiance to religion as a matter of choice, it is possible to argue that some statistical evidence does point towards the endurance of religiosity at the same time that there are indisputable indications of decline in traditional Christian beliefs. From the early 1980s, in the case of Britain, the European Systems Study Group found that although the beliefs associated with traditional Christianity had declined, some 60 per cent of those surveyed defined themselves as 'a religious person', 50 per cent claimed that a belief in God was significant to them, just under 50 per cent believed in existence after death, and around 20 per cent admitted to a religious experience sometime during their life. However, perceptions of God and the afterlife were far from in accordance with traditional Christian doctrine and indicated a complexity of beliefs which displayed a misunderstanding of basic Christianity or were, to one degree or another, influenced by other faiths. At the same time, evidence has pointed to a growing interest in alternative religions. For instance, research in the USA has indicated an increase in the proportion of the population opting for a faith outside of the three major traditions (Protestantism, Catholicism, and Judaism) at around 9 per cent (Roof & McKinney 1985, 28).

Evidence of a sustained religiosity, despite the decline of traditional Christianity, is also presented by Stark and Bainbridge (1985) in their survey of religion in the USA and Western Europe. They argue that the fact their survey findings show that those who report no religious affiliation or belief are more likely to express interest in some form of unorthodox or fringe supernaturalism such as astrology, transcendental meditation, and yoga, is a clear sign of the endurance of religion. Stark and Bainbridge present their findings within the framework of what they see as a growing spiritual marketplace in Western societies. Religion is now increasingly marketed, and likewise 'consumed', at a time when there is the observable reduction of, to use another economic metaphor, the Christian 'monopoly'.

For Stark and Bainbridge, there now exists the endless potential for religious growth in satisfying personal spiritual, material, and psychological needs. While such human needs have always existed, there is in the West an increasingly complex set of personal requirements. This explains the appearance of new and innovating cult movements. Generally free of the deficiencies of the older religious traditions, namely Christianity, the new religions are in line with the priorities of individuals in Western societies and 'fill a gap in the market'. The Unification Church, ISKCON, and, more recently, the New Age movement, provide testimony of the rekindled vitality of religion. According to Stark and Bainbridge, these expressions of religion are far from superficial and insignificant forms of faith. Indeed, they are fraught with great meaning and provide more than psychological and social needs. They offer the universal functions of religion in presenting the answers to the ultimate questions which have plagued humanity from time immemorial: the purpose to life, suffering, and the possibility of existence after death.

Variations on a theme

The notion that alternative religions are filling the gap left by historical Christianity and are increasingly attractive in the growing spiritual marketplace is plausible enough in explaining the rise of new forms of religion. There are, however, limitations in this appraisal since the framework does not do justice to the vast range of 'alternatives' now on offer, which are by no means novel or innovating expressions of religiosity. Neither does a supposed marketplace of religion fully explain why some alternatives have proved to be more popular than others, or why a number are enjoying growth while others decline. To fully comprehend their appeal it is necessary to range wider.

Some of the 'alternatives' are derivatives of Christianity but outside its historical traditions and doctrines. Those such as the Church of Latter-day Saints (the

Mormons) have endured for well over a century, and some considerably longer. A few, including the Jehovah's Witnesses, boast a membership counted in millions and are organized on an international scale. Not infrequently, these movements can be placed under the sociological rubric of 'sect' in that they often constitute breakaway factions from established Christianity. More often than not, they display a high level of tension with society and are antagonistic towards established religion. Such sects tend to be exclusive and elitist, embracing what they perceive to be the uncompromising truth. The processes which lead to the emergence of the sect are complex but do indicate a dissatisfaction with, and critique of, traditional Christianity. The apparent proliferation of these sects may indicate the weakness of mainstream Christianity and offer an alternative to it through a set of beliefs and practices perceived by the established churches as at least unorthodox and frequently heretical.

As much can also be said regarding Christian fundamentalist movements, although they are frequently observably *within* the remit of historical Christianity. Fundamentalism, to oversimplify a complex phenomenon, claims 'absolute answers', protects the very triumphalist myths supposedly eroded in the post-modern society, and espouses an uncompromising set of doctrines. It may well be that the need for such all-encompassing religion still remains attractive to a number of people in the uncertainty generated by a culture of relativism. Fundamentalism, then, offers an anchor of certainty in a world of uncertainty. Nonetheless, while it may arguably satisfy the needs of some in the spiritual marketplace, it must also be seen as a broader movement which responds to the challenges of the secular world that eats away at the legitimacy and former privileges of Christianity. In the USA, in particular, this has rendered Christian fundamentalism a highly visible, if still marginalized, expression of religiosity.

There is yet another strand of alternative religion which has its own, largely independent origins. We have already noted the increasing influence of religious beliefs originating from outside the Western cultural context and their impact on innovating forms of religiosity. At the same time, religious imports are not infrequently associated with a variety of ethnic minorities that are to be found in Europe and North America. Sometimes these minorities are constituted by migrants who have been refugees from war and civil upheaval, or have sought asylum from political and even religious persecution. Whether Asian Kenyans fleeing to Britain in the 1970s, Vietnamese to the USA and Europe in the 1980s, or a variety of peoples from Eastern Europe in the 1990s seeking release from ethnic persecution, the West has been regarded by many as a haven. The great majority of migrants, however, originate from Third World countries and have responded to the demands of the modern global economy. Since the mid-twentieth-century, the Western nations have called on labour migrants from various regions of the globe for their economic expansion. As a result of this migration, the populations of the West are now, ethnically speaking, increasingly heterogeneous.

It is evident that Western societies have become not only pluralist but also multicultural and that there are implications for the variety of religions to be found. Today, there are currently well over 3 million Muslims in the USA, with smaller communities of Hindus, Buddhists, Sikhs, and Jains (Waugh *et al* 1983). Comprising part of the British population of some 55 million people are approximately 1.1 million prac-tising Muslims, 400,000 Hindus, and 250,000 Sikhs located in London and other major urban areas (Brierley 1991a, 233). In Britain, most Muslims have the status of citizen, almost 50 per cent have been born in the country, and many others are growing up in a society to which they have purposefully migrated (Anwar 1995, 48). Undoubtedly, the faiths of these ethnic minorities have added substantially to the rich tapestry of alternative religions.

Problems of objectivity

So far we have discussed a number of the theoretical and conceptual difficulties encountered when generally analysing religious life. We have also set some broad parameters related to alternative religions, which will be explored more fully in the chapters to come. This introductory chapter can be concluded, however, by briefly considering the problems related to objectivity, in particular, whether a value-free stance is possible and indeed desirable in discussing the vast variety of religions which come under the remit of 'alternative'.

As already noted, attitudes towards alternative religion today in secular Western societies are frequently associated with controversy at worst, or ridicule and scepticism at best, while stigmatizing labels abound. Thus, there are considerable repercussions for how the 'alternatives' are perceived. This is particularly true of those forms of religiosity that are often designated 'cults', 'sects' or 'fundamentalist'. Although these are socio-logical categories, albeit sometimes contended, they are frequently used in society at large as little more than labels which suggest extremism and intolerance. On the other hand, people may think of alternative religion in terms of new forms of religiosity. This may include the New Age movement, which is often viewed as rather 'wacky' or super-ficial even by supposedly objective academic writers on the subject.

Broader societal attitudes may impinge on even the most well-meaning and objec-tive survey of today's religion or be part of a more critical appraisal. Moreover, it is clear that a discussion of religion in the Western world is invariably intertwined with the theme of secularization, which is frequently given to denote the decline of reli-gion, and the related theme as to whether this should be a welcomed trend in the contemporary world. In short, it might be argued that religion and superstition, whether defined as 'mainstream' or 'alternative', are something that the human race could best do without. Of course, a conviction that secularization is inevitable is not the same thing as flagging up the merits of a religionless society. Nonetheless, at least some of the sociological literature overviewed in these pages does subscribe to such a view. A more neutral approach is endorsed by other commentators. However, the latter is less easy to achieve than might at first be expected. It is obvious that even in the *description* of at least some of the 'alternatives' a degree of subjectivity might be apparent and this will become evident throughout this volume.

Finally, religion, by its very nature, is not like other social phenomena. It involves seemingly curious beliefs, practices, experiences, and references to a supernatural realm, which is understood by those with faith as impinging upon this world. Yet, sociology is forced to analyse, explain, and describe with models and social variables alien to the believer. The 'process' of 'conversion', for example, is frequently accounted for in terms of social background, the influence of social networks, personal crisis, and, indeed, any other consideration except the actor's own narrative of his or her experience. Some of these more reductionist aspects are considered in this book. At the very least, in line with good sociological tradition, it is prudent and fair to admit to such limitations. Yet, to some extent at least, this dilemma is addressed by considering the beliefs and practices of the 'actors' involved in the alternative religion, alongside the sociological theorizing and empirical research.

Summary

The purpose of this chapter has been to discuss briefly issues related to matters of definition and to consider the changing cultural environments in which alternative religions now seem to proliferate and which enhance problems of definition. Secondly, we have briefly raised the question as to how to categorize these religions. Thirdly, we have overviewed problems of objectivity in analysing and even in describing alternative religions. These themes will arise again in subsequent chapters as we explore the various types of 'alternatives'. This enterprise commences in the next chapter with a discussion of those broadly defined as 'cults'.

Further reading

Bainbridge, W. (1997) *The Sociology of Religious Movements*, New York: Routledge.
Bancroft, A. (1985) *New Religious World*, London: McDonald.
Barrett, D. (1998) *Sects, 'Cults' and Alternative Religion. A World Survey and Sourcebook*, London: Cassell.
Gee, P. & Fulton, J. (eds.) (1991) *Religion and Power: Decline and Growth*, London, British Sociological Association, Sociology of Religion Study Group.
Hinnells, J. (1998) *A New Handbook of Living Religions*, Harmondsworth: Penguin.
Parsons, G. (ed.) (1994) *The Growth of Religious Diversity: Britain from 1945. Volume II, Issues*, London: Routledge.

2 Cults

By way of definition, perhaps no category of religion has created so much confusion as that of the 'cult'. Frequently it is a term interchanged freely with that of 'sect' or a variety of other labels, most of which have negative connotations. All such classifications of cults are usually associated with deviant forms of religiosity which, more often than not, are in conflict with their social environment. Partly, this generalized appraisal results from a widespread ignorance which associates the cult with dangerous religious movements that embrace a bizarre set of beliefs, led by unscrupulous, often psychologically disturbed, individuals. Media sensationalizing stories of so-called 'brainwashing', financial extortion, and abduction of members add to this rather disparaging picture. While there are certainly cults that may display at least some of these characteristics, they are relatively few. The whole area of cults therefore deserves clarification and a broader assessment.

Cults defined

To some extent the confusion as to what a cult amounts to has not been aided by the sociological enterprise. Sociology has defined and accounted for cults in very different ways. This is largely because they are extremely complex religious phenomena, and not infrequently sociologists appear to be discussing very different things. Indeed, in the hands of some commentators the 'cult' can range from so-called 'doomsday cults' such as Heaven's Gate or the Branch Davidians, to those which scarcely seem to be religions at all and merely offer strategies of psychotherapy, positive thinking, or some other means of developing human potential. These diverse expressions make the categorization of a religious group as a 'cult' difficult to apply and a balanced appraisal practically impossible to achieve.

Perhaps we can start our discussion with a dictionary definition. According to the *Concise Oxford Dictionary* a 'cult' is a 'system of religious worship; homage, to person or thing'. With this definition the cult would seem to have a private, eclectic quality, attracting a loose association of members. Thus, cults are popular, non-official expressions of religion, which grow up inside or outside established faiths. In traditional Christianity, perhaps the most obvious cult using this definition is that of the Virgin Mary, or the veneration of various saints. Historically, as with those within the

Roman Catholic Church, many cults arose from beliefs related to particular local holy persons and often included a pilgrimage to a holy site. Such cults are by no means limited to Christianity, since some parallel ones, with the same function and expressed in similar ways, can be found in most of the world faiths. In Islam, for instance, there is the convention that all Muslims, if possible, should make a pilgrimage to Mecca and Medina at least once in their lives. The cult then, according to our dictionary definition, is a universal and cross-cultural religious phenomenon.

Other, more sociological, interpretations of cults are more restricted and have tended to view them as relatively new expressions of religion, emerging largely since the mid-twentieth-century, and essentially a product of the social environment of the West. Typical of this approach is that of Colin Campbell (1972), who speaks of the growth in Western societies of a 'cultic milieu' made up of a wide variety of occult beliefs and practices, techniques of divination, alternative therapies, and complementary medicine. Campbell, as with Troeltsch before him, predicted that many such cults in the West would increasingly be identified by numerous forms of mysticism. Although this would seem to run counter to the increasing rationalism of modern society, Troeltsch maintained that mysticism would become attractive because of its 'radical religious individualism' (Troeltsch 1931, 377). For Troeltsch, this personalized form of religion is not essentially an inward-looking and selfish expression of religiosity but one which is idealistic and aesthetic. It follows that it is opposed to institutionalized forms of religion and the exclusive dogma of both the Church and sect. At the same time, cultist mysticism embraces some aspects of contemporary culture and, in doing so, appeals to a largely urban middle-class clientele. Troeltsch's prediction regarding the growth of such religion appears, to some extent at least, to be fulfilled with the emergence of the New Age movement (considered in Chapter 8) and similar forms of religion that appeal to a more affluent constituency.

More recent accounts of the contemporary cultic milieu contend that it includes those expressions which are not necessarily 'religious' in the conventional sense but may involve a very secular range of activities. This is suggested by Steve Bruce's definition of the cult, which makes no explicit reference to religion. For Bruce, a cult is 'a small loosely knit group organized around some common themes and interests but lacking a sharply defined and exclusive belief system. Each individual member is the final authority as to what constitutes the truth to salvation.' (Bruce 1996a, 82) Bruce's description is partly derived from the work of Roy Wallis (1976a) and his distinction of four major types of religious organization, namely, Church, denomination, sect, and cult (see Table 3). In this typology, Wallis attempted to categorize different types of religious organization based on how they saw the external world and how they perceived themselves within it. Hence, the important considerations become, firstly, whether a particular religion regards itself as respectable or deviant and, secondly, whether it perceives itself as having a unique grasp of the 'truth' and how to gain salvation.

For Wallis, the cult, like the denomination, does not claim a unique monopoly of religious truth. By contrast, the Church and sect do make exclusive claims for their organizations, and for that reason they may display a certain instability. This means that, under pressure, the latter tend toward significant divisions and fragmentation,

Table 3 Types of religious organizations

	External conception	
	Respectable	**Deviant**
Uniquely legitimate	Church	Sect
Internal conception		
Pluralistically legitimate	Denomination	Cult

Source: Adapted from Wallis, R. (1976) *The Road to Total Freedom: A Sociological Analysis of Scientology*, London: Heinemann, p. 13.

with sects often breaking off from a Church and, over time, one sect may secede from another. Cults, like denominations are more stable. Yet they are relatively weak religious organizations because their beliefs and practices are hardly distinguishable from a large number of similar groups within their respective categories.

Wallis notes how many cults do not have a strict membership, or impose a restricted set of beliefs on their followers. He points out that many permit members a fair degree of freedom to work out their own path to salvation. Moreover, it is conceivable that members may drift into and out of a number of cults without crossing any very clear threshold in either direction. It is also possible to be associated with a number of different cults simultaneously.

Bruce comes to similar conclusions. The modern cult, like the denomination, is tolerant and understanding of its members' needs. In fact, it is so tolerant that it scarcely has a membership in any meaningful sense. Rather, it has 'customers' who pick and choose the portions of a 'product' which best suit them. However, in contrast to Wallis, Bruce believes that this is one of the reasons why cults are often short-lived and unstable. They have a tendency to split over divergent opinions or are unable to command the obedience of members. Hence, they do not have the long history and tradition of the Church or denomination (Bruce 1996a, 89–90). Bruce suggests that in the contemporary spiritual marketplace cults find that members are selective in their acceptance of doctrines. Adherents pick specific elements and may even merge them with what they have acquired from other cults. Given this interpretation of cults, then, it is difficult to see them as all controlling, abusive, and threatening. Indeed, it is an account that is radically different from the common-sense, more popular, viewpoint.

A third way that the term cult is used is with reference to NRMs. In fact, the two terms are frequently interchangeable. This, of course, again suggests that cults, almost by definition, are a fairly new religious phenomenon. From the 1960s, in particular, the designation 'cult' has frequently been employed to describe a wide range of new religion. The Unification Church, for example, is generally put under the remit of an NRM. Yet, even in sociological circles, it is not uncommonly designated as a 'cult', and a rather undesirable one at that. Some sociologists would argue that it is really a matter of scale and that when cults grow beyond a certain size of membership and organization it is legitimate to refer to them as a 'movement'. Hence, many NRMs begin as cults but develop to embrace tens of thousands of members, subsequently become highly structured, and achieve a global significance with representation in many different countries.

The social significance of cults

Not only are there disagreements between sociologists as to what constitutes a cult, there are also wide-ranging speculations as to why they appear to have proliferated in Western societies over recent decades. Much of the discussion related to the relevance of cults goes right to the heart of debates about secularization. Bruce (1996a, 4–5), for instance, regards them as largely insignificant and only important to the extent of marking a decline of 'real' religion. He writes:

> the direct social impact of these cultic preferences is slight. The small numbers of people who get involved do so in a highly selective and picky way. Like the sovereign consumers they believe themselves to be in other spheres of their lives, they feel able to decide what works for them and how involved they will become.

Bruce argues that this is in complete contrast to the traditional role of Christianity and other established religions. The cultist milieu is constantly influenced by the fads and fashions of today's culture. From this perspective, questions must be asked about their true level of spirituality. Bruce is adamant that they offer no great system of morality, have no clear-cut framework of beliefs and practices, and have no major social relevance. In short, they are marginalized, superficial, and relatively insignificant forms of religion. Moreover, they are frequently a mirror of cultural developments and reflect, through their preoccupation with self-improvement, human potential and healing techniques, the this-worldly concerns of contemporary secular society, albeit given a spiritual gloss.

An entirely different perspective on contemporary cults is offered by Stark and Bainbridge (1980), although they too acknowledge cults to be essentially a product of today's world. Cults have grown in the West precisely because they have adapted to people's spiritual, emotional, and practical needs. However, far from being marginal and superficial, cults are innovating forms of religiosity and are concerned with particular requirements generated by the modern condition. They are enthused with great meaning and significance for those involved and this is evident in the different ways that they deal with 'rewards' and 'compensators'. At this point a broader under-standing of Stark and Bainbridge's work on the universal nature of religion must be appreciated. These renowned sociologists start with the premise that human beings are calculating actors and are primarily motivated by what they believe to be 'rewards' and try to avoid what they regard as 'costs'. 'Rewards' are defined as those things which humans desire and are willing to incur some cost to obtain. These may be specific goals including good health or material enrichment, or they may be more general concerns such as answers to questions of ultimate meaning. Yet individuals are often thwarted by what they desire, not infrequently in terms of wealth and status, which are always in short supply. They may subsequently turn to 'compensators'.

For Stark and Bainbridge a compensator constitutes the conviction that a reward will be obtained in the distant future or in some other context which cannot be verified. It amounts to a kind of 'IOU'. In short, individuals believe that if they act in a particular way they will eventually be rewarded by God, gods, or some other supernatural entity. This is the essence of religious belief – it provides an unverifiable future, especially after death. It compensates for what cannot be obtained in the here and now. At the same time, as part of a uniquely religious quest, people may seek to answer the ultimate questions which have plagued humanity from time immemorial. Is there a purpose to life? Is there an existence after this life? Why is there suffering? Thus, the human need for religion endures even in the face of rationalism and science. Since it deals with ultimate questions of human existence, religion will still frequently be formulated in transcendental or supernaturalist forms and display a belief in spiritual entities. Nonetheless, many of its expressions have changed. At the same time, many cults proliferate as a means of dealing with the very different needs of individuals in today's society, perhaps related to psychological and emotional needs, the fulfilment of human potential and matters of health and healing. While older and established forms of religion cannot provide for such needs, neither, generally speaking, can sects (although they may provide for the needs of some).

Stark and Bainbridge (1985) identify three types of cult according to their degree of organization and by way of the 'rewards' and 'compensators' they offer their followers. In doing so they present probably the most elaborate sociological appraisal of contemporary cults.

- Firstly, there are *audience cults*. These are the least organized and involve little interaction between members and leaders. While wishing to adhere to a cult representing their interest, a member's commitment may amount to no more than mail ordering and attending the occasional specially organized event. It is tempting to put at least some strands of the New Age movement under this remit since it relies considerably on a variety of publications and such 'plastic media' as audio and video cassettes.

- Secondly, there are what Stark and Bainbridge designate *client cults*. These are rather more organized and structured – offering services to their followers which, in past times, tended to focus on astrological prognoses, healing miracles, or various forms of spiritualism. Today, they generally specialize in the area of 'personal adjustments'. Thus, 'clients' are individuals rather than comprising well-integrated communities. The emphasis is not so much on enhancing the spiritual, but the worldly opportunities of the membership. This may again plausibly apply to some aspects of New Age religiosity with their emphasis on holistic therapy, healing, and a spiritualized human potential.

- Thirdly, there are *cult movements*. These involve followers to a greater extent and amount, as mentioned earlier, to what are otherwise known as NRMs (discussed at length in Chapter 5). Such cults seek to satisfy all the spiritual needs of their members and forbid them to adhere to other faiths. While some demand little more than a commitment to a set of beliefs and the occasional attendance at meetings, others may endeavour to completely dominate the individual's life. Not infrequently, client cults develop into cult movements for their most devoted followers.

Stark and Bainbridge have also attempted to provide three contrasting models describing the *process* by which cults emerge. In doing so they show the dynamics behind the growth of cults, the significance of the leadership, and the appeal to the rank and file membership.

- Firstly, there is the *psychopathology model*. The leaders of such cults tend to be mentally unbalanced. S/he concocts novel and innovating compensators and accepts them as rewards. Stark and Bainbridge (1987, 159) argue that mental illness can primarily be interpreted as a mode of behaviour which fails to conform to whatever a society regards as normal or acceptable. The relevance of mental illness is that it liberates the cult leader from conventional ways of comprehending the world and thus allows considerable innovation and creativity. As their behaviour is not limited by social conventions, cult leaders are relatively free to devise new patterns of behaviour and establish wholly innovating compensators and religious ideas which they are subsequently able to persuade others to accept and which, in turn, become incorporated into a new religious cult.
- Secondly, there is the *entrepreneurial model*, which perceives some cults to be rather like businesses established by individuals with flair and talent. These cult leaders personally profit by offering innovating compensators in return for rewards from their followers. In many instances this may be financial, but could also include power, status, or personal admiration. Cult leaders are not always calculating and manipulative individuals. Indeed, Stark and Bainbridge distinguish between honest cult founders who offer only those compensators which they themselves subscribe to, and more unscrupulous ones who do not themselves countenance what they offer to others. Often, the leader may have had previous involvement in one or more cult. This provides him/her with the skills and knowledge needed to establish and continue a successful religious movement to which they may append elements of the beliefs of their earlier cults. They may even add on their own doctrines and thus create a whole new synthesis of beliefs and practice.
- Finally, there is the *subculture/evolution model*, which utilizes sociological work on deviant subcultures. Cults under this heading are likely to be relatively isolated from mainstream society by way of interaction and exchanges, novel explanations and, therefore, novel compensators, which are very much at odds with the values of the outside world. The cult grows through a process by which new compensators are collectively invented and where a membership is acquired through a series of small steps consisting of exchanges in which the cult offers more and more rewards in return for greater commitment. If the process goes on for some time a new cult may emerge which amounts to a marginalized subculture relatively insulated from society and with a highly integrated membership. Stark and Bainbridge argue that such a cult will tend to generate compensators of an increasingly general kind and therefore qualify as a full-blown religious cultist movement.

Cults and cultural innovation

In line with other commentators, Stark and Bainbridge (1980) view cults, unlike sects, as not primarily schisms arising from established religions. Instead, they are forms of 'cultural innovation' and are largely unconnected with existing faiths. Occasionally, however, cults may break off from other cults. Stark and Bainbridge acknowledge that this brings a conceptual problem since if such a group develops from another it becomes rather like a sect – a distinction which they are keen to differentiate from their definition of a cult. Nonetheless, they insist that cults of all kinds, in much the same way as sects, are likely to express a fairly high degree of tension with their social environment since they may offer a very different set of values. While some may borrow from the dominant cultural themes of Western society, others may be completely new by way of core beliefs and practices. Others still may constitute cultural importations derived from entirely different social and religious contexts. It is the latter which have arguably become of greatest significance although they overlap with a number of developing aspects of Western culture.

Since the 1960s, a range of eastern mystical cults has been introduced into the West. This is an indication of the wider effects of the process of globalization. Profound changes have taken place internationally in recent decades and there have been significant implications by way of economics and culture. It is clear that the world is now a smaller place and that national, political, and cultural boundaries are breaking down. This has repercussions for religious life too. Hence, today it is increasingly obvious that a discussion of religion in any particular society, or indeed any political-geographical region of the world, including the industrialized nations of North America and Europe, can only be within reference to the dynamics of globalization.

Globalization has ensured that religions originating outside the West now come to have a considerable impact, especially over the last forty years or so. The major trend, as far as Campbell (1999) is concerned, is that of *Easternization*. Campbell goes so far as to argue that traditional Western culture has been undermined by an 'eastern' one. Hence, easternization has come in the wake of the decline of traditional Christianity and offered challenges to rationalism as a pre-eminent mode of thought. One of the most evident ways that this can be seen is within the realm of cultist religion. In the 1960s and early 1970s, there was a vast extension in the missionary endeavour on the part of many eastern religions that seemed to dovetail with the popularity of experimentation in such areas as humanistic therapy, psychedelic drugs, and the counterculture generally. Magnifying and hastening the impact in the USA, from which so many cults seem to emerge, was the rescinding in the United States of the Oriental Exclusion Act, which permitted numerous eastern religious teachers and leaders to enter the country (Melton 1987).

Easternization does not, however, simply result from the introduction and spread of eastern imports. Campbell maintains that there is good evidence to suggest that this fundamental change has been assisted by social transformations increasingly observable *within* Western societies. To generalize, these are largely developments in consciousness including beliefs in the unity of man and nature, holistic views of mind, body, and the spirit, the perceived limits of science and rationality, and the alleged virtues of meditation and other psychotherapeutic techniques. Campbell argues that in many respects the eastern paradigm is more congruous with some aspects of current Western societies – particularly the expanding interest in environmentalism and holism, popular beliefs related to reincarnation, human potential, as well as the growth of what he calls 'life-affirming' cults. Eastern mysticism, principally expressed in Hindu and Buddhist thought, thus overlaps not only with contemporary alternative thinking, but some of the evolving core values of the West.

Cult controversies

We have already noted that a certain degree of notoriety and controversy surrounds cultist expressions of religion. While a number of sociologists suggest that they are a relatively benign social phenomenon, others, including Stark and Bainbridge, argue that at least some cults will display a relatively high level of tension with society. While this tension may arise from their innovating and apparently bizarre range of beliefs, and perhaps the manipulations of the entrepreneurial leader, it may also commence with negative public perceptions and governmental response.

Clearly, some cults attract a great deal of publicity and controversy. Much of the focus in this respect is on *cult movements* – those with uncompromising beliefs, demanding full commitment from their membership, a leadership claiming obedience, and displaying a high level of conflict with the outside world. However, cult controversies and debates surrounding the attempt at recruitment are not new since they were also evident in the nineteenth and early twentieth-centuries (Bromley & Shupe 1979). The charges then, as very often now, are ones of control, deprivation, and systematic brainwashing; sexual abuse; deluded charismatic personalities (often with the felt need to overcome their own personal crisis); dangerous conspiracy theories; the view of the world which divides it into 'us' and 'them' and good and evil; and the exploitation of vulnerable and emotionally unstable people – those on the street, and with alcohol or drug addiction problems. In most cases, accusations of abuse, frequently directed towards one or other of the larger movements, are unjustified. This is not to suggest that the more dangerous cults should be underestimated. Nonetheless, they constitute only a very small minority. Most offer something meaningful and constructive to their membership who are neither coerced, manipulated, or exploited. Few cults deteriorate into violent confrontations with civic authorities. Nonetheless, some have fallen foul of officialdom for various reasons.

One movement which has found itself in continual difficulty is the Unification Church. In the USA, the Attorney General spent four years investigating the movement before finally concluding, in 1988, that it should be permitted to claim the status of a registered charity. There have been frequent court cases in the USA brought against the Church, which have tended to be initiated by ex-members with a personal grievance or by relatives of current members. In 1982, the movement's leader, Sun Myung Moon, was prosecuted for non-payment of taxes on interest in his personal bank account. As a result, he was fined $13,000 and gaoled for 13 months. Largely as a result of his reputation Moon is banned from entering Britain and a number of other European countries. Another cult, the Rajneesh movement (now Osho International), has also been plagued with controversies throughout its short history. A good deal centred on the movement's late, charismatic leader and guru, Bhagwan Shree Rajneesh. Criticisms were directed at his considerable wealth and accusations abounded that much of it came from the financial exploitation of his followers. In addition, critics pointed to what could be interpreted as unpaid labour in his commune, and the non-payment of taxes. There are also claims that he rigged local elections in the USA, as well as allegations of his sexual exploitation of some of his female followers.

Another of the more controversial movements has been the Children of God (COG). Possibly the first anti-cultist group, FREECOG, was established as early as 1972 specifically for parents to 'rescue' their teenagers from what amounted to one of the largest strands of the Californian Jesus movement. Perhaps the most serious accusation against the COG was that of sexual abuse. The leader David ('Mo') Berg shared the wives of some members of the movement and, from 1976, encouraged his followers to practise sexual exploration. Some ex-members allege that he advocated group sex, and the sexual involvement of children, alongside the notorious policy of 'flirty fishing' – a kind of prostitution in order to win converts.

Such controversy frequently suggests that some of the new religions are particularly abusive to women. Many of these religions have been found to be attractive to females since they offer opportunities to become more involved in a wider range of activities than that offered by many mainline religions. However, there is a more negative side. Puttick (1999, 147) perceives the dangers of corruption, particularly sexual abuse, in the master-discipleship relationship. She points out that abuse in the past may have arisen from manipulative Asian gurus who exploited the increasingly sexually permissive culture of the West. However, Puttick argues that cases of sexual abuse are largely the result of the not infrequent development of harem-type structures where women are encouraged to compete for the gurus' favours.

At a broad level, cases of control and abuse are not easily explained. Nevertheless, the more notorious movements do have specific characteristics which are likely to generate abuse. Among the more obvious are the charismatic leadership and the hierarchical nature of some cults. In the case of Berg, the leader of the COG, abuse may have emerged from the need to re-establish control of the membership as a result of the process of bureaucratization within the movement. Wallis (1982) explains that the organizational growth of the COG undermined his charismatic authority. Berg thus condemned local leaders for building institutional structures which challenged the purpose of the movement but, in reality, presented alternative centres of power to his own. To negate this development he attempted to reinstate his charismatic authority. This led to the expulsion of some members and the stricter control of those that remained. Appealing to the rank and file membership over the heads of the leaders, Berg also proclaimed new prophetic insights. This greater degree of regulation and authoritarianism arguably led to excessive abuse.

The emphasis on abuse by unconventional cultist groups tends to distract attention from the fact that cults can develop within established Christian churches and prove no less harmful. The *Nine O'clock Service* based in Sheffield, England, is one example. Originally this movement in the Church of England in the 1990s was regarded by many as a model to attract the young back to the churches with its contemporary music, light shows, and images of the 'rave' culture at a large conference centre that was used for worship. Initially, the charismatic young leader, Christopher Brain, was highly successful in drawing those, particularly women, who had become disenchanted with the more traditional forms of worship. The *Nine O'clock Service* was eventually disbanded after adverse media attention and an official enquiry, when accusations of sexual improprieties were verified in what had grown into an abusive cult.

Doomsday cults

In the history of dangerous cults, the USA has long proved to be fertile ground. Profoundly disturbing to the nation in the 1960s were the activities of Charles Manson's nihilistic terrorist group. Based in Death Valley, California, what began as a hippie commune deteriorated into something akin to a dangerous cult, with Manson's followers believing him to be an incarnation of both God and the Devil who preached that murder merely liberated the victim's soul. Subsequently, the group slaughtered several prominent individuals before facing trial and conviction. Although not strictly speaking religious in orientation, the cult did set the scene for later so-called 'doomsday cults' and has continued to haunt the American psyche. It also appeared to set the agenda for how other cults, malignant or otherwise, have been publicly perceived and dealt with by civil authorities and media coverage.

Epitomizing the activities of dangerous religious cults were the disastrous events surrounding the People's Temple. On November 21, 1978, there were global news reports of a massacre deep in the jungle of the South American Republic of Guyana. It amounted to the bizarre killing of an estimated 917 members of the Temple, many of whom were American citizens. Some two hundred died voluntarily as part of a suicide pact. Most of the other members were executed by gunshot. The dead included children, most of whom had died drinking a lethal concoction of an orange drink styled 'Kool Aid' to which had been added potassium cyanide and tranquillizer drugs. Matters came to a head in November 1978 when US Congressman Leo Ryan visited the community, accompanied by four pressmen, to investigate complaints of brutality and the assertion that people were being kept in Jonestown against their will. A small group of members agreed to return with them to the USA. When attempting to leave, the party was assassinated. The mass suicides and executions of cult members were discovered the next day.

The events which led up to the horrific climax began three months earlier when self-styled Revd Jim Jones, a man of compelling personal attraction and impressive rhetoric, who claimed to have spiritual healing powers, led his faithful flock to the proclaimed paradise in Guyana in order to start a new life and to prepare for Armageddon (the end of the world). Jones had initially founded his movement in California, attracting mainly poor people from ethnic minorities with the promise of a world in which all would live as equals in an egalitarian Christian community (although Jones was inspired as much by Marxism as any form of Christian fundamentalism). Jones insisted that his movement would be spared the coming nuclear holocaust. At its height the People's Temple was undoubtedly a success, claiming congregations of some 3,500 worshippers.

Jones had established churches in San Francisco and Los Angeles and gained support for his goal of helping the poor and underprivileged. He had fooled many influential figures including the then Vice President, Walter Mondale, and became active on the margins of the Democratic Party. Despite this shroud of respectability, however, Jones relied on heavy-handed techniques and intimidation to maintain order and loyalty among his followers, including beatings and physical restraints against leaving the cult. When the cult's financial affairs were investigated it was discovered that Jones had amassed a personal fortune of over 5 million dollars.

There are other examples of cults ending in tragedy. In the early 1980s, a cult named the Temple of the Sun (or the Solar Temple) was founded in Europe and North America and grew to around 3,000 adherents. It was the inspiration of a Belgian doctor, Lue Jouret, and a failed French property dealer, Joseph di Mambro. These men preached a doomsday message and recruited membership from influential and affluent families on both sides of the Atlantic, chiefly from Switzerland, Canada, and France, who gave considerable personal assets to the cult. The Temple of the Sun claimed to be descended from the charter of the medieval Knights Templar, and had a preoccupation with a forthcoming apocalypse, and sustaining the belief that its followers could be saved by fire. It brought together eastern mysticism and aspects of Roman Catholicism, while Jouret claimed that he was a time traveller who would lead the faithful to a new life on a planet that was orbiting the star Sirius.

Seventy followers committed suicide in 1994. Their deaths followed the cult's murder of a family who tried to leave and whose relations subsequently alerted the authorities. More or less simultaneously, at a cult-owned property at Cheiry in the Swiss mountains, twenty-two adults were either shot dead or injected with fatal drugs. Further south, at Granges-sur-Salvan, another twenty-five corpses were found burned beyond all recognition. A year later, suicides by sixteen more members were discovered, burned as before, and laid out in the shape of a star. Letters found bore witness to the cult's beliefs that death was merely a gateway to a better life that awaited them elsewhere. Hence, the suicides were part of a purification ritual of fire before journeying to a new spiritual life on the planet's home world. The fact that so many apparently intelligent and professional people gave themselves over to ending their lives violently is an obvious indication of the charisma of the cult's leadership.

Also usually added to the list of perilous cults is that of Heaven's Gate, which was founded in 1970 by Marshall Applewhite and Bonnie Nettles (who began as Bo and Peep). It amounted to a UFO cult which, like others, believed that extra-terrestrials would visit Earth, make contact with human beings, and bring them knowledge of a higher realm of existence. Failing the arrival of a spaceship in the Colorado Desert, the group virtually disappeared before establishing what became known as their 'monastery' near San Diego. Here, followers were cut off from contact with the outside world as friends and family became increasingly concerned with the bizarre behaviour of

Applewhite. The cult brought in a prohibition on sexual activity and even the castration of male followers. In the months leading up to the final disaster in 1997, the leaders taught that the spirit could be freed from the limitations of the human body by suicide. Belief in a perfect cosmic realm and Christian references were merged together. Thirty-nine members, including Applewhite himself, committed suicide. A harrowing videotape which they left behind shows that death was voluntary and willingly accepted as the way to a better existence.

Although the ill-fated end of those cults discussed above can be blamed on the unscrupulous designs of leaders and seemingly unconventional beliefs, too much condemnation is frequently heaped upon the movements themselves, and rarely on the repercussions of the way that they respond to the real or perceived threats from the outside world. This was evident with the events surrounding the Branch Davidians. The cult was originally formed as an offshoot of the Seventh-day Adventists (SDA) in 1929, when it was known as the Davidian Adventists under its founder Victor Houteff. The movement splintered from the SDA when the leadership felt that the half a million strong membership had become too worldly and that what was needed was the whittling down to the biblical 144,000 Servants of God mentioned in the Book of Revelation.

In the spring of 1935, the cult commune was relocated to a 189-acre site just outside the small town of Waco in Texas. It remained in the area until it came under the control of David Koresh in 1986, who led the group to its disastrous end in 1993. Koresh, in the minds of his followers, was the new messiah, preaching an apocalyptic message largely based on the prophetic text of the Books of Daniel and Revelation. He introduced ideas of polygamy, the community education of its children, violent resistance to outside authorities, and the core teaching of the final message of God through himself as the 'Seventh Seal' of the Book of Revelation. It was by this new message that the faithful would be saved from God's wrath. Koresh identified himself as 'the Lamb of God' who would open the seven seals, after which Christ would return to earth and the war of Armageddon would be unleashed, a conflict in which the Branch Davidians would play a key part (the settlement at Waco being renamed 'Ranch Davidians').

In April 1993, the federal authorities found justification for besieging the heavily armed camp at Mount Carmel after tip-offs that the cult possessed illegal firearms. The storming of the commune ended in the death of four officers from the Federal Bureau of Alcohol, Tobacco and Firearms, as well as six Branch Davidians. The assault was repelled and a stand-off ensued that lasted for fifty days. It provided abundant and often grim media fodder for millions of people worldwide. The episode drew attention to the heavy-handed and ill-considered exercise of the Federal authorities. Indeed, Waco became a metaphor for how not to deal with a marginalized cult (Tabor & Gallagher 1995; Gallagher 2001).

Such dangerous cults are by no means limited to the USA and Europe, although even in non-Western countries it is noteworthy how Christian millenarian beliefs have fuelled the activities of at least some. In contemporary Japan, cults have flourished with approximately 180,000 registered with the state authorities. The Aum Shinri Kyo movement is one of a handful that have proved dangerous. This cult, which has adherents in the West, attracted global notoriety in 1995 when its members orchestrated a gas attack on Tokyo's subway leading to twelve deaths and thousands of people being hospitalized. Representing a mixture of Christianity and traditional Japanese faiths, the cult aimed at world domination and attempted to convince the human race to move from its materialistic path and thus to escape divine retribution which, according to the prophecy of its leader, Shoko Asahara, would occur in 1997 (Reader 2001).

Despite the wide variety of beliefs and practices of these 'doomsday cults' they do appear to have a number of characteristics in common. Anthony and Robbins (1997) include a dualistic worldview among them. Here, the cult divides the world into good versus evil. Hence, the Branch Davidians, for example, saw themselves as Christ's elect and the outside world as 'Babylon'. The religious movement and its leaders are idealized, while its enemies are demonized. Thus, the hostile activities of civil authorities can enhance this worldview by forcing the group to look inwards and rally around the leadership.

Secondly, there is, more often than not, a charismatic leader who casts himself (and it is usually a male) in the role of a prophet or even a messiah. As we have seen with the COG, leadership based on charisma is inherently less stable than other forms of leadership. It is legitimized by the extraordinary qualities he is supposed to possess. Often innovating in terms of teachings, the charismatic leader frequently puts himself beyond moral restraints, whether sexual, financial, or violence directed towards others. This seems to be compounded when the leadership is put under stress and may include such factors as declining physical and mental health (Robbins & Palmer 1997). The more destructive movement would also seem to be one encapsulated in a community of believers who have cut themselves off from contact with family and friends. Members become highly dependent on the cult and the leadership not just for material existence but for the enforcement of their worldview. This is why members often find it very difficult to leave.

Societal reaction to cults and new alternative religions

While not discounting the internal dynamics of a cult which can generate tendencies towards self-destruction, a number of other pressures stem from secular society and the state in engaging with religions on the margins of social life. Sometimes antagonisms emerge when the cult deliberately contravenes civil law. In the early 1940s, for example, the Jehovah's Witnesses were involved in the so-called 'saluting the flag controversy' in the USA. This focused on the movement's refusal to observe the Pledge of Allegiance to the American flag, which, after a long legal campaign, was upheld by the Supreme Court in 1943. Although, in this case, the episode did not result in open conflict, the worldview of the Witnesses is one which sees political institutions in the hands of Satan and legal moves against them would have been interpreted as deliberate persecution. For the most part, however, a religious group may have done nothing to contravene legal statutes. Their mere existence may be enough to arouse a public response and bring a negative reaction from civic authorities.

So controversial has the area of minority religions become that today most Western societies have a set policy orientated towards them. To be sure, wide differences in the attitude to cults and new religions are evident. This ranges from extensive, if at times reluctant, toleration in the United States and Britain, to a systematic hostility manifested so vigorously in France and, in the late 1990s, from the Swedish government. In France, policy was framed largely as a response to events such as those surrounding the Temple of the Sun in Switzerland. The 1996 parliamentary report entitled *Cults en France* listed 172 potentially 'dangerous' religious collectives varying from Buddhist groups to Evangelical Christians, as well as numerous NRMs. The French Parliament has also established the Observatory of Cults to monitor developments. An even more extreme state report was issued in Belgium in 1997. It listed 189 minority religions, which even included several Roman Catholic orders, a variety of Christian evangelical groups, and Hasidic Jewish communities. Ironically, given the wide criteria used in the report to define a cult, even the government agency which issued the report might have been designated as cultist in nature!

A novel approach to minority religions has been taken by the Federal Republic of Germany. There, religious organizations with public law status enjoy the benefit that the state will collect taxes on their behalf from their members. To achieve public law status, a movement must prove its durability. It is required to show that it is well organized, with a sizeable membership and sound finances. It must also have been in existence for at least thirty years. Thus the law is designed to exclude short-lived 'volatile cults'. The 1998 report published by the government appeared more liberal than that of other countries. It affirmed the constitutional guarantees of religious freedom, called for no new legislation, but did confirm the government's interest in intervening in cases of suspected crimes or acts by a cult detrimental to its own membership. However, this was not before the raids by state authorities on Pentecostal churches and an intense government campaign against the Church of Sociology, which, in 1997, was placed under surveillance by the secret police. In the mid-1990s, governmental committees in France, Germany, and Belgium were established to enquire whether so-called sects or cults are damaging to the health of a population. These have run into the problem of what exactly is meant by mental health, how to detect it among their members, and whether so-called 'bizarre' behaviour is dangerous for members (Kranenborg 1996).

The debate as to the merits or otherwise of the more organized fringe religions is often clouded by cultural and ideological considerations. To question why anyone would wish to abandon all the attractions of secular society and join a cult is clearly a reflection of mainstream public opinion about their desirability (Snow & Machalek 1984). However, such opinion can itself be heavily influenced by various factors. Bromley and Shupe (1981) have argued that many groups are the subject of crude stereotyping and unsubstantiated myths propagated by anti-cultists in an attempt to agitate public indignation. Arguably, these anti-cultist crusades are in many ways more dangerous and threatening to civil liberties than the movements they attack. Frequently they appear to exaggerate the numerical significance and social impact of various movements and, according to Bromley and Shupe, implausibly claim that anyone is at risk of falling foul of their techniques of brainwashing. The reality is that the alleged abuses perpetrated by the new religions are not those imagined in the great scandals reported and amplified by the media. Usually they are just minor offences such as street soliciting for funds while concealing the movement's true identity and intentions.

While the media can have a significant role to play in amplifying deviance, anti-cultist groups can also be important in forging public opinion. Some groups have a particular motivation in attempting to forge a good public image for themselves. This is the strategy undertaken by some Christian evangelical groups. Often with titles which give no indication of their true origin, they may form anti-cultist organizations against their rivals and even attempt to win converts from the membership of movements such as the Mormons or Jehovah's Witnesses.

By and large, sociologists who have studied NRMs have found no widespread evidence to substantiate coercive tactics or brainwashing among the larger groups (Bromley & Shupe 1981; Downton 1979). Particularly impressive here is Eileen Barker's work (1984) on the Unification Church. The Church's 'workshops' are often cited as a means of pressurizing people to join. They appear to include constant attention or 'love bombing' followed by the withdrawal of affection, endless rounds of activities, and seclusion from the outside world. Barker studied those who failed to be converted as well as those who were. Nine out of ten of those who attended two-day workshops and who were subject to the same experiences did not join and there appeared to be no difference in their social background when compared to those who did. Neither did Barker find any attempt by the Unification Church to coerce members to remain in the organization by physical restraints or by isolating them from the outside world.

More evidence against the brainwashing thesis is how rapidly new members of many religious groups decide, of their own accord, to disengage (Barker 1984). Mounting testimony from studies of many of the NRMs of the last four decades indicates that far from being the malleable, passive, gullible individuals portrayed in the media, recruits to these religions are active, meaning-seeking people who exercised considerable volition in deciding to convert to a new religion. Furthermore, a striking fact concerning membership of NRMs is its transitory nature. Sensationalist media stories convey the impression that converts are trapped, indeed, 'lost' indefinitely. In fact, much testimony suggests that allegiance to an NRM is temporary (Wright 1988). For instance, Barker (1985) found that in the case of the Unification Church only about 5 per cent of those initially attracted to the movement were still members two years later, while the membership of the Jesus Fellowship in Britain has an annual turnover of some 12 per cent (Hunt 1998).

The emphasis on the alleged negative psychological effects of joining a cult tends to draw attention away from the fact that leaving it can also precipitate damaging psychological conditions. A Dutch study of former members of NRMs found that only around half of the respondents in the survey had psychological problems when joining. Moreover, many successfully dealt with their difficulties in their time with the cult, only to have them resurface again after being forcefully removed (Derks 1983). A similar correlation appears in studies of the so-called 'cult withdrawal syndrome'. Psychologists affiliated with the anti-cultist movement hypothesize that NRMs use 'mind-control' techniques that produce negative psychological and emotional states including nightmares, hallucinations, altered states of reality, and violent outbursts (Conway & Siegelman 1982). Other studies found that persons who were forcibly deprogrammed were significantly more likely to experience troubling psychological symptoms than were persons who left the groups voluntarily and were not subject to any so-called 'exit counselling' (Lewis & Bromley 1987).

Summary

Early on in this chapter it was recognized that the category of 'cult' is one which is extraordinarily difficult to pin down. This is an observation that must be continually reinforced. In many ways the term remains highly unsatisfactory. It denotes a variety of religious groups ranging from *audience* and *client* cults, with little by way of a structured membership or coherent beliefs, to those with a highly integrated membership, clear and uncompromising doctrines, and a general orientation that bring them into tension with society. The following chapters will explore these subcategories at length and detail those cults related to the NRMs, the New Age, and human potential and healing groups. Some of the characteristics of the cult are also implicit in a number of the less obvious expressions of religiosity, such as UFO cults, and these too will be discussed in subsequent chapters.

Further reading

Barker, E. (1986) 'Religious Movements: Cult and Anti-Cult since Jonestown', *Annual Review of Sociology*, **2**, 329–46.

Beckford, J. (1983) 'The Public Response to the New Religious Movements in Britain', *Social Compass*, **30** (1), 49–68.

Beckford, J. (1985) *Cult Controversies: The Societal Response to New Christian Movements*, London: Tavistock.

Evans, C. (1973) *Cults of Unreason*, London: Harrap.

Introvigne, M. (1995) 'Ordeal by Fire: the Tragedy of the Solar Temple', *Religion*, **25**, 267–83.

Loftland, J. (1966) *Doomsday Cult: A Study of Conversion, Proselytization, and Maintenance of Faith*, Englewood Cliffs, NJ: Prentice-Hall.

Melton, G. (1998) 'Modern Alternative Religions in the West', in G. Hinnels, *A New Handbook of Living Religions*, Harmondsworth: Penguin.

O'Donnell, J. (1993) 'Predicting Tolerance of NRMs', *Journal for the Scientific Study of Religion*, **32** (4), 365–89.

Stark, R. & Finke, R. (2000) *Acts of Faith: Explaining the Human Side of Religion*, Berkeley: CA: University of California Press.

3 Sectarianism

Much like cults, the popular appraisal of sectarianism is one of an unorthodox, bizarre, marginalized, or even dangerous religious phenomenon beyond the remit of the established faiths and at odds with mainstream society. Although oversimplified, this view amounts to one which is at least partly shared by sociological definitions of sects that generally categorize them as movements that have broken away from mainstream Christianity. Whether they are bizarre in terms of beliefs and practices is an entirely subjective view. Very few, however, can be regarded, by any criteria, as constituting some kind of social threat.

Although it is often assumed that there is a recent discernible growth of sects, they are by no means new. The Christian Church, over two millennia, has been littered with examples of breakaway sectarian movements. In fact, of all the major world religions, sects appear to be most common to Christianity. This is undoubtedly because of the emphasis that the faith has historically placed on 'correct' beliefs and doctrines, while it has proved to have developed a wide range of organizational types compared to other world faiths. Sects are also fairly frequent within Islam and this is because, like Christianity, it is a 'religion of the Book'. The significance is that the stress placed on the written Word of God lends itself to differing interpretation of the text and, hence, a tendency towards sectarian divisions.

In simple terms, Christian sects may be understood as religious movements which seek to restore 'lost' or neglected beliefs and practices and to recapture the vigour of what is discerned by those involved as the 'true' faith abandoned by the established churches. This self-assigned mission can bring sects into contention with organized religion and the secular realm. Many other major faiths such as Hinduism do not exhibit the same degree of tension with the world and, although it is by no means unknown, tend not to generate sectarian divisions (Martin 1965, 10, 22). Moreover, within Christianity, Protestantism, itself originating as a sectarian schism during the Reformation, is especially prone to breakaway factions. The freedom of conscience allowed to the believer and the pluralist nature of Protestantism have ensured that sects are historically far more prevalent than other strands of Christianity largely represented by the Roman Catholic and Orthodox churches.

Sects defined

There are many reasons why a large body of sociological literature has been produced on sectarianism. Sects are of interest because they offer the opportunity to analyse processes of conversion, the dynamics of membership, so-called 'deviant' beliefs and practices, and the social and ecclesiastical developments which generate this distinct and frequently marginal form of religious organization. The common starting point for a discussion are the writings of Max Weber (1965), who defined sects as off-springs from older, more established religions. This is how he saw the emergence of Christianity. Initially, the faith had begun as a breakaway sect from Judaism and was an innovating form of religion which provided for the needs of people in a particular time and place.

Weber explored the emergence of sects largely with reference to his concept of the 'routinization of charisma'. 'Charisma', for Weber, denotes the belief in supernatural or extraordinary powers often associated with religious leaders and prophets and, in the case of Christianity, to a messiah. Sects generally put a stress on extraordinary spiritual powers and the closeness of the transcendental realm. The relevance of charisma here is that it expresses a profound spirituality and brings an effervescence which generates an innovative faith. While at least some religions may begin as sects, there is a tendency for them, over time, to take a greater organizational form, to establish ecclesiastic structures and create codified doctrines and, in short, become a Church.

Weber maintained that as religions become more institutionalized they tend to inevitably lose the initial spark that began them. The authority of the charismatic leader, after his death, becomes routinized in the hands of a priesthood that is generally responsible for the performance of sacraments and rituals. This is usually accompanied by an increasing compromise of the faith with wider society. Under such conditions the sect emerges as a breakaway party of believers who endeavour to revitalize the faith by taking it back to what is understood to be its 'true' origins, frequently without the encumbrances of institutionalized religion. Typically, there is an attempt to restore 'correct' doctrine and a search for a primal spirituality. Also, as already suggested, the sect is commonly led by a charismatic prophet, or at least a much-venerated leader.

In his analysis of the processes which lead to the development of sects, Troeltsch (1931) elaborated and modified the work of Weber. Troeltsch's significant contribution was in producing an organizational model which differentiated between sects and established churches on the basis of various criteria. The key considerations are the extent of organizational differentiation, specialization, and hierarchy, and the orientation towards society. However, Troeltsch began with the assumption that distinct religious outlooks will be expressed in different forms of religious organization. Working largely within the framework of Christianity, he identified two broad inclinations in the early church which precipitated unique types of religious organization.

One type of organization emphasized the need to establish an egalitarian community outside mainstream society. This orientation tended to deliberately limit bureaucratic structures and hierarchy. The other stressed the independently structured community that endeavoured to make use of the surrounding social institutions for its own advantages. The former displayed a radical tendency and the latter a conservative one. While the conservative tendency associated with the Church came to dominate, the radical variation expressed itself in unique ways, notably monasticism and sectarianism.

According to Troeltsch (1931, 331) the Church comes to largely accept the legitimacy of the social order (an orientation legitimated by scriptural reference) and attempts to have authority over every aspect of life. It also endeavours to influence the state and appeal to the dominant classes. In this way it forms an integral part of the status quo. In contrast, the sect, which throughout the history of Christianity has typically broken away from the Church and condemned its worldliness, has attracted the lower classes, who feel oppressed by the state and are frequently opposed to the prevailing social order. In turn, the established churches label the sect as extremist and heretical. These labels, however, much like that of 'sect', can plausibly be seen as negative ones imposed by those religious establishments who have the power and legitimacy to apply them.

For Troeltsch, the major attributes of sects are as follows.

- Firstly, they are fairly small religious collectives and their members are well integrated within them. Like cults, sects have generally tended to be less complex organizations than churches and denominations and have little by way of an internal hierarchy.
- Secondly, rather than drawing members from all strata of society and being closely connected with the state, sects tend to appeal to the lowest strata.
- Thirdly, sects reject the world and the culture of mainstream society, and frequently see established state and religious authorities as oppressive and persecuting.
- Fourthly, sect members are expected to withdraw from the outside world.
- Fifthly, sects insist that members remain strictly committed to a rigid set of beliefs and demonstrate their allegiance.
- Sixthly, members join voluntarily as adults rather than being socialized into the religious group. When children of sect members grow up, they are expected to either accept the teachings of the community or leave.
- Seventhly, sects believe that they have a monopoly of the 'truth' or at least claim that they have superior beliefs.
- Finally, sects have no hierarchy of paid officials or priesthood.

Troeltsch's two-fold typology has proved a useful tool in understanding transformations within the history of Christianity and obviously still has some application. There are abundant examples of sects which have broken away from mainline Christianity and some are considered below. However, the evidence suggests that religious organizations display a greater complexity than Troeltsch had allowed for. In particular, sects may be discovered *within* Churches rather than breaking away from them. One example is found in Harper's (1974) analysis of Roman Catholic charismatics. He found that they display a commitment to a sect type of organization that has a small, non-institutionalized, voluntary membership which is subject to strict regulations. Yet, this is achieved within an existing Church structure. The movement emphasizes religious socialization, a rather tentative allegiance to the Catholic Church and its dogma, an emphasis on the 'Pentecostal' conversion experience as a necessary 'badge' of belonging, and the stress on continued interaction between members, ranging from loosely organized prayer cells to large-scale renewal conferences. The movement thus provides an example of how 'alternative' religion may be hidden within mainstream religious institutions.

This existence of sect-like organizations within Church structures is, of course, not new. The monastic variant of the sect typified by Roman Catholic monasteries and nunneries still endures as it has for centuries (Hill 1971). This variant can be seen as a particular expression of what is generally known as the 'intentional community', where members of a sect choose to live together communally and are generally separated from the outside world in order to preserve its distinctiveness. Most are outside established Church structures and are typified by a variety of Anabaptist groups, including the Bruderhof and Amish, and the more recently established neo-Pentecostal communities. While such collectives tend to last longer than the non-religious intentional communities which became so popular in the 1960s, they have proved increasingly hard to sustain economically and have less appeal in the highly individualistic societies of the Western world. A good example of a successful Christian community, however, is the Jesus Fellowship (discussed in detail in Chapter 7) – a British variant of the Jesus movement which emerged in the late 1960s. It carries many characteristics of the sect, although it is more conveniently placed under the rubric of an NRM.

Church-sect transformations

Niebuhr's work (1957) marked a significant stage in the discussion of sect transformation. His emphasis was on what he believed to be an endless cycle of Church-sect evolution. For Niebuhr, the sect was not capable of surviving for very long. It would either adapt itself to prevailing circumstances or die. Moreover, there was the 'problem' of the second generation. In short, the next generation of adherents to the sect would generally fail to have the zeal and commitment of the first. Simultaneously, a this-worldly asceticism engendered a prosperity for later generations that would raise them out of poverty and provide them with a sense of greater integration into wider society. As the sect developed into a worldlier Church, a new sect might emerge as part of a relentless and inevitable process.

Bryan Wilson (1970), however, opposes Niebuhr's view that sects are inevitably short-lived. The evidence indicates that some sects do survive for a long time without becoming either a denomination or a Church. According to Wilson, the key factor is the way that a sect answers the question 'What shall we do to be saved?' One form, the 'conversionist sect', is inclined to evolve into a denomination. The goal of this type of sect is to make as many converts as possible by way of revivalist preaching. Becoming a denomination and developing the organization structure necessary for proselytization does not have to undermine this objective. The other type of sect, the 'adventist sect', such as Jehovah's Witnesses and SDA, like many others that arose in the nineteenth-century, await the return of Christ who, it is believed, will establish a new world in which sect members are guaranteed a place. These sects preach a separation from the world. To become a denomination they would have to compromise this premise. In discussing changes within contemporary Western societies, Wilson also recognizes that the process of sect transformation to denomination was speeding up and that this was a sign of the potency of secularity in eroding away at the sectarian structure.

In turn, Wilson's work on sects has influenced other writers. A chief inspiration is his emphasis on the separateness and distinctiveness of the sect and its claim to uniquely possess the 'truth'. One of the most innovating works in this respect has been Robertson's four-fold classification of religious organizations, which spells out the difference between sects and other organizations and how likely sects are to develop under particular circumstances (Robertson 1970). Robertson's classification uses two groupings of distinction to constitute four categories of organization (Table 4). Firstly, there is 'inclusive membership' – membership open to anyone, as opposed to 'exclusive membership' where some test or condition of eligibility is required. Then, there is what he designates the self-conceived basis of legitimacy, which the sect takes as either a claim to the only possession of 'truth' ('unique legitimacy') or, alternatively, an acknowledgement that other religious groups also possess at least aspects of it ('pluralist legitimacy').

Table 4 Classification of Church, denomination and sect

		Self-conceived basis of legitimacy	
		Pluralist legitimate	**Uniquely legitimate**
Membership principle	**Exclusive**	Institutionalized sect	Sect
	Inclusive	Denomination	Church

Source: Adapted from Robertson, R. (1970) *The Sociological Interpretation of Religion*, Oxford: Blackwell, p. 123.

Sects and deprivation

The link between sectarian membership and deprivation has been an important and enduring aspect of the study of sects. As we have seen, in such works as that of Troeltsch and Niebuhr, deprivation is usually given to mean material poverty and social marginalization. For those who have little stake in society the sect brings a new status. Often, through millenarian themes which stress the immanent arrival of the kingdom of God, it constructs a new set of values that are in conflict with the world, frequently attacking injustices and the sources of poverty and alienation.

The clear identification of the sect with the lower classes and, indeed, the Church with middle or dominant classes is harder to sustain today, although the typical sectarian tension with society remains. In the 1960s, as part of the wider picture of profound religious and social change, sects appeared to be proliferating. In the USA, at least, the growth seemed to be more obviously linked to the recruitment of marginal and disadvantaged groups. For instance, the Black Muslim movement provided for the needs of many poor blacks. Although it started in the 1930s among Afro-Americans, the movement proliferated at a time of pressure for civil rights from the 1960s onwards and began to also attract middle-class adherents. In time-honoured tradition, the movement has since splintered into various factions. Some have returned to Sunni Islamic orthodoxy while others continue to be politically motivated, advancing black rights in what is perceived to be a white-dominated society.

In explaining the rise of sectarian type groups, Glock (1958) expanded the notion of deprivation. This was in order to understand how sects, in numerous ways, provide a channel through which their members are able to transcend their feelings of deprivation by replacing them with a sense of religious privilege. This privilege comes through sectarianism, with its emphasis on belonging to an 'elite'. Thus we can understand how adherents to sects may be drawn from a variety of social backgrounds. Here, sect members no longer compare themselves in terms of their relatively lower economic position, but by way of their superior spiritual status.

According to Glock, the major forms of deprivation that sects address are as follows:

- *Economic deprivation*   a subjective criterion by which people feel themselves underprivileged in terms of the distribution of material wealth.
- *Social deprivation*   underprivilege in whatever society regards as important such as prestige or power, often in modern society youthfulness, male superiority, or reward by merit.
- *Organismic deprivation*   when a person's level of mental or physical health does not match up to society's standards.
- *Ethical deprivation*   when the individual feels that the dominant values of society no longer provide a meaningful way by which to conduct life and there is a felt necessity to find another set of values.
- *Psychic deprivation*   which results from a consequence of severe and unresolved social deprivation. The individual is not missing the material advantages of life but its psychological rewards are felt to have been withheld.

Religious solutions to this range of deprivations are more likely to occur where the nature of the deprivation is inaccurately perceived or where those experiencing the deprivation are not well placed to work directly at eliminating the causes. Conversely, the resolution is likely to be secular, without reference to the supernatural, in a situation where deprivation is correctly assessed by those experiencing it and they have the power to overcome its causes directly. Religious resolutions, then, are likely to compensate for feelings of deprivation rather than to eliminate its causes. However, sects may bring resolutions more effectively than secular ones, particularly in the case of ethical and psychic deprivation. Different sects invariably cluster around distinct deprivations. For example, *organismic deprivation* may attract beliefs about alternative forms of healing. Some sects also tend to last longer than others. Those dealing with merely ethical deprivation are inclined, according to Glock, to be rather short-lived.

Sects as an integrating force

A related interpretation of the emergence of sects (and cults for that matter) conjectures that they are foremost a response to the problems of social dislocation and a failure to develop a sense of belonging to wider society. For instance, the Holiness movement, a breakaway faction within Pentecostalism, spread rapidly in the 1930s among rural people who had migrated to urban neighbourhoods (Holt 1940). The movement provided a locus of belonging, identification, and stability for those who found themselves in an alienating environment. Similarly, the emergence of sects in New York State over a fairly long period in the first half of the twentieth-century may have correlated with the uncertain conditions caused by dramatic economic fluctuations at the time (Barkun 1986). Sects, therefore, bring certainty in a period of uncertainty and ambiguity. They also allow members to protest against the environment in which they find themselves, while simultaneously overcoming some difficulties of dislocation by establishing a new community in small, close-knit networks and operating as a kind of surrogate family.

The level of tension that sects exhibit towards society may vary considerably. Hence, Stark and Bainbridge (1985, 135) distinguish between those sects with 'extremely high tension' and those with 'very high tension'. The former engenders both ridicule and serious antagonism, even to the point of a great deal of state and legal intervention in their affairs. They may frequently be associated with socially unacceptable practices typified by polygamous Mormon communes and/or all groups which are millenarian in orientation, such as Jehovah's Witnesses. Those with 'very high tension' are the ones regarded as quite deviant and display considerable friction with society, for example, many Pentecostal groups with their emphasis on such religious phenomena as 'gifts' of healing and speaking in tongues.

While the subject of sects is usually addressed in terms of exclusion and social deviance, some sociologists speculate that they can provide the function of helping to integrate people into society and may in fact contribute towards social stability. In this regard, the so-called 'moral regeneration theory' advances the view that religious sects generate the process of reaffiliation with the social order and bring conforming behaviour under the influence of new social bonds. For instance, Akers (1977) argues that persons outside society, lacking ties to the moral order, are strongly reattached to the social mainstream by virtue of their recruitment into the intensely integrated moral community represented by the sect. It can even be argued that the very deprivations that cause people to join sects are abated by membership, enabling them to improve their material circumstances and thus have a greater stake in society. This may include, for example, an ascetic orientation towards hard work and thrift, or practical financial help given to members.

In terms of personality traits, sect members tend to be over-conventional and cling rigidly to social rules and regulations. At least this is the finding presented by Johnson

(1961) of Pentecostalism in the USA. He indicated that while Pentecostals could be perceived as a 'deviant' sectarian minority, there was also evidence of strong conformity to mainstream values. The cultural values more readily endorsed tended to be those which were held to have made the USA great – especially the ones interpreted as in line with the teachings of Christianity, including hard work and personal success. In much the same way (as discussed in Chapter 7), the 1970s Jesus movement appeared to reintegrate social outcasts back into society and inculcated its young, former counter-cultural membership with at least some dominant American values (Adams & Fox 1972).

Recruitment to sects

A fair amount of sociological work has been orientated towards finding out why some sectarian forms of religion are clearly more successful than others. The focus has largely been on how those which are successful at recruiting then consolidate and deploy their members, and how they sustain their organization and arrange leadership structures. Surveys conducted include those of Jehovah's Witnesses (Beckford 1975) and the Jesus movement (Davies & Richardson 1976). One of the most acclaimed studies however, is Gerlach and Hine's (1970) work on Pentecostalism. Here, it was found that the movement displayed various organizational factors which allowed it to spread and consolidate (these were also discovered to exist within political Black Power movements as well). They involved:

- Firstly, the relationship among networks of local groups of the movement, which provided a flexibility that promoted the movement's spread.
- Secondly, the recruitment was along the lines of pre-existing social relationships, including social class, family, and friends.
- Thirdly, an emphasis on a clearly defined commitment, act, or experience.
- Fourthly, an ideology offering a simple, easily communicated interpretive sense of sharing, control, and promised rewards, and a sense of personal worth and power.
- Finally, the emphasis was on the perception of a real or imagined opposition which brought both unity and purpose.

Although sociological studies are concerned with what religious organizations do to promote growth, a related sociological interest is in *how* people come to join sectarian forms of organization. Here, some sociologists have put an emphasis not on the attraction of particular doctrines, the members' social background, or psychological frame of mind. Rather, those such as Snow and Philips (1980) are concerned with the importance of personal links or, at the very least, 'emergent personal ties'. Personal links can stem from street evangelism should a cord be struck on a face-to-face level with potential converts. Hence, some sects, like Jehovah's Witnesses, put a great deal of stress on evangelizing for new converts. In doing so, they may purposely play up the 'coincidence' of meeting in the street as 'God's will' and refer to a crucial turning point for the convert in their life. Winning converts in this way also reinforces the collective's worldview as being part of God's supposed elect. An integral part of this is that sects, as well as other religious movements, will frequently stress the alleged deteriorating state of the world and hope that this corresponds with the individual's own situation. Beckford has pointed out that Jehovah's Witnesses often approach strangers about common worries such as war, economic problems, or rising crime. The emphasis is on order-threatening conditions which may magnify the potential convert's feelings of dissatisfaction, fear, or anxiety – feelings they may have previously felt only vaguely in their life (Beckford 1975, 174).

Very frequently there are generations of people who join the same sectarian group. This is obviously achieved through religious socialization by parents or close relatives. Other close social networks and relationships with somebody in the religious group are also important in explaining why a new convert will join. The importance of such connections is in promoting the withdrawal of the individual from his/her former way of life by encouraging the renouncement of competing relationships and discouraging interaction with the outside world, family, and friends. This amounts to a resocializing of members into the religious group, which is integral to learning to act, look, and talk rather like other members and displaying outward signs of commitment.

Accounts of conversion to sects and other similar movements, typified by Beckford's work (1978) on conversion to Jehovah's Witnesses, also tend to put an emphasis on a learning process. It includes a study of personal accounts of conversion which, according to Beckford, is 'skilfully accomplished by actors' – the slow acceptance of the movement's version of its own rationale. The convert slowly abandons his/ her former worldview, social relationships, and activity patterns. Conversion is 'achieved' and 'organized'. The individual's conversion account depends on the guidelines of the Witnesses' all-controlling body – the Watchtower organization based in New York – and its exclusive ideology. This ideology (even if it changes over time) is all-embracing and disseminated via literature and the activities of the Watchtower organization generally. To be a full member of the Jehovah's Witnesses is to subscribe to a worldview and make use of particular rules in certain situations. To be converted is to internalize such rules through a 'progressive enlightenment' – an acceptance of the Watchtower as God's visible organization and spiritual elect, as a kind of theocracy, and publisher of God's intentions. Beckford (1983) observed that in his research on Jehovah's Witnesses and the Unification Church it was not uncommon for members to alter their views over time and even pass through distinct phases of commitment that vary in style and strength. He concludes that conversion entails an interaction during which the recruit constructs or negotiates a new personal identity.

Some major Christian sectarian movements

While we may accept the view of those such as Niebuhr that the emergence of sects is a relatively normal aspect of the development of religion (particularly within Christianity), there have been periods in history when sects have proliferated in greater number. Certainly, the Reformation generated numerous new sects. The spirit of dissent against the Roman Catholic Church and the rise of different interpretations of Christianity undoubtedly brought about their development. Amish and Hutterites, Baptists, Presbyterians, Shakers and Quakers, and other sects within Protestantism rapidly expanded with the new-found freedom of the period. In turn, especially throughout the eighteenth and nineteenth-centuries, sects broke away from the original sects and in doing so created an increasing fragmentation of religious life in many Western societies.

The late nineteenth and early twentieth-centuries also saw the rise of countless, almost exclusively, Protestant sects. Although sects have developed more recently, in many respects this period marked the heyday of sectarian divisions. The Church of Jesus Christ of Latter-day Saints (the Mormons), the SDA, Christadelphians, and Jehovah's Witnesses were but a few that appeared at this time. Many of those of the nineteenth-century initially materialized in the USA and subsequently spread globally over the next one hundred and fifty years (Wilson 1970). Some of these sects have come to have a membership counted in millions. They appear to have enjoyed prolific growth over the last thirty or forty years and now constitute an important element of the constituency of 'alternative' religions. To one extent or another, the majority of the movements overviewed below display many, if not all, of the characteristics outlined in the typologies of those such as Weber and Troeltsch, while others make important departures. The way that some have subsequently developed has also opened up a number of other interesting issues.

The Brethren movement

The Brethren movement has always displayed fairly straightforward evangelical Protestant beliefs. There are, however, some doctrines and conventions which appear to take at least one major stream of the movement off in a sectarian direction. The Brethren originated with a small group of believers in Dublin in 1827. Their meetings were held along the lines of what was assumed to be the New Testament church: a group of brothers meeting in God's name, a simplicity of worship, and no established form of ritual. There was an opposition to all the trappings of denominationalism and a rejection of an ordained ministry. Like other sects at the time, the early Brethren believed that the restoration of these practices suggested the imminent return of Christ, although what appeared to be the evils of an increasingly secular society also confirmed this assumption.

John Nelson Darby (1800–82) joined this small Brethren group after relinquishing his role of curate in the Episcopalian Church of Ireland. He moved to Plymouth in 1930 and established a congregation there. Hence, the group became known as the Plymouth Brethren, although the movement has generally disliked this designation. Darby took his message to Western Europe as well as other countries as far flung as Australia. His major theological contribution was that of Dispensationalism. This dogma insists that God deals with man through seven stages: the Age of Innocence, before the Fall, and then the Ages of Conscience, Human Government, Promise, Law, and Grace (the Atonement of Christ). The seventh and future age to come is the millennial reign of the messiah. In turn, Dispensationalism, in one form or another, has been preached by many evangelical churches. Hence, it is no longer an exclusively Brethren doctrine. Darby was also an early pioneer of the pre-millenarian doctrine of the 'Last Things'. He taught that the saved will be caught up in the Rapture before Christ's return, and so will be spared the great tribulation (spoken of in the Book of Revelation), whereas others, including Jehovah's Witnesses, believe that the elect will have to suffer such a tribulation and great persecution.

In many respects, today's Brethren movement is well within that branch of Protestantism frequently referred to as Conservative Evangelicalism. This constituency is the strict inheritor of the Reformation; it is vehemently anti-Roman Catholic, Trinitarian, and insists on the assurance of salvation by faith alone. What is distinct about the Brethren communities however, is that they continue to reject many of the creeds and believe that the bible is the sole source of authority for their teachings. Yet, for over 150 years, the Brethren has been a divided movement. In 1848 it split into two, the larger portion calling itself the Christian Brethren or the Open Brethren, to distinguish itself from Darby's faction, the Exclusive Brethren. The Open Brethren now operates much like a confederation of independent evangelical churches, although it depends on the individual congregation whether outsiders are allowed to join in the Eucharist. In the USA, there are claimed to be some 65,000 devotees, to be found in as many as eight subdivisions of the movement.

In Britain, during the 1960s, some Brethren were instrumental in the creation of British Restorationism, which came to constitute a distinct strand of neo-Pentecostalism outside established church structures and one which developed its own unique set of beliefs (see Chapter 5). More recently, some churches refer to themselves as 'Progressive Brethren' and display all the trappings of the contemporary church 'scene', including the drums, guitars, and other musical instruments. It also presents an image orientated towards the young – the next generation of believers. Those who head the movement have concluded that it has to move with the times if it is to survive. It is this more modernist and culturally accommodating stance that will probably guarantee the continuation of the movement.

The Exclusive Brethren, by comparison, now appears to epitomize the classic sectarian form of organization and a declining one at that. Members keep themselves apart from every other Christian church or denomination. They hold their exclusivity by refusing to share the Eucharist with those outside the sect – 'in view of maintaining suitable conditions for partaking of the Lord's Supper' (Barrett 1998, 70). They exclude from their fellowship those who do not share their doctrines and decline to adhere to absolute standards of purity. Members separate themselves from the corruption of the world, including the sinful influences of television and other forms of modern entertainment. Socializing with anyone outside the fellowship is prohibited. The children of the sect are educated in state schools, but do not take part in competitive sports or any extracurricular activity, and they are strongly discouraged from making any friends outside the group. University education is not sanctioned since it is believed that student life is full of evil and temptation. Despite the attempt to ensure the next generation of Brethren through the strict control of members and inculcation of doctrine, the Exclusive wing appears to be in terminal decline on both sides of the Atlantic. Typical of many such forms of sectarianism, this demise, alongside perceived growing heresy and increasing evil in the world, is regarded as a 'sign' of the Last Days. Nevertheless, God's promise is also vindicated by the continuation and loyalty of a small and upright 'remnant'.

Christadelphians

The Christadelphians were founded in America by John Thomas in 1848. After much study of the bible, Thomas carved out his own set of doctrines and established a unique variant of Christianity. Typical of sectarian organizations, he believed that his teachings were a return to original New Testament beliefs. In 1849, he published a book, the *Hope of Israel*, in which he wrote that the 'Last Days' had commenced and this resulted from his conviction that before the return of Christ, Israel would be restored. While there had been earlier attempts by Christadelphians at predicting the Second Coming, in 1868 and 1910, this practice has now been abandoned and the movement has come to believe that no one knows the date of Christ's return. In their millenarian teachings today the Christadelphians are broadly similar to most evangelical churches, although far more emphasis is put on the restoration of Israel since it is believed that the Jews have their own destiny that runs parallel to the historical purpose of the Christian Church. In a rather formal and sober way, modern Christadelphians will frequently stage local lectures on the subject of the restoration of Israel, along with other biblical themes. This, in addition to public exhibitions of their bible collections, is their principal means of evangelism.

While Christadelphians are stronger now in Britain than the USA, Thomas had initially established churches on both sides of the Atlantic. In these congregations he set up no central authority or priesthood, and each was self-governing. This is a working structure which still endures. At a global level only the subscription to *The Christadelphian Magazine* unites the wider movement. Christadelphians pride themselves in being ardent students of the bible, which they believe to be the indisputable word of God and from which they take all their teachings. They display some sectarian characteristics, but not all those found in other Protestant groups. The attitude towards sexuality is not liberal, nor do members vote or take active part in political activities, but they refrain from discouraging interaction with non-members.

While displaying a greater degree of toleration regarding mainstream Christianity than do other sects, Christadelphians see themselves as having little in common with the traditional churches. Doctrinally, the fundamental divergence is that there is no acceptance of the Trinity, but neither are they Unitarians. They subscribe to the view that Christ was literally the 'only begotten Son of God' but not himself God. Hence, they do not endorse the doctrine of the divinity of Christ. The Christadelphian teaching on the atonement is fairly similar to orthodox Christianity: being sinless Jesus could offer himself as a sacrifice to man. However, he would not have been able to do this if he himself had been God. The other person in the Christian Trinity, the Holy Spirit, is merely seen as 'God's own radiant power': he is not some third person in the Godhead.

Christadelphians do not believe in Satan as a personal devil but only a metaphor for the evils of human nature. They also deny the immortality of the soul or eternal punishment in a literal hell. Heaven, for the saved, will be on earth after Christ's return. The unsaved will simply not be resurrected. From time to time, in their doctrines, the Christadelphians are divided over certain issues. A major source of division has been in regard to the conscientious objection to war. A minority refused to fight in the Second World War, while others were prepared to do so on the grounds of a 'just war'.

The Church of Jesus Christ of Latter-day Saints

The Church of Jesus Christ of Latter-day Saints (the Mormons) has established itself, particularly in the USA, as one of the largest religious movements outside main-stream Christianity. From its beginnings, it has grown to have a global membership. Like many other revivalist evangelists at the time, its founder, Joseph Smith (1805–44), came from New York State. In the early 1820s, Smith laid claim to a number of visions. In one of these, in 1823, the angel Moroni informed him about some golden plates buried in a local hillside. In 1827, according to his assertions, God allowed him to dig them up and he began the work of translating them.

When the translation was finished the angel allegedly took the golden plates away, although much of the revelation was published in *The Book of Mormon* (1830). Its subtitle, *Another Testament of Jesus Christ* indicates the Mormon conviction that the volume authoritatively adds to the traditional Christian revelation. This makes the movement a distinctive form of sectarianism in that it has an extra-scriptural authority which separates it from traditional Christianity. The book tells of two migrations to the American continent, the earlier one by the Jaredite people after the fall of the Tower of Babel, and the second by a group of upright Jews whose leader was known as Lehi. Two of Lehi's sons were Nephi and Laman. The descendants of Nephi, the Nephites, were godly. The Lamanites were evil, and were cursed by God so that their skin turned dark, and they became the ancestors of the Native American Indians. According to *The Book of Mormon*, after his resurrection Jesus visited America and preached to the Nephites. The Lamanites eradicated the Nephites around AD 428 on the hill where Smith found the golden plates. These plates, which related the history of the migrations and American settlements, were written by the prophet Mormon and his son Moroni, who were the last of the Nephites.

After a period of persecution, the leadership of the Mormons fell into the hands of Brigham Young. The church's unconventional beliefs and the common practice of men having more than one wife (since relinquished) were the basis of such persecution. It was Young who led over 30,000 Mormons from Nauvoo, Illinois, to Salt Lake City, Utah, in 1848. This journey of 1,400 miles is remembered in Mormon history as the 'Great Trek'. About half the population of Salt Lake City is today constituted by members of the Mormon Church.

The Mormon Church regards itself as a restoration of the early Christian Church and as the sole true faith. Although many Mormon beliefs are similar to that of mainstream Christianity, there are some radical departures. A unique practice is that baptisms are performed for deceased ancestors, with tens of millions who never heard the Mormon 'truth' now baptized. Each member researches his or her family tree at least four generations back. Hence, the Mormon genealogical database at Salt Lake City is the largest in the world. A further departure from the Christian mainstream is the teaching that God is not an immaterial spirit but a being with a physical body. One consequence is the belief that Jesus was conceived in a physical union between God and the Virgin Mary. Mormons also believe that our souls existed before we were born. On a planet orbiting the star Kolob, God and his many wives have children: these are spiritual beings without bodies. When a child is about to be born on earth, one of these spiritual beings inhabits the child, the spirit and the body becoming a living soul.

Mormons maintain that, with his death, Jesus paid the penalty that man inherited from the fall of Adam and Eve. His sacrifice will redeem man from sin if we believe in him and keep his commandments. However, unlike evangelical Protestants, Mormons believe that salvation comes through both grace and works. Thus, the Mormon Church lays great stress on morality and disciplined behaviour. Sex before marriage and infidelity within marriage is condemned (marriages are usually consecrated for eternity), as are homosexual practices. Tobacco, alcohol, and other drugs are prohibited, along with the drinking of tea, coffee, and cola drinks, because of the stimulants they contain.

As with other sects, the Mormons believe that they are not only reviving the beliefs of the early Christian Church, but many of its practices deemed as being lost over two thousand years. One is temple worship, and the Mormons have constructed some very large and beautiful buildings, which are occasionally open to the public. Another form of restoration is the priestly structure within the organization. Besides the posts of elder, deacon, and overseer, which are to be found in the New Testament, there is also a lineage of priests which is reminiscent of Old Testament customs. As far as the latter is concerned, Joseph Smith claimed to have rejuvenated the office alongside restoring the 'keys' of the kingdom' – a reference to Jesus' statement to the apostle Peter that he (Jesus) was the rock upon which the Christian Church would be built.

The temple is central to the life of Mormons. Its function revolves around the restoration of the so-called 'ordinances'. There are three such ordinances: endowment, the sealing of marriage, and the sealing of ancestors. Ideally, endowment should be practised by each member once in a lifetime. This entails going through the various rooms of the temple in a spirit of contemplation. The endowment climaxes in the Celestial Room, which is usually placed at the top of the temple and is the most splendid of all the rooms and a rough equivalent of the 'holy of holies' in the temple of Solomon as described in the Old Testament. The second ordinance is the sealing of marriage, which is expected to be not only for life but all eternity. The third, the sealing of ancestors, is related to the baptism of the dead and, in essence, secures the spiritual well-being of the dead.

The Mormon Church is organized into 'wards' – congregations of between 200 to 600 members led by a bishop in a hierarchical, structured movement. There is also a lay priesthood. Although the level of commitment that a local Mormon group expects of its members varies considerably, the church purposely emphasizes networks and peer relationships in sustaining both organizational cohesion and a distinct worldview. This has partly accounted for its prolific growth. Although suffering persecution, controversy over polygamous marriages, considerable doctrinal disputes, and internal leadership conflicts, the Mormons have grown rapidly (sending out international ministries as early as 1840). In 1997, the movement claimed to have nearly 10 million members, with a little under half to be found in the USA. The movement has made particular inroads into Mexico and Latin America and, since 1945, appears to be doubling its membership every fifteen years. *The Book of Mormon*, which is read alongside the bible, has sold 78 million copies.

Jehovah's Witnesses

The Watchtower movement was initially founded by Charles Taze Russell (1852–1916), a controversial figure, who developed a number of the millenarian ideas that were popular in the 1870s among some Christian circles. In 1871, he published the first issue of *Zion's Watch Tower and Herald of Christ's Presence*. A decade later, the Watchtower Bible and Tract Society was formed. It is still the official name of the huge New York-based publishing operation at the heart of the Jehovah's Witnesses organization. In 1918, J.F. Rutherford succeeded Russell. He was to add greatly to the doctrinal writings of the movement and it was Russell who coined the famous slogan 'Millions now living will never die', which is still used. The name 'Jehovah's Witnesses' was officially adopted in 1931.

The Jehovah's Witnesses is one of the largest international sectarian movements. Like the Mormons, the Witnesses appear to enjoy a prolific growth rate. For example, at least according to the organization's own statistics, the movement has expanded in Britain from nearly 98 thousand in 1980, to nearer 118 thousand in 2000. There are now some 4 million Jehovah's Witnesses in over 200 countries across the world. For several years the rate of global growth was around 5 per cent annually. In the post-war years this expansion can at least be partly attributed to the emphasis on door-to-door evangelism that underlines the importance of personal contacts. However, the growth has not been straightforward. In recent times the expansion has been more in non-western societies, while in the mid-1970s, after the failure of prophecy, there was a noticeable drop in membership worldwide.

Like the Mormons, the Jehovah's Witnesses are extremely well organized, which largely accounts for the movement's success. The Watchtower Bible and Tract Society is authoritarian and patriarchal. It has strict rules of membership and keeps its adherents constantly active and involved in evangelism. Also, like the Christadelphians, there is no official priesthood. Rather, there is a strong emphasis on the 'priesthood of all believers' and all are given a missionary task. Certainly, Beckford's (1975) in-depth study of the Witnesses shows that the members are strongly motivated and goal orientated as a result of effective socialization into the movement. In terms of social composition, Ninian Smart (1971) generalizes that the membership is relatively poorly educated with a strong lower middle-class component which he believes, in the classical interpretation of sectarianism, is a compensator for one form or another of deprivation. However, much remains unsubstantiated and there is the acute danger of stereotyping members into preconceived sociological categories.

In many respects, the Jehovah's Witnesses epitomize the sectarian form of organization. As with other schismatic groups, the movement likes to present itself to the world as the restoration of something older, seceding from a religious tradition which has drifted into worldliness, and not as an entirely new phenomenon. Hence, the Jehovah's Witnesses prefer to describe themselves not as a variant of Christianity, but as the 'Truth' (Beckford 1990). In line with other movements of sectarianism, this has often been accompanied with claims to restoring the first-century Church after two thousand years of apostasy and heresy. Like other such sects, the Jehovah's Witnesses also tend to emphasize simplicity of worship, with no ritual or set form of service, since it is envisaged as a return to first-century practice.

The development of a specialized ministry, bureaucracy, and formal organization seems to accompany Church-like forms, but not sects. Yet, this is not always the case, and certainly the Jehovah's Witnesses is a highly differentiated and complex organization, while also retaining a negative view of society. Hence, the movement is best described by what Nelson (1968) calls the 'established sect', which denotes large, enduring, and highly organized groups that retain their sectarian orientation.

Also in line with other sects, Jehovah's Witnesses stress a number of particular beliefs which are held to be a badge of a self-assigned elite status and which help constitute the boundaries with other Christian groups. Many of these core teachings are outside the traditions of historical Christianity and amount to a theology that is very rationalistic and devoid of mysticism. Thus, the movement in many ways follows the Protestant evangelical tradition of the Reformation. There is an emphasis on the written 'Word' of God, at least as it is translated by the Watchtower organization. The Witnesses have their own version of the bible, *The New World Translation*, which supports key doctrines (most not accepted by the great majority of biblical scholars) such as the created nature of Christ. This view towards Christ, theologically speaking, is Arian – regarded by the established Church as a fourth-century heresy. Hence, the Witnesses reject the Trinitarian Nicene Creed as man-made and having parallels in Hinduism. Like Christadelphians, the Witnesses believe that the future for the righteous will be on a new earth, rather than heaven.

For Jehovah's Witnesses there is every attempt to make the movement different from what is perceived as the corrupt historical Christian Church, which is an integral part of 'Babylon' or the world order and of the dominion of the anti-Christ. There is also a preference for seeing Christ as having died on a 'stake' rather than a cross. Above all, there is considerable stress on reclaiming the true name of God, 'Yahweh' or 'Jehovah', after centuries of it falling into neglect. Hence, the organization's name is taken from the Book of Isaiah (43:10–12), which declares 'Ye are my witnesses, saith the Lord' (Jehovah). Another controversial area is that of rejecting blood transfusions, which is based on the Jewish law of the Old Testament forbidding the eating of blood from living creatures. This restriction has now largely been reduced to a matter of individual conscience. Less well known is the refusal to take up arms for any earthly government since they are perceived to be in the hands of Satan.

By various criteria the Jehovah's Witnesses are clearly sectarian. Members, in many respects, separate themselves from this world, taking seriously Christ's command to his followers that they are to be 'no part of the world'. The Witnesses interpret this as meaning that they should not be a part of political affairs since this is Satan's domain. This represents a clear dualism, a world of good and bad, where members of the Watchtower organization belong to Jehovah's theocratic rule. Being 'no part of the world', however, does not mean that certain worldly activities are not acceptable. Thus, the movement's members have no difficulty with earning an income through employment in the outside world, and their children are allowed to attend state schools. However, other worldly activities are denied and this includes celebrations and holidays. Hence, Christmas, birthdays, and national festivals are not celebrated. Many such festivals are seen as so much selfish indulgence, while the refusal to sanction Christmas comes from the conviction that it is a pagan festival (the fact that most other churches allow it is a sign that they are under satanic influence).

Like many sects that began in the nineteenth-century, the Jehovah's Witnesses are strongly millenarian, believing in the invisible return of Christ and the setting up of his kingdom on earth. Here, a great deal of emphasis is put upon the Old Testament Book of Daniel and the New Testament Book of Revelation. According to teachings derived from this scripture, the Witnesses identify six world powers throughout human history: Egypt, Assyria, Babylon, Medo-Persia, Greece, and Rome. A seventh power is expected and is generally believed to be the USA, in conjunction with Britain. It is these powers that are anticipated to dominate world affairs for a short period before the final battle of Armageddon between godly and satanic powers. The former will inevitably win, with the Watchtower organization assumed to be the means by which God creates his new world order.

Predicting dates of the arrival of God's kingdom has always been a strong theme. The problem, however, is that such date fixing of the end of the world may ultimately be self-defeating. Initially, the early Witnesses were convinced that the end would begin to occur from 1874. Various other dates were predicted at the turn of the nineteenth-century, before the year was moved to 1914. Christ was to return openly, and then the organization insisted that it was an 'invisible' return when the advent failed to materialize at that time. This date was also said to mark the beginning of the End and those who witnessed 1914 would not die out before the arrival of God's kingdom. In a sense, the movement did strike lucky since the First World War appeared to fit the apocalyptic scenario.

With the generation that was alive in 1914 now dying out, the Watchtower organization is presently confronting a doctrinal dilemma. It is forced to admit that 'Not all that was expected to happen in 1914 did happen, but it did mark the end of the Gentile Times and was a year of special significance' (*Jehovah's Witnesses in the Twentieth Century* 1989, 7). In effect, this means the beginning of the transition period from human rule to the Thousand Year Reign of Christ. Other attempts to set dates – 1920, 1925, 1940, 1975, and 1984 have resulted in disappointment and sometimes revision of doctrines. Currently it is accepted that no one knows the date of the end of the world. More broadly, some of the teachings related to the Last Days are not that different from those of other evangelical Christians, including the pre-millenarian emphasis on Armageddon. However, much is made of the 'little flock' of 144,000 who will go to heaven and rule with Christ, while the 'great crowd' will remain on earth and be ruled by God's organization. It is possible that this doctrine developed when, by the 1930s, the membership had exceeded this number. Thus, while there is no distinction between clergy and lay people in the movement, a kind of spiritual elite is discernible.

Quakers

The term 'sect', as we have noted, tends to be a derisory one. Nonetheless, while refuting the designation, some religious movements would arguable recognize a number of the sociologically defined characteristics as a virtue. Others, however, would reject the label and its descriptive elements altogether. The Quakers are a good example. Although once fitting squarely into the rubric of a sect, it is less easy to substantiate that this is so today. In fact, the development of Quakerism displays one of the possible future pathways for a sect.

George Fox established the Religious Society of Friends, or Quakers, as they soon became known, around 1650. They gained their nickname because of the tendency to quake with fear in the presence of God. The distinctive form of worship, then as now, is a silent awaiting on the Holy Spirit, perceived as guiding with an inner light which dwells in the heart of each individual Christian and is maintained to be the only true authority. In the early days, if not today, the movement was also associated with speaking in tongues. An observance that continues, however, is that Quakers do not accept the authority of any church minister and refuse to swear oaths of any kind. Initially these beliefs meant that the Quakers were unorthodox and often ostracized by the wider Christian community.

The Quakers were the most radical sect in seventeenth-century Britain. During the civil war period the movement came very close to being a mass movement. Civil authorities at the time feared that as a popular form of religiosity it could become revolutionary in form. Its egalitarian ethos and challenge of church tradition, instilled fear in many with a vested interest in the socio-economic and political status quo. With numbers perhaps as high as 60,000, the first Quakers shared the typical social background of other sectarians of the time; they were what Gilley and Sheils (1994, 202) refer to as 'classic "middling sorts" of industrious peasant farmers, craftsmen and small traders, with the nearest smattering of gentry'. The liberating possibilities of Quaker doctrine were evident in the advocacy for a greater equality in property owning, calls for fair prices and wages, and contempt for the idle rich. Their simple and dowdy dress and refusal to bow and scrape to the established order was regarded as particularly shocking. Early Quaker attitudes towards women were also radical. They had women's meetings and a women's ministry, as well as insisting upon a woman's consent in marriage.

The basic belief of the Quakers today as then is that each person should worship God in his/her own way and this has led to ecumenical and conciliatory attitudes towards other Christians and even other faiths. The authority of any 'Church' is rejected, as is any ritual or sacrament, including those which most Christians would regard as central to the faith – perhaps most significantly, baptism and the Eucharist. Since Quakers refuse to embrace a codified creed, it is difficult to pin down any precise theology.

The Quakers have earned a great deal of respect from outsiders because of their commitment to social issues. In the past this has meant advancing prison reform and the abolition of slavery. Today the emphasis is on international peace and nuclear disarmament. The membership of the Quakers has been significantly reduced over recent decades even if the composition of the congregations is still observably solidly middle-class. Today, the ethereal beliefs have attracted those of a New Age tendency, leaving traditional Quakers unsure of quite where the movement is heading. While many Quakers have always embraced a 'low' Christiology, emphasising Jesus' human rather than divine nature, over the decades the movement seems to have increasingly departed from its Christian heritage.

Seventh-day Adventists

Seventh-day Adventism is now accepted by many as a mainstream denomination rather than a sect on the grounds that there are few beliefs and practices which designate it as such. The main difference from mainstream church doctrine is that the Christian holy day should be Saturday not Sunday. This is based on Old Testament scripture and one of the Ten Commandments rather than Christian tradition. Although Adventists teach obedience to the Hebrew law, and are more legalistic than other branches of Christianity, the movement nonetheless stresses that salvation does not come through keeping the law or by 'works' but through Christ's atoning death.

There are two other unorthodox SDA teachings and these relate to the eternal fate of believers and non-believers. Firstly, it is taught that the dead remain in their graves rather than going straight to heaven or hell. When Christ returns to establish his kingdom, the saved will be resurrected to everlasting life. Secondly, SDA do not believe in everlasting punishment for non-believers; eternal death means absolute destruction – what is often referred to as 'annihilation theology'. Although not standard Christian doctrines, both teachings are accepted by a significant number of mainstream theologians and lay Christians.

Seventh-day Adventism initially grew out of the broader Adventist movement of the early nineteenth-century when William Miller, an American Baptist minister, attracted thousands of followers with his message, based on prophecies in the biblical books of Daniel and Revelation, that Christ would return in 1843. When it did not happen, he recalculated it to be the year following. Believers sold their properties and possessions in readiness. Once again, nothing occurred and the event became known as the 'Great Disappointment'. In this way the SDA are a good example of a movement that has had to deal with what has come to be known as *cognitive dissonance*.

The importance of cognitive dissonance brought on by failed expectations of this kind has been the subject of sociological enquiry. The classical study by Festinger *et al*

(1965), *When Prophecy Fails*, has often been read as demonstrating one reason why some sects endure. The argument is that, paradoxically, sectarian movements are strengthened by the failure of prophecy. Festinger *et al* used cognitive dissonance theory, one based upon a social-psychological foundation, to explain the behaviour of members of a flying saucer cult rather than a Christian sect. Nonetheless, the crucial point is that far from abandoning their beliefs, the movement's members increased their efforts to proselytize in order to bring more people into the church and thus reduce the dissonance between the leader's prophecy and the failure of the cataclysm to appear as predicted. Failure led to a stepping up of the proselytizing effort since if more and more people are encouraged to join the group, a belief system becomes psychologically more plausible to the existing membership.

While the study has been criticized as having numerous methodological problems (Bainbridge 1997, 134–8), not least of all the possibility that the mere presence of the research may inadvertently encourage a greater evangelizing effort, there is further historical evidence of how the failure of prophecy can lead to the growth of a sectarian organization. A good instance would, indeed, be that of the SDA. The movement has flourished, despite the Millerites, as they were often known, further subdividing into different sects. It has been global zealous evangelizing missions that have sustained the movement despite the failure of prophecy.

At the same time, there were other ways by which the SDA dealt with the failure of prophecy. One was the claimed divine insight provided by Hiram Edson the day after the Great Disappointment. Edson maintained that Christ had not returned to earth in 1844, but had entered his heavenly sanctuary to cleanse it and divide out the 'sheep' from the 'goats' in preparation for the Judgement of God. Another, a teaching put forward by Joseph Bates in 1846, was that Christians must obey the Jewish Sabbath – hence the present core teaching which separates the SDA from other Christian groups. Edson's revelation was confirmed by another SDA prophet, Ellen White, who lay claim to a number of visions related to the end of the world. Significantly, one insisted that sometimes God allows his prophets to make errors and fail in their predictions in order to test them and his church. Later prophets are permitted to discover these mistakes. This strategy again would appear to be linked to the need to deal with cognitive dissonance.

As we have seen above, Niebuhr identified an endless cycle of Church-sect evolution. The SDA movement would be a prime example. Although originating as a sect, numerous small factions have subsequently broken away from it. Since the 1980s, various organizations have sprung up which are often referred to as 'independent ministries'. These ministries have the avowed aim of bringing Adventists back to the 'pillars of the faith'. One, known as 'Hope for Today', calls for members to come out of 'apostasy' back into the 'truth' because the official Adventist church is perceived to be in danger of becoming part of 'Babylon' – the evil world order (Porter 1992, 199).

Interestingly, the SDA movement has become more worldly in its concerns. It has publicly campaigned against smoking and drinking alcohol, and encourages a vegetarian diet. The church also runs many hospitals and health centres offering both orthodox and alternative medicine. All of these areas reflect a genuine concern to make a humanitarian impact upon the world. The SDA church therefore provides the rare example of a sect that is millenarian in orientation, but one which also concerns itself with improving the world as it is.

Swedenborgians

Emanuel Swedenborg (1688–1772) was a Swedish nobleman, the son of a Lutheran bishop, who had launched himself upon a spiritual journey. In his writings he insisted that he was going back to the first principles of Christian doctrine and sought to redefine many of the issues central to the faith, such as the Trinity, the nature of Christ, and the essence of man's relationship with God. As part of this enterprise, Swedenborg claimed mystical revelations, particularly through dreams that showed him various spiritual truths. While Swedenborg himself did not found a movement, a number of individuals inspired by his work did so shortly after his death.

Swedenborg taught that there is only one God and that as Jesus he came into this world. This amounted to what is referred to as Monarchianism – designated a heresy by the second-century Christian Church. Here, there is believed to be only one God, not three-in-one. God, rather like a stage actor, plays three parts: Father, Son, and Holy Spirit. As was the case with leaders of other sects, Swedenborg tied millenarianism teachings to the notion of re-establishing the original church. Hence, he taught that the Second Coming of Christ took place in 1757 and that this marked a new dispensation and the beginning of the New Church. One aspect of this was perhaps Swedenborg's principal visions of the New Jerusalem descending to earth from heaven. For Swedenborg this constituted a new dispensation in which the human race took a vital evolutionary step in its spiritual development.

For Swedenborg, the bible was to be understood chiefly for its spiritual teachings and not generally to be taken on a literal basis. This meant that only certain books of the bible are divinely inspired. In the New Testament this amounts to the four Gospels and the Book of Revelation. Swedenborg also taught that the soul is immortal and that after death it goes to a spirit world and eventually to heaven or hell. When the physical body dies, the spiritual state of every individual will become apparent in the spiritual realm. Only those who have faith in Jesus and have shown a benevolent spiritual disposition will go to heaven. The whole purpose of creation is to share heavenly joy with as many people as possible. This universal principle of love is revealed in Jesus Christ as 'Divine Humanity'.

Despite sectarian inclinations, Swedenborg insisted that God shares his knowledge with humanity through the laws, myths, and poetry of many religions. This universal and mystical element, along with Swedenborg's alleged clairvoyant powers, and notions of spiritual evolution, has meant that he has been an inspiration for some in the New Age movement. The overall membership, however, remains small, with several thousand adherents in the USA and somewhat fewer in Europe. Nonetheless, the movement is now enjoying something of a revival in ex-communist Eastern Europe. For the rest of Christendom however, Swedenborg's teachings are at worst a heresy, and at best a curiosity.

Unitarians

Unitarianism represents one of the great heresies of Christian history, at least according to mainstream Christianity. Like the Jehovah's Witnesses, it embraces Arianism – the rejection of the deity of Christ. This was a theology which survived until the sixth-century and enjoyed a brief revival during the Reformation. In the eighteenth and nine-teenth-centuries, Unitarianism was particularly strong in New England, USA, and, as with other strands of Christianity, seemed to construct a doctrine that was compatible with scientific rationalism and the modernist theology that was developing in the Western world. It also embraced a philosophy of advancing education, morality, and social activism, while endorsing a spirit of Christian freethinking.

Like the Quakers, the Unitarians have no formal creed and insist that no one has the right to impose a set of beliefs on anyone else. However, there are a discernible number of key doctrines. The broad conviction is that there is one God, not three, or one-in-three. The Father is God, Jesus was a man, and the Holy Spirit is God's influence in the world. The belief that Jesus was merely an exemplar by way of a holy and perfect man is central to Unitarian belief. Jesus' death on the cross was nothing to do with atonement, but merely an example of love and sacrifice.

While undeniably there is wickedness in the world, human beings are, according to Unitarians, essentially good rather than sinful. There is no hell, no everlasting suffering for non-believers, although there is some disagreement as to whether a heaven exists in the traditional sense. The church also embraces a number of liberal themes. It actively welcomes gay members and puts a great deal of emphasis on social rights and equality. Today, as with the Quakers, many Unitarians see no reason why religious truths cannot be found in the sacred texts of other world religions, while some members are becoming increasingly interested in the New Age and Green Spirituality. In most Western societies, Unitarians are represented by a very small membership. There are, for example, only around 8,000 Unitarians in Britain.

Worldwide Church of God

For half a century the Worldwide Church of God (WWCG) and its founder, Herbert W. Armstrong, were almost synonymous since the vision of the organization is largely his. It is one which, until relatively recently, had displayed a strong sectarian orientation. According to Armstrong, the Christian Church lost its way around AD 70, although there have always been small remnants that followed the original, 'true' faith. The WWCG identifies certain religious movements throughout history that have carried the 'correct' version of Christianity. This includes the Gnostic-influenced Cathars, the Lollards, and the seventeenth-century Sabbatarians. What they all held in common was their keeping of the Saturday Sabbath, the inclusion of the name 'Church of God' in their title, the rejection of the Trinity, and their persecution by the established church.

In every such example, so the WWCG insists, either mainstream Christianity destroyed the small group of true believers, or Satan encouraged the beliefs to be watered down or distorted. This is argued to have been the case in the nineteenth-century with the SDA. The latter is perceived as especially relevant because

Armstrong had been a member of the SDA, or at least one of its churches which kept the significant name, the Church of God. In 1931, he became an ordained minister in the church and in 1934 began publication of the magazine through which the WWCG is best known, the *Plain Truth*. Armstrong left the SDA when his teachings, particularly on British-Israelism, departed from theirs. He then established his own church.

The WWCG displays a strange mixture of sectarianism and American culture, but this is not uncommon in the history of Christianity in the USA. Armstrong had faith in the American Dream and maintained that success breeds success. His 'Seven Laws of Success' epitomizes the enculturation of American conservative religion. It is a formula for achievement and is not unlike the notion of the 'seed-faith giving' espoused by evangelists like Oral Roberts that has, in turn, inspired the health and prosperity gospel of the present-day Faith movement (see Chapters 4 and 11). It is a teaching that insists that if you give God your best, he will give you his best. With this philosophy Armstrong built an economic empire around his church. It became controversial, however, when there were allegations that the church used powerful psychological techniques to extract more and more money from its members through tithes and 'free-will' offerings.

In the last few years, many of the WWCG's beliefs have been modified, although one or two of the fundamental tenets are still to be observed. It still promotes the validity of the Saturday Sabbath, even if its insistence that this was the mark of the true Christianity has been watered down. The other main practice which still exists is the church's observance of the Old Testament feast days. At one time this was compulsory. Among the dogma now more or less abandoned is the belief that the dispersed 'Lost Ten Tribes' migrated to Europe and then to the USA. This was far from a new idea and once accompanied nineteenth-century British imperialism. It was one which insisted that the Hebrew people became the British nation and that its rise to global power fulfilled biblical prophecy. Lack of credible evidence means that this core teaching has been dropped. The interest in prophecy that the church still retains, however, is very much linked to a preoccupation with the Last Days and even the date setting of Christ's return. Another concern of the church has been in criticizing the theory of evolution, although this has been somewhat modified with the recognition of the validity of scientific evidence. When all is considered, perhaps the most significant change has come with the acceptance of the Trinity and in this respect the movement has moved closer to the traditional Christian doctrine related to the atonement.

Some of the main criticisms of the WWCG made by mainstream Christianity in the past centred on its legalism, its strict observances of Old Testament law, and its teaching of salvation through a combination of faith and works. At the same time, while its reforms have brought it closer to traditional Christianity, cliques have broken away in order to adhere to the earlier doctrines; these include the United Church of God, founded in 1995. Although such breakaway groups appear to be part and parcel of classic sect development, the establishment of these new factions also arose as a reaction to the original movement succumbing to scientific evidence and the criticisms of other Christians. In turn, the sectarian schisms have undermined the parent church as an international organization, and with declining income its influence and membership appears to have waned.

Summary

This chapter has attempted a broad discussion of the nature of sectarianism. It is a form of religiosity frequently believed to be expanding in Western society. However, this is not largely a result of the classical Church-sect split, but of the increasing secularization of society. Any religious group, Christian or otherwise, that seeks to uphold its core beliefs, particularly if they are at odds with the cultural values of wider society, will necessarily find itself thrust into a marginalized social position. For conservative varieties of Christianity this appears to have been enhanced by the increasing liberalization of today's mainline churches. This is why many churches in the USA and elsewhere have come to display sectarian characteristics and a recourse to fundamentalism without necessarily literally developing as sects. For those that do so, the primary, close-knit relationship of members will be an important part of the sectarian orientation because it supports the believer in the face of real or perceived opposition in the secular world. Simultaneously, the experience and worldview of the sectarianism helps maintain the believer's assurance of having the 'truth' and being sustained as part of what Peter Berger has referred to as a 'cognitive minority' (Berger 1967, 163). Precisely what the broad challenges are that have engendered the growth of sects and Christian fundamentalism is the subject of the next chapter.

Further reading

Barrow, P. (1991) *Mormons and the Bible: The Place of Latter-day Saints in American Religion*, Oxford: Oxford University Press.

Hoekema, A. (1963) *The Four Major Cults: Christian Science, Jehovah's Witnesses, Mormonism, Seventh-day Adventists*, Exeter: Paternoster.

Mullan, W. (1983) *The Mormons*, London: W.H. Allen.

Wilson, B. (1961) *Sects and Society: A Sociological Study of the Elim Tabernacle, Christian Science and Christadelphians*, Berkeley, CA: University of California Press.

Figure 1 *The Family*, pamphlet on 'Flirty Fishing'

Figure 2 Rooms in Masonic Temple, Salt Lake City

Figure 3 Cover of *Plain Truth* magazine of the Worldwide Church of God

Source: *Plain Truth*, June 1987

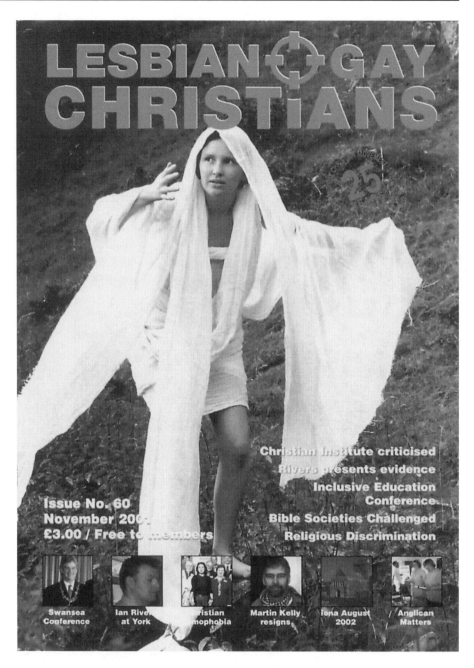

Figure 4 Cover of *Lesbian and Gay Christians* magazine

Source: *Lesbian and Gay Christians*, November 2001

4 Christian fundamentalism

The term 'fundamentalism' is far from an endearing one. Like those of 'cult' and 'sect', it suggests a religious bigotry at best, and fanaticism at worst. The fact remains, nonetheless, that as a form of religiosity it is poorly understood by both Western governments and the general public at large. Frequently, it is a term used interchangeably with others, above all, that of sectarianism and perhaps justifiably so. It is often the case that fundamentalism is articulated by sectarian types of religion, and may take, by way of organization, sectarian forms. In the West, fundamentalism has also emerged as a social movement that has attempted to alter state policy and to change the moral attitudes and behaviour of wider society. Understandably, some evidence of the growing support of Christian fundamentalism in Western societies, and the apparent success of its moral campaigns, has led a number of sociologists to argue against the 'hard' secularization thesis, which insists on the declining social impact of religion. Yet, as we shall see, the evidence of fundamentalism's social repercussions is rather mixed.

Fundamentalism undoubtedly enjoys a global significance. In recent years it has expressed itself in various forms and is frequently associated with many of the major world religions including Hinduism, Islam, Judaism, and Sikhism. This apparently near universal rise of fundamentalism, particularly since the 1970s, suggests that it marks a response to a common set of challenges. The emergence of Christian fundamentalism in the West over the same period, especially in the USA, is no exception. Simultaneously, however, it may also be seen as a reaction to unique circumstances in Western secular society. This chapter, then, considers the origins of fundamentalism, its social and political implications, and whether it can rightly be regarded as a marginalized expression of religion or, alternatively, something considerably more significant. An overview of fundamentalism and other global religions will be discussed later in Chapter 12, which is concerned with religion and ethnicity.

Fundamentalism defined

Fundamentalism is a slippery term and has come to stand for rather different things. To a considerable extent, this is because definitions are intrinsically linked with explanations as to its rise. In the context of the USA, Roof and McKinney (1987) categorize fundamentalist churches as merely one part of the conservative wing of Christianity, which also includes Southern Baptists, Evangelicals, Nazarenes, Pentecostal/Holiness churches, Assemblies of God, Churches of God, and Adventist churches.

This emphasis on the Protestant conservative segment of Christianity by Roof and McKinney, and others, is at least partly influenced by how fundamentalists have perceived themselves. The self-designated term was first proudly proclaimed in the USA by Protestant conservatives, who published a series of pamphlets between 1910 and 1915 entitled *The Fundamentals*. These works called for a return to what were beheld to be the core doctrines of the Christian faith. However, the boast of restoring a pristine religion is one also advanced by other global religions such as Islam, Hinduism, and Judaism. Neither do conservative Protestants have a monopoly of fundamentalism within the Christian tradition. Movements of Catholic 'fundamentalism' have been observable throughout the church's history, and have gained ground since the 1970s. The contemporary Catholic variety has, in many respects, responded to the same challenges as Protestant fundamentalism, although the aims and visions are not infrequently radically different.

Fundamentalism as anti-modernism

Rather than using the term 'fundamentalist', some commentators have preferred the designation of 'neo-traditionalism' to refer to movements which appear preoccupied with self-consciously attempting to represent or reassert an authentic religious tradition in opposition to the modern world (Sharot 1992, 25). Hence, it is frequently seen as a form of Christianity primarily concerned with the reclaiming of traditional moral and religious values, and in organizing protest against changes that have taken place and those who support such changes. Over the decades, puritan Protestant fundamentalism has attempted to battle the declared corrupting effects of popular culture by organizing moral crusades against ballet, brothels, contraception, gambling, television, erotic literature, and even ice-rinks. In more recent times it has campaigned against abortion, pornography, and the alleged decline of the family.

Not only does fundamentalism perceive external evils, but also enemies 'within'. Thus, it is simultaneously concerned with defending the inerrancy of scripture or articles of faith and opposing liberalism and modernism *inside* the Protestant tradition. This is how Barr (1978) approaches the subject. For him, fundamentalism in the original Protestant sense of the term, is a formal belief system predicated on the assumption that the bible is without error and that its 'truths' have everlasting validity. There are a number of key doctrines associated with this orientation and these include: God as the Trinity, the Virgin Birth, the deity of Christ and his resurrection, and the truth of miracles as related in the bible. In turn, such dogma has become a way by which the fundamentalists distinguish between themselves as upholders of the faith and the liberals who they not infrequently label as apostates and even heretics.

Although the Christian churches have long been wracked by doctrinal and ecclesiastical differences, a new source of divergence became significant in the nineteenth and early twentieth-centuries with the traditionalist-modernist division that was often observed through conservative-liberal theological debates and sectarian schisms within the churches. The debate was stimulated by changes in the modern world and the challenges they offered to the Christian faith. In the nineteenth-century, liberal theologically orientated churchmen anticipated the difficulties for the survival of Christianity posed especially by the separation of Church and state. To retain cultural power and influence, liberal Christianity endorsed a process of accommodation, engaging with dominant scientific and rational outlooks. Central to the liberal agenda, at least within Protestantism, was also the felt need to be 'relevant to modern man' by providing a Christian gospel that was pertinent and meaningful in the modern age.

The liberals sought to retain the essentials of the faith while reducing the supernaturalist component, which was now to be judged in the light of human reason. Typically, biblical miracles were reinterpreted as metaphors or said to express some profound moral message. By comparison, the conservatives mobilized themselves to resist such changes and held on to what was understood to be the major fundamentals of the faith. This conservative reaction was often articulated within Protestantism by sectarian schisms and fundamentalist forms of Christianity. The latter poured scorn on the accommodating stance of the more liberal Protestant denominations and seminaries and resisted attempts to refine the faith by incorporating contemporary scientific beliefs such as evolutionary theory.

The major concern for liberal Christianity has been in forging a relevance in the contemporary world and in being sensitive to its changes. This has meant embracing a spectrum of issues that matter on an individual, national, and global scale. There has subsequently grown up a number of broad-based inter-denominational liberal organizations such as the Christian Education movement, and many 'single-issue' groups including Christian CND, the Lesbian and Gay Christian Movement, and Christian bodies concerned with environmentalism, racism, and the various loosely-knit Christian feminist networks. These all constitute vibrant areas of the religious fringe in their own right, with an implicit agenda: pro-ecumenism, pro-women's ministry, pro-liturgical reform, and pro-critical theology. They have all been vehemently opposed by fundamentalism.

It is apparent that fundamentalism has met with various levels of success in Western societies (Larkin 1974). In the USA, it appears to be relatively popular. By contrast, in Europe there is rather mixed testimony. There is some evidence to suggest that the attempt of liberal Christianity to be relevant and practical may have had the unintended effect of alienating people. Alternatively, in other cases, it is conservatism that has met with this reaction. Sihvo (1988) argues that in Finland many people are convinced that the Lutheran Church has become too secularized. Thus, it has little to say in terms of religious conviction. As a result, those leaving the churches may adopt more fundamentalist forms of religion as an alternative to giving up religious conviction altogether. In the Netherlands, by comparison, Goddijn (1983) maintains that both the Dutch Reformed Church and the Roman Catholic Church have been conservative in social issues and taken an uncompromising and authoritarian approach. This has resulted in diminished church attendance. As these churches have reacted strongly to secular developments, church members who are progressively minded have left because the dogma espoused is irrelevant to their lives. Yet, the picture is not always quite so clear cut as the above evidence suggests. As Gee (1992, 141) points out, it is sometimes misleading to differentiate between individual 'liberal' and 'conservative' churches and congregations as if there were some distinct dichotomy. A survey of many would reveal a wide diversity of perspectives from extremely conservative to incoherently radical in the same congregations.

A phenomenological approach

If fundamentalism is primarily a religious movement responding to modern developments, it is not a united movement – certainly within Protestantism. Fundamentalists may disagree among themselves and sometimes very vociferously. Marty (1978) notes that various factions are often deeply hostile to each other, even if there is a measure of broad agreement on the nature and location of fundamental articles of faith and their general orientation in opposition to all things modern. The source of this division is usually that of biblical interpretation. Hence, distinct strands of fundamentalism may interpret the bible in different ways. Each may claim a 'correct' view of scripture and regard this as a sign of their special relationship with God.

The disagreement about scriptural interpretations means that fundamentalism does not amount to a tightly integrated dogmatic system, nor one necessarily derived from a biblical literalism. This evidence has led Martyn Percy (1995) to conclude that it should primarily be comprehended as a distinct worldview. Fundamentalism is therefore best understood as a construction of reality and the world that displays certain characteristics. According to Percy, it constitutes a self-enforcing view of the universe which feeds back and shapes subjective experiences and provides a complete 'world' in which individuals and religious communities exist, magnify their identity, and process their 'cosmic experience'. Frequently, this includes a backward-looking interpretation for present practice and belief. Fundamentalists will embrace the claim to an exclusive validity via selected biblical references which establish the absolute authority of a religious collective. They perceive God working through them and regard themselves as his elect and the means by which he is believed to mediate his past, present, and future designs. All other religious traditions, even within the same faith, are outside this self-designated elect. Percy's analysis of fundamentalism is an important one. It allows us to understand fundamentalism as a unique religious phenomenon in different religious traditions. It is, above all, a frame of mind and distinctly restricted religious disposition.

The New Christian Right and political activism

As a result of losing the debate over evolution, as exemplified by the so-called 1925 'monkey trial', and the repeal of prohibition legislation in the USA, the credibility of fundamentalism was severely undermined. In the modern world, dominated by technology and science, it appeared to be an increasingly anachronistic form of Christianity in both North America and Western Europe (Simpson 1983). However, since the 1960s, the fundamentalist constituency has become more active and more vocif-erous. This rise of conservative Protestant religion, particularly in the USA, with its strong commitment to doctrine and its refusal to compromise, nonetheless took many sociologists by surprise. Equally astounding was the tenacity of its political activity in the form of the New Christian Right (NCR) which arose in the 1980s.

Whereas in the 1950s and the 1960s, religion was generally seen as a relatively benign force in society, by the 1980s, particularly in the USA, it had become an increasingly politicized topic. This was witnessed in acrimonious arguments related to such controversies as abortion, lawsuits over the teaching of religion in public schools, and the mixing of politics with religion in many areas of civic life. Clearly, Christian fundamentalists have been at the forefront in advancing many of these issues. They have embarked on political and moral campaigns in order to bring salva-tion to the world and advance the interests of their own constituency. Throughout the nineteenth and early twentieth-centuries, fundamentalists sought to influence the social agenda in an increasingly pluralistic and multicultural society. However, while condemning the alleged sin of modernity, not all fundamentalists have resorted to political activism to support their cause. Some have turned their backs on the world and left it to its own moral mire and destruction. This includes many conservative Evangelicals and Pentecostals. For them, political campaigns to change what is regarded as a satanically dominated world system are seen as irrelevant. A number of fundamentalists have chosen not even to evangelize it – seeing it as beyond redemp-tion. Those that have been politically active from the 1970s constitute the so-called 'New Fundamentalists'. What is unique about this movement is its ability to bring a fresh unity to the different strands of conservative Protestantism that became leagued behind a common cause.

In the USA, the NCR has attempted to transform sectarian dissent into political action. Ministries such as that of Jerry Falwell mobilized the Southern Baptist and inde-pendent Evangelical groupings, and gained four million members including 70,000 church ministers (Liebman 1983). The aim, as Falwell's book *Listen America* explained, was to take America's so-called 'Moral Majority' 'back to God, back to the bible, back to morality' (quoted in Willoughby 1981). These fundamentalist 'moral entrepreneurs' appeared to be particularly successful and this was partly because they exploited the increasing public disenchantment with America's political institutions after the Water-gate scandal and other episodes of political corruption (Simpson 1983).

Another explanation as to the rise of the Christian fundamentalists in America focuses on the decline of the so-called 'civil religion'. A civil religion has been perceived as a form of religiosity that brings social cohesion even in highly secular, advanced industrial societies. In short, it displays the beliefs and rituals of a nation and is said to be more significant than particular beliefs and cultures, whether they be those related to social class, ethnic community, or specifically religious denomina-tional divisions. Much ink has been spilt on USA civil religion and this is invariably due to the need to explain how the country has welded together numerous diverse social groups. Bellah (1967), for instance, sees American civil religion as related to the Judaic-Christian faiths, but subsequently given a uniquely USA-style dimension.

When deconstructed, therefore, American civil religion is saturated in biblical symbolism. There is, for example, a cultural reference to the chosen people, the promised land, and a new Jerusalem – themes often discernible in major civic ceremonies such as presidential addresses.

Despite a preoccupation that American commentators have displayed with analysing civil religion, the general concept is now less easy to substantiate, particularly with the moral flux that has disrupted Western societies since the 1960s. This was identified by Bellah in his later work, *The Broken Covenant* (1975). According to Bellah, the USA is now wracked by social divisions and increasing pluralism, engendering the need for new integrating forces of religion. This theme is also developed by Anthony and Robbins (1990), who assert that in order to bring social stability, conservative Christianity has attempted to reinvigorate the nation's civil religion. This is essentially why fundamentalism appears to be infused with American cultural values. It is American 'fundamentalism' as much as Christian fundamentalism. Anthony and Robbins also identify the same tendency among some NRMs, many of which have given birth to fresh American myths as a response to the nation's general moral confusion. For Anthony and Robbins, one such religion is the Unification Church. This appears to be fairly successful in America because it places a great deal of value on family life, has an anti-abortion stance, advances the entrepreneurial spirit, and displays a fundamentalist belief system which holds that there is a global struggle between communism and the 'God-fearing world', the foremost representative of which is the USA.

Who are the fundamentalists?

Another way of explaining the rise of fundamentalism is to trace *who* precisely is involved in the movement. There are different accounts of this subject of membership. The work of Marty (1978) suggests that, ironically, fundamentalists are not necessarily inspired by religious considerations. He argues that those who advocate fundamentalism do so largely as a smokescreen since they are, in reality, encouraged by their psychological dispositions and may be interpreted as a product of social forces and historical events. In short, they have some motivation other than their stated conviction to change the world in religious terms. Marty's assertion is that Christian fundamentalism attracts those people who are relatively deprived. As we have seen in the previous chapter, sectarianism can give a new social status to those who, for various reasons, feel relatively deprived. If Marty is correct, so too can movements of fundamentalism.

Studies on fundamentalism and the issue of deprivation conducted in the USA have tended to focus on the declining middle classes who are driven on by the problem of status discontent. Much work was inspired by Gusfield's (1963) suggestion that those involved in the USA temperance movement in the 1920s were experiencing a decline in social group status that was only retained through a symbolic crusade seeking public affirmation of their group's values over those of their opponents. To put it succinctly, those whose status is threatened by changing cultural norms attempt to assert their values politically in order to re-establish the ideological basis of their social position and prestige (Lipset 1963). This kind of theorizing has also been more recently utilized to account for the activities of anti-abortion and anti-pornography fundamentalist campaigners (Zurcher & Kirkpatrick 1976).

Another argument which proposes that fundamentalists are not quite what they appear or claim to be is based on evidence centring on who has subscribed to the New Religious Right since the 1980s. Although religious views appear to be the motivation, they sometimes constitute no more than a shroud by which to advance more hidden interests or conservative views of the world. Religion then, is often a powerful and attractive resource. Himmelstein (1986), for instance, regards it as a source of traditional images such as that of the family and conventional female roles within it. Fundamentalism may therefore be seen as a network from which political traditionalist movements can be mobilized to resist change in these areas. Similarly, Wald *et al*'s (1989) study of the US Christian right wing found that it was constituted by individuals with authoritarian personalities who were dissatisfied with the amount of social respect given to groups representing traditional values such as the work ethic and the alleged virtues of family life.

There is yet another approach as to who constitute the fundamentalist constituency. The differences between supporters and non-supporters of the NCR are perhaps less matters of economic class and social status, than of cultural (Christian) lifestyles (Johnson & Tamney 1984). In other words, it is primarily the belief system and values that are most significant. Hence, the NCR may be primarily a political defence of a set of lifestyle criteria. Fundamentalism, at least in the USA, forms one side of the so-called 'culture wars' of religious conservatism versus the pluralist, permissive, liberal, and secular society. To put it simply, there are different worldviews.

This latter interpretation of fundamentalist activism comes closer to Percy's understanding of fundamentalism. Thus, moral campaigns are a means by which a religious cognitive minority engages with the secular world and whose motivation is no more than what it says it is, religious. In other words, religious conviction can run parallel to secular motives and the symbolic use of targets constituted by controversial political and moral issues, and may provide motivations outside and beyond economic and status considerations. There are no 'real' sociological factors, then, other than the actor's explicit meaning. While socio-economic circumstances may produce a susceptibility towards taking social action, an individual's motives invariably come from within a distinctly religious view of the world.

On both sides of the Atlantic, the grievances of fundamentalists have, over the decades, been fairly consistent: complaints concerning adherence to the bible, moral decline in society, and the inevitability of God's judgement. Hence, the so-called 'permissive society' of the 1960s onwards provides the indication of a turning away from God and the assurance that judgement and punishment will follow. It is what Thompson (1997) has referred to as the 'Ezekiel factor'. The most important consideration here relates to collective judgement, since fundamentalists believe that the Old Testament prophet Ezekiel cautions that, no matter how pious they are, God's people cannot isolate themselves in seeking salvation while his judgement falls on others. Also, tied in with this biblical interpretation, there is a distinctively pre-mille-narian scenario of 'sign watching' for the End Times: one which perceives moral decline, apostasy, and heresy as signs of Christ's second advent, all of which feeds back and enforce a unique worldview.

Fundamentalism appraised

There are different ways by which the impact of Christian fundamentalism can be gauged. One, as suggested by the evidence below, is that it is the more conservative Christian churches which have been growing, most notably in the USA. The steady expansion of these churches after 1950 was linked to the declining membership of the liberal churches and the marked demobilization of long-established denominations (Bibby 1978). Although the evidence is sometimes questioned (Smith 1992), the conviction of a good number of American academics is that people have been steadily leaving the liberal churches for the attractions offered by the more conservative variety. In 1967, evidence of this was that the conservative Southern Baptist Conven-tion overtook the Methodists as the largest Protestant denomination. Churches within the Convention have increasingly displayed all the characteristics associated with sectarianism (Ammerman 1990). Survey data in the USA also estimates that conservative Protestants make up nearly 19 per cent of the American population, while up to one-third of Americans claim to be 'born-again' Christians – usually the self-assigned badge of conservative evangelical Christianity (Hunter 1987).

In terms of social impact, conservative Protestants have, according to James Hunter (1987), succeeded in widely publicizing and advancing their views in the USA. By the early 1980s, they had established 450 colleges and 18,000 schools, set up 275 periodicals, founded 70 evangelical publishing houses, and opened 3,300 Chris-tian bookshops. Nonetheless, Hunter does not suggest that the expansion of conser-vative Protestantism disproves that there is a general decline of religion in Western societies like the USA, but he maintains that the process is complicated by discernible cycles of secularity and religious revival.

Although highly vociferous and attracting a good deal of media attention, Steve Bruce (1988) argues that the net result of NCR activity is minimal. Very few of its representatives who stood for election to national office were elected. Only half a dozen members of the senate supported the NCR and they failed to get any significant federal legislation enacted. Opinion polls showed no major public shifts towards their views on moral issues over a number of years. In Bruce's assessment, the NCR achieved little more than to flag itself up as a distinct interest group, which attempted to defend its religious rights in an increasingly pluralist society.

In some respects, such moral activism as that engaged upon by the New Right may be doomed to failure. This is plausibly because fundamentalists in the West are oper-ating within increasingly secular societies. In attempting to mobilize support for their objectives, religious organizations are less effective than secular organizations as a result of the tendency of the former to follow vague, universal, and usually moral goals, which are often abstract, unattainable, and unwinnable. In many ways, the aim of the NCR to bring a religious revival and reversal of the permissive and increasingly materialistic and individualistic society that had evolved from the 1960s seems particularly unrealistic.

The effects of such moral and political campaigns, however, should not be underestimated. In Britain, in the 1960s and 70s, the equivalent movement to the Moral Majority in the USA established the Festival of Light and the National Viewers and Listeners Association (Caulfield 1975). In turn, they founded groups, including CARE (Christian Action Research and Education), that used printed media and campaign posters for their moral campaigning, and to good effect. Such groups were sufficiently weighty to convince local councils to refuse certificates for controversial films including *Caligula* and *The Life of Brian* in the 1970s, and to close 500 sex shops. They also influenced the 1982 and 1985 Cinematographic Acts, which seriously restricted the expanding sex cinema industry. In terms of legislation, the British groups were arguably more successful than the NCR in the USA.

On occasions, campaigning by fundamentalists has deteriorated into 'moral panics' – a concrete expression of an over-exaggerated fear of the decline of moral values. Periodically, this has serious repercussions. Thompson draws our attention to the example of 'satanic panics'. False signs of satanic ritual abuse identified by Christian social workers operating in Britain magnified the belief that abuse was rampant in the early 1990s. The accusations (sometimes directed towards parents) were never proved. A prophecy that 50 satanic cults in Scotland would be exposed by Christians had catastrophic consequences (Thompson 1997, 178). In 1995, eight children were returned to their families in Ayrshire, Scotland, after being taken into care by social workers. Many other similar cases followed throughout the country. The parents were cleared of any guilt. Nonetheless, families were left emotionally damaged and their children traumatized after being searched for signs of sexual abuse. Similar occurrences have also been documented in the USA, where considerable money and power were gained by groups combating non-existent satanist activities (Victor 1992).

In appraising Christian fundamentalism there are also a number of other considerations. While fundamentalism appears to be marginalized and at odds with the world, it may be more accommodating than is often supposed. It criticizes secular humanism, liberal theology, and moral permissiveness, but will embrace certain modern developments for its own ends. For instance, it may utilize technology for evangelizing campaigns (Sharot 1992, 32–6). Thus, while fundamentalist evangelicals have opposed some modern advances, including that developing in the mass media such as the cinema, television, and radio, they have long recognized the significance communication technology has for successful evangelism. This tendency is succinctly described by Bauman (1990, 72) when he suggests that fundamentalists frequently attempt to 'have their cake while eating it'.

One such means of evangelism is television. In the USA, over 34 million households tune into the 'electronic church' – Christian television shows with popular, usually fundamentalist preachers (Hadden & Shupe 1987). While this may appear to be a significant figure, studies indicate that those who *frequently* watch are almost exclusively already committed conservative Christians and that the programmes probably do little other than simply affirm their existing beliefs (Stacey & Shupe 1982). Indeed, this tendency proves the need of Christian fundamentalism to constantly reaffirm the worldview of its adherents. As Ammerman (1990) suggests, this is largely achieved by immersion into the 'appropriate' religious audio recordings and reading matter, even to the point of cooking with a Christian cookbook. If this surmising is correct, fundamentalist activity does little more than convince its followers of their distinctive worldview.

Fundamentalism is often on the receiving end of 'bad press'. This is obviously so with its more extremist or even violent expression. Among the many radical right-wing Christian sects is that which calls itself the Militia. In May 1998, one of its members reduced the Federal Building in Oklahoma City to rubble in what he stated was an act of revenge against the federal government. The Militia's belief is that the government, the gun control lobby, genetic mutations, UFO activity, and certain military bases throughout North America are all part of a grand conspiracy to over-throw the USA and organize it as a communist-style state. There are other similar groupings too. Inspired by a distinct worldview, one based on theories of satanic conspiracy and millenarianism, the Christian Patriot movement typifies right-wing Christian identity movements that have sometimes turned to violence in order to further their ends against what they see as social and moral evils.

These groups are really quasi-military organizations, or what are sometimes referred to as 'survivalist cults', which stockpile food, weapons, and provisions for after the global apocalypse that they believe will inevitably come through nuclear war, environmental disaster, and racial conflict. Their literature often offers doomsday warnings that are anti-Catholic, anti-Semitic, and racist. Other examples of those that are motivated by the 'End Times' worldview are American fundamentalists such as the group that call themselves the Concerned Christians. They have raised money to help Jewish extremists to reclaim the Temple Mount in Jerusalem, which is the site of one of Islam's holiest shrines. The Mount is anticipated by the Concerned Christians to be the location of Christ's Second Coming.

The global significance of Christian fundamentalism

Much is made in the media regarding the influence and alleged dangers to the West of Islamic and other forms of religious fundamentalism. However, relatively little is discussed in relation to Western Christian fundamentalism being exported across the world. Such fundamentalist groups may not offer a terrorist threat, but they do have other important repercussions. While such expressions of sectarianism as Jehovah's Witnesses and Christadelphians have long exported their variety of Christianity glob-ally, by the end of the twentieth-century and into the twenty-first, new forms of Protestant evangelicalism have come to the fore. These have substantially increased the global significance of Western, particularly USA-style, religion. It is apparent that the peoples of the world, perhaps more than ever before, are now subject to the beliefs and ways of life espoused by North American Christian fundamentalism. For example, in 1990, the USA evangelist Pat Robertson launched his 'Project Light', a television revival directed at the whole of Central America. Broadcasting on Guatemalan television with a programme put together at the Christian Broadcasting Network in Virginia, the campaign reached over 60 per cent of the Guatemalan audience, a record for any kind of programming.

A recent detailed account of the global spread of USA evangelism is Brouwer *et al*'s work *Exporting the American Gospel* (1996). Here, it is argued that Western countries have come to dominate the world's productive resources, manufacturing, banking, and commercial institutions. For Brouwer *et al*, the global diffusion has meant that new forms of Christian fundamentalism have emerged that largely result from distinct economic developments. Such transformations amount to what they call 'fundamentalist Americanism' – the belief peculiar to USA Christianity that simultaneously sanctifies American imperialism and the American gospel of success, wealth, and prosperity.

No strand of fundamentalism expresses this so well as the so-called 'prosperity gospel', which is advanced by what is commonly known as the Faith movement. Across the world, hundreds of thousands of people subscribe to the teachings of those such as Kenneth Hagin and Kenneth Copeland in the USA. The Faith movement is not a unified one, but is constituted by hundreds of large-scale ministries that frequently cooperate in terms of personnel and in distributing tract, books, and audio and visual tapes. They are typically highly efficiently organized and tend to be very alike in form, direction, and genre. Based on well-trained pastors, congregations, and bible schools, they annually turn out hundreds of graduate pastors who advance the central tenets of the Faith gospel across the globe.

In style, form, and a number of key teachings, these ministries are discernibly derived from the Pentecostal movement (although many Pentecostals would disown them) and the healing revivals which sprang up in North America after the Second World War. What is unique about the teachings is that they insist that health and wealth is the automatic divine right of all bible-believing Christians. A number of the leading exponents of the Faith gospel claim that neither Christ nor his disciples were poor. In the view of one principal Faith minister, Fred Price (speaking on the TBN programme Ever Increasing Faith in November 1990), they exemplified the hardworking artisan. Through faith in God they achieved the just rewards of their labour and therefore provided the model lifestyle for all true believers.

The Faith ministries have made some inroads into Western Europe. Their expansion, especially since the 1980s, can be attributed to economic changes and accompanying cultural transformations. As far as the American ministries in Sweden are concerned, Simon Coleman (1991) speculates that they can primarily be understood as a carrier of the North American obsession with money and success. In the case of Sweden, throughout the 1980s, this occurred at a time when free enterprise was increasingly encouraged by the state, alongside the growing cultural emphasis on consumerism and individualism.

Further afield, the Faith teachings have appeared to carry American values into many of those nations which constitute the world's emerging economies. They have enjoyed a prolific growth in the wake of the collapse of Soviet domination, where the free market has increasingly replaced the state economic monopolies, and in Latin America and the Pacific Rim, as well as Third World Africa (Hunt 2000). Chapter 11 has further discussion of some of the teachings and practices of the Faith movement.

Fundamentalist movements within Roman Catholicism

Some of the developments of Protestantism have been mirrored within the Roman Catholic Church. From the mid-1960s, exemplified by Vatican II, Catholicism observably set out on the road that Protestantism had taken earlier in its search for accommodation with secular culture and offered at least a dialogue with other faiths. Indicative of this new progressive spirit was that, during the 1960s, there was the rapid translation of Latin Mass to the vernacular throughout many nations of the globe. The church has also increasingly engaged with the world outside its boundaries. For instance, since the 1990s a high priority has been given to supporting or instigating international peace initiatives. This was seen with the establishment of diplomatic relations between Israel and the Vatican, and the latter's support of peace initiatives in Northern Ireland and between Spain and the Basque separatists.

As Hornsby-Smith suggests (1987, 89–115), these international developments were accompanied by the dismantling of the defensive walls around the previously distinctive Catholic subculture in Western societies. There has thus been strong evidence of a substantial convergence towards the values of the general population on matters such as contraception and divorce and, to a lesser degree, abortion. Today, a liberal or 'progressive' wing has developed in the Catholic Church. This has brought a critical orientation towards its authority, as well as advocating liturgical change, a community emphasis, a this-worldly religious stance (including a socio-political commitment to overcoming such problems as poverty), and the rejection of traditional sexual and marital regulations.

The more liberal wing has shown itself in the development of movements on the fringe of the church and some have come to exert considerable influence. One is the Cursil, which stresses individual assertiveness and the relevance of the faith to everyday life as a reaction to the conservative orthodoxy. There are also numerous smaller progressive movements, which prefer a lower profile. Dobbelaere (1992, 121) identifies these as constituted largely by educated upper middle-class people in their late middle age. Even though they regard themselves as Catholics, they tend to be an intelligentsia situated on the margins of the church. These are people who wish to make Catholicism meaningful and relevant and are no longer satisfied with its authoritarian structure and antiquated cultural language. In addition, some Catholics have even set up their own 'deviant' groups, such as the Association of Separated and Divorced Catholics.

The decline in membership, falling church attendance, loss of authority, the diminishing involvement of lay people, and the demise of the distinctive Catholic subculture resulted in more reactionary tendencies by the mid-1970s. In many countries, particularly those with a Catholic minority, the church stood firm against the temptation to compromise with the emerging post-Christian culture and held a hard line against theological and moral liberalization. This period of reaction was symbolized by the encyclical *Hananae Vitae* of Pope Paul VI in 1968, which reaffirmed the ban on contraception, while the rejection of women priests was confirmed in 1976.

One of the strengths of Roman Catholicism is its ability to prevent sectarian breakaways and to retain internal unity. Hence, those conservatively inclined elements that extol a traditional and 'fundamentalist' expression of the faith tend to work *within* the structure of the church. As part of this broad reaction, factions within Catholicism have grown up in order to hold tight to and advance traditional dogma and practice, and emphasize loyalty to papal authority. One example is Opus Dei ('The Works of God'), which connects the traditional religious values of private prayer, religious devotion, spiritual guidance, and impeccable moral standards. After the Jesuit order, Opus Dei is probably the best known of the movements which seek to maintain the purity of the faith against both internal and external liberal influences. It was founded in 1928 by a Spanish priest, Monsignor Josemaria Escriva de Balaguer y Albas (1902–75), who took a direction towards becoming a saint when he was beatified in 1992. There are around 80,000 members worldwide, including an archbishop, some 15 bishops, and 15,000 priests.

Over the last two decades, there has been a great deal of controversy concerning Opus Dei. Many articles and at least one book have described it in terms usually applicable to a cult. It is interpreted as politically right wing and excessively authoritarian. The movement appears to impose strict forms of behaviour, such as members sprinkling holy water on their beds at night, encouraging chastity, strict penance including the wearing of a *cilice* or spiked bracelet, and in demanding severe mortification. Rules and regulations circumscribe every aspect of life, including censoring what its members read. It separates children from parents, and men from women. Finally, it also seems to be difficult to leave the organization. If members do so, they may find themselves shunned by their former associates. Opus Dei has been described as a secret society, a church within a church, with a disproportionate amount of power in the Vatican (Barrett 1998, 122).

Opus Dei is not the sole ultra-orthodox movement within the Catholic Church and it is not the only one that has found itself in controversy. There are Focolare, founded in 1943, the Neocatchumenate, founded in 1964, and Communion et Liberazione, also established in the 1960s. They appear to be particularly attractive to the more affluent Catholic youth and support traditional social policy. Like Opus Dei, each is outside the normal diocesan structure of the church and has been criticized if not for being cultist, then for bringing divisions within individual congregations. In addition, there are Catholic movements dedicated to the cult of Mary. This includes the Army of Mary that was established in Quebec in the 1960s. In many respects it is an unorthodox movement with teachings contrary to that of the Catholic Church. One principal goal is to establish the Virgin as part of the Godhead and effectively undermine traditional teachings on the Trinity. It is possible that the movement could be excommunicated; if so, it could provide the very rare example of a sect breaking away from Roman Catholicism, albeit through forceful expulsion.

Summary

This chapter began by suggesting that 'fundamentalism' is a slippery term to come to grips with. It is open to interpretation, and most of the important contrasting accounts have been considered here. It is also a broad term and this is evident in the fact that it can refer to movements of very different faiths. Hence, we will return to this subject in the discussion of ethnic and world faiths (Chapter 12). Even with references limited to Christian fundamentalism there is some disagreement between academics studying religion as to which groups should be included under the rubric of 'fundamentalism'. A case in point is the Pentecostal movement. While some sociologists regard it as fundamentalist in orientation, others prefer to see it as something rather different: as a movement of renewal and revivalism. It is the Pentecostal movement, in its different expressions, which is the subject of the next chapter.

Further reading

Ammerman, N.T. (1990) *Bible Believers: Fundamentalists in the Modern World*, New Brunswick, NJ: Rutgers University Press.

Barr, J. (1978) *Fundamentalism*, London: SCM Press.

Bruce, S. (1988) *Rise and Fall of the New Christian Right in America*, Oxford: Clarendon Press.

Hadden, J. & Shupe, A. (1987) 'Televangelism in America', *Social Compass*, **34** (1), 61–75.

Lang, K. & Lang, G. (1960) 'Decisions for Christ: Billy Graham in NYC', in A. Vidich & D. White (eds.) *Identity and Anxiety*, New York: The Free Press.

Marty, M. (1978) *Fundamentalism*, Boston: Beacon Press.

Percy, M. (1995) 'Fundamentalism, A Problem for Phenomenology', *Journal of Contemporary Religion*, **10** (1), 83–91.

5 Pentecostalism and movements of Christian renewal

Movements of renewal and revival, both inside and outside the established churches, litter the history of Christianity in the West. Since the Reformation there have been revivals of piety, such as those of the seventeenth-century Puritan movement, and the holiness and Methodist movements of the early eighteenth-century. In the USA, in the nineteenth-century, there were a number of apparently spontaneous revival movements, typified by the New England 'Great Awakenings' and that of Cane Ridge, Kentucky. These movements were by no means limited to Protestantism. The Orthodox and Catholic churches have, throughout their histories, also experienced movements of revivalism and renewal. These movements not uncommonly attempted to regalvanize existing communities of believers or developed into sectarian schisms. In many cases, as with the Great Awakenings in the USA, they appeared to spread rapidly through entire towns and villages, and frequently involved large-scale conversions and great spiritual excitement bordering on what could be interpreted as mass hysteria.

In many respects, revivalism is often viewed as an essentially North American heritage. Here it is traditionally linked to a code of personal piety and the denouncement of evil in the world and strict isolation from it. Revivalism is seen as a popular form of religion associated with a stern opposition to such personal sins as drinking, smoking, and gambling. Perhaps, above all, there is the insistence upon the conscious commitment to Jesus Christ as one's 'personal saviour'. In many of these regards, revivalism shares a style of religion without being fundamentalist, although many contemporary fundamentalists fashion their religion in terms of American-style revivalism.

The most significant movement of revival over the last hundred years is that of Pentecostalism. Today, it constitutes the fastest growing wing of Christianity and indeed of any expression of religiosity in the world other than Islam. While, in many respects, it has been on the fringes of mainstream Christianity in the West, traditional churches and denominations have frequently assimilated many of its beliefs and practices, albeit in diluted form. This movement has not only impacted in Western industrialized nations, however. Third World countries, notably Latin America, Africa, and the Far East have seen a rapid expansion. Indeed, all over the world Pentecostalism has penetrated just about every Christian tradition with its message of spiritual renewal and revival. Thus, with some justification one of its leading apologists, Peter Wagner (1992), has argued that on a global dimension it is the most significant non-political and non-military movement of the latter half of the twentieth century. Numerically speaking, a realistic appraisal estimates that its size is in the region of 619 million or 29 per cent of the entire Christian population of the world (Barrett 1988).

The Charismatic Renewal movement

The Charismatic movement of today (otherwise known as neo-Pentecostalism) began as a fresh version of an older religious manifestation. The earlier Pentecostal movement, with its own legendary origin at the Azusa Street mission in San Francisco, in 1906, and its counterpart in Britain during the Welsh and Sunderland revivals, is now typically referred to as 'classical' Pentecostalism. In time-honoured tradition it was, in essence, a sectarian movement which set its face against the established denominations of the time and eschewed institutionalized ecclesiastical arrangements. Its distinctive features were the doctrine of 'baptism in the Spirit' and an emphasis on the charismata (the 'gifts of the Spirit'), including speaking in tongues, prophecy, and healing. As the movement grew, in typical sectarian style, Pentecostalism drew up boundaries with what it regarded as nominal Christianity and refused fellowship with the established churches. Over the decades, however, the major Pentecostal churches, as with other revivalist churches before them, became more institutionalized and had themselves virtually grown into denominations, including the Assemblies of God, the Four Square Gospel Church, and the Elim Church, although numerous independent Pentecostal churches still exist. While fundamentalist in orientation, Pentecostalism was initially disowned by the established evangelical bodies because of its emphasis on the charismata and what appeared to be an excessive emotionalism at the cost of sound biblical doctrine. Today, Pentecostalism still rests uneasily in the fundamentalist camp.

In a very short time, classical Pentecostalism had disseminated itself across the world, revitalizing churches and founding its own with a powerful missionary endeavour. The more contemporary Charismatic movement has continued this self-assigned world mission with considerable success. This has been attributed not only to its powerful spirituality, but also to its theological flexibility that has brought about substantial enculturation in different global contexts (Martin 1990; Cox 1994). By the end of the twentieth-century, the two movements had become virtually indistinguishable with a constant interaction of dogma, practice, and personnel.

In the mid-twentieth-century, the Charismatic movement, with its alleged beginning within Episcopalian circles in Van Nuys, California, rapidly spread across the USA, to Europe and beyond, permeating various Christian traditions. Since the 1960s, it has considerably influenced many mainstream churches and generated numerous independent Christian fellowships. While the spread of the movement might partly be attributed to the encouragement of a number of widely dispersed church leaders, renewal was also instigated at grass root level, with the impetus coming from ordinary people responding to their personal experiences and fulfilling their own needs.

Throughout both Roman Catholic and Protestant traditions, the Renewal movement advocated the return to the pristine spiritual condition of the first-century church. Like its predecessors, Renewal confronted increasing secularization, rationalism, disbelief, and pluralism. For many church leaders it appeared to be a force capable of arresting the long-term decline of Christianity in the West. It was able to simultaneously attract people indifferent to mainstream denominations and to infuse elements within almost every denominational community with a spiritual revival capable of transcending established ecclesiastical loyalties. On the other hand, it was often divisive and some church leaders frequently feared the threat of entire local congregations going over to Pentecostalism and losing respect for traditional authority and liturgy (McBain 1997).

Besides the felt need to respond to the modern world, there has been no clear agreement, at least by Charismatics in the established churches, as to what their movement signified. Some believed that God was preparing to bring spiritual life back into the denominations that were marked by stagnation and worldliness. Others put the emphasis on the universal Church rediscovering Christian unity. Roman Catholics and Protestants came together 'in the Spirit' to discover what united rather than separated them and gained the strength to reassert themselves in an ever increasing secular world. This was sometimes accompanied by a sense of exclusiveness, even elitism. The first Pentecostals saw their movement as the 'Latter Rain' – of God pouring out his Spirit in the 'Last Days'. In the second half of the twentieth-century, those who were charismatically inclined used terms such as 'revival', 'awakening', 'outpouring', and many believed that renewal signified a return to the early church experience. At times, the hopes of renewal and revival were linked to millenarianism. A sense of unity, spiritual experience, and the gifts of the Spirit all seemed to point towards the restoration of God's true church.

A principal platform for renewal was the attempt at reconciliation and cooperation between the traditional denominations. This spirit of reconciliation also extended to the older Pentecostal churches hitherto largely outside the fold of the 'respectable' churches. From the other direction, a number of leading Pentecostals opened up channels with the established churches. More widely, the ecumenical spirit of renewal brought an acceptance of the institutional basis of the existing denominations and this was an important factor in the growth of the Renewal movement. There was the belief that the various denominations should establish common ground and interests rather than found new structures outside the mainstream churches. This inclination can also be interpreted as an extension of earlier ecumenical initiatives, and ecumenicalism, as Bryan Wilson has argued, is indicative of an underlying weakness of contemporary Christianity, rather than a sign of its strength and endurance. Denominations that once felt sufficiently strong to bicker about their doctrinal differences now attempted to find strength in unity (Wilson 1966).

Within twenty years, the Renewal movement in the churches had begun to run out of steam. Its influence continued to spread, although it was the image and culture of the movement that was influential, such as its distinctive songs and lively worship, rather than the stress on the charismata. From the 1980s, the dedicated Charismatics, for their part, increasingly found common cause with their cousins outside the established denominations – the growing independent and confederations of neo-Pentecostal churches (the communication between the two camps was often through bible conventions). Typical were developments in Britain. Since the 1960s, parallel to Renewal in the mainline churches, there had developed 'house churches', or what was then known as the Restorationist movement. Today, these independent churches constitute, in the case of Britain, 14 per cent of all Christian churches. Frequently included in their titles are 'Community Church', 'Family Church', or 'Christian Fellowship'. Such churches are now the fastest growing segment of Christianity in many Western countries and in the Third World.

The nature of Pentecostalism

Precisely what the Pentecostal movement amounts to today is a matter of conjecture. Certainly, it is a different movement than the one that arose in the mid-twentieth-century. Once it had core distinguishing features, including the emphasis on speaking in tongues and the 'second baptism' in the Spirit as its badge of membership. However, the entire Pentecostal movement is evolving so rapidly that it is not entirely clear whether these distinctive hallmarks still hold. This is because, on a global scale, the very ability to enculturate, which has led to its rapid growth, has also frequently transformed the movement out of all recognition.

The appeal of contemporary Pentecostalism in Third World countries has been interpreted by David Martin as a result of its ability to offer a popularized form of (largely) Protestant Christianity, which satisfies the requirements of the impoverished masses. In short, it furnishes means of social and psychological survival by offering a safe subculture or 'substitute society', which provides for spiritual and material needs (Martin 1990, 258). Indeed, so significant has Pentecostalism proved to be that in some parts of the world, particularly Africa and Latin America, its Protestant forms are rapidly replacing traditional Roman Catholicism as the principal expression of Christianity.

Exactly how neo-Pentecostalism relates to contemporary Western society is a fascinating question. Arriving at a categorical answer is not easy since the movement is one of contradictions and paradoxes. The main contradiction is that it appears to resist secularizing forces while simultaneously endorsing some aspects of present day culture (Hunt *et al* 1997). In various respects the movement tends to be anti-modern. It seems to be close to Christian Protestant fundamentalism since it condemns the more permissive attitudes of the modern world. It is also inclined towards a biblical literalism, even if the movement interprets the bible in terms of its own experiences. In fact, Chalfont *et al* (1987) regard Pentecostalism as a particularly powerful form of fundamentalism. They argue that it demonstrates the appeal of a close relationship between evangelism, a literal interpretation of the bible, and religious experience including tongues, healing, miracles, and other paranormal experiences. Such experiences, interpreted through a scriptural fundamentalism, not only carry profound religious significance and meaning, but simultaneously demonstrate the 'power of God'. This is the basic recipe for Pentecostal growth.

Harvey Cox (1994, 81–3) agrees that Pentecostalism is backward looking when he speaks of its 'primal spirituality'. In short, the movement attempts a restoration of the spiritual power which began the faith. It seeks a return to archetypal religious experiences exemplified by the emphasis put on the charismata. There is, Cox states, the 'primal hope' that looks forward to the dawn of a new age, a millenarian heaven on earth. This brings the movement close to what Peter Berger refers to as an 'inductive possibility'. In *The Heretical Imperative* (1979), Berger outlines the three possible responses of Christianity to the challenges of the modern world. Firstly, there is an accommodation to the world and a demystification of biblical myths evident in liberal theorizing. Secondly, the faith is defended through a biblical literalism. This response is displayed in conservative and fundamentalist interpretations of the bible. Thirdly, there is an attempt to rediscover the spirit that began the faith and to live out the experience of early Christianity. It is the latter, an 'inductive possibility' that appears to characterize Pentecostalism.

At the same time, contemporary Pentecostalism in the West does manifest a specific orientation towards secularity. Andrew Walker (1997), a long-time observer of Pentecostalism, believes that it displays a great deal which is 'thoroughly modern' since it accommodates the world as much as rejects it. While it centres upon a strong supernatural element and frequently arrays a biblical literalism, it has not, by and large, opposed science and critical rationalism. It uses hi-tech modern approaches to evangelism and embraces such cultural concerns as healing, human potential, and therapeutic techniques (considered in more detail in Chapter 11).

While the Charismatic movement clearly attempted to revitalize Christianity, it had, from the very beginning, also constituted part of a wider cultural milieu. Although it moved rapidly from sectarian to more world-accommodating forms, this apparent transformation had always belied the tendency to follow the contours of Western culture. Certainly, there is much which appeals to certain aspects of the post-modern world. In fact, some opponents of the movement, as well as academics, believe that it has strong overlaps with the New Age: its esoteric nature, its spontaneity, and notions of an imminent new world. It also seems to appeal to a similar clientele.

Who are the Pentecostals?

Neo-Pentecostalism in Western societies, unlike its 'classical' predecessor, has continued to attract a fairly distinctive middle-class element. Indeed, the movement has always found it very difficult to transcend its white middle-class enclaves (McBain 1992). There are good grounds for arguing that such esoterically inclined revivalist movements as modern day Pentecostalism may be perceived as a historical phenomenon and should be understood within the framework of Troeltsch's (1931) typologies of Christian organizations. While Troeltsch was primarily concerned with the categories of Church and sect, he also established a third type of religious expression, which he called 'mysticism'. In this form, doctrine and worship give way to purely personal and inward spiritual experience and conviction. Historically, this was rather unique in that it was related to the expansion of individualism and the growth of urbanization from the Middle Ages in Europe.

Troeltsch maintained that this Christian mysticism is characterized by a free community of believers with little by way of organization, and appeared to be particularly attractive to the prosperous middle-classes. More recently, this typology has been exploited in understanding contemporary expressions of faith. For instance, Thompson (1974) considers the Charismatic Renewal movement, at least within Roman Catholicism, as close to Troeltsch's notion of mysticism. He sees it as a loosely structured movement operating within church institutions, and based on a form of mysticism that is particularly attractive to middle-class people with their concern with individualism and personal development.

Other explanations have been furthered to explain the appeal of neo-Pentecostalism to the middle-classes, and these tend to highlight aspects of social deprivation. Wallis (1976b, 227) and Martin (1978, 41–3) both suggest that movements such as neo-Pentecostalism provide a form of escapism and help their followers cope with their negative worldly experiences. They compensate for the difficulties thrown up by the modern world, notably rationalization, social isolation, alienation, and mark a response to the bureaucratization of professional life. Whatever the precise explanation, however, the tendency for the movement to appeal to the middle-classes appears to fulfil the 'market model' in that certain types of religion suit the requirements of particular social groups, be they material, psychological, or spiritual.

In terms of marketability, it is also evident that many contemporary Charismatic churches in the West have become what Harvey Cox calls 'designer churches' that wish to be judged by the speed of growth of their congregations, funds available, attractive buildings, prestigious leaders, and other hallmarks of success which reflect the wider enterprise culture (Cox 1994, 272). Such churches have become increasingly world accommodating, displaying a willingness to employ marketing techniques to evangelize and appeal to their members.

Evidence suggests that many Charismatic churches today are not winning a great number of new converts. What they appear to do, however, is to attract members from other (non-Charismatic) churches. This amounts to church switching, or what North American sociologists have referred to as the 'circulation of the saints' (Bibby 1978). In this respect, a study by Mauss and Perrin (1992) of the highly successful confederation of Charismatic congregations, the Association of Vineyard Churches, shows the attraction to middle-class people. The thrust of Mauss and Perrin's account results from a debate with the influential work of Kelley (1978) on successful religious movements. They argue that Kelley is broadly correct in that 'seekers' in the spiritual marketplace are looking for 'the essential functions of religion', that is, 'making life meaningful in ultimate terms' (Kelley 1978, 166). However, they say that he is largely wrong in that successful churches do not demand personal commitment and self-sacrifice through a change in lifestyle. Kelley believed that conservative religion makes demands on members in terms of belief and commitment. Charismatic churches, according to Mauss and Perrin, offer a convincing belief system, a sense of being caught up in a successful movement of revival, but are not strict about lifestyles or commitment. There are the additional attractions of emotional healing, contemporary music, and a middle-class cultural milieu that allows the opportunity for like to be with like. In short, middle-class people will be attracted to churches with members of a similar background to themselves.

If Mauss and Perrin are correct, Charismatic churches are often world accommo-dating and open-minded, and do not demand a great deal of conformity. Moreover, on many issues their theology cannot easily be distinguished from popular secular values and the orientations of non-Christian alternative religions. Miller (1997) substantiates this tendency. What he designates as 'New Paradigm Churches' – his description of the independent, so-called 'mega-churches' and 'post-denominational churches' – combine a biblical literalism with a more self-centred spirituality. The attraction of those such as Vineyard, as well as Calvary Chapel and Hope Chapel in the USA, is the emphasis on personal conviction and spiritual experience. A century on, these neo-Pentecostal churches are a very different kind to the first Pentecostal congregations with their stress on purity, sectarianism, and biblical fundamentalism.

Miller believes that the new churches, while offering a satisfying spirituality, help people feel 'comfortable' with church life. This tendency is also evident in the working philosophy behind Charismatic evangelizing initiatives. Recently, Charis-matic churches (and some non-Charismatic churches) have embraced the so-called *Alpha* programme. *Alpha* amounts to a large-scale evangelizing campaign endorsed by well over 7,000 churches in Britain and thousands more worldwide. Much heralded in many quarters of Christendom, practically all churches and denomina-tions have praised the value of *Alpha* and have come to widely accept it as one of the last words in contemporary evangelism.

Alpha is based on a course run at local churches and amounts to a ten-week crash course in Christianity. The rationale is to present the opportunity for the unconverted to delve into the basics of the faith. It brings a popularized expression of Christianity which is shaped considerably by the Charismatic movement. *Alpha* also musters a great deal of what has been learned by Charismatic churches over a number of years about how to spread the 'good news'. Hence, it utilizes techniques which are very much state of the art, such as applied sociology, psychology, and business and organizational strategies. Numerous market techniques have been developed in order to enrol people on the *Alpha* course: poster campaigns and television advertising, video presentations, free meals, and numerous commercial materials such as books and magazines. There is also an intrinsic recognition that converts are won through networks of family and friends (that 'alike attracts like') and that there is the need to bridge church and secular culture by making people 'feel at home' in the church environment. However, while the evidence is pres-ently slim, it is clear that *Alpha*, despite its almost scientific approach to church marketing, has failed to win over a significant number of new converts (Hunt 2001a).

Strands within neo-Pentecostalism

To speak of neo-Pentecostalism at the beginning of the twenty-first-century as constituting a 'movement' is rather misleading. Besides mainstream Charismatic Renewal, there are now various distinct strands observable within it. Some had emerged around the same time as the Renewal movement but outside the established churches, while others have developed more recently. These strands display unique attributes but continue to overlap and influence each other. They are distinguished by theological, organizational, and cultural differences, although many of the identifiable aspects of neo-Pentecostalism remain. Such divisions are consistent with the ever-fragmented nature of Pentecostalism since the early twentieth-century, but they do not necessarily appear to conform to the internal characteristics associated with sectarianism.

In the USA, the division within neo-Pentecostalism is a rather exaggerated development of what has happened elsewhere. Here, there are somewhere in the region of 60,000 independent Charismatic churches. Many have established networks between them so that they constitute loose, overlapping ministerial associations without the bureaucratic encumbrances of traditional churches and denominations. Well-known examples include the Charismatic Bible Ministries (1,500 ministers), Christ for the Nations (600 churches), Rhema Ministerial Association (1,500 churches), and the large, umbrella type Network of Christian Ministries which brings together leaders of other, smaller strands. In the USA, the independent churches are the basis of Christian life for some 14 million Charismatics compared to merely 6 million in the established denominations. The Vineyard church alone, based in Anaheim, California, claims over 280 local assemblies.

Restorationism and the house church movement

The Restoration movement was once described as 'the most significant religious formation to emerge in Great Britain for over a century' (Walker 1985, 28). The movement has also had rather smaller representation in other countries, including the USA and South Africa. What was distinctive about this movement was that it sought not just to bring spiritual renewal but to create independent churches with unique ecclesiastical structures. This was believed to be in line with what its advocates interpreted as the first-century church, that is, its unity and authority being in the hands of 'apostles'. In doing so, Restorationism denounced the historical churches as 'the abomination of the denominations'. Evolving from the independent fellowships, such as those of Sidney Purse and G.W. North, Restorationism in Britain developed sectarian characteristics. A central belief was that God was returning the church to its original spender, imparting a greater measure of the spiritual gifts including prophecy and healing, and preparing the church to reign in God's coming kingdom. The evil world, 'Babylon', would be overcome by the restored church, which would win mass converts in the Last Days.

The heyday of Restorationism was the 1970s. In retrospect, it appears to have been not only a form of sectarianism but in many regards yet another NRM, and seems to have had much in common with numerous others. At a time of decline in established religions, the new, often syncretic types of religiosity filled the vacuum. Eileen Barker (1992) argues along these lines when she speaks of the attractions of the new religions to those who sought a dynamic expression of faith. The successful ones were frequently those that were appealing in terms of what they offered the individual believer, especially by way of human fulfilment. According to Barker, what such forms of religiosity had in common were the promise of community and a sense of belonging, of creativity, self-development, religious experience, and the endeavour to build one variety or another of the kingdom of heaven on earth. Moreover, the theme of overcoming the forces of darkness and the expected mass revival imperative to Restorationism was indicative of the triumphalism and success-orientated philosophies of so many forms of non-Christian NRMs.

Very quickly, the Restorationist movement mutated into the so-called 'New Churches' (a self-designated term which was preferred for greater respectability). These churches have increasingly endorsed aspects of today's culture and technological advances which could enhance the cause of winning souls. Contemporary dress and music, and state-of-the-art church buildings, alongside aspects of commercialization, constitute what has rapidly become part of a Christian consumer subculture as these mega-churches increasingly inspire, and even dictate the tone of the rest of the Charismatic movement with which they have opened up close contact. Hence, today some British Charismatic churches, notably Baptist, have a dual membership to their denominations and one or other of the federation of New Churches. This is not to say that more sectarian forms of New Church, such as Bryn Jones's Covenant Church in England, do not remain. Nonetheless, those churches, including New Frontiers, Ichthus, and the Pioneers, have attempted a wider popular appeal. The irony is that, as groups or networks of churches, they increasingly display common qualities, practices, and a sense of identity which means that the New Churches have come to form the type of denomination that they were once so critical of (Wright 1997, 74–5).

The Third Wave movement

Another important strand of neo-Pentecostalism (although it often denies that label) that has developed in the last twenty years is the Third Wave movement. This strand was believed, by those involved, to be the third wave or 'movement' of the Holy Spirit in the world throughout the twentieth-century before the return of Christ. The first wave was perceived to be the early twentieth-century Pentecostal movement, the second was the mid-century Charismatic movement, and the third, beginning in the 1980s, was understood as bringing together all true 'born-again' evangelical Christians, of different persuasions, united in a common cause of evangelism. According to one of its leading exponents, Peter Wagner (1988), the Third Wave meant, above all, the movement's recognition of the power of the Holy Spirit and an enlightened comprehension of the church's historical role before the Second Coming of Christ.

The most significant figure in this movement was the healing evangelist, the late John Wimber, who headed the Association of Vineyard Churches. Although his impact in the USA was slight, his effect on the white middle-class Charismatic movement proved, on a global scale, to be considerable (Hunt 1997). Wimber, through his 'Kingdom' or 'Signs and Wonders' theology, typified much Third Wave thinking. His view was that the Church had lost contact with supernatural 'power' and the 'signs and wonders' that accompanied the evangelizing endeavour of the early Christians. In a secular society, he argued, it was necessary for the contemporary Church to restore supernatural phenomenon such as miraculous healing and prophecy, and to launch an attack on satanic forces through strategic 'spiritual warfare'. All of these themes often took their own trajectories. For example, the Prophetic ministry, typified by the mission of the so-called Kansas City Prophets in the 1980s, constituted an attempt to return the lost art of prophecy to contemporary Christianity. In whatever way they were expressed, however, this preoccupation with these 'proofs' of the authenticity of Christianity can be seen as an attempt to bring power back into the Church that had, in many Western societies, become essentially 'powerless' (Hunt 2001b, 338–9).

The Third Wave movement, like other strands of neo-Pentecostalism, also saw itself at the forefront of God's plans. In doing so, it appeared to rewrite hurch history in order to interpret the movement as central to divine designs. Again, this reflected a wider tendency among many new forms of religion that has been recognized by sociologists such as Richard Fenn (1990). Fenn has argued that a major characteristic of NRMs (Christian or otherwise) in the post-modern world is that they tend to reinvent history and make their movement applicable to it. The speed of social change and the decline of cultural continuity breeds an ignorance of the past, including religious history. In turn, new narratives are constructed by which religious collectives frequently perceive themselves as restoring, reforming, or reviving the true faith. While this appears to be the case with some strands of neo-Pentecostalism, the New Age movement may also conform to this tendency (see Chapter 8).

The Vineyard movement, and the international churches that are associated with it, proved to be the principal carriers of an extraordinary esoteric phenomenon, which swept through tens of thousands of Pentecostal churches worldwide. The so-called Toronto Blessing first appeared in the Airport Vineyard Church in Canada in the early 1990s and lasted for several years until it eventually petered out by the end of the decade. The 'Blessing', as it was more popularly known, became associated with remarkable expressions of ecstatic and esoteric phenomena. It was identified with shaking, trembling, twitching, hysterical laughter, sobbing, and barking and other animal noises. To some extent, the Toronto Blessing resulted from the psychological pressures built up by the prolonged hope for revival in the wider Charismatic movement (Hunt 1995). From another perspective, the phenomenon expressed a newly discovered unity. It constituted an ecumenical movement of sorts in that Charismatic churches of different persuasions were involved. Another interpretation by Philip Richter (1995) focuses on the esoteric phenomenon itself. Richter saw it as essentially 'learned' – an imitated ecstatic religious phenomenon which began in Toronto. Primarily a package of ecstatic manifestations, the Toronto Blessing was then exported as far afield as Europe, Latin America, South and West Africa, Australia, and Japan. Although an extremely complex phenomenon, its global dissemination was either largely through a 'pilgrimage' to the Toronto church by church leaders and lay people, or via electronic communications in the form of national and international phone calls, faxes, and e-mail, as well as magazine articles, television coverage, popular paperbacks, and the World Wide Web.

Reconstructionism

While it can be identified as a branch of the New Christian Right in the USA, Reconstructionism is also a strand of the neo-Pentecostal movement that has become heavily involved in political campaigning. Reconstructionism teaches that conservative (Protestant) Christians could transform North American society (and ultimately the world). This would create the basis for Christ's millenarian kingdom on earth through a God-mandated set of social, economic, political, and legal principles of the books found in the Old Testament. Like Restorationism in Britain, Reconstructionism aims at establishing the kingdom of God on earth. There is the belief that the powers of good will overcome the strongholds of evil including earthly governments. The 'true' Christian Church will reconstruct God's reign as in the Old Testament and the ancient proscriptions found in Judaic law will apply in this new kingdom. This will include such extreme measures as the execution of homosexuals. Shupe (1997) interprets the movement as a particularly aggressive form of Protestant fundamentalism that is aggrieved at the major developments within secular society.

Social activism

Aspects of social concern and activism are closer to certain streams of Charismatic churches in the USA. One is a strand commonly known as 'Kingdom Now', which includes the 10,000-member Chapel Hill Harvester Church in Atlanta (Georgia), and the Full Gospel Tabernacle in New York. These churches urge the active Christian penetration of secular society for the sake of a social gospel and structural transformation rather than the typical moral crusade of American fundamentalism. In this way the church is believed to become the visible expression of God's dominion of the world. Kingdom Now has some similarities with what was British Restorationism. Behind such social projects is the aim to win over converts. Thus, social activism is a mere strategy for evangelism. In some respects, this tactic also draws close to nineteenth-century liberal Christianity.

The black Pentecostal churches

The appeal of Pentecostalism to the black community is generally well known. This has been so with both classical Pentecostalism in its early stages and as a distinct strand within the neo-Pentecostal movement in recent decades. If a broad statement can be made, it is that existing accounts of Caribbean and African churches have tended to cluster around a number of themes which focus on the role and purpose that such churches provide for underprivileged black communities and in helping them to cope with felt discriminations and deprivation in the Western context. There are, however, various explanations as to why this has been the case.

Troeltsch's (1931) view that sectarianism was attractive to a particular clientele, that is, lower social groups, was certainly evident in the early days of Pentecostalism. There have been times when classical Pentecostalism has attempted to orchestrate political and social protest against the disruptive conditions of economic life and actively sought to improve the worldly circumstances of the poor (Bastian 1983). For the most part, however, during its first decades of existence, Pentecostalism provided the means by which those of a low social class background could come to terms with their plight, rather than overcome it by worldly means. This notion was most clearly seen in Anderson's (1980) Marxist interpretation of the movement and its spread in the 1920s and 1930s, which saw Pentecostalism as a distraction of the working-class from its politico-revolutionary path. Even less radical perspectives have tended to understand it as historically linked to the tendency of the movement to allow deprived social groups to construct an alternative lifestyle and subculture in which to passively withdraw from the world, rather than making an outright protest against it (Calley 1965).

In the USA, the leadership of the early Pentecostal movement came from various classes and races, but the great bulk of the membership was either black or derived from the poor white urban and rural working-class (Tinney 1971). The rapid early spread of the movement in the USA was later interpreted as marking a response to the social problems generated by urbanization, poverty, and the break-up of well-established communities (Schlsinger 1932). A variation on this theme is that Pentecostalism amounted to an attempt by some social groups experiencing acute societal maladjustment and culture shock to recapture a sense of security through religious revival and reform at a time of rapid change (Holt 1940).

Studies of exclusively black Pentecostal churches have followed in much the same vein, although some research also focused on these churches in providing places of welcome and community for migrant groups. This was especially so for the first waves of immigrants into countries such as Britain and older black communities in the USA. In Britain, from the 1950s, they helped Afro-Caribbean and West African immigrants to overcome a feeling of unfamiliarity and hostility that many faced in the workplace, in the housing market, and on the streets. This was exemplified by Calley's (1965) work, which showed that the West Indian Pentecostal sect represented a deliberate attempt to create an ethnic enclave, to enhance group solidarity, and to construct a refuge from wider society. Many also sought a distinct and more lively expression of Christianity than that which could be found in the traditional denominations, in which some blacks also faced less obvious forms of discrimination.

By way of belief, practice, and cultural orientation, the new generation of black churches at the beginning of the twenty-first-century is, in many regards, very different from the earlier Pentecostal congregations. Today, within the broad family of Pentecostalism, these churches constitute one of the fastest growing wings. Many are inspired by the Faith ministries of the USA and their 'health and wealth gospel' that has impacted in Africa. However, some, particularly the West African churches, are unique because they are 'planted' out of Africa, predominantly from Nigeria. There is a certain irony here. Christianity, the religion originally exported from the West, is now returned through the process of 'reversed globalization'. Influenced by the North American prosperity gospel, but with distinctly African cultural attributes, the indigenous African churches have developed a number of the key doctrines for the needs of their own people, mixing purity with a work ethic and teachings of human potential. In turn, these churches have embarked on missionary endeavours across the world, including countries of the West. In Nigeria, such churches as the Redeemed Christian Church of God (now with a global membership of some two million) have established congregations in the USA, Western Europe, the Far East, and Australia. While seeking to win converts of all ethnic backgrounds, their main appeal, however, is to more prosperous Nigerian ethnic enclaves that have settled in these countries (Hunt 2001c). This new movement, in turn, exemplifies the wide diversity of neo-Pentecostalism, its ability to incorporate a variety of beliefs and practices, and to appeal to millions of people on a global scale.

Summary

Pentecostalism, in many respects, does not fit easily into any category of alternative religion. Some commentators readily see it as an NRM because it has characteristics in common with movements arising since the 1960s that are not Christian in orientation. Simultaneously, certain aspects of neo-Pentecostalism are fundamentalist in orientation, but it does not, as we have already observed, sit neatly within the fundamentalist camp. It could also plausibly be regarded as a form of sectarianism that has developed within and outside the Christian Church. Moreover, Pentecostalism, whether 'classical' or 'neo', has the tendency for sect proliferation, with one sect breaking off from another. Exemplifying this is so-called Oneness Pentecostalism which divided from the Assemblies of God in 1916. There are now some 90 Oneness Pentecostal denominations in 57 countries. In the West, the movement is particularly strong in the USA and Canada. Central to the movement is the belief in the unity or 'oneness' of God rather than the Trinity. The Oneness Pentecostal movement adds to the vast richness of the wider Pentecostal movement. Yet, despite its infinite diversity, Pentecostalism is the fastest growing variety of Christianity on a global scale. For that reason it is difficult to designate it as an 'alternative' in quite the same way as other expressions of religiosity.

Further reading

Anderson, R. (1980) 'Visions of the Disinherited: The Making of American Pentecostalism', *American Historical Review*, **87**, 1–48.
Cox, H. (1994) *Fire from Heaven*, Reading, Mass: Addison
Harrison, M. (1974) 'Sources of Recruitment to Catholic Pentecostalism', *Journal for the Scientific Study of Religion*, **13** (3), 49–64.
Hocken, P. (1994) *The Glory and the Shame: Reflections on the Twentieth Century Outpouring of the Holy Spirit*, Guildford: Eagle.
Hunt, S., Hamilton, M. & Walter, T. (eds.) (1997) *Charismatic Christianity: Sociological Perspectives*, Basingstoke: Macmillan.
Martin, D. (1990) *Tongues of Fire: The Explosion of Pentecostalism in Latin America*, Oxford: Blackwell.

6 New Religious Movements

A copious amount of literature has been produced over the last thirty or forty years on the NRMs. Partly this is because their rise seems to argue against the broad secularization thesis since they have emerged at a time when mainline religion has declined. At the same time, the intense interest has arisen because many appear to be innovating and novel forms of religion not witnessed before – at least within the Western context. The new religions have also drawn a broader public interest largely because of the controversy and notoriety that surrounds their more 'cultic' expressions.

Although a good number of the NRMs had sprung up from the mid-1960s to the early 1970s, they are not entirely 'new' social phenomena even if many arguably enjoy a greater social significance than earlier movements. Innovating forms of religion that were outside mainstream Christianity have been part of the religious scene of Western societies for at least a century and were usually manifest in the form of mysticism or occultism based largely on one variety or another of the major eastern religions. In the USA, in particular, such religions have proved to be a familiar aspect of religious life and frequently proliferated during periods of religious enthusiasm over the course of nearly two centuries (Melton 1987).

From the mid-1960s, the new religions found a ready acceptance in the USA, and from there many of the larger ones, such as the Unification Church and the COG, spread to other countries, frequently winning thousands of converts and becoming truly global movements. Since that time, NRMs have come and gone with some regularity so that today it is difficult to approximate their number. One estimate is that there are now some 2,500 new religions in the Western world (Barker 1999,16). Without doubt they are of a vast variety in terms of their beliefs, practices, and outlooks. For this reason, one of the major preoccupations of sociologists specializing in the area has been in trying to place them into distinct categories.

Varieties of NRMs

A common way of categorizing the new religions is one that has been heavily influenced by models of sects and cults – in particular, their orientation towards the world, that is, whether they embrace or reject it. This is how Wallis (1984) proceeds in his classification. NRMs, he argues, can be divided into three broad groupings. Each category displays different attitudes towards the outside world and this is evident by way of their principal beliefs and the kind of people that any given movement attracts.

There are, firstly, *world-rejecting* movements. These carry a clearly defined perception of God(s), a strong system of morally ascribed rules, and often a puritanical set of beliefs. The teachings will be critical of, and in conflict with, wider society. Thus, the movement will earnestly seek to change the world and usher in a new spiritual order. Members will be expected to separate themselves from outside society. This may lead to a sect-like organization, sometimes a communal lifestyle, and the designation of the world beyond its boundaries as 'Babylon' (in a biblical sense given to mean an evil abomination and perhaps false religions). Very often, there will be a strong charismatic leadership and clear organizational hierarchy. Falling within this category would be such NRMs as the Family (previously the Children of God) and other groups emerging out of the broader Jesus movement.

Secondly, there are *world-affirming* movements. In many ways these hardly appear to be religions at all and this brings them close to Stark and Bainbridge's (1985) definition of 'client' and 'audience' cults. Typically, adherents to these movements do not really constitute a membership in any meaningful sense, but are customers who are often literally buying a 'service' such as healing or realizing personal abilities. Some of these movements may be totally new and innovating in their beliefs. Alternatively, they may derive from traditional global religions, usually forms of eastern mysticism, or offer syncretic variations. Sometimes world-affirming movements are orientated towards improving the nature of society as well as the lives of their adherents. For instance, Nichiren Shoshu, an innovating form of Buddhism, offers a faith which impacts on many dimensions of the individual's life and, so it is argued by the movement, indirectly enhances wider society as members provide an example of spiritual living to others.Very often world-affirming movements display very little by way of organization, collective worship, or a framework of belief. Neither do such NRMs systematically attempt to convert people in the traditional sense of the term. However, they are 'religious' in as much as they claim to provide pathways to spiritual or superhuman powers. These movements are inclined to affirm the world as it is and tend to endorse the dominant values of Western society, notably those of positive health and human perfection. Ideas of 'salvation' and spiritual development may be evident. Yet, these are frequently projected through the prism of personal advancement and the realization of human potential. These movements are largely indifferent to the truth claims of other religions and rarely boast that they have a monopoly of spiritual truths.

A third type of movement is what Wallis refers to as the *world-accommodating* NRMs. These neither completely embrace nor reject the world, but they may display elements of both. At times they tend to adopt a rather elitist standpoint which is accompanied by the self-designated mission of restoring an older religion. The Charismatic Renewal movement, as a revivalist movement within Christianity, would provide a prime example. Other movements in this category may begin within an established religion but develop to make significant departures from it. For instance,

Subud claims origins within Islam but has observably modified its principal beliefs and practices. Unlike world-rejecting varieties, the world-accommodating movement often tolerates other faiths and is thus more pluralist in outlook and closer to denominations in the Christian sense. Beliefs and practices are rarely totally unorthodox. Wallis believes that this means they have a certain social respectability. For that reason (as discussed below) they seem to attract particular types of people, while there is the tendency of such movements to separate the religious and worldly in a distinctive way so as to serve the spiritual needs of the membership.

Wallis realizes that no religious group fits neatly into one or other of these categories. A good number mix aspects of each type and display different levels of endorsement or rejection of the world. Typical is the Healthy Happy Holy Organization (3HO) that was originally derived from Sikhism. Occupying the middle ground allows the followers of 3HO to combine elements of an alternative lifestyle with conventional marriage and employment. Like world-accommodating movements, it employs techniques that are believed to bring happiness and good health, while appealing to those who otherwise lead conventional lives. Simultaneously, 3HO has some characteristics in common with world-rejecting movements. Hence, it displays a clear concept of God, while members dress in distinctive white clothes and turbans. However, while members may opt to live in communes (ashrams), they do not embrace the total sharing of possessions. Some restrictions are placed on the lifestyles of the membership. This includes vegetarianism, and the abstinence from alcohol and tobacco.

The 1960s and getting saved from them

The reasons why NRMs arose where and when they did, from the 1960s and 1970s in the USA and Western Europe, has attracted a great deal of sociological speculation. The general argument is that they were a product of profound social and cultural changes at the time. However, there is some disagreement as to what the most significant factors were. The theories that have been developed can be generalized as follows.

Firstly, that NRMs should primarily be understood as a product of the counter-culture rebellion of the 1960s (Bellah 1976; Wuthnow 1976). In the West, many young people sought an alternative lifestyle to an increasingly materialistic and individualistic society. The counter-culture offered a critique of technical rationality, a scientifically dominated culture, established social institutions, and dominant forms of morality. Numerous NRMs, which developed at the end of the 'hippie' decade of the 1960s, articulated a more effective criticism, while also marking an attempt to restore a supernatural view of the world. This they often did by offering a stringent set of beliefs and a communal and alternative lifestyle.

A very different perspective that accounted for NRMs during this period stressed that they were able to provide a firm set of moral standards at a time when Western society was finding it increasingly difficult to do so. Modernity was becoming more and more pluralistic and people's experience of the world had radically diverged because of social mobility and economic specialism. This meant that a coherent moral system was being eroded and this was evident in the decline of traditional, particularly civil religions. As we have seen (in Chapter 4 under The New Christian Right and political activism), according to Anthony and Robbins (1982), society must find a way of providing an unambiguous set of moral standards and sense of belonging. Those NRMs such as the Unification Church, as well more mystical forms, brought, in their different ways, a sense of belonging and a system of moral guidelines. These movements, therefore, contrary to popular opinion, actually provide a positive function in overcoming alienation and the anomic tendencies of the contemporary world. Bromley and Shupe (1981) also largely argue along these lines. They insist that NRMs may be seen as part of a normal cycle of religious movements in the USA, in which periods of social instability are followed by a time of religious revitalization that, in the long run, brings a greater stability. From the 1960s, NRMs have aided social integration by reintroducing individuals involved in the counter-culture back into society.

Yet another contrasting view is one that suggests such movements do not so much reintegrate people back into society but provide an alternative basis of belonging in a largely rootless culture. Exploring the so-called 'decline of community' thesis, Gordon (1974) and Marx and Ellison (1975) point out that many NRMs have an emphasis on building a community by offering bonding, fellowship, and the sense of belonging lacking in wider society. This is achieved through an emotional and ecstatic religious experience in movements which combine all the attributes of a surrogate family through a collective lifestyle, along with a set of universalistic values and beliefs that are often expressed as a spiritual force working in the lives of all members.

Alternatively, pre-dating more stringent theories of post-modernity, some earlier commentators established a link between the new religions and a search for self-identity that is precipitated by a contemporary world dominated by bureaucratic structures and fragmented social roles. NRMs are said to address this need by promoting a holistic conception of self, especially through therapeutic movements and mystical cults (Westley 1978). Cult-like groups offer the ability to control and change one's social identity and self. In comparison, the more sect-like groups address the search for self-identity by consolidating all of the individual's fragmented social dimensions into a single, central, religiously defined self, which is strengthened by the strict control of an authoritarian structured movement (Bird 1978; Dreitzel 1981).

The problem with these above explanations is that they offer a rather sweeping account of the new religions which hardly does credence to the vast variety of movements that can be found. Furthermore, the explanations often become entwined in wider debates about the legitimacy and desirability of such religions. Just as important, the notions of a 'crisis' of *modernity* precipitating social and/or individual psychological malfunctioning that are implicit in many of these approaches have their limitations. Some of the social changes considered significant are long-term processes in the West and do not fully explain the proliferation of NRMs from the 1960s. Since innovating forms of religiosity are far from new, they can scarcely be explained by the unique developments arising in the second half of the twentieth-century. Conscious of this, Glock and Bellah (1976) argue that the pressure for profound religious change had been building up, especially in the USA, long before the 1960s. However, the trigger for NRMs, and the counter-culture that generated it, was the protest movement against the Vietnam war and issues of civil rights which effectively brought challenges to dominant culture to the fore.

The difficulty is that this view constitutes a rather parochial attitude. Although it is widely held that cults and NRMs are common in the USA and are somehow linked to changing and historical developments in the country, Stark and Bainbridge (1980) have found that there are proportionately more NRMs in some European countries (this claim in turn is hotly contested). They claim that in the late 1970s in the USA, there were only 2.3 cult movements per million inhabitants, compared to 3.2 in England and Wales. Neither can the emphasis upon the so-called 'crisis' of contemporary society explain the relative decline of NRMs since the 1980s, despite ever-changing aspects of technological and economic life. Nor, for that matter, can they always account for the variety of NRMs, especially those such as the Unification Church, which in many respects embrace the dominant culture of the USA.

More recently, NRMs such as the Divine Light Mission (DLM) and ISKCON have been interpreted as partly embodying a retention of certain counter-culture values, but are translated into a new idiom that rejects its anarchic, ill-disciplined, and often destructive lifestyle. This was Tipton's view in his suitably entitled *Getting Saved from the Sixties* (1982), where he considers three very different groups in California including one derived from the Jesus movement, a Zen meditation group, and a human potential therapeutic group. Largely middle-class in composition, Tipton regards the membership as 'survivors' from the 1960s and a counter-culture that was an inadequate basis for a new lifestyle which, however, these new religions could provide. This kind of theorizing, nonetheless, has its own limitations. If a number of the movements did recruit heavily among ex-participants in the counter-culture this was not true of all (Barker 1984). Moreover, Rochford (1985) found that while early recruits to ISKCON, better known as the Hare Krishna movement, had been involved in the counter-culture, the later members were not. Nor do the doctrines of all these NRMs embody particularly counter-cultural values (Wallis 1984).

NRMs and contemporary society

While the NRMs may deal with the range of deprivations generated by Western societies since the 1960s, whether of moral flux, the breakdown of social bonds, or alienation, there is much regarding some of the movements, particularly recently, which is clearly in line with Western culture and fulfils cultural-specific needs. This observation brings us close to Stark and Bainbridge's (1980, 1985) account of new cult movements. They see the new religions as generally free of the deficiencies of the older religious faiths since they deal with the needs of individuals in the contemporary West. The new religions thus fill the 'gaps' left by more traditional forms. A similar viewpoint is advanced by Wilson (1982), who argues that NRMs cannot be fitted under the rubrics of 'sects' or 'cults' because in many ways they have different functions; in particular, they offer 'proximate means to salvation'. In short, Wilson maintains that NRMs provide a surer, swifter, more convincing assurance of salvation from whatever the individual seeks to be released, whether from sickness, unhappiness, relationship problems, perceived evil forces, or practically any negative experience. They achieve this far more convincingly than traditional religious forms.

For commentators such as Stark and Bainbridge, the growth of the new religions is additionally enhanced by the breakdown of religious 'monopolies', that is, traditional Christianity, and the growth of a 'spiritual marketplace' in North America and Europe. This development is, however, by no means limited to the West. In modern Japan, as Finke (1977) points out, thousands of new religions, such as Soka Gakkai, have emerged with the decline of state-subsidized Shintoism. The new voluntarism now evident in religious life – where 'choice' is the operative word – also suggests that people are more likely to join a group for personal advantage and instrumental reasons. This is in contrast to the previous basis of belonging: social pressures and collective concerns. Thus, the contemporary world heralds a more profound individualism and utilitarianism that overspills into the religious domain, whatever the form of spirituality preferred (Wuthnow 1993, 39–40).

Today, there are good grounds for arguing that in the spiritual marketplace it is the *world-affirming* forms of NRMs that are increasing in popularity at the expense of the more *world-rejecting* and *world-accommodating* types. It is the former which is more compatible with the conditions of Western society and prevailing cultural values. This type of movement also demands a much lower level of commitment than the other expressions and they are less stigmatized. In addition, they may offer, as Marx and Ellison (1975) suggested as early as the 1970s, strategies related to human potential, a sense of community and fellowship on a part-time basis, without the less attractive full-time, more utopian and demanding aspects of the authoritarian-orientated movements.

Wallis (1984) also recognized such a tendency. What he referred to as 'epistemological individualism' is increasingly articulating itself in religious terms in a consumer society where there are ever changing tastes and fashion. It follows that world-affirming groups become more popular at the expense of world-rejecting movements, since they offer immediate gratification for those who take part. However, as Heelas (1988) maintains, world-rejecting forms will continue to endure because they still provide for the needs of some people and resist the tendency towards weak commitment and marketable strategies.

Evidence to support the increasing domination of world-affirming groups has been presented by Khasala's (1986) survey of the 3HO Foundation and Vajradhatu (a Tibetan Buddhist church whose members are mostly well-educated, middle-class, white Americans). These groups have become less world-rejecting. They have developed an ideological orientation that supports worldly success as a spiritually relevant enterprise and thereby identify no dilemma between embracing both the spiritual and the earthly realms. It is not, however, primarily a matter of a sectarian type of religion becoming more worldly as a result of an inevitable process. Rather, the evidence suggests that the transformation is brought about by a pragmatic leadership decision in response to changing social and economic conditions in an attempt to promote the survival of the movement. The opting for worldly success establishes a firm basis on which the religion can grow. At the same time, it provides otherwise deviant groups with a strong image of legitimacy and this is enhanced by the emphasis on individualism, enterprise, and success.

Accounting for success

It is broadly accepted that NRMs, as cultist forms of religiosity, are highly precarious types of religious organizations. Their characteristic pluralist doctrines and their members' general individualistic mode of adherence, alongside problems of authority, frequently renders many of them more unstable than other types of religious collectivity. However, some have become particularly successful and endure, while others fairly rapidly decline and die. Although a number of new forms of religion can stabilize as what might be referred to as 'established cults' (Nelson 1968), as has spiritualism for nearly 150 years, most which do endure typically undergo transformation from cult to sect. This is typified by the Jesus movement, Scientology and the Unification Church. The reason why some continue is of particular interest to sociologists of religion.

Success is obviously partly linked to the appeal of NRMs for their membership. At the same time, accounting for the growth of such movements has often led to an examination of the resources which they have at their disposal. The emphasis is therefore on the restraints within which religious organizations work and the causes of success and failure, including the charisma of religious leaders and activists in mobilizing resources such as people, money, publicity, and the media. In this regard Loftland (1979) has shown how even apparently small, peripheral, and fairly insignificant NRMs can attract members by manufacturing favourable images of themselves. This includes projecting their movement as one that is growing in popularity, as a tool of the divine will, and the active engagement with evil powers within the framework of a wider cosmology. It is obvious that a belief system, particularly when it constitutes an entire worldview, is imperative for unifying individuals within the group by spelling out the principal aims of the movement and the appropriate means by which they are meant to be realized. However, commentators have suggested that stringent worldviews also become a commodity in the 'theological marketplace' in winning over converts. In short, people are attracted by dynamic religious teachings, particularly when they display a relevance in their lives (Greeley 1990).

In exploring a number of other important 'resources' relevant to the growth and endurance of some NRMs, we may cite the examples of the COG and the Unification Church. The former originated in Los Angeles in 1968, with a membership of only a dozen people; it was merely one of several factions of the Jesus movement that sought converts among 'hippies' on the West Coast. By the mid-1970s, the COG could claim to have 4,500 adult members and a representation in over 70 countries. Davies and Richardson (1976, 338) attribute this growth, compared to other strands of the Jesus movement, to 'the rational approach to governance that has been developed over a period of years'. The year 1972 marked a major exportation of members of the COG to Europe (especially England and Holland) and Latin America. Until 1973, the evangelistic style that the COG advanced was mostly street witnessing through a strong music ministry, which set biblical themes to rock music. Rapid growth continued, which can be put down to a number of variables. These include financial resources derived from possessions of members, gifts from parents, and above all by selling evangelizing literature that is printed in 28 languages. Secondly, there is also a conscious attempt to be less vigorously 'American' and assimilate other cultural patterns. Thirdly, there is the deliberate endeavour to gain greater respectability by associating with other Christian churches.

In their study of the Unification Church, Shupe & Bromley (1979) examined emergence of the organization from the 1960s, when it was on the margins of the counter-culture, to its prolific spread in the 1970s. Important resources utilized included the positive image of the charismatic leadership, the organizational zeal and personal wealth of Sun Myung Moon, the adoption of American cultural values, personalized recruitment strategies, and entering into dialogue with secular authorities. The church was able to concentrate on a growing population of young people who were socially isolated, in full-time education, and living in urban areas. At the same time, other religious institutions, particularly the traditional churches, were unable to meet the needs of this young element. The movement has also come to own numerous businesses including pharmaceuticals, manufacturing, and the *Washington Post* newspaper, which are able to sponsor its activities. In addition, it has a number of 'front' organizations, the International Conference on the Unity of Sciences and the World Peace Academy among them.

This last strategy underlines the fact that another important resource is the image of respectability. The reputation of an NRM may be enhanced if it can demonstrate its ties to an ethnic community and/or a major world religion. To improve its image, ISKCON has emphasized its relationship to the wider Hindu community (Carey 1987). It claims to have a priestly function derived from its roots in the ancient tradition of Vausnava Hinduism, which cultivates worship of the god Vishnu and his *avatars* (incarnations), Krishna and Rama. This had the effect of moving the cult towards the structure of a type of denomination – hence an attempt to court a greater respectability in the eyes of the outside world (Rochford 1985). Scientology, by way of another example, seeks respectability in combating drug abuse through its organization Narconon. In this way, it seeks to project a good public impression in an attempt to throw off the rather stigmatized image that it has acquired. Another movement attempting to generate a good image has been the Soka Gakkai. An offspring from the Nichiren Shoshu faith, it has founded a university campus in California and regularly awards honorary degrees to royalty and politicians.

Who joins NRMs?

Social class

Who is attracted to the new religions and why? Clearly there is an overlap here with some of the explanations that account for their growth in Western society over the last few decades. There is more to consider, however. Many sociological studies point to the social background of those converted and the attractions of specific movements. The findings often contradict the popular conception that converts are derived from the poorer sections of society or those on the margins of social life, as is frequently the case with sectarian expressions of religion. This is not to suggest that this has failed to be the case with some world-rejecting movements. One example is the British-based Jesus Fellowship, a community-orientated fundamentalist group, which claims a membership of some 2,500 (Hunt 1998). At the core of the movement are leaders who are committed Christians, derived from the well-educated middle-classes who have sought a deeper expression of spiritual life. Beyond this central group is the bulk of the rank and file drawn from the 'underclass' of young homeless people, often with a background of alcoholism, drug abuse, or family break-up. The Jesus Fellowship offers shelter, rehabilitation, a puritan lifestyle, and moral support to what it calls 'generation X'. A slogan of the fellowship is one borrowed from the Salvation Army in the nineteenth-century: 'Those who do not belong to anyone else belong to us'.

While world-rejecting movements are perhaps those best suited to providing some compensation for a sense of deprivation in this world, Wallis found that they were by no means dominated by lower-class individuals. This was clearly in marked contrast to earlier sectarian-orientated groups and has been verified by other accounts. Studying what might be interpreted as a world-rejecting movement, Wallis found that participants in the Jesus movement were largely of middle- and upper-class backgrounds. Similarly, in Britain, Barker (1984) discovered that recruits of the Unification Church appeared to be mostly of middle-class origin, while she refuted the suggestion that those who might be thought to be most vulnerable – the young, socially isolated, deprived, or those not succeeding in their lives, were particularly attracted.

These findings raise the obvious question as to why often affluent, well-educated, middle-class young people with so many worldly opportunities before them should be particularly attracted to NRMs of a world-rejecting nature. The question is particularly pertinent since these people would presumably be the most resilient to NRMs, which are supposed to be coercive and manipulating. A simple answer would be that such individuals are those more fully involved in the counter-culture and experimentation. Indeed, there is evidence of the link with the middle-class young who were more wrapped up with the 'hippie', drop-out, drug counter-culture of the 1960s and 1970s. The longer period of higher education and an unparalleled growth in affluence and job security during this time encouraged a spirit of experimentation (Ellwood 1973; Downton 1979). There is, however, more to consider, since a number of movements have survived beyond these decades.

There appears to be a link between the membership of NRMs and various forms of deprivation experienced by the middle classes. Wallis (1984) touches upon this in his account of recruitment to world-accommodating religions, including his analyses of neo-Pentecostalism (discussed in the previous chapter). He claimed that members are generally those who have some stake in the world. However, a number of movements help individuals to cope with their social roles, above all by offering the safe haven of a subculture that they can retire too. Often unconcerned with trying to alter the world or furthering the worldly opportunities of members, such movements seem orientated to dealing with the negative effects of modern society. For many members, according to Wallis, there may be a feeling of being spiritually deprived in an existence which they see as too materialistic, lonely, and impersonal.

Other studies have discovered that members of world-affirming types tend to be rather older than other NRMs (Alfred 1976; Babbie & Stone 1977). The average age of participants in human potential groups was found to be 35, while Ellwood (1973) discovered that 43 per cent of members of Nichiren Shoshu were over the age of 36. These recruits were also inclined to be even more predominantly middle-class and affluent than those of other movements. Many of them were undoubtedly well educated, professionally qualified, and had begun promising careers. The key may be, as Wuthnow (1978, 21) suggests, that experimentation with eastern religion, such as Transcendental Meditation, Yoga, and Zen Buddhism shows a certain amount of upper middle-class intellectual and cultural sophistication and a high level of education.

While usually not appealing to the needs of the more economically deprived sections of society which are, more frequently, provided by world-rejecting groups, the world-accommodating varieties offer a kind of spiritual substitute for those who otherwise lead fairly mundane respectable lives. In contrast, although open to all types of people, the attraction of world-affirming movements is often to wealthier social groups who have a significant interest in the world as it is. Members seek no compensation, only religious expressions which enhance their lives by providing a spiritual path to guilt-free, spontaneous self-advancement, largely through human potential therapies.

The young and NRMs

Besides social class background, age is an important variable when considering the attraction of many NRMs. Judah (1974) found that 85 per cent of ISKCON members were under 26 years old, while only 3 per cent were over 30. Ellwood (1973) discovered that participants in the Jesus movement were mostly aged between 14 and 24. In her study, Barker (1984) concluded that the average age at which recruits joined the Unification Church was 23, and that about 80 per cent of members were between 19 and 30.

To some extent, the attraction of the young can be explained by many of the considerations above. NRMs provide a sense of purpose, of belonging and identity. At the same time, traditional mainline Christianity seems to be of less and less appeal to this age group. The European Values Survey (Stoetzel 1983; Harding *et al* 1985) clearly indicated that belief in the Christian God is declining among the young but increases up the age scale, as does belonging to church institutions. This is so for various European countries irrespective of denomination and other social variables such as gender and social class.

Evidence suggests that the culture of church life has contributed to the decline of young people belonging to Christian denominations. Philip Richter and Leslie Francis' interviews of those leaving churches in Britain discovered that they did so because they were found to be dominated by older people and that church displayed a culture that was 'old fashioned'. Moreover, those who did not leave the faith entirely gravitated towards those churches which were described as 'more lively', 'exciting', 'creative', 'youth-orientated', and 'alternative' (Richter & Francis 1998, 124–5). It is possible to suggest that many of the NRMs also display some of these attractive attributes, while avoiding some of the negative aspects of traditional Christian churches.

Women and NRMs

Women appear to be over-represented among the ranks of NRMs. However, this is also the case with mainline churches and is true of women of all age groups. In explaining their over-representation in Christian churches, Walter (1990) believes that much can be accounted for in terms of a search for solutions to a number of negative social and psychological experiences. Feelings of anxiety, a range of emotional difficulties generated by domestic roles and over-dependency on the male sex, and a search for self-assertiveness are frequent concerns which need to be psychologically addressed. In addition, compensators might be sought for such deprivations as poverty, low status, and lack of opportunities, again linked to the limitations of female social roles and child-rearing responsibilities in particular. Feasibly, NRMs also deal with these social and psychological deficiencies – and perhaps in a more effective way than the established Christian churches.

The NRMs, then, may have their unique attractions for women. One observation is that many offer women what the mainline religions do not. Evidence suggests that traditional Christianity has continued to advance conservative attitudes towards the social roles of women. Here, there is little that is unprecedented. In the nineteenth-century, a number of new religions emerged which reinterpreted women's roles – often giving women significant leadership positions and ritually expressing their needs and experiences. This was typified by various metaphysical movements and those such as theosophy and spiritualism, which have continued to offer women opportunities denied to them by traditional Christianity.

In the Christian churches men have historically held all important leadership roles and performed religious symbolic functions, while women have been given lesser functions and excluded from positions of authority. True, the liberal wings of established religions such as Christianity or Judaism have embraced numerous positive changes for women. Nonetheless, many of their congregations are still out of step with wider, more tolerant cultural attitudes. By contrast, numerous new religious groups are willing to reflect the changing attitudes and experiences of women in the outside world. Less orthodox forms of religiosity, including the Mormon Church, have recently developed alternative gendered spiritualities. Similarly, many of those movements rediscovering witchcraft and paganism, as well as what has come to be known as spiritual eco-feminism, have embraced the cause of women. In such movements the teachings and practices might be loosely defined, but they certainly express an aversion to hierarchy and the regulations of male-dominated institutions.

Many new expressions of religiosity provide women with more liberating roles, pathways to self-transformation and image construction, and furnish an alternative source of authority and power through distinctive beliefs, rituals, and symbols. For the most part, they are consciously articulating alternative spiritual beliefs and practices which envisage and celebrate positive images of women, such as homage to a female deity, rituals of female empowerment, and moral norms which do not promote female submissiveness. At the very least, they may also permit women to take the position of power and leadership denied by more orthodox forms of religiosity. Most appear to advance positive images for women by focusing on non-hierarchical relationships; a few, however, envisage inverting male-female and status roles.

Susan Palmer's (1994) work on the roles of women in seven unorthodox religious movements in the West provides one of the few extensive treatments of the link between NRMs and gender identity. Palmer explores the innovative roles that many NRMs supply. They allow women to experiment with new concepts of gender and sexuality. In ISKCON, for example, women are defined solely as 'mothers'. Unmarried or childless women hold the same status in the movement. A number of the more mystical NRMs believe that a woman transfers her spiritual qualities not just to her male partner but to the whole community. Through this transfer, she may earn respect and offer authority within the organization. Another example is the Hindu-based Brahma Kumaris movement, which displays an implicit female ideology. As adherents to the organization, women occupy considerable power and status. In fact, it offers a complete role reversal: men look after the practical aspects of living, thus freeing women for higher spiritual duties, while the male pupil and female mentor is not uncommon (Puttick 1999).

Puttick argues that some NRMs may attract women who have achieved secular/professional success and are now looking for a spiritual dimension to their lives. As a whole, the beliefs and practice of these movements, as far as gender is concerned, are more fluid and flexible, sometimes with a focus on androgyny, and they usually include women in the leadership positions that they also enjoy in secular life. NRMs such as the Osho, the Brahma Kumaris, and many Buddhist and Pagan groups offer equal opportunities with no 'glass ceiling', and the possibility for women to combine work, marriage, and motherhood with spiritual growth.

Men too have developed their own spiritual groups and these also appear to be linked with identity construction. The contemporary men's spirituality movement however, does not seem to have any particular grass-root basis. Many of those that have endured are more like the 1970s support groups that rejected the approach of the newer movement towards articulating a spiritual/ritual expression of a new masculinity in which there is an attempt to 'get in touch' with their feminine side. Such groups include, at least in the USA, the Brothers of the Earth and the Radical Faeries. For the most part, the male movement appears to be largely an entrepreneurial effort in which, for the cost of subscription, men are brought together in a group setting for an orchestrated spiritual experience. These movements are premised on the basis that, although men's status and roles may be acceptable, individual men are not functioning well psychologically – indeed, some may be emotionally and socially crippled because they have been inadequately socialized into masculine social roles.

NRMs: conversion and disengagement

A good deal of the sociological research into NRMs has been concerned with not just the question why some members join, but *how*? Findings have often focused on conversion processes and, in doing so, have considerably enhanced our understanding of religious conversion per se. Many of the theories related to conversion discussed below obviously dovetail with the subject of sect/cult recruitment considered in Chapter 3.

Membership and conversion to NRMs are often perceived as one and the same thing. Moreover, the adoption of a distinctive religious view of the world and a new organizational allegiance is frequently seen as the result of some conversion experience. In short, there is a change in consciousness, a transformation of one's self-image and meaning system, or what Snow and Machalek (1983, 264) refer to as a change in one's 'universe of discourse'. Whether the conversion experience is rapid or slow, complete or partial, such radical conversion transforms the way in which individuals perceive the world, including the social world and their place in it.

The 'causes' of conversion

Initially, theories of conversion were inspired largely by the accounts of American POWs during the Korean War. These theories became known as the 'brainwashing' or 'coercive persuasion' model of conversion and were typified by Sargant's work (1957), which examined under which circumstances people may be persuaded to accept beliefs alien to them. Hence, the emphasis tended to be on the proselytizing endeavours of the religious group which the individual elected to join. This downplayed the individual as an autonomous actor searching for a spiritual truth and claims to a subjective spiritual experience. Frequently, references to conversion appeared to take place during carefully orchestrated settings, for example, the evangelical revival meeting. Hence, claims to conversion, sociologically speaking, are frequently explained as little more than an emotive response to contrived situations and the compliant conformity to group pressure (Lang & Lang 1960). Contrary evidence has, however, been found. As Barker (1983) discovered to be the case with the Unification Church, only some of those exposed to such pressures decide to convert. At the very least, studies of members of NRMs show that the relationship between membership and conversion is not a straightforward one (Snow 1976).

The publication of the Loftland-Stark conversion model in 1965 inspired a great deal of sociological thinking, particularly in the area of cults and new forms of religiosity, and moved beyond the simple assumptions advanced in earlier works. For Loftland and Stark, conversion was a 'process' involving seven requisites. In turn, empirical research has further explored specific aspects of this 'process' and singled out what is anticipated to be the most important variables. They are as follows:

- Firstly, people have unresolved tensions and contradictions in their lives. The emphasis here is on the individual's personality, experiences, and personal problems. This kind of variable has proved attractive in later studies because it meshes with the Western cultural emphasis on individualistic motivations and experiences. Some commentators have focused on personality disorders. For example, Levine (1980, 146–51) believes that the appeal of contemporary cults is in offering security and a purpose for those who cannot deal with individual responsibility and the demands of wider society. Others sociologists, including Greil and Rudy (1984), put an emphasis on variables such as marital strain, the loss of a family member, unemployment, or the pressures of living, such as the felt need to succeed in higher education. Frequently, this approach takes on board the significance of social class, gender, age, and level of education in framing such experiences.

- Secondly, for Loftland and Stark, we must take into account the ways open to dealing with personal problems. An individual may already be predisposed to coping with their difficulties with reference to religious views of the world.

- Thirdly, it follows that s/he will probably seek a resolution to problems through the appeal of religious ideas and beliefs. Other research has also emphasized this dimension (Harrison 1974). Conversion and recruitment is likely when a potential convert's perspective is congruent with that of a religious collective, even when the specific content of the group's beliefs may be unfamiliar. The key point is that a convert's personal experiences are interpreted in terms of the belief system of a religious movement. In short, unique personal and situational factors can predispose people to conversion by making them aware of the extent to which their prior meaning system fails to explain or give meaning to experiences and events. S/he may try alternative beliefs and practices until finding one which strikes a chord.

- Fourthly, there is the fairly predictable 'turning point'. The would-be convert comes to a crucial juncture in their life. Many appear to describe a crisis which may disrupt a person so completely that the individual has difficulty integrating events into their previously held meaning system. Hence, serious illness or unemployment may become turning points. There is, however, nothing predetermined about such a development and very diverse individual responses are possible.

- Fifthly, there is the relevance of 'affective bonds'. This means the important emotional networks open to a religious group. During what amounts to socialization into the movement, recruits learn to redefine their social world. Relationships previously valued become far less important, and patterns of behaviour once undesirable become desirable. This process results in a whole new way of experiencing and negotiating the world and oneself in it.

- Sixthly, there will be the negation of relationships outside the religious group. At the same time as establishing affective bonds, the recruit also weakens or severs those relationships that support the old self. This might be easier if the individuals attracted to the group are already socially isolated. The religious group becomes the most important focus of life. The religious seeker is now a fully-fledged member.

The Loftland and Stark model appears impressive. Nonetheless, it has its weaknesses. Snow and Phillips (1980), for instance, found that of the seven suggested prerequisites for conversion, only one, intensive interaction, was applicable to conversion to the Nichiren Shoshu Buddhist group in the USA. A similar attempt to test the theory was conducted by Greil and Rudy (1984), who examined case studies of the conversion process in ten very different religious groups ranging from the Mormons, to Hare Krishna, to evangelical Christian groups. They conclude that several components of the model had to be rejected for conceptual reasons. For instance, there is no way of knowing whether 'tensions' distinguish converts from non-converts, since not all those experiencing personal problems turn to religious groups to resolve them. On the other hand, other components are to be found in some types of groups but not others. For instance, 'neutralization of attachments', where conversion involves a radical transformation of social roles, could be found more obviously among evangelical Christian groups, but not necessarily with those based on eastern mysticism. Only the 'formation of affective bonds' and 'intensive interaction' with group members seem to be indispensable prerequisites for conversion. Thus, any group which seeks to successfully convert people must be structured so as to foster interaction with members.

Learning processes

An alternative account of conversion is the 'role theory' model. Here, conversion is identified as a kind of learning process, although the emphasis is once more on the interaction with the group's members. The model developed by Bromley and Shupe (1979), based on a study of the COG, Hare Krishna, and the Unification Church, was primarily concerned with levels of psychological commitment to a religious movement. Bromley and Shupe note that frequently there is no great depth of individual dedication or commitment, feeling of belonging, or intense individual religious experience, while little may be known of the movement's beliefs. Rather, conversion is a 'structured event' arising from relationships with members and roles within the group. Affiliation is an 'exchange process' which involves a link between problem-solving strategies and norms and values of the group whereby the individual's needs become shaped by the group. One becomes a convert through five stages:

- Firstly, 'predisposing factors' such as alienation or social availability.
- Secondly, 'attraction' – levels of motivation, and experience of role models in the group.
- Thirdly, 'incipient involvement'. This refers to the group's claims to compliance and greater depth of individual involvement.
- Fourthly, 'active involvement', for instance, witnessing, evangelizing, and fund-raising.
- Finally, 'commitment', which includes opportunities for leadership, the acceptance of a 'master theology', the submergence into a subculture, the idea of being part of a world-saving elite, and a large number of collective experiences and activities.

Social networks

The emphasis on interaction has been given greater attention with the social network approach to conversion. Here, the stress is on the relevance of group interaction and emotional bonds. Indeed, some sociologists have argued that this is more important than social factors such as gender or age, or a life crisis in determining differential recruitment (Snow & Machalek 1983; Oegema 1987). What is advanced as being of greatest importance is the formation of bonds and intense interaction with members of the religious group and that this interaction is generally along pre-existing lines of social relationships which are significant and meaningful to the individual and hence easing the process to membership. Nonetheless, not all those with personal links to religious groups are converted. Snow and Machalek (1983) deem it necessary to consider 'socio-spatial factors' to account for why some join while others do not when introduced to a religious movement. The key point is that potential converts have more free time, discretion over choice, and are less bound up within relationships that inhibit commitment.

Several social processes enable the individual to make the transformation to a fully-fledged life in the more world-rejecting movement. Group support is particularly significant in establishing the welcoming bonds which affirm the new self and in accepting a distinct meaning system. As the recruit gradually withdraws from competing social relationships, the new group's opinions become increasingly important. Intensive interaction and close affective bonds with group members are central to the conversion process because they link the individual's new identity with the organization's perspective and goals (Greil & Rudy 1984). Nonetheless, there is contrary evidence. Not all of these contributing factors are present or significant for all movements. As we have seen, Jehovah's Witnesses, for example, recruit very little from pre-existing networks of social relationships and more from 'cold' evangelizing (Beckford 1975).

The convert's point of view

The preoccupation with social variables, roles, and networks in explaining conversion means that there has tended to be a neglect of accounts provided by the converts themselves. In their later work, Snow and Machalek centre on what individuals themselves claim about their experiences rather than reductionist explanations focusing on sociological 'causes'. They suggest that this process of conversion is more fundamental than beliefs or identities (Snow & Machalek 1983, 170). They are concerned with those they call a 'social type' of person. In other words, conversion is experienced by particular types of people. This approach is founded on an analysis of the accounts and reasoning of converts and is supported by the actor's own underlying experience of conversion, which displays certain 'rhetorical indicators'. Based primarily on Snow's (1976) study of the Nichiren Shoshu Buddhist movement, Snow and Machalek suggest that converts may be identified firstly by 'the adoption of a master attribution scheme'. While people always try to make sense of themselves and others and experience the world as a common cognitive process, what distinguishes the convert from non-converts is that when asked to account for the state of the world, self, or others and their actions, converts inevitably resort to one (religious) attribution system. In short, they explain the world and their part in it in a distinctively religious way.

Secondly, for Snow and Machalek there is the importance of 'biographical reconstruction'. This denotes the idea that individuals who experience the radical change of conversion reconstruct or reinterpret their past life perspective from the present. This does not necessarily entail a wholesale fabrication or distortion of one's previous life, but rather a restructuring in which previous important occurrences may be de-emphasized and less significant ones elevated to greater prominence.

Thirdly, there is the 'suspension of analogical reasoning'. This can be seen as a technique for affirming the sacredness of one's beliefs over the worldliness and irrelevance of all others, thereby insulating and protecting beliefs and self from the contamination of association with alien worldviews and non-believers. Fourthly, there is the embrace of a 'master role'. Here, the convert comes to see him/herself in terms of the role of convert and member of a particular group. All other roles become subordinate to it. Hence, while a person may be a 'son' or 'daughter', a 'student' or 'professional person', it is by being a member of a religious group that a convert primarily constructs their identity.

In turn, Staples and Mauss (1987) present a critique of Snow and Machalek's alternative theory of conversion. They believe that Snow and Machalek fail to distinguish between conversion and commitment. Conversion is, above all, primarily a change in self-consciousness. It is a way that a person thinks or feels about him/herself. Snow and Machalek do not go far enough in acknowledging this. By using a small sample of evangelical Christians, Staples and Mauss indicate that while some aspects of the first, third, and fourth of Snow and Machalek's rhetorical indicators were present, the second was often conspicuously missing to the point of denying a conversion experience. Whereas Snow and Machalek view particular kinds of rhetoric to be a reflection of some underlying changes in consciousness, Staples and Mauss see particular types of language and rhetoric as tools that individuals use to achieve transformation of self. While Snow and Machalek tend to view conversion as something that 'happens to' a person, Staples and Mauss understand the person to be an active participant in the creation of a 'new self'. Rhetoric is the convert's own account of conversion and is often framed in this way, and it is seen as an individual choice. This decision is said by the convert to be beneficial, with an emphasis on a wonderful new way of life. With sectarian and many NRM groups this is often imperative – affirming a worldview which is frequently in conflict with the outside world.

Disengagement from the new religions

The preoccupation with the subject of who joins NRMs, and the processes by which they do so, means that the area of why and how people may come to leave the new religions (and others) has been rather neglected. As in the case of theories of conversion, those related to disengagement from the religious group have tended to see it as a 'process'. There are various trains of thought. One simply suggests that much may be similar to an individual's disengagement from social roles elsewhere. In contemporary societies people frequently go through role-exit experiences, for example, they may change their job or exit the role as a parent or student and assume new roles. Such role exiting tends to be a rather lengthy and sometimes a difficult period of transition.

Alternatively, leaving a new religion may very often be a reversal of the process related to how the member came to join in the first place. Thus, Ebaugh (1988) conjectures that exit involves the pushes and pulls of various social influences. Individuals weigh the advantages and disadvantages of being in or out of the NRM just as they did so when enlisting. This is a process perhaps more applicable to the world-rejecting movement. Typically, members reach the decision to leave the group only gradually, but just as their retrospective accounts of conversion are transformed to fit their new beliefs and image of self, so too is ex-members' narrative on decisions to leave. However, what we do know is that accounts of exit frequently include first doubts, the seeking and weighing of role alternatives, a turning point, and the establishment of an ex-role identity. By contrast, Wright (1987, 1988) identifies five factors that contribute to the conditions under which defection is likely to occur. This involves the following:

- Firstly, the breakdown in members' insulation from the outside world. At some point there will be comprehensive contacts with people external to the group.
- Secondly, a failure of the group to provide for the needs of the member as promised and when equated with the effort invested in membership.
- Thirdly, the perceived lack of success in achieving world transformation as promised by the movement.
- Fourthly, a failure to meet affective needs of the primary group.
- Finally, inconsistencies between the actions of leaders and the ideas they symbolically represent. The level of emotional attachment to the charismatic leader will also be an important variable.

Summary

It is evident in the above survey that NRMs have attracted a great deal of attention from sociologists of religion over the last three or four decades – perhaps even more so than mainstream religion. Certainly, they are a fascinating field of enquiry. Research has told us a great deal as to why they have arisen, how they might be classified, why some endure while others do not, who joins and why, and the processes by which people become members and converts on the one hand and the means by which they leave on the other. Although these are important considerations, details of beliefs and practices are frequently overlooked or neglected. The next chapter considers some of the major movements and examines such beliefs and practices. By endeavouring to do so it may provide a sense of what it means to belong to such movements.

Further reading

Barker, E. (1978) 'Living the Divine Principle. Inside the Reverend Sun Myung Moon's Unification Church in Britain', *Archives de Sciences Sociales des Religions*, **45** (1), 75–92.

Barker, E. (1983) 'New Religious Movements in Britain: the Context and the Membership', *Social Compass*, **30** (1), 33–45.

Beckford, A. (1978) 'Through the Looking Glass and Out the Other Side. Withdrawal from Reverend Moon's Unification Church', *Archives de Sciences Sociales des Religions*, **45** (1), 95–127.

Beckford, A. (1983) 'Young People and New Religious Movements. An Introduction', *Social Compass*, **29** (4), 5–19.

Beckford, J. (ed.) (1992) *New Religious Movements and Rapid Social Change*, London: Sage.

Beit-Hallahmi, B. (1993) *The Illustrated Encyclopedia of Active New Religions, Sects and Cults*, New York: Rosen Publishing Group.

Nelson, G. (1987) *Cults, New Religions and Religious Creativity*, London: Routledge & Kegan Paul.

Parsons, A. (1986) 'Messianic Personalism: A Role Analysis of the Unification Church', *Journal for the Scientific Study of Religion*, **25** (2), 141–62.

7 Some major New Religious Movements

A distinctive approach to the categorization of NRMs is that advanced by Eileen Barker (1985) who classifies them according to the religious tradition from which they are ultimately derived. The Family, and other similar strands of the Jesus movement which originated in the Californian counter-culture in the late 1960s, obviously have a Christian (if distinctively Pentecostal) origin. Zen groups have their roots in Buddhism, and Hare Krishna and the disciples of the Divine Light Mission stem from Hinduism. Some NRMs are more syncretic and merge together different religious traditions. A prime example is that of the Unification Church, which mixes Christian ideas with elements of Taoism and Confucianism. Others have a pagan, occult, or witchcraft source. Alternatively, a number of NRMs display little connection with previous religions but are part of the human potential movement, with Scientology being an obvious example.

Barker is aware that some groups are so idiosyncratic that they defy any classification and by way of beliefs and practices are genuinely new expressions of religion. Nonetheless, her classification will inform our outline of the beliefs and practices of a number of the major movements discussed below. Those chosen are among some of the largest and are selected as representative of their kind. Those related to neo-Paganism or human potential, and others which could plausibly be placed under the rubric of quasi-religions, will be considered in later chapters.

NRMs derived from Christianity

The Jesus movement emerged in the late 1960s in California and subsequently spread throughout the USA, to Europe, and beyond. Reflecting the counter-culture in which it originated, the movement placed an emphasis on informality. The early congregations did not possess their own buildings and meetings for worship were often held in the open air or in all kinds of rented venues. For the young, informal dress and the application of rock music to gospel themes were important attractions in the West Coast cultural milieu. Common to all of them was communal living, which reflected both the counter-cultural experiment of the time and the attempt to restore first-century Christianity. There was also a preference for spontaneity and for expressing the gifts of the charismata, including healing, prophecy, and speaking in tongues. The tone and content of the preaching tended to be fundamentalist. What was produced was thus a curious mixture of counter-cultural themes and 'old-time' American gospel evangelism.

During the 1970s, the Jesus movement succumbed to its own sectarian divisions, which were often vehemently opposed to each other. Those factions that did survive until the end of the decade either joined the established Pentecostal churches, or began to create churches of their own. These, in turn, occasionally grew to become 'mega' churches with thousands of members. Calvary Chapel in California, for example, is one of the best known. This has increasingly meant that the original adherents to the Jesus movement found themselves becoming part of the more respectable and culturally accommodating evangelical groups proliferating in the USA. A few, however, stood the test of time and have clung tenaciously to their original beliefs and practices. The first two considered here have origins in the USA: the Family and the Messianic Communities. A third, the Jesus Fellowship, represents a British counterpart to the North American movement. A fourth is the London Church of Christ, which has origins in the USA but is based in Britain.

The Family

The Family was formerly the COG, whose original founder was David Berg (or Mo David, as he was more popularly known). Under his leadership the movement enjoyed considerable growth for nearly twenty years, initially in the USA, and then in Europe, Latin America, and elsewhere. Today, by its own estimates, the Family claims to have representation in 106 countries worldwide and a membership of just over 10,000 drawn from some 90 nationalities (*The Family: Moving Into the 21st Century*).

In many respects, the beliefs of the Family are in line with those of conservative Christianity: the doctrine of the Trinity, the divinity of Christ, his atonement, and the acceptance of the bible as the inspired word of God. Like other groups that emerged at the same time, the movement has a strong evangelical tone. In the early stages it had a significant youthful appeal and was discernibly neo-Pentecostal in orientation. Today, many of its members are older and of a wider social mix, while two-thirds of the current membership are children, and this can be explained by the strong emphasis on family life.

At the same time as being observably fundamentalist, the Family also makes important departures from traditional evangelical Christianity. There has always been a great deal more emphasis than most evangelical groups on the significance of the Last Days, and the belief that Christ would shortly return to establish the kingdom of God on earth. Here, the founder Berg had a central role to play. Even since his death in 1994, members of the Family have insisted that Berg was a specially chosen prophet who was predestined by God to proclaim the message of the End Times to the human race. Since his death, his wife, Maria, has largely been recognized as a prophetess and leader of the Family.

The Family has, in addition, evolved its distinctive teaching of the 'Law of Love'. Members believe that this 'Law' is the supreme tenet upon which all Christian life and relationships should rest. Only those acts inspired by unselfish love are acceptable in dealing with other people. Where this has placed the movement into controversy, however, is the application of the Law of Love to sexual relationships. There is the belief that all heterosexual relationships between consenting adults are permissible to God, irrespective of marital status, as long as they are motivated by unselfish love. This liberal sexual attitude has also been extended to winning converts through so-called 'flirty fishing'. In the past this amounted to the practice (now abandoned) of female members offering sex to potential converts in return for joining the movement or financial support.

For several decades, the Family has been one of the most controversial groups. The first ever official anti-cult organization, FREECOG, was set up to counter its influence and win back young members for aggrieved relatives. Not only sexual controversies, but also alleged coercive means of winning over members, authoritarian control, and 'brainwashing' have been to the fore. Because, according to ex-members, sexual relationships have extended to children, over 600 of the movement's younger generation have been taken into care by various authorities in different parts of the world. Fear of the lack of education and social and physical well-being has also spurred such draconian measures. Today, the movement has changed its ways and manufactured a fresh image. Perhaps partly as a response to the allegations of sexual misconduct, but mainly because of the threat of AIDs, the Family now has very strict rules on sexual relationships, which are to be only between Family members.

Like other strands of the Jesus movement, the Family has always placed an emphasis on communal living. The communities – or homes – are where the fully committed members live. They can range from four to several dozen people residing together. While each is self-governing, the Family has a broad charter (since 1995) which outlines most of the important principles, aims, and beliefs of the movement and offers guidelines for communal life. One third of those who live in the movement's community houses have done so for a period of between sixteen and twenty years. The Family does not, however, actively encourage people to join its communities. Like other intentional communities, anyone who wants to engage must first spend some months acquainting themselves with the Family's beliefs and lifestyles. There is a trial period of three weeks, after which members of the community will vote on the applicant's suitability. This is followed by a six-month probation.

The Community's income is derived mainly from donations and from sale of its posters, music cassettes, and videos. From time to time, members in the community may take on a secular job to bring in more income if required. Each community gives 10 per cent of its income each month to World Services, more or less the central authority of the movement, which is responsible for publications and starting new communities. As well as evangelistic work, members of the Family help in providing humanitarian aid, which in the past has meant sponsoring food aid after natural disasters.

The Messianic Communities

The Messianic Communities (previously known as the Northeast Kingdom Community Church) has a membership as high as 1,500. The movement, in the early years at least, was in many ways not that different from similar groups of the time, a good number of which have not survived. However, the survival of this particular movement can be attributed to its sect-like qualities and relative insulation from the world. At the same time, it embraces a unique theology which provides a syncretic form derived from numerous origins.

In 1971, the charismatic leader of the movement, Elbert Spriggs, felt a divine calling in which God demanded that he establish a new form of religious life. His original ministry, based on a coffee shop and small health foods business, expanded to a community lifestyle in five houses which served as the foundation for evangelizing out-reach. The community began to solidify and expand. In 1978, Spriggs received an invitation to visit their community in Island Pond, Vermont from a band of Pentecostal-type Christians who had experienced similar hostility with local churches. By 1980, the rest of his community (which had by this time expanded to include several hundred members who were running a delicatessen business in Tennessee, Alabama, and Georgia) sold their property and moved to Island Pond.

The Messianic Communities have followed a path of Restorationism or, to put it literally, the attempt to restore and continue the primitive Jewish/Christian Church of the Book of Acts, both theologically and in terms of lifestyles. The generalized belief is that the early church was corrupted by the Roman Empire and, subsequently, over the last two millennia, it has been undermined by false teachings and worldly materialism. It follows that the historical role of the Messianic Communities is to restore the 'true' first-century church in the Last Days.

Although the Messianic Communities claim that they are returning to the 'true' doctrine of the Christian Church, the teachings espoused do make radical departure from orthodox historical Christianity. Most of this is in terms of the broad eschatology which, in turn, belies the sectarian aspects of the communities. According to the teachings there will be two divine judgements. Those under covenant with God, that is, members of the Communities, will be judged first, with the righteous among them going to rule over the recreated earth with Yahshusa (Jesus). Unbelievers who were never exposed to the 'true' message will be judged separately – together with those of other faiths and those who through no fault of their own have never heard the message (including Catholics). These people will be judged according to their deeds rather than their beliefs. Most Protestants are expected to be judged along with unbelievers, as they are not perceived by the Messianic Communities as living under the covenant.

The exclusivity of the Messianic Communities' sectarian nature can be seen in the unique millenarian role which they ascribe to themselves. The significance of spiritual perfectionism in the eschatological teachings of the Messianic Communities is that it is confidently believed that very soon the restored church will be able to send out prophetic emissaries to preach during the final ingathering of souls before the Second Coming of the messiah. Derived from esoteric passages of the Book of Revelation, it is believed that this spiritual elite will number 144,000 pure male virgins – 12,000 from each tribe. The Messianic Communities are also Sabbatarian, keeping the Jewish Sabbath. Most of the members adopt Hebrew names. This sense of restoration extends to food and dress as well. Food is a cross between rural cooking and health food since, according to the community, it makes sense for people in God's kingdom to be healthy. Much of the music is based on Israeli folk songs. Women are expected to dress modestly and men follow the Jewish practice of growing long beards and leaving their shirts untucked 'to hide their form'.

Although the Messianic Communities have flourished for most of their existence, there was no easy or straightforward development and there have been several difficult periods that threatened their survival. In the early 1980s, a number of members left as a result of persecution and economic hardship. After 1982, the church members also lost a series of child custody battles due to their unconventional lifestyles and damaging rumours regarding child-rearing practices. In 1984, there was a much-publicized raid on the community located in Island Pond by a hundred state troopers in order to take forced custody of the children.

The membership of the Messianic Communities is distributed among some twenty widely dispersed colonies which, nevertheless, have relatively good communication systems between each. Roughly half of these communities are in the USA, with the others to be found in Canada, England, France, Germany, Spain, Brazil, and Australia. Economically, these communities are extremely diverse. Each is typically based on multi-family households which are, for all intents and purposes, economically independent of wider society. While members may at times work as semi-skilled and skilled day labourers, particularly when starting up a new evangelizing out-reach, each collective attempts to support itself through agriculture and a number of cottage industries (Bozeman 1997).

The Jesus Fellowship

The Jesus Fellowship emerged in 1968 as a consequence of a Pentecostal-style revival based at a Baptist chapel just outside Northampton, England. It grew to attract new converts drawn principally from 'bikers', drug-abusers, and 'hippies', and as it did so it established a number of communal houses with economic support derived from a farm that was bought in the area. Frequently surrounded by controversies related to unconventional Christian living, the fellowship was expelled from the Baptist Union and, in 1986, from the Evangelical Alliance (the umbrella organization of many British evangelical churches). In many respects, however, the movement was not that different from other New Churches that sprang up at the time, although it did differ in its emphasis on communal life and a membership that was not predominantly middle-class in composition.

As a result of controversy and persecution, the Jesus Fellowship grew more defensive and introspective to the extent that it became, if temporarily, sectarian in nature. Retreating from secular society and those who persecuted it, the movement increasingly designated the outside world as 'Babylon'. Perhaps paradoxically, this was also a period of sustained membership growth and the stepping up of proselytizing missions into urban areas through its evangelical wing, the Jesus Army. This evangelism has largely been conducted via street work (along with colourful painted double-decker coaches), marquee campaigns, local initiatives, church planting, renewal weekends, and 'celebration rallies'. Many of these activities attract several thousand people and tend to be calculated to appeal to the contemporary 'rave' culture, complete with the light shows and rock music, of a younger generation.

Although in many respects orthodox Christians, the Jesus Fellowship believes that community life is a natural outcome of the Christian experience. It is also seen as part of an End-Time vision, a theological view that tends towards post-millenarianism, the creation of the Kingdom on earth *before* the Second Coming of Jesus Christ. Those in community are expected to lay aside personal interests and accept a common purpose. Hence, domestic arrangements reflect the Jesus Fellowship's understanding of the basic values of the kingdom of God: a new society of simplicity and equality. Practically speaking, all households conform to set patterns of consumption and activities to which members are obliged to adapt. Those in community (and indeed members not in community) are also understood to assume a new identity when joining. This is indicated by the adoption of a new 'virtue' name, where a person's first name is followed with that such as 'Intrepid' or 'Resolute', which are meant to characterize certain personal qualities.

Today, the New Creation Christian Community (NCCC), as the Jesus Fellowship's communal element calls itself, is no longer limited to its centres of Northampton and its locality. The fellowship claims that there are over 800 people (including children) living a community life in houses of various sizes modelled on the experiences of the first-century church. There are now over 60 large houses and 20 smaller ones which have been purchased all over Britain, so that the Jesus Fellowship has a presence in numerous major cities and towns. Like many intentional communities, entrance into the life of the NCCC is gradual and follows a period of mutual adaptation. Those committed Christians seeking a communal existence, in much the same way as new converts off the street, are afforded a welcome, drawn into the fellowship and offered membership, with a personal decision expected within six months.

Generally speaking, in most houses of the Jesus Fellowship communal life is a Spartan existence and involves a simple lifestyle. There is no television or radio, and rarely any newspapers to be read. Most possessions are divested when entering the community, except for clothes and a few personal items. In many ways the NCCC is also self-sufficient. A community distribution centre at one of the larger properties just outside Northampton has been functioning for several years by way of providing the food, clothing, and other basic daily needs of the numerous households through a national transportation and distribution network.

Today, only a third of the Jesus Fellowship's 2,500 adherents live in community. It is apparent that the church has come to recognize that not all members find it appropriate to respond in the same way. It now provides four different styles of covenant membership with different levels of commitment: those who live in their own home, have their own jobs, and participate in various non-church as well as church activities; those who possess their own homes but retain a lifestyle of simplicity, discipleship, and sharing; those who live in NCCC households, sharing all wealth; and those who live at a distance from a congregation and cannot regularly participate in meetings. This flexibility of membership probably largely explains why the Jesus Fellowship has endured while other similar movements have not survived.

The Central London Church of Christ

The Central London Church of Christ (CLCOC) is another of the more controversial Christian movements to be found today. It was established in 1982 by Douglas Arthur and James Lloyd with some other ministers who came to Britain from the Boston Church of Christ (which is part of the so-called 'Crossroads movement'). The organization has also been known as the International Church of Christ. The growth of the movement has largely been obtained by church 'planting' in major cities, first in the USA and then across the world.

Many of the movement's beliefs are similar to those of mainline conservative evangelicals. However, it insists that a person cannot be a Christian unless baptized as a believing adult by conversion and that it is possible to lose one's salvation. The movement has a hierarchical structure and is dominated by males in the major leadership position. An important characteristic is the practice of discipleship – members all have a 'discipler' who is expected to help them to learn how to become better Christians by discussing details of their daily lives and offering advice. This is a controversial practice not dissimilar to the 'shepherding' policy enacted by the Jesus Fellowship.

Discipline is another important feature. Members of the CLCOC are expected to spend considerable time in prayer and bible study each day, and there are several services and meetings to be attended throughout the week. Sometimes fasting for several days is encouraged. The membership in London is now approaching some 2,000 and many members live in community flats. The majority of adherents are young and under thirty. Like similar movements, the CLCOC takes many converts from 'off the street'. However, they do not necessarily stay long and it is possible that half of those that have joined the movement have subsequently left. Also, similar to other such Christian groups, there is a strong emphasis on the conversion experience and the conviction that every believer should be an evangelist. It is the strategy of aggressive proselytism that has become the subject of considerable concern for critics of the movement and its rigorous attempts to win converts among university students has meant that it has been banned from some campuses.

NRMs derived from Hinduism

Numerous NRMs claim an origin in Hinduism, although there are problems in referring to some of them as 'new' or 'alternative'. One of the difficulties is that Hinduism, as a world faith, is so diverse in its beliefs and practices that it is difficult to identify a Hindu mainstream and its 'alternatives'. Moreover, it is difficult to separate the 'old' and the 'new', in short, to put many groups under the heading of NRMs. While there are important Hindu scriptural texts, the faith is not the 'religion of the book' in the same way as Judaism, Christianity, and Islam. Hinduism is characterized by its mysticism, which means that many beliefs and practices are open to variation, and teachings open to interpretation. Some of these problems will arise in the discussion of the NRMs to follow.

The Divine Light Mission

The leader of the Divine Light Mission (DLM), the Guru Maharaji, was 13 years old when he spectacularly rose to fame in the early 1970s. It was his young age which made him different from other eastern gurus who had established similar Hindu-inspired movements at the time. He was the son of Shri Hans Ji Maharaji, who began the DLM in India in 1960, based on the teachings of his own variety of enlightenment through the acquisition of spiritual knowledge. When his father died in 1966, the Guru Maharaji announced himself the new master and started his own teaching. His global tour in 1971 helped to establish a large following in Britain and the USA. In 1973, he held what was intended to have been a vast, much publicized event in the Houston Astrodome. 'Millennium '73' was meant to launch the spiritual millennium, but the event attracted very few and had little wider influence.

Perhaps because of this failure, Maharaji transformed his initial teachings in order to appeal to a Western context. He came to recognize that the Indian influences on his followers in the West were a hindrance to the wider acceptance of his teachings. He therefore changed the style of his message and relinquished the Hindu tradition, beliefs, and most of its original eastern religious practices. Hence, today the teachings do not concern themselves with reincarnation, heaven, or life after death. The movement now focuses entirely on the 'Knowledge' (formerly called mahatmas), which is a set of simple instructors on how adherents should live. This Westernization of an essentially eastern message is not seen as a dilemma or contradiction. In the early 1980s, Maharaji altered the name of the movement to Elan Vital to reflect this change in emphasis. Once viewed by followers as Satguru or Perfect Master, he also appears to have surrendered his almost divine status as a guru. Now, the notion of spiritual growth is not derived, as with other gurus, from his personal charisma, but from the nature of his teaching and its benefit to the individual adherents to his movement. Maharaji has also dismantled the structure of ashrams (communal homes).

The major focus of Maharaji is on stillness, peace, and contentment within the individual, and his 'Knowledge' consists of the techniques to obtain them. Knowledge, roughly translated, means the happiness of the true self-understanding. Each individual should seek to comprehend his or her true self. In turn, this brings a sense of well-being, joy, and harmony as one comes into contact with ones 'own nature'. The Knowledge includes four secret meditation procedures: Light, Music, Nectar, and Word. The process of reaching the true self within can only be achieved by the individual, but with the guidance and help of a teacher. Hence, the movement seems to embrace aspects of world-rejection and world-affirmation. The tens of thousands of followers in the West do not see themselves as members of a religion but the adherents to a system of teachings that extol the goal of enjoying life to the full.

For Elan Vital, the emphasis is on individual, subjective experience rather than on a body of dogma. The teachings provide a kind of practical mysticism. Maharaji speaks not of God but of the god or divinity within, as the power that gives existence. He has occasionally referred to the existence of the two gods – the one created by humankind and the one which creates humankind. Although such references apparently suggest an acceptance of a creative, loving power, he distances himself and his teaching from any concept of religion. It is not clear whether it is possible to receive Knowledge from anyone other than Maharaji. He claims only to encourage people to 'experience the present reality of life now'. Leaving his more ascetic life behind him, he does not personally eschew material possessions. Over time, critics have focused on what appears to be his opulent lifestyle and argue that it is supported largely by the donations of his followers. However, deliberately keeping a low profile has meant that the movement has generally managed to escape the gaze of publicity that surrounds other NRMs.

The International Society for Krishna Consciousness

ISKCON was founded by A.C. Bhaktivedanta Swami Prabhupada (1896–1977) in 1966. Born in Calcutta, he became a follower of the Gaudiya Mission, a Hindu revivalist movement. In 1933, the leader, Bhakti Siddhanta, charged him to carry Krishna Consciousness to the Western world. When finally allowed into the USA in 1965, the movement soon gained a following among counter-culture activists in New York and San Francisco, to whom it appeared to offer a meaningful lifestyle. It also attracted some celebrities, among them the Beatles' member, George Harrison, who helped promote its publicity, especially with his Hare Krishna mantra, which reached number 12 in the records charts. Over time, ISKCON has attracted its own controversies, especially those related to maverick gurus within the movement and the abuse of females under their guidance. However, ISKCON has rooted out those gurus who have attracted the greater notoriety. The major problem seemed to be that the concept of a spiritual mentor was based on the model of a charismatic authoritarian figure, which did not lend itself well to the Western context.

Unlike many other forms of Hinduism, Krishna Consciousness teaches a relationship between individuals and a personal god, Krishna, who is believed to be the eighth reincarnation of Ishnu. ISKCON however sees Krishna as the original form of Vishnu (Rama was another avatar of Vishnu, as was the Buddha). Krishna is regarded as the supreme Godhead. This is effectively a monotheistic form of Hinduism, known as Vaishnavism (worship of Vishnu). Krishna is the sustaining energy of all creation. Yet, rather than an unknowable god, which the more mystical Hindu movement teaches, Krishna is also personal and cares about every *jiva*, every living being.

The last reincarnation of Krishna is believed to have been the Bengali holy man, Chaitanya Mahaprabhu (1486–1533). There was a long-established tradition of Vaishnavism in both the north and south of India. Chaitanya began a reformed branch of this known as Gaudiya Vaishnavism or Vaishnava Bhakti (loving devotion and complete surrender to Krishna). Bhakti Hinduism has been a widely respected form of the religion since Chaitanya's death. Hence, far from being an NRM, ISKCON is merely a modern version of a 500-year old tradition, concentrating its attention on the West rather than the East.

ISKCON devotees believe that by living an existence of deep spirituality they can achieve pure, blissful consciousness in this life. The ultimate purpose of man, in this or any other world, is to serve God, and chanting the Hare Krishna mantra, repeating the names of God, helps the adherent to attain a deep love of the divinity. Devotees lead an austere life and at their initiation, when they take their vows, they are given Indian names. Those who choose to live in the temples are expected to chant the Hare Krishna mantra 1,728 times a day – once per bead, for 16 rounds of 108 beads – to purify consciousness. This is known as *japa* and takes about two hours a day, first thing in the morning.

The appearance of ISKCON members is quite conspicuous. Some shave their heads, though this is no longer very common among those not living in a community. All wear the *sikha*, a small plait or pigtail, to show that they have a spiritual calling but still remain an individual. Members also usually wear a *tilaka* (a white stripe of clay from a sacred lake in India) on their forehead and on seven other points of their body. This is frequently referred to as 'the footprint of Lord Vishnu' and marks the body as the Temple of God. Men wear *dhotis* – saffron for celibate men, white for married men – while women wear saris. These are seen as spiritual clothing and close to the traditions of India, perceived as the original spiritual culture. The ability to play drums and cymbals – *sankirtan* – is an essential part of the teaching. It accompanies the chanting of the name of God that purifies the heart and is regarded as a form of enjoyment, celebrating the pleasures that Krishna himself partook of. Desires themselves are not to be denied. Unlike Buddhism, therefore, which attempts to negate desires, Krishna Consciousness endeavours to transform them in creating a personal identity that seeks attachment to God.

Sai Baba

The Sai Baba movement originates in the Saivite tradition and is based on the Indian guru of that name. The movement was brought to the West by Gujaratis from East Africa, to whom it belonged as part of their own religious faith. Of all the famous Hindu miracle workers, Sai Baba is probably the most famous. He has also proved to be probably the most venerated and sought after yogi of recent times – followers seeking him to bless rings, pendants, and lockets, which enables mysterious ash, known as *vibhuti*, to be made manifest with its miraculous and healing powers. Sai Baba, like other Hindu gurus, developed a reputation for his distinct holy life as a child, and by the age of 16 he was said to have the ability to materialize objects. From 1958 onwards, he evolved the teaching of 'upadesh', the doctrine of erring humanity. His fame spread rapidly, and within a very short time a community complex was established at Prasanthi Nilayam which, in 1967, became an independent town. From that time he conducted tours, and by 1980 there were 3,600 principal centres and over 1,000 sub-centres. Sai Baba's attraction grew as religious seekers in the West became increasingly interested in meditation, vegetarianism, and paranormal phenomena. The movement established its own base in Britain in 1966 and became the centre of focus for Hindu devotees who had immigrated from India.

There is much about the Sai Baba movement that is cultist in the sociological meaning of the term. Although it has organization structures, the wider following is loosely organized and there is no one stringent set of practices. The movement centres on the leader who is believed to be divine – offering his own distinctive teachings and demanding obedience. He is supposed to be an incarnation of a previous guru, also known as Sai Baba who, in turn, is reckoned to be an incarnation of the Hindu-Sufi mystic poet Kabir (1398–1518 by tradition). All these men are said to have possessed the full range of *siddhis* (supernatural perceptual states), being able to control the weather, command astral travel, and materialize in other forms. Sai Baba provides little by way of teachings and most of his activities are limited to blessings of devotees. However, he continues to teach four important principles for his followers: Satya (truth), Dharma (duty), Shanti (peace), and Prema (divine love). Collectively they are said to bring an answer to all human problems and to show the way forward to man's enlightenment, progress, and destiny.

Although Sai Baba has attracted little attention from anti-cultist groups, in the West, he is not without his critics. It has been argued that he is little more than a showman and a charlatan who makes extravagant claims to his divinity and supernatural powers. Others have denied his 'true' spirituality since he by no means discourages his followers from seeking the material benefits of the world. Perhaps, above all, his critics fear that he has fooled gullible people by stage-managed 'miracles' producing holy ash, ikons, and jewellery.

Shri Swaminarayan

Lord Swaminarayan, the founder of the Swaminarayan faith (also known as Bochasanwasi Shri Akshar Purushottam Sanstha), has attempted to bring a moral and spiritual renaissance in a worldwide movement that claims to have over 1,720 centres, 1,550 youth forums, 2,300 child forums, and over a million followers. It is involved in local and international projects through a dedicated volunteer force of 25,000 young people and 699 *sadhus* (holy men). The movement boasts that within England alone it has reached out to over 5,000 families in 30 centres with a project for spiritual, educational, and cultural regeneration.

It is believed that the Swaminarayan is the incarnation of the Supreme God who appeared on earth in 1781, in the North Indian village of Chapaiya. A series of divine miracles accompanied his childhood with an alleged ability to elevate people to new spiritual heights through trance. At the age of eleven he renounced the world to perform penance and to redeem souls. Travelling to practically every region of India, his following quickly spread to over two million people and during his lifetime he was worshipped as the Supreme God. Since his death, in 1769, his adherents have maintained that Swaminarayan's presence on earth has remained through a hierarchy of enlightened gurus and is today represented by his fifth successor, Pramukh Swami Maharaj. Like those before him, Swami leads a simple and austere life and attempts to represent the Hindu tradition in all its purity. Hence, the movement he heads can be seen largely as a form of Hindu revivalism rather than a NRM. At the same time, he recognizes the validity of all earnest forms of worship, whatever the faith. He has embarked on over fifteen preaching tours covering 43 countries and has established temples in many of them, including North America and Europe.

In the West, Swaminarayan's followers have sought to radically change a society that is perceived as politically corrupt and spiritually bankrupt. They have preached love and non-violence, and sought to eradicate addictions, superstition, and 'harmful' beliefs. There is also the call for the unity of the human race irrespective of creed, race, colour, and nationality. In the new century, London can boast the Shri Swaminarayan Mandir – the first traditional Hindu Mandir temple in Europe. It has a prayer hall capacity to accommodate over 2,500 worshippers. This movement, which started some two centuries ago and which began as one dedicated to revitalizing Hinduism, now has its own web site and in many other respects has all the trimmings of a contemporary religious movement.

Brahma Kumaris

Brahma Kumaris is a widely respected movement, not least of all because of the dedication of its followers to teachings of purity, chastity, and peace. Many of its adherents have worked within the broader interfaith movement, having played a part in such initiatives as the World's Parliament of Religions in Chicago in 1993, and having worked closely with the World Congress of Faiths and the International Association for Religious Freedom. The movement also has a close association with India. The headquarters of the movement is situated there, while its founder, Dada Lekhraj, spent his life working in the Indian subcontinent. He had made no attempt to evangelize the West; that became the mission of some of his followers, who have succeeded in making the movement attractive to Westerners and, indeed, on a global level.

Dada Lekhraj (1876–1969) originally lived in Hyderabad and grew to multimillionaire status by specializing in the diamond trade. In his late sixties, he had a series of visions which were so significant as to lead him to abandon his business in favour of the spiritual life. These visions were said to provide insights into God's divinity, the nature of human spirituality, and the means by which the physical world would become transformed. From a small group of some 300 followers in the late 1930s, the Brahma Kumaris movement has developed. In 1952, Dada Lekhraj (also known as Brahma Baba) expanded his movement from Pakistan to the Indian subcontinent. After his death his followers continued this expansion in London and Hong Kong in 1971. By the end of the decade there were centres in over 40 countries, and by the mid-1990s there were somewhere in the region of 3,200 centres in 70 countries, with over 450,000 followers.

The Dada Lekhraj movement today insists that the courses offered in the Brahma Kumaris World Spiritual University is open to people of different religious and political affiliation. It presents a unique range of teachings that originate in the founder's visionary experiences. Dada Lekhraj himself did not claim to be a guru or to be the incarnation of some spiritual lineage. However, since his revelations are believed to have originated directly from Shiva, they are imbued with authority and relate to God, humanity, and the future of the cosmos.

Dada Lekhraj taught that each individual could be likened to an invisible luminous energy, much like a tiny star. These 'stars' centre around Shiva, who is the brightest luminary, followed by Krishna, and then Lakshmi. These various beings of light once wished to visit the physical world: Krishna and Lakshmi went first, followed by others in physical bodies. This world was originally a paradise, but those who entered it came to desire material things and to acquire wealth, possessions, power, and the destructive influence of sex.

Adherents to the movement see the spiritual quest as the need to find 'identity transference', to become perfect individuals that deny the seducing and corrupting desires of the world. There is the requirement to find the 'true self' in the soul and not the body. The former has three separate attributes – mind, intellect, and impressions – that operate together on interconnected levels. There thus needs to be a control of the mind that is the basis of emotions, desires, and sensations; a mastering of the intellect as the centre of processes of thought and decision; and the domination of impressions that, as a result of actions, may form negative habits, tendencies, and personal traits. Because the soul becomes attached to the physical world, reincarnation occurs.

Along with other Hindus, the Brahma Kumaris believe in the law of karma, and that the individual is reborn according to one's state of consciousness. Added to this is the conviction that man is moving towards a new Golden Age – the *sat yuga* (dawning). Greed, desire, hatred, and lust will give way to compassion, humility, and the spiritual life. The means of achieving this Golden Age is spiritual. The most important consideration here is the practice of Raja Yoga. This is a simple practice where the adherent does not have to assume any specific physical posture. Rather, the follower merely sits in silence before the image of Dada Lekhraj, which is projected onto a screen. This is believed to bring a mystical union between the individual soul (*atman*) and the supreme soul (*paramatman*), so that God comes to dominate the mind of the follower. Integral to the Raja Yoga are five 'affirmations'. Firstly, there is the affirmation of the individual's soul as an eternal infinitesimal point of light; secondly, the affirmation of one's nature as purity, love, and peace; thirdly, the acknowledgement that one has come from the world of souls and that one returns there; fourthly, the affirmation of the human soul as the child of God who teaches and guides; and finally, the acceptance of the necessity to live in peace and to do good.

Healthy Happy Holy Organization

Strictly speaking, the Healthy Happy Holy Organization (also known as Sikh Dharma) (already partially overviewed under Varieties of NRMs in Chapter 6) is a spin-off of Sikhism and is considered here largely because Sikhism was originally a breakaway sect from Hinduism. Founded in the USA in 1971 by Harbhajan Singh Khalsa Yogiji, the movement is best known through its educational branch, 3HO. It now claims 5,000 Western adherents scattered over 17 countries. It is distinguished by its followers' white apparel, including turbans for women as well as for men, and by a rigorous discipline of yoga and meditation.

The organization emphasizes health, based on the practice of Kundalini Yoga. New converts undergo a baptism (*Sikh amrit*) and ceremoniously accept the five 'Ks' in the same way as Khalsa Sikhs (see Chapter 11). There are believed to be some 4,000 members, mostly based in North America. While life in communes (ashrams) was once popular, they have declined over the last decade, and with this has come a decline in the popularity of 3HO.

NRMs derived from Islam

Another world faith which several of the NRMs are said to have origins in, or have beliefs and practices which can be traced back to, is Islam. While Islam does have its mystical wing in Sufism, it has a clear ecclesiastical structure, a profound sense of a united community, and a codified set of beliefs found in its holy scripture, the Koran. This means that compared to Hinduism it is less likely to lend itself to considerable innovation and interpretation. Nonetheless, the Subud began in Islam, although it has now departed from it considerably. Similarly, the Baha'i Faith has some roots in Islam. However, Subud and other similar movements, by proclaiming that there were significant prophets after the Prophet Muhammad, cannot be seen as somehow 'inside' Islam since they make major departures from it.

Subud

Broadly translated, *Subud* means 'to follow the will of God'. Beginning in Indonesia, in 1924, the movement was founded by Muhammad Subuh Sumohadiwidjojo, who was originally of the Muslim faith. He laid claim to a series of powerful spiritual transformations as a result of experiencing the inner power of God. By the 1930s, he had gained the conviction that he should pass on this experience to others; in 1933 he set up Subud. Over the next twenty years he worked quietly, propagating the faith in Indonesia. First in Britain in 1956, then in America and Australia, Subud spread rapidly, and the movement now has around 10,000 members in over 70 countries.

Subud firmly claims that it is not a religion in its own right; it has no priests, no rituals, no dogmas or doctrines. Like Sufism, it is a more mystical expression of Islam, claiming that God's 'spiritual energy' can be experienced through 'spiritual exercise' (*latihan*). Some three months after first attending Subud meetings, a new member stands in a group, including some experienced 'Helpers', and the latihan occurs. The first time is known as 'The Opening'. The experience varies for different people, and this is part of the basis of the religion. Some will experience joy, others peace; some an inner vibration, others a quiet simplicity; some will laugh, cry, dance, or pray. All are viewed as equally valid experiences. The latihan lasts for about thirty minutes and is usually conducted twice a week within the group. Once members are experienced, they can undertake initial latihan once a week on their own, at home. For everyone, the pace of development depends on their own inner capacity, but in time each member is put increasingly in touch with their nature and talents, as well as experiencing spiritual comfort, guidance in life, and an inward security. The acquaintance with latihan is not always pleasant, especially when the power of God is believed to be acting directly on the inner person and may be purging out the spiritual negativity within.

Subud has now so departed from Islam as to encourage members to stay in the religion to which they originally belong. This is because they are directly in touch with the power of God: believers become brothers and sisters in spiritual unity, whatever their chosen religion. All that is required is complete surrender to that particular faith. Essentially, believers must become their own selves and develop their inner self if they are to find their way to God.

The Baha'i Faith

In some respects it is misleading to refer to the Baha'i Faith as an NRM since it can be dated back to the mid-nineteenth-century. However, the designation can perhaps be justified in terms of its incredible recent growth and not insignificant impact in the West. In 1963, the global membership was estimated at 400,000. By the end of the twentieth-century this was calculated to be in the region of five million.

The Baha'i Faith began in Persia in 1844 when a young Muslim merchant, Mirza Ali Muhammad (1819–50), started to preach that the Day of God was at hand. He proclaimed himself to be the 'Bab' or 'Gate' and announced that he was the forerunner of one greater than himself who would initiate a new age of peace and justice. Although initially within Islam, his teaching increasingly departed from it and he finally announced that Babism was a new religion in 1848. He was martyred in 1850. After the death of Bab, one of his closest followers, Mirza Husayn-Ali Nuri, took over the leadership of the Bab community, and in 1863 he advanced himself as the Baha'u'llah ('the Glory of God'), the one whom Bab had foretold. He was succeeded by his son and great-grandson, each of whom played a key role in the evolution of the faith.

The Baha'i Faith is monotheistic. It believes that from time to time God dispatches his prophets or messengers to earth in order to communicate with the human race. This has included Abraham, Krishna, Zoraster, Buddha, Jesus, and Muhammad. In recent times he has sent two others, Bab and Baha'u'llah. Each has revealed God to the people of a particular time and place and cultural context. Every messenger builds upon the messages of those gone before, leading to new spiritual heights and bringing moral and social teachings designed for a particular age. However, behind the prophetic messages are the same God and the same spiritual realities. The movement teaches that when the human body dies, the soul is liberated from the physical world and begins its progress through the spiritual realm. Hence, life in this world is but a preparation where one can develop and perfect spiritual qualities needed in the next life. Heaven can be seen partly as a state of nearness to God, while hell is a condition of remoteness from God. What awaits each individual is a result of the natural consequence of the individual's efforts, or otherwise, to develop spiritually.

The Baha'i Faith, which is effectively a world religion, is unusual in having no priesthood or set liturgy for services. Its organization is extremely democratic in structure. Much of its appeal is to members of the other 'Religions of the Book': Judaism, Christianity, and Islam. This is largely because the Baha'i Faith is a continuation of the same theme: one God, the Creator, who cares enough for the world that he sends messengers. In its own way it also attempts to fulfil many of the prophecies of the major religions. Hence, there is a continuity as well as a familiarity about the faith. More recently, it has appealed to those interested in the New Age movement. Both overlap in their syncretism, while seeking a new age, spiritual truths, and universal peace, and embrace other similar concerns such as vegetarianism (although this is not insisted upon). The Baha'i Faith is also very strong on the equality of all races and gender, and is keen on extending education, especially in Third World countries, if it is based on spiritual principles. Although the Baha'i Faith claims that it has never splintered into sects, in fact there have been several. These have included the New History Society created in 1929, the World Union of Universal Religion and Universal Peace in 1930, and the Baha'i World Federation founded in 1950.

Syncretic movements

Clearly, some significant NRMs do not fit under any of the above headings and would appear to be more syncretic in form. Here, we have to be cautious. While it will be argued below that the Unification Church has elements from several world religions, it does tend to regard itself as 'Christian'. Hence, from the movement's point of view it should not fit under the rubric of 'syncretic movements'. Nonetheless, it can be argued that this is its true designation, and as much can be said about the other NRMs discussed here, Rastafarianism and the Rajneeshes.

The Unification Church

The Unification Church is one of the best known and more successful NRMs. Its founder, Sun Myung Moon, teaches the unification of world Christianity, which he believes has gone astray, and stresses the imperative of its restoration. Moon was born in what is now North Korea in 1920. At the age of 16, he claimed a vision of Jesus Christ, who told him that he must further the building of God's kingdom on earth. Although having no formal theological training, Moon spent nine years in prayer and intensive bible study. In 1945, he began preaching in South Korea. In 1948, he moved back to North Korea where he was imprisoned by the communist authorities. He was liberated by UN troops in 1950 and resumed preaching.

Although it has moved considerably from orthodox Christianity, the Unification Church still regards itself as Christian. It believes the Judaic-Christian bible to be the inspired word of God, even if it is not regarded as word-for-word infallible. Moon, who claimed himself as the new messiah in 1992, sees his historical mission in re-establishing its 'correct' teachings. However, his interpretation of Christianity is so unorthodox that mainstream churches will have nothing to do with his movement.

In *Discourse on the Principle*, his most authoritative work, Moon discusses the fall of man, philosophizes on the meaning of life, the work and death of Christ, and how and where Christ will return. He also outlines his key teachings and the 'fuller revelation'. God's original plan was for men and women to have a flawless relationship with him. When Satan tempted man and Adam fell, the perfect 'family' of God, man, and woman was destroyed. The original, ideal trinity is redefined by Moon as God, man, and woman united in perfect, unsullied love. This was lost in the Garden of Eden. Satan, who was originally placed in Eden to serve the first two people, fell in love with Eve and seduced her. Eve, repenting her sin, told Adam what she had done. She then had sex with him to try to put things right, when at that stage in their relationship they should still have been coexisting as brother and sister, not husband and wife. Moon re-established this bond in his perfect marriage and offspring, which restored man's true relationship with God. While these teachings have a strong Christian orientation, Moon also integrates Taoist and Confucian elements. As we have seen (under The New Christian Right in Chapter 4), the desire to be morally and culturally appealing, particularly in the USA, has also meant that the movement has adapted a politically rather right-wing platform.

According to Moon, God has periodically sent prophets to guide his people back to him. Jesus was one. However, he did not come to earth to be crucified: he came as the messiah to re-create the lost ideal family. The plan was that he should marry and have children, re-establishing the ideal trinity through the perfect family, for all mankind. Again, the plan was thwarted. He was not recognized for whom he truly was and was murdered. Jesus' resurrection brought only partial redemption to mankind. After the crucifixion, God gave the Holy Spirit as a mother spirit, or feminine spirit, to work with the resurrected Jesus in Eve's place. Just as children are born through the natural mother, the Holy Spirit gives spiritual rebirth.

To complete the work Jesus was unable to finish, it was necessary for a messiah to come again. His purpose is to marry and re-establish the trinity both physically and spiritually. This is what Moon claims to have accomplished. Through the messiah's perfect marriage, the fallen nature of mankind can be transformed once more to the ideal trinity of God, man, and woman. Moon is able to pass this on through the renowned large-scale marriage ceremonies performed under the auspices of the Unification Church. Each couple, blessed by God through Moon, is now in the right relationship with God and their children will be born without the sin of Adam and Eve. This is the principal aim and duty of Moon's church. It is an aim achieved through arranged marriages, often to a person from another nationality, with Moon responsible for most of the matches, praying over photographs and being guided by God to put suitable couples together. In 1992, 30,000 couples were married in one vast ceremony and in 1995, 364,000 couples were simultaneously blessed at 52 locations around the world. Spouses are given time to get to know each other before the marriage and have the option of declining the chosen partner.

Three missionaries of the Unification Church were initially despatched from Korea to the USA in 1959 and the first church was established in California. The movement grew only slowly at first and it was not until Moon moved to New York State in 1972 that it enjoyed substantial growth. By 1976, the membership in the USA had expanded to 6,000, rising to 10,000 by the end of the twentieth-century. The movement has become a focus of cult controversies and for many of the same reasons as other NRMs. There were accusations of sleep deprivation, indoctrination, brainwashing of its members, and excessive authoritarianism. In the USA and Europe, young converts were sent out on the streets selling flowers or candles, to raise money for the movement, as a form of disciplinary training, and to win over new recruits. For those living in community, lectures, study sessions, and worship might continue for hours. These practices have subsequently been diluted, while most of the members are now married with families and live in their own homes. There are currently approximately a quarter of a million members of the Unification Church worldwide, mainly in South Korea, Japan, the USA, Europe, and South America.

Rastafarianism

Rastafarianism is often regarded as an NRM. Yet, it pre-dates the NRMs of the 1960s by some forty years. Quite what it amounts to, however, has been a matter of conjecture. Some commentators have attempted to highlight the millenarian aspects of the movement and see it largely as a sect (Barrett 1977), while others have focused on its socio-political dimensions (Campbell 1980). This disagreement as to what the movement signifies suggests that numerous factors can account for the development of Rastafarianism. This is true both of its origins in colonial Jamaica where, in particular, economic deprivation had at least some role to play, and its popularity among alienated young blacks, especially in Britain.

It is clear that Rastafarianism has an eschatological vision of redemption located in Ethiopia as a solution to the concerns of black people in the African diaspora. In this context, the teachings of Marcus Garvey were important at the early stage of the movement's development. He predicted that Ethiopia would become the centre of black redemption. This, according to Garvey, appeared to have become evident when Prince Ras Tafari (1891–1975) was crowned Emperor Haile Selassie in 1930. Black nationalists throughout the world celebrated his coronation and much was expected from his rule. Furthermore, the titles and attributes claimed by Selassie – King of Kings, Lord of Lords, and Conquering Lion of the Tribe of Judah – seemed to correspond with New Testament messianic texts. Many of these titles were those ascribed to the returning messiah. The prophecies of Garvey led several black ministers to preach that salvation was at hand: Selassie would lead the black 'race' out of 'Babylonian' captivity. After establishing a community of followers in Kingston, the founders of Rastafarianism set about preaching to the black communities in Jamaica. The threat to the white powers in Jamaica led to the leaders being imprisoned in 1943.

Rastafarianism has no one creed, practices vary, and different leaders have different messages. Many teachings are derived from the bible. One is the central belief that God's chosen people were black, not white. The bible provides a history of God's oppressed peoples throughout history. It is interpreted to show that God has appeared in human form – Moses, Elijah, Jesus, and finally as Haile Selassie (Ras Tafari). He is the returned messiah, the saviour of the oppressed black race. This belief is accompanied by that of reincarnation. Black people are said to be the reincarnation of the ancient Israelites, exiled from their homeland. Most Rastafarians embrace eschatological expectations. Some hold that Selassie will be resurrected, others that he will return from heaven. With him will come the establishment of the promised land, to be founded in Ethiopia. Others see 'Ethiopia' as a metaphor, symbolizing a new age for black people without the physical return to Africa. Whatever the precise rendering of doctrine, the final release from the oppression of the whites will be forthcoming.

It is mainly disadvantaged black youths from the inner cities who join the Rastafarian movement (Cashmore 1983). Members frequently smoke ganga (a form of marihuana grown in Jamaica) as a sacrament – a ritual. The Rastafarians provide an example of a language ('soul language') that is unintelligible to most outsiders. It has been interpreted as a speech symbolizing an identification not only with other believers but those who see themselves oppressed (Barrett 1977). The substantial immigration which took place in the late 1950s and 1960s included Afro-Caribbeans, some of whom brought Black Power ideologies, including Rastafarianism, with them. Its appeal was highlighted by the popularity of the reggae music of Bob Marley. Above all, Rastafarianism stands for the fullest cooperation and relationship between the governments and people of Africa. It sees itself as a movement for all black people of whatever social status and constitutes a search for cultural identity and racial security.

Rajneeshes

Bhagwan Shree Rajneesh began lecturing and preaching throughout India in the mid-1960s, promoting meditation and free love. In 1969 he settled in Bombay, then in Poona in 1974, attracting large numbers of followers. Like various other leading gurus of the time he moved to the USA, setting up a large community in Oregon in 1981, which became known as the 'City of Rajneeshpuram'. He preached his message almost exclusively to the affluent, arguing that the poor find it difficult merely achieving the basics of life and thus have no time or inclination for spiritual development. Rajneesh's own opulent lifestyle was the subject of notoriety, including his collection of 91 Rolls Royces. In failing health, Rajneesh eventually returned to India where he died in 1990. After his death, Osho International, as his movement became known, re-established itself in Rajneesh's original commune in India and continues to propagate his teachings. However, the movement has declined since 1985, and some would argue that it is now, for all intents and purposes, defunct.

The name Bhagwan is translated in various ways, with 'the Blessed One' being the most respectable interpretation, although Rajneesh suggested that it was derived from words for the female and male genitalia. The philosophy he taught was based on the premise that the legitimacy of the religions traditionally taught in the East and West must be questioned. However, it is extremely difficult to pinpoint what the movement or its guru actually stand for and the teachings advanced often appear contradictory. Put succinctly, they seem to be a mixture of an entirely original, even idiosyncratic philosophy and deep spiritual insights.

Many of the teachings appear ambivalent and this is, in fact, intended, since in all he taught Rajneesh was opposed to all doctrine and indoctrination. For Rajneesh, God is everywhere, in everything; every part of life can be a communion with God, and the divine is the innermost core of the world. Hence, the teachings amount to a mystical rather than an intellectual enterprise. Spirituality may be learned, but it cannot be taught, at least, not as a set of rules. Rajneesh rejected discipleship as a guru in the typically eastern style and saw his commune as one of like-minded spiritual travellers rather than a church.

The movement has offered courses in meditation, dance, mysticism, and a variety of spiritual, psychological, and alternative healing practices. One of its more unusual practices (although with counterparts in contemporary psychotherapy) is the encouragement of people to let their emotions free: to scream and shout, to flail around, to express their anger and frustrations. One of the central meditation practices of the movement is the Mystic Rose. This involves laughing for three hours a day for the first week, crying for three hours a day for the second, and sitting in silence for the third. Another practice is Dynamic Meditation, which consists of five phases including breathing, catharsis, and jumping up and down on one's heels shouting Sufi mantras. Many other forms of meditation are taught, but the primary principle is that meditation should be a part of every aspect of life.

Within the ashram, Rajneesh also promoted free love, encouraging people to view sex as a powerful affirmation of spirituality. To teach that it was a sin was the false doctrine of religions of both East and West. In general, he criticized both. Eastern spirituality he saw as dead, it repressed emotion, while Western man had lost track of spiritual consciousness. In the West, man has become increasingly rational and denied his inner spiritual self; life is shallow and materialistic. From the 1980s, however, the movement began to emphasize that there was nothing wrong with material possessions and the guru encouraged his followers to enjoy all aspects of life. Above all, Rajneesh saw his movement as an experiment. The principal things that it experimented with were aspects of most of the major religions. Whatever was good in any tradition was worth advancing. Hence, his movement was a synthesis of all paths.

Summary

There is a very real sense in which it can be said that the above account of the beliefs and practices of NRMs scarcely does them justice. For this reason further reading is very much recommended. Moreover, it might be argued that to classify them under the above headings is not entirely satisfactory. Indeed, these headings should only be regarded as a broad rubric by which to understand some of the origins of these movements. Nor is the list exhaustive since smaller groups are not overviewed. However, some of these will be considered in the forthcoming chapters related to the New Age, esotericism, neo-Paganism, ethnic religions, and quasi-religions. The fact that NRMs turn up under all types of categories is indicative of their vast diversity.

Further reading

Barker, E. (1992) *New Religious Movements: A Practical Introduction*, London: HMSO.
Beit-Hallahmi, B. (1993) *The Illustrated Encyclopedia of Active New Religions, Sects and Cults*, New York: Rosen Publishing Group.
Driel van, B. & Belzen van, J. (1990) 'The Downfall of Rajneeshpuram in the Print Media', *Journal for the Scientific Study of Religion*, **29** (1), 76–93.

Forem, J. (1974) *Transcendental Meditation*, London: Allen & Unwin.

Gadhia, D. (1989) *The Divine Grace of Lord Sri Sathya Sai Baba*, Wolverhampton: Sri Sathya Sai Bab Centre.

Gordon, D. (1974) 'The Jesus People: An Identity Synthesis', *Urban Life and Culture*, **3** (2), 159–78.

Hatcher, W. & Martin, J. (1986) *The Baha'i Faith: The Emerging Global Religion*, San Francisco, CAL: Harper & Row.

Hunt, S. (1998) 'The Radical Kingdom of the Jesus Fellowship', *Pneuma*, **20** (1), 21–42.

Knott, K. (1986) *My Sweet Lord: The Hare Krishna Movement*, Wellingborough: Aquarian.

Palmer, S. (2001) 'Peace and Preparations for Yahshua's Return: The Case of the Messianic Communities' Twelve Tribes', in S. Hunt (ed.) *Christian Millenarianism: From the Early Church to Waco*, London: Hurst Publishers.

Rieu, D. (1983) *A Life with a Life: An Introduction to Subud*, Tunbridge Wells: Humanus.

Sontag, F. (1977) *Sun Myung Moon and the Unification Church*, Nashville, TN: Abingdon.

Whaling, F. (1995) 'The Brahma Kumaris', *Journal of Contemporary Religion*, **10** (1), 3–28.

8 The New Age

Recent developments in contemporary religion have thrown existing categories of NRMs into question. This is particularly so with the growth of the so-called New Age movement which provides a rich variety of cultural phenomena and exemplifies the cultist milieu of fringe religion. The various interrelated strands which constitute the movement display a profoundly eclectic and syncretic pattern of beliefs and practices. At the same time, so it might be argued, the New Age has impacted significantly at various societal levels. The evidence advanced is that this apparent mix 'n' match form of religiosity has proved to be highly attractive to people as an alternative to mainline religion, while a number of its key ideas have discernibly permeated various aspects of social, political, and economic life.

If a brief introductory statement can be made regarding the New Age movement it is that many of the beliefs and practices are not new but, simultaneously, there is much which is contemporary. It thus amounts to the bringing together of numerous overlapping teachings that encompass a wide range of activities. Many are aimed at establishing what adherents claim to be 'a new spirituality' and the rediscovery of a lost sacredness in the world and human society. Indeed, the movement itself is perceived as indicating a change in man's consciousness. As one advocate puts it: 'A new spiritual awakening is occurring in human culture [that] represents the creation of a new, more complete worldview [that] is opening up to us the real purpose of human life.' (Redford 1995, xv, xviii)

What is the New Age movement?

'New Age', then, is a term used to describe a very wide expression of spirituality which has become increasingly popular since the late 1980s. Although the movement could be seen as merely an extension of the new religions of the 1960s and 1970s, many of its origins can be found in the esoteric culture of the mid- to late nineteenth-century, when spiritualism and occultist practices flourished in Western Europe and North America. Yet, there are sufficient differences of belief and structure to justify the New Age as a completely distinct form of religiosity in its own right and not merely a continuation of older expressions of religion. These different interpretations of what the movement amounts to result from an attempt to understand its eclectic nature. There are few clear divisions and boundaries between its major strands and little by way of organizational arrangements. In short, the New Age constitutes a true cultic mix from which people pick and choose from what is on offer. It follows that because the movement has various threads and a complex make-up, it is impossible to gauge its size and its membership or, as it is succinctly put by Michael York:

> The major difficulty in assessing anything about the New Age is that the movement comprises a disparate and, at best, loosely co-ordinated confederation of contrasting beliefs, techniques and practices. There is no central authority capable of speaking for the movement as a whole. There is likewise no central register which can supply membership for the overall movement. And there is no central co-ordinating agency able to ascertain who is and who is not a New Ager. The New Age is largely a perpetually shifting and *ad hoc* alliance of exegetical individuals and groups, audience gatherings, client services, and various new religious movements that range between the cultic, sectarian and denominational. Even when viewed from 'outside', as in sociological observation, there is little agreement concerning what constitutes the New Age and who is and who is not to be included.
>
> (York 2001, 226)

It is clear in his account that York regards the New Age as defying many of the accepted definitions of cult, sect, and 'movement'. While they may be applicable to some strands of the New Age, they are not to others, and others still defy any organizational types (York 1996, 315–31).

How then, might the New Age be categorized? It is obvious that it does not constitute a unified, coherent, or highly mobilized movement. At the same time it lacks the sectarian, hierarchical structure and authoritarian charismatic leadership of many earlier NRMs. Rather, like 'client' and 'audience' cults, the New Age is heavily reliant on magazines, books, and audio and visual cassettes to reach its adherents, as well as a loosely structured lecture circuit. Yet, it is also cultist in the sense that it frequently appears to be in tension with society and opposes many of its core values, not least of all a rampant materialism and rationalism. In this way, the New Age would seem to be part of the great counter-current of modernity, namely the nineteenth-century Romantic movement, which opposed the rationalizing tendencies of the time (Turner 1991).

For the New Age, rationalism is perceived as having profound limitations. Hence, some people seek a mystical and meaningful spirituality beyond the restrictions of the secular world. In so doing, the New Age brings a search for the authentic self and the pursuit of a genuine form of spirituality. This is why Woodhead and Heelas (2000, 113) have argued that it could be described as incorporating a number of 'expressive spiritualities'. Inherent here is the suggestion that it is a form of religion which seeks an inner quest for freedom and self-expression. It seeks to express what one truly is, to live life as the manifestation of one's true nature, and to affirm oneself as bound up with the natural or 'real' order as a whole. The emphasis then, is on the self and self-discovery within a holistic frame of reference which embraces the universe and this world through an essential 'truth' and unity. At the same time, the New Age is a highly optimistic, celebratory, utopian, and spiritual form of humanism. As Paul Heelas (1988), puts it: 'Ultimacy – God, the Goddess, the Higher Self – lies within, serving as the source of vitality, creativity, love, tranquillity, wisdom, responsibility, power and all those other qualities which are held to comprise the perfect inner life.'

New Age: the religion of post-modernity?

Precisely what the New Age amounts to depends at least partly on an interpretation of contemporary culture in the West and the movement's relationship with it. From one point of view, the New Age may be said to display cult-like characteristics in the sense that it often embraces a range of counter-cultural values. It rejects the rational scientific worldview which dominates Western culture as the only way of interpreting the world, and seeks to show the legitimacy of other bodies of knowledge such as alchemy and astrology. However, many of these features would appear to be *congruent* with developments with the nature of post-modern society. If this perspective is adopted, then the discussion as to the nature of New Age is rather more complex than perhaps at first supposed.

There are several commentators who see the New Age as exemplifying the spirit and even the inherent contradictions of post-modernity. From one viewpoint, it is the definitive religion of the 'gaps'. Heelas (1996), for instance, believes that the disintegration of the certainties of modernity has left a situation in which post-modern religion flourishes. In this sense, mystical or New Age spiritualities, or what he terms 'self-religions', have emerged to fill a spiritual vacuum and satisfy the need for meaning which traditional religions can no longer provide and which give way to those in line with contemporary culture.

According to post-modernist writers, religion in the emerging age frequently expresses individualistic religious 'experience', reflecting today's culture with its attraction of the fleetingly dramatic, titillating, and exotic (Roof & McKinney 1987). Such an emphasis on experience may be at the expense of codified beliefs that inform traditional religion. Much is typified by the New Age movement. Michael York therefore argues that many expressions of New Age and neo-Paganism come to assert that belief per se is not essential to religious orientation. In short, it is experience, through various forms of mysticism, which is at the core of the new spirituality (York 1996, 56). The New Age also has a profound subjectivism and relativism which endorses post-modernity. If spiritual knowledge comes from learning to listen to an inner voice, the light within, then each person's revelation is as good as any other.

Post-modernity also suggests a mix 'n' match religiosity congruent with the spirit of post-modernity. Lyotard (1984), for instance, argues that the collapse of modernist social and cognitive structures means that post-modernity includes a willingness to combine cultural expressions from various symbols or frameworks of meaning, perhaps from different parts of the globe, even at the cost of disjunction and eclecticism. Post-modern culture simultaneously includes a celebration of spontaneity, fragmentation, superficiality, irony, and playfulness. It follows that for post-modernist theorists, like Lyotard, contemporary forms of religion would embrace many of these features. Moreover, diversity of discourse and the abandonment of unitary meaning systems would allow syncretic elements of religion to flourish – a tendency enhanced by the collapse of the boundaries between 'high' and 'popular' types of religion, which mirrors the disintegration of distinctions between different cultural systems. The term which is often utilized in this context is that of the '*de-differentiated*' society – *the* key characteristic of post-modernity. In short, there is the breakdown of social divisions, which effectively erodes the significance of distinctions between autonomous cultural spheres. De-differentiation of the cultural realm means that people do not have to worry about contradictory commitments to particular cultural formations. Instead, they can draw on a cultural 'reservoir' in constructing lifestyles and worldviews. So it is with New Age religion, which brings together different religious elements.

Another reason why the New Age epitomizes the mix 'n' match religiosity of today can be observed in its belief system, which frequently attempts to reconstruct past religious myths. In the post-modern world the speed of social change and decline of cultural continuity breeds an ignorance of history, including religious history. In turn, religious chronicles may be reinvented through new narratives, with religious movements frequently perceiving themselves as restoring, reforming, or reviving the true faith or spirituality. This is evident in some of the central beliefs of New Age as discussed below. It is also arguably discernible in some of the revivalist and sectarian Christian movements already considered in previous chapters.

A related and distinctive dimension of most strands of the New Age is their pluralistic outlook. This is displayed in two principal ways. Firstly, it tends to array syncretic characteristics. Its adherents may participate in a variety of groups at one and the same time. Secondly, there is a great deal of toleration of the beliefs of other religions. To some extent this is why the New Age frequently plunders other religions for a spiritual core. This undoubtedly underlines the movement's strong root in theosophy and the idea that all religions have some essential common 'truth'. Some of the aims of the Theosophical Society (see Chapter 9 under Esoteric movements) have been adopted by the New Age. This includes the attempt to form a universal brotherhood of man, irrespective of race, religion, or class; to study ancient religions and philosophy; to investigate the laws of nature; and to reveal and develop the divine psychic powers of human beings. There is also the accompanying belief that not only is man evolving, but that each individual person is progressing, through reincarnation, to a higher spiritual state.

New Age: empowerment and identity

Various other sociological explanations have been advanced for the rise of the New Age movement. One suggestion is that it reflects a kind of individual and collective anxiety generated by the way that society, political institutions, and economic activity are organized and advocates a future way forward. It arose in the 1980s with the approach of a new millennium. This engendered a mentality that expected the old order to give way to a new epoch for the human race (Friedrich 1995). Yet another perspective sees it as marking a growing dissatisfaction with the material world – one wracked by war, crime, inequality, and pending environmental catastrophe. Hence, the popularity of the New Age paralleled the preoccupation that some evangelical Christian groups had with the Second Coming of Christ at the same time (McDonald 1994).

These are all broad and sweeping explanations. More narrowly, it is possible to regard the New Age movement as being in line with the contemporary religious marketplace. Among its attractions is the emphasis on man's potential, and this is generally associated with holistic philosophies which see human beings as constituted by mind, body, and spirit (see Chapter 11). The movement is therefore opposed to everything which threatens an organic unity. This emphasis on holism leads to the popularity of alternative healing and is carried by the numerous cults of the movement which, in Bruce's words (1996a), comprise its 'circulatory system'. These are a loose set of organizations with little personal commitment expected and which provide services for individuals to improve their lives in an infinite variety of ways. The New Age, then, offers a radicalized version of human potential, resting on spiritual rather than psychological foundations.

In exploring this link between the New Age and human potential, Heelas (1988) speaks of the 'humanistic expressivism' of the movement. This means the focus on the interior life, self-exploration, and self-development rather than a collective attempt to construct a new world order. It is this emphasis on the self which arguably differentiates the New Age from earlier NRMs such as the Unification Church. Yet, as we have already noted, many NRMs were increasingly stressing ideas of the development of 'self' for materialistic and psychological ends and we have observed this tendency with those such as the 3HO Foundation and Vajradhatu. The New Age, however, plausibly takes this to its logical conclusion by merging physiological, emotional, and spiritual powers. There is an attempt to find the 'true' self and to be liberated from oppressive and corrupting socialized identities. It follows that the New Age anticipates a 'new order', an aspiration that is itself a reflection of the post-modern condition with its largely optimistic philosophy that the self is perfectible and improving, while individuals are continually empowered.

Heelas (1988) attributes the increasing popularity of the New Age movement to the ability to empower people's lives, rather than to transcend them. The emphasis is on a spirituality through the notion of a process of self-development, or what he calls 'self spirituality'. Thus, self-development, in terms of the enhancement of the 'higher self', takes on a spiritual quest. It is a development of mental, physical, and spiritual perfection through quasi-religious therapeutic cults. Here the 'self' is regarded as potentially perfect and divine-like and it is where 'salvation' is translated into 'human potential'. This is evident in the claim that the self is potentially or actually perfect and indestructible. For this reason, New Agers appear to readily accept the belief in reincarnation, although this can vary in explicitness from those people who claim to remember the experiences of previous lives to those who simply think that death is not a reality.

The development of the self is also tied up with the transformation of identity. Here again much would seem to be in line with post-modernity. According to several commentators, contemporary culture brings a utilitarian selfhood – an expressive form of being and emphasis on 'experience' and an 'off-the-shelf' image. It establishes the freedom for individuals to create and sustain the self-image of their choice. This emphasis on self and the body is particularly significant since it gives way to the preoccupation with identity construction.

For Wuthnow (1988), the focus of contemporary forms of religion with identity is intimately bound up with economic change. The significance of identity construction in the sphere of religion results from the fact that people no longer have an immutable position in a fixed status order in a socially mobile society. Social class, the base of previous identity, has been eroded and replaced by the significance of the individual's lifestyle and sense of self-identity. Wuthnow argues that the contemporary market economy has increasingly encouraged a culture of choice, which is specifically geared to lifestyle preferences. Thus, the purchase and display of consumer goods has an ever more important role in the social construction and negotiation of identity. As far as the New Age is concerned, spiritual, personal, and social identity is continually structured through holistic therapy and healing and relates to themes such as gender identity, as discussed below (see also Chapter 11).

Reid (1996), in appraising the link between New Age and identity, takes a more phenomenological approach. Her argument is that all human religion is a reflection of the 'divine other', and its sole purpose is to contribute towards a divine image of the world. This kind of perspective starts with the assumption that the human community is the only one possible in relation to which individuals may derive a sense of meaning. Nevertheless, this instance underscores the point that religion is a process of negotiation with some manner of 'significant other' that leads inward towards a form of self-definition. Reid argues that when we look at New Age spirituality, we can discern the movement advancing towards fully locating the sacred life within the realm of consciousness. The New Age is therefore very much an individual approach to spirituality.

In line with contemporary culture, argues Reid, New Age religion is a personal, potentially transformative experience. This is very much in contrast to traditional experiences of religion, which were historically concerned with the power that society, history, and God exert over human meaning of the world. At the same time, this has been a slow historical process. Certainly, the Enlightenment, to a substantial measure, contributed to this shift in focus. Medieval Europeans understood their universe in terms of a divine order. God had created every object in the universe, and purposely placed each in relation to every other. With the Enlightenment, however, this transcendental order began to dissolve. The human being slowly became defined not in terms of a position in relation to something other than itself, but in terms of an internal ordering of consciousness. This is a fundamental assumption of the New Age and has been enhanced, according to Reid, by the tendency of Western man to conflate psychological and religious language. In general terms, religion has become a mode by which to achieve psychological gratification and a path to happiness and health.

Inherent contradictions of the New Age

While there is a great deal that is innovating about the New Age, and at the same time it puts an emphasis upon personal growth, there is much within the movement that tends to create pseudo-anthropological legitimization for many of the core beliefs and practices (McGuire 1992, 282). This is evident in the broad conviction that earlier 'simple' societies understood essential truths about healing power, gender, and the environment, which modern societies have lost. Thus, there is an observable tendency to borrow myths, legends, rituals, and symbols from ancient Celtic, Mediterranean, Polynesian, Tibetan, Eskimo, Aborigine, and Native American culture. It is from many of these that the New Age has taken ideas of Mother Earth as a religious system which developed from being close to the land (Johnson 1996). To this are added shamanism, neo-Paganism, Wicca, and Druidism (discussed in more detail in the next chapter). Also, typical of many new forms of spirituality is the reinvention of polytheism (Ellwood 1996). These restored 'truths', however, are not always historically accurate and, as Bowman (1993) suggests, with reference to the New Age's depiction of Celtic religion, there is a certain amount of idealization and reinvention of past religious forms that do not always truly reflect these ancient faiths.

On such evidence, argues Bruce (1996a, 206), the New Agers can be said to take the best of both worlds. There is a fair amount that is explicitly contemporary and in some respects the movement sets its face against tradition, even if ideas, practices, and therapies make reference to it. Much is in opposition to the scientific method, which perpetually destroys old knowledge and replaces it with the new. By reasoning backward from the observation that modern societies have many defects, New Agers conclude that pre-modern cultures must be morally and ethically superior and had insights into workings of the material world now lost. Paradoxically, however, many New Age techniques and methods are often legitimated by a scientific rationale. Hence, it rejects but borrows the language of science in strategies of healing and spiritual exercises. The contradiction, as Bruce (1996a, 209) points out, is that New Agers combine criticism of the scientific and medical establishments with the belief that they are doing what will some day be recognized as science. Yet the movement tends to have little interest in conventional notions of (scientific) testing. Bruce writes:

> That one or two people assert that a therapy worked for them is enough to establish its efficacy. New paradigms are not covered by painstakingly trying to explain observations that do not fit with existing well established theories, but by revelation, metaphor, and textual synthesis from a variety of archaic traditions.
>
> (Bruce 1996a, 225)

Strands of the New Age

In the New Age movement there are various divergent religious or psycho-religious systems and even secular ideologies that vie for a prominent place. These ideologies may be put on a gradient between the two poles of the New Age. One pole centres on the 'ecstatic' and includes gurus, channelling, psychics, witches, crystal healers, and other visionaries. The other pole is constituted by social transformationist philosophies that are more concerned with ecology, social conscience, feminism, and compassion for all of creation. Even this division, however, obscures the complexity of the strands which form the movement. Of these, some are constituted by ancient beliefs, albeit modified; others are more recent. Those such as neo-Paganism, occultism, mysticism, the spiritual-psychic, and human potential elements, all of which have impacted on the movement, are discussed in more detail in subsequent chapters. However, this chapter concludes with an overview of a number of discernible strands which may or may not overlap with these spiritualities. They include the feminist, environmentalist, eastern mystical, and New Age-Christian wings.

Eastern mysticism

While interest in eastern spirituality has been observable in Western societies for centuries, it has enjoyed a renewed popularity since the 1960s. This has perhaps been most clearly expressed in various forms of Buddhism, Sufi Islam, and Taoism – all of which have their unique appeal. Buddhism in Britain, for example, may be regarded as one of the fastest-growing religions. Since the late 1960s, over 70 new Buddhist groups have been established, including 24 since 1985. Inherent in the popularity of the mystical elements of these expressions of eastern religiosity is a rejection of the Judaic-Christian-Islamic emphasis on the redemption of this world through a personal saviour relationship with the one God, since this tends to eclipse concerns with cosmic order and processes. Hence, there is the attraction of the sacred scriptures of Hindus, Buddhists, and Taoists. These are frequently transformed into the framework of the New Age, which, for the most part, is non-monotheistic. None of this is particularly new and, in many respects, the popularity of eastern mysticism marks a resurrection of the 1960s counter-cultural concern with alternative religions of this type.

Much of the New Age's embrace of eastern mysticism is directed towards self-spirituality and world rejection. It has a close relationship with ancient notions of the mystical transformation of the person, the collective, and the cosmos, but is now linked to a philosophy of human spiritual evolution. At the same time, suitably transfigured, these older religions dovetail with the more contemporary interest in the awakening of potentials and abilities. Nonetheless, it is eastern mysticism that genuinely furnishes the New Age with its supernaturalistic element. In this regard, York (1995, 37) sees it at the heart of what he calls the 'spiritual camp', which occupies the middle ground between the 'service' extreme of the human potential element at one pole, and the call for social improvement, and the esoteric tendencies at the other. Furnishing this spiritual camp are the teachings of many eastern gurus, some of which have been encountered in previous chapters. These gurus include Maharishi Mahesh Yogi, Bhagwan Rajneesh, Swami Muktananda, and Meher Baba. To this list can be added prominent Western figures identified with distinct schools of mysticism, typified by John-Roger Hinkins and the Movement for Inner Spiritual Awareness. All of these filter into the New Age in discernible and less discernible ways. This spiritual camp of the New Age, according to York, centres on self-discipline as a means of encountering an experience of the union with the divine and a sacred reality. Its techniques are essentially those of human potential without the supernaturalist intervention associated with the more occultist wing, while its primary focus is towards individual development rather than social change.

New Age environmentalism

There is a strong overlap in the New Age with the so-called 'green' revolution in its concern with mind, body, and spirit. Yet this environmental awareness is manifest in different ways. This includes involvement in such movements as Friends of the Earth, green consumption, or the exclusive purchase from ethical investment companies. The emphasis on environmentalism perhaps also gives the New Age its most radical edge, with the protest of its 'eco-warriors' against the erosion of the countryside and the exploitation of nature and natural resources, joining, for example, protests against motorway construction or the extension of the urban environment.

This focus on environmentalism follows from the assumption that there is an essential harmony between the individual and the cosmic order. There is, however, a particular emphasis taken by New Agers. Environmental problems and their solutions are closely linked to personal problems. Thus, it is claimed that emotionally, intellectually, and spiritually balanced people do not make excessive demands on natural resources. At the same time, the planet is seen as an organism – a self-regulating environmental system – and the New Age environmental movement seeks to protect the planet out of respect for a superior being. The earth is thus revered as Gaia, an animate organism upon which all life depends, and nature is regarded as sacred, harmonious, and providential.

Teachings on New Age environmentalism have partly been drawn from the great religious traditions as well as pagan inspirations. Gaia, for instance, was the goddess of all life for Homeric Greece. From Buddhism it takes the view that a concern with the environment has direct application to Buddhist principles of an awareness of the effects of one's actions in the world. Simultaneously, as Heelas (1996, 56) notes, the interest that New Agers have with the environment stems from an anti-modernist stance. They do not accept the premises of a society based on economic growth and they have thus broken with the traditional values of capitalist society. Rather, they seek a new relationship to nature, one's body, towards sexuality, to work, and to consumption. Accordingly, argues Heelas, the New Age can be thought of as a new social movement. More pertinently, it is one which focuses on spiritual environmentalism, eco-feminism, and various forms of healing. In this way the New Age again marks the continuation of the counter-culture of the 1960s with its 'small is beautiful' mentality and an emphasis on alternative economics and an ecologically sustainable economy. The paradox, however, as Heelas suggests, is that since the counter-culture collapsed in the 1970s, the cause of an environmentally friendly economy is now carried on by fewer people through the matrix of the New Age movement.

The emphasis on environmentalism also ties in with the theme of healing. New Agers seek fresh ways of relating to the environment: ways which will preserve the earth from the damages inflicted by industrial capitalism. This involves adopting ways of life, of production and consumption, which are environmentally sound. In turn, these ways of life will contribute to the completeness of the spiritual existence as lived by the individual. Many New Agers would also subscribe to a 'deep ecology' – the view that nature should be valued for its own sake rather than for its utility value. Those who seek natural fulfilment as humans will at least partly find it in the appreciation of nature.

New Age feminism

New Age feminism may be interpreted as a kind of spiritualized version of a secular ideology that has come to prominence since the 1960s and adds to the growing list of various forms of feminism. One of the main strands of spiritual development in the new religions generally is a highly feminist path with its emphasis on receptivity, love, and devotion in a discipleship to a god and guru. In this respect, the New Age movement is close to some earlier NRMs such as ISKCON, which embraces a feminist approach to spirituality (Puttick 1999, 146). However, the feminist expression of the New Age does not constitute a unique wing within the movement. Rather, it permeates different expressions of it such as neo-Paganism and Wicca.

Those spiritualities akin to the New Age, including the Wiccan (witchcraft) movement, remove women from what they see as the constraints of Christian gender roles and sexuality (Crowley 1994, 116). Typically, they attempt to link biology or anthropology with gender issues and there are frequent references to men's or women's 'nature' – a common core nature that has been distorted by modern society (McGuire 1992, 283). This relates to the preoccupation with identity which encourages the search for some lost, ideal human experience and the marked attempt to return to a previous spiritual state that is exemplified in the New Age approach to gender issues.

The New Age has rekindled an interest in the goddess and female spirituality and this ensures that women are prominent among the fully engaged participants. This is most evident in its neo-pagan element, which brings a form of polytheistic Nature religion based on the worship of the Mother Goddess. For many of the New Age feminist persuasion, the essential reference is to 'the Goddess' as an expression of the natural realm, a metaphor for harmony of the self and nature. According to New Agers of this persuasion, neo-Paganism is part of a gendered self-fulfilment. The goddess lies dormant within all women and has, historically speaking, been crushed by patriarchal culture. The goddess, often represented by Gaia, is benevolent, life giving, and in harmony with all of creation. The assumption is that there needs to be an influx of feminine energy to balance the patriarchal society and to bring an equilibrium of male and female energies – a philosophy which often seems close to Taoism.

There is also eco-feminism, although this dovetails with aspects of Wicca and neo-Paganism. It is a theme developed by feminist New Agers, who argue that women should quest for a pure, original female consciousness, incorporating the natural order of which they are a vital part. In doing so, they will invariably counteract the patriarchal aggression which has so harmed the earth. It is clear that the attraction of New Age feminism is not that different from what is offered by many of the earlier NRMs. The New Age permits a greater level of involvement than traditional religion. Nonetheless, the movement brings a more radical and more focused celebration and veneration of female attributes than is coherently articulated through its various strands.

The New Age-Christian wing

At the same time that it is pluralistic in outlook, the New Age rejects organized religion, typically that of the Judaeo-Christian tradition, which is seen as socially and spiritually destructive. Thus, much of the New Age seeks to restore a pre-Christian form of religion to draw on the wisdom of ancient civilizations and native peoples untouched and untainted by Christian authority and morality. However, representative of the multidimensional nature of the movement, there exists a New Age-Christian wing, which largely constitutes a modification of traditional Christian beliefs by converging biblical text with esoteric sources. For instance, a key teaching is that the advent of the New Age will be apocalyptic and characterized by terrestrial and social upheaval in what is typically a pre-millenarian form of Christianity. Here, Christ's physical return is predicted to follow a period of catastrophes which will inaugurate the New Age millennium.

Various individuals have inspired such teachings. However, perhaps the best known is Matthew Fox, who founded the Institute in Culture and Creation Spirituality in Chicago in 1978. Influenced by Teilhard de Chardin and Meister Eckhart, he has developed a 'creation spirituality', which teaches a combination of Christian mysticism, feminism, and environmentalism. Members of the Institute include a Zen Buddhist, a yoga instructor, and a Wiccan leader. As a Dominican priest, Fox advances the New Age critique of the materialist nature of Western civilization and sees the virtues of paganism in relation to the care and veneration of the earth. Similarly, he advocates the opening up of Christianity to the alleged virtues of eastern mysticism. He adds to this the Old Testament call of the prophets for social justice. Because of many of these teachings, Fox has long been disowned by the Roman Catholic Church.

One of the principal organizational expressions of the New Age-Christian wing is the Church Universal and Triumphant (originating in the late 1950s). It sees Jesus as a great 'Ascended Master' in his time on earth but maintains that his teachings were corrupted by the New Testament writers (York 1995). Although partly inspired by theosophy, the church has its own theology and embraces aspects of Gnostic Christianity. The church teaches that there is an element of Christ, a divine spark, in all human beings. This is at the heart of all religions and was the primary message of Christ. Jesus, however, was not God the Son, in the orthodox Christian sense, but a man completely in touch with his divine spark. There are other Ascended Masters too and these include prophets and leaders of many other religions. According to the church, human beings, by uniting with their Christ consciousness, can halt the relentless wheel of reincarnation. Spiritual progress comes through following the examples of past Ascended Masters. Typical of the New Age, it does not expect its members to embrace all its beliefs but recommends a search for what truths can be found in other religions.

Another organized expression of the New Age-Christian wing is the Emissaries, which could be regarded as one of the earliest articulations of the New Age movement. The movement's members live in a dozen or so communities of 20 to 50 people in North America, Britain, and elsewhere. It is based on personal renewal and honouring of the sacredness of all things. It was founded in 1932 in Tennessee by Lloyd Arthur Meeker (1907–54). Searching through the world philosophies and religion for a purpose in life he found none which satisfied him and came to the realization that he must seek a life of peace and value. Meeker then developed his ideas into a more comprehensive system. It amounts to a very practical spirituality, based on the recognition that God works through individuals in the here and now. Partly inspired by the Christian ideal of loving each other, all are responsible for divine action occurring in the world that operates through human beings. Hence, the stipulated goal of the Emissaries is to assist the spiritual regeneration of the human race.

According to the Emissaries, it is the very individuality of each human being which displays the power and diversity of God, and in a community of such people the whole is greater than the individual. The divine energy is a power that is almost tangible and is sometimes referred to as the 'Substance'. Members also have a practice called 'Attunement' – a meditative technique for aligning body energy with universal energy to increase divine awareness within. Since all are created in the divine image, human beings have the capacity to manifest the divine nature on earth.

In Britain, as in other Western countries, there are a number of sites that advance a New Age Christianity. One is St James's Church, Piccadilly, London, which has found itself in conflict with traditional evangelical groups. Its former rector, Donald Reeves, developed a philosophy which is carried forward by the church. Reeves speaks of the need to refer to God as Mother in order to break away from the patriarchal dominance of traditional Christianity. He also advances many of the virtues of New Age thinking and calls for a more open-minded Christianity that is liberal in its attitudes to the religious faiths of the modern multi-ethnic society. At the same time, he is careful to steer away from paganist elements of the New Age movement.

Of similar nature, at least in terms of teachings, is the Omega Order, a semi-monastic community based in the west of England and led by Peter Spink. It regards itself as both a contemplative and teaching order that is heavily influenced by the writings of Teilhard de Chardin. In this respect, the Omega Order advances elements of traditional Christianity, a philosophy of the unity of mystics of different faiths, and those teachings of New Age which recognize an imminent human spiritual awakening that will take man on to a new evolutionary stage. Spink himself has been particularly influenced by Indian mysticism, which he sees as a counterpoint to the deadness of institutionalized Christianity.

Who are the New Agers?

As suggested above, the concept of membership is very difficult to apply to the New Age. If contemporary religion is characterized by an individual seeking after the 'truth', then this would appear to be exemplified by the New Age. Thus, because it is chiefly organized around audience and client cults, its popularity cannot be measured by estimating the membership of particular organizations. Moreover, there is little by way of a well-developed research literature or sound statistics on who joins the New Age. It is probable that different elements of the New Age attract particular types of people and that New Age 'travellers' and 'eco-warriors' may have little in common with well-heeled middle-class subscribers to its client and audience cults. However, a fairly wide assumption is that, rather like the earlier NRMs, most of the adherents are derived from the middle-classes. By contrast, working-class people are likely to be under-represented. Popular in south-east England, and in cosmopolitan cities such as Amsterdam, Barcelona, or San Francisco, the appeal is to an urban, relatively prosperous constituency. Thus, the movement is unlikely to appeal to those from well-established and rural communities.

For the most part, then, the New Age is open to those who have sufficient means to embark on voyages of self-discovery. For this reason, Bruce (1996a, 218) speculates that it is specifically appealing to the university-educated middle-classes working in the expressive professions: social workers, counsellors, actors, writers, and artists – the bottom layer of the privileged classes. The attraction of the New Age for women is also fairly implicit. Bruce's rough count of some 500 people entering the hall for the Mind, Body, and Spirit convention in 1993 in London gives a female to male ratio of about 2 to 1 (Bruce 1996a, 220).

More empirically based evidence is presented by Michael York (1995, 187–8), who quotes the New Age Spirituality Survey and other findings. These show that 73 per cent of New Agers are female, 23 per cent between 18 and 34 years old, 42 per cent between 35 and 49, and 35 per cent over 50. In terms of education, 18 per cent have attended high school, 18 per cent have a degree, and 12 per cent a higher degree. By way of occupation, 25 per cent have a professional/technical background, 19 per cent are retired or unemployed, 13 per cent are clerical, 12 per cent are in the service industries, 11 per cent are managerial, and 6 per cent are involved in sales work.

New Age travelling

In Britain, in the early 1980s, disaffected, largely young town dwellers, those alienated by urban and consumer society, took to the roads in old buses, vans, and trucks to search for a fresh and meaningful way of life. Very different from the middle-class adherents to client cults, this more impoverished and experimental constituency was, however, attracted by aspects of the New Age and neo-Paganism. Centres of attention were the Druid monument at Stonehenge and Glastonbury ('the lap of the Mother') in the west of England, which long had a mystical significance. The 1984 gathering at Stonehenge (which proved to be the last because of a legal ban) attracted an estimate of 30,000 people. They were by no means all New Age travellers, but a good contingent was.

This faction also became part of the wider Peace movement of the 1980s as the international Cold War worsened. Focuses of protest were the RAF cruise missile bases, one of which became the site of the Rainbow Field Village. Little about the movement was in common with the witchcraft or magic as practised by more organized New Age groups. If any deity was worshipped it was the Earth Mother, along with a desire to recapture a Celtic past. All in all, ritual tended to develop spontaneously with circle dancing, chanting, drumming, and the use of mantras. This movement has been described as not so much an alternative lifestyle but a new form of tribalism (Kemp 1993, 49–51).

Levels of involvement

As we have seen (in Chapter 5), it is the world-accommodating religious movements which appear to be enjoying the greatest adherence. To some extent this is exemplified by the emergence of the New Age. It is a movement which does not insist on one hundred per cent commitment, although this may be the choice of some. For the most part, the religious consumer will be as dedicated as s/he likes and will take out of the New Age what is to their advantage. This is essentially why the practices and beliefs are also extremely varied. It is, in this respect, the polar opposite of that other alleged growth area – religious fundamentalism. The New Age allows various levels of commitment. Heelas (1996, 117–19) distinguishes them as follows:

- *The fully engaged*   those who are deeply committed and have given up conventional lifestyles for a spiritual quest and are often practitioners providing services to clients, or organizers of New Age events.
- *Serious part-timers*   those whose spirituality is compartmentalized as part of their life, albeit a relatively serious one. New Age activities do not prevent adherents from living conventional lives and following conventional careers.
- *Casual part-timers*   this includes people who are interested in exotic and esoteric things as consumers, but fail to get seriously involved. This group is the smallest but, for Heelas, threatens the movement with its inherent superficiality.

It is this variation in commitment which enhances the consumer choice, as well as the range of ideas, which makes the New Age so typical of contemporary forms of religiosity.

The impact of the New Age

The annual Mind, Body, and Spirit convention, held in London, began in 1977 as a one-day event with only a small number of exhibitors. In the late 1980s, the convention was extended to five days. By 1993, over one hundred individuals and organizations presented their products or ideals on stalls. At about the same period, the number of bookshops in the USA known to specialize in New Age materials doubled over the previous decade (Brierley 1991b). On such evidence the New Age seems to be enjoying an increasing popularity and, for Bainbridge, this growth is possibly strongest where Christianity is weakest. He writes: 'With its ties to pseudoscience and Asian religion, the New Age is clearly the most formidable thorough-going religious culture that currently exists in modern society [and] presents a direct spiritual challenge to traditional Christianity.' (Bainbridge 1997, 391)

As we have seen, the New Age is perhaps the ultimate mix 'n' match religion. This makes it a leading competitor in the religious marketplace. At the same time, it is apparent that the New Age carries with it certain distinctive features which are in line with the contemporary world and may anticipate *the* growth area of religiosity – at least into the near future. This is marked, above all, by a discernible pre-occupation with the enhancement of self and the development of what Heelas (1996) calls the 'de-traditionalized spiritualities of life', where ancient religions are reinvented for the needs of individuals in contemporary society. Furthermore, there is, he suggests, a move away from the holistic frameworks which characterized the early movement to a concern with all aspects of human potential and perfection, identity construction, and even worship of the self. The New Age has thus evolved to become, perhaps, the form of religion most removed from traditional Christianity with its codified doctrinal system and abstract morality, but is that most in line with contemporary needs.

The New Age movement is also indicative of the long-term demise of religion in its collective-expressive form. Unlike traditional Christianity and the NRMs which emerged in the 1960s, it is typified more by 'individual-expressive' types. From one perspective, this increasing individual and privatized articulation of religiosity is linked to the prevalence of choice in a consumer-dominated society. There is more to the equation however. Even when the New Age movement was in its infancy, Fenn (1990) argued that the form of religion most compatible with today's world is that which grants a restricted scope to the sacred and advances a low degree of integration between corporate and individual value systems. It is occult and esoteric religion which best exemplifies this form of religious culture. Since it can be practised without coming into conflict with everyday occupational roles it confines itself to very particular times, places, objects, and issues. Such religion provides an ecstatic and magical form of activity and an opportunity for the individual to indulge in the irrational against the enforced rationality of formal and bureaucratically structured organizations and roles of everyday life. While New Age is sufficiently more than a range of mystical and occultist activities and links the individual to a broader global and cosmic order, there is much in Fenn's analysis that does effectively account for the movement's growth and direction.

If the New Age movement is predominantly a form of religiosity which may be marked by its transitory nature in the sense that it is constantly influenced by the fads and fashions of today's culture, the question may legitimately be raised as to its true level of spirituality. Some have doubted whether there is a great deal to be observed. Like many of the new religions over the last forty decades, there may be evidence of what Bryan Wilson (1979, 96) scathingly calls so much 'pushpin, poetry, or popcorn'. This is, of course, a matter of opinion. Certainly, those fully engaged in the movement would point to a profound spirituality and earnest attempt to live the religious life and deny accusations of superficiality. Indeed, many would regard it as offering a 'true' spirituality that is radically different from traditional Christianity with all its institutional and cultural encumbrances.

While movements such as the New Age appear to have deeply private dimensions, it is possible to suggest that they impinge, in many discernible ways, into the public arena, with a distinct social and political agenda. Beckford (1992) admits that the number of activists and true believers deliberately pursuing or cultivating the principal ideas of the New Age may be relatively small. However, he contends that the movement's holistic consciousness has already made incisive inroads into public thinking about such issues as ecology, peace, gender, and health. It has made its way into mainline religion and other social spheres: medicine, sport, leisure, education, dying and grieving, self-help, animal welfare, and social work. Success can also be measured by the growth of green politics and green products – taking the movement from the alienated fringes of public life to its centre.

The New Age also increasingly appears to have practical application, including the employment of its techniques in management training – advancing those which are mood-altering, induce behavioural change, and bring about the alleged spiritual development of human resources (Roberts 1994). All this suggests a growing recognition, in each of these spheres, of the strength that can be derived from emphasizing the whole person, the interconnectedness of the human and non-human environment, and the essential global nature of social and natural processes. The thrust, then, is towards a transcendent, but not necessarily supernatural, point of reference.

Bruce (1996a, 225) suggests, however, that such influences should not be overestimated. Even when the New Age does have a major impact on the lives of individuals, there is little or no effect on the world at large. The same comment can be directed towards the NRMs of earlier decades, but this is even more the case with New Age. The latter cannot aspire to promote radical and specific change because it does not have the cohesion and discipline of a sect. Despite its rhetoric, which speaks of community, New Age is the embodiment of individualism. Indeed, Bruce (1996a, 205) puts across a generally disparaging view of the New Age and its wider social impact:

> In so far as Western European governments are now interested in ecology, it is because appeals have been successfully made to self-interest and not because we have come to believe that the world is really a super organism called Gaia.
>
> (Bruce 1996a, 225)

Summary

In many respects, the New Age would appear to be a movement of contradictions. This should not necessarily surprise us. Of all the 'alternatives' it is perhaps the expression of religion that is most suited to the contemporary age. In responding to the needs of individuals in the spiritual marketplace it brings together a *bricolage* of beliefs and practices from different sources. Hence, some of its expressions reflect the prevailing ethos of today's culture, while other aspects resist it. Indeed, the beliefs and practices of the movement are so broad that it is difficult to be sure what to include under the heading of New Age and what to exclude. In the next chapter we will consider neo-Paganism and esoteric movements which overlap with the New Age, although some of their participants would prefer not to be identified with the movement.

Further reading

Hanegraaff, W. (1996) *New Age Religion and Western Culture: Esotericism in the Mirror of Secular Thought*, New York, Leiden: E.J. Brill.

Heelas, P. (1988) 'Western Europe: Self-Religions', in S. Sutherland & P. Clarke (eds.) *The World's Religions*, London: Routledge.

York, M. (1995) *The Emerging Network: A Sociology of the New Age and Neo-Pagan Movements*, Lanham, MD: Rowman & Littlefield.

9 Neo-Paganism and esoteric spiritualities

There is a not insignificant overlap between the New Age movement considered in the previous chapter and popular esoteric, occultist, and neo-pagan varieties of religion. However, those who subscribe exclusively to these forms of alternative religion are likely to object to being placed under the rubric of New Age. This is not so much because they are not 'new', but because their distinctive beliefs and practices suggest that they should be dealt with separately in order to give them full justice. At the same time, these often ancient expressions of religiosity tend to dismiss the central concern with what the New Ager frequently refers to as the 'higher self' in preference for a veneration of gods, goddesses, and other supernatural forces, or at least hidden spiritual powers. Nor, for that matter, do pagans follow the dictates of gurus or masters, or a particular book, all of which are common to some strands of the New Age. For these reasons and others, neo-Paganism, occultism, esotericism, and related 'alternatives' deserve a separate account. However, even these classifications of alternative religions are unsatisfactory since they disguise the variety and complexities to be found within each. For example, it is probably correct to speak of 'neo-Paganisms' rather than to refer to 'neo-Pagan' because contemporary pagans, between and within the various strands, disagree about belief and cosmologies, practices such as shamanism, and concepts such as 'magic' and 'nature'.

Neo-Paganism

The word 'pagan' originally meant 'country-dweller' – or, more specifically, 'the beliefs of the country of the people'. The ancient Romans applied the term to nations, especially those on the periphery of the Empire, who embraced what was perceived as the peculiar and ancient superstition of their communities. More often than not this included one variety or another of the worship of the Earth Mother goddess and/or a pantheon of gods. Today, the term neo-Paganism has a rather different connotation. Those who practise it maintain that 'neo' or 'new' denotes a revival and reconstruction of ancient Nature religions adapted for the contemporary world. Although as a contemporary movement neo-Paganism can be traced back to the nineteenth-century, it was the counter-culture of the mid-twentieth-century which increased its popularity, particularly in the USA where a rediscovery of the ancient cultural traditions of the Native American Indians became popular.

This brief overview suggests that neo-Paganism displays a remarkable diversity. Indeed, practically everything that can be termed neo-Pagan is eclectic since it is derived from various sources. Hence, shamans, witches, Druids all have different characteristic religious elements. These are often based on diverse national traditions, and within each broad group there are many different emphases. Nonetheless, there are discernible overlaps between the principal strands. There are, for example, links between some traditional forms of Wicca and Druidism, and between both of these and shamanism. This will become evident in the survey of each of the major strands of neo-Paganism presented below.

For dedicated neo-Pagans, spiritual activities are an important part of their lives. Some are more dogmatic in their beliefs and practices than others. They may maintain household altars and shrines; they will be involved in meditation, communication with the gods, rituals, and celebrations. The practice of magic is common to most strands and is generally used for beneficial purposes, for individual healings, blessings, and personal transformations. Other practices, through so-called 'circle work', involves raising group energy for healing, attempting to change weather conditions, and incantations for protecting the earth and its wildlife. Typifying the range of involvement is witchcraft, whose beliefs and practices are followed with varying degrees of seriousness and involvement. At one end of the spectrum are people for whom witchcraft is undoubtedly something of a fad or rather superficial form of entertainment. For others, there is an earnest belief in witchcraft outwardly expressed in the performance of spells for health, protection, or success. They might also ascribe special importance to astrological events such as solstices or eclipses. This greater involvement may include belonging to covens, which have developed their own rituals and their own set of beliefs over the last few years, based in part on earlier traditions.

Generally, because of its vast diversity, there is a lack of any central organization for the neo-Pagan movement: adherents tend to be based in non-hierarchical small groups. This prevents the movement from becoming dogmatic and authoritarian but it also makes it impossible to estimate how many people are involved. Nonetheless, umbrella organizations have emerged over the years. In the USA there are several different nationwide federations of neo-Pagans. One such is the Universal Federation of Pagans established in 1991. Another is the Covenant of the Goddess, which is a legally recognized Wiccan church, although in its attitude towards associated congregations it appears to operate more like a federation and in the same way as some Christian denominations. The Covenant only has as much sovereignty over congregations as to function effectively. Federations and other umbrella groups serve a number of goals: the exchange of views, mutual support, publications, and central information for the media and official bodies.

In Britain, the Pagan Federation and PaganLink work towards establishing the same rights for neo-Pagans as for members of other religions, including hospital and prison chaplains, and weddings and funerals. Once dominated by the Wiccan movement, they now put more emphasis on non-Wiccan neo-Pagans. Also in Britain there is the Church of All Worlds, founded in 1968. It has no particular dogmatic system or creed beyond a claim to being neo-Pagan. This is given to mean the reconstruction of ancient Nature religions and the combining of the mystic, environmental, and spiritual disciplines of many cultures, ranging from world religions such as Hinduism, to shamanism, science fiction, and transpersonal psychology. There is a strong emphasis on feminist and environmentalist principles. The membership is currently around 650. There are also over three dozen branches across the USA and Australia. The mission of the Church of All Worlds is to promote information and experience to reawaken Gaia and reunite humanity through tribal communities responsible for the care of the earth and the evolution of human consciousness. Another widespread organization which cuts across many of the divisions within the pagan world is the Fellowship of Isis, which has over 11,000 members in 72 countries and is headed by Olivia Robertson and her brother, Lord Strathlock, from Clonegal Castle in Ireland. The aim of the Fellowship is to restore the veneration of the goddess in her many forms.

Some organizations are concerned with certain strands within neo-Paganism. They tend to be rather small. In Britain, the House of the Goddess is fairly typical. It constitutes a contemporary pagan association and temple established in the mid-1980s (York 1995, 116–17). The original inspiration was Dianic and the temple was built and consecrated by women (although men can now be associated). Typical of contemporary homespun religion, it is based in a wooden 'hut' in the garden of a suburban terraced house in South London. Its founder, Shan, works as a healer and counsellor, and conducts weddings, divorces, and funerals. She also specializes in circle work, which amounts to an introduction to neo-Paganism for the uninitiated. The idea is that the 'graduate' can then approach other neo-Pagan traditions if they wish to move beyond an introductory background. A similar circle is based around Kevin Carylon, a male witch based in Sussex, England, who calls his brand of witchcraft the Covenant of Earth Magic. It seems to have acquired a certain notoriety over the years, attracting frequent press coverage, and condemnation from local clergy.

Many forms of neo-Paganism have been faced with the dilemma of finding the desirable balance between relaxed spontaneity and practical organization. Over the decades, many groups have disintegrated because they have refused to become institutionalized. This has been particularly so with the Wicca movement, although there are exceptions. In existence today there is, for example, the Association of Cymmry Wicca, which traces its origins back to a centuries old Druid-based Welsh Wicca. Founded in 1965, it established an American branch and claims a total membership around the world of over 15,000. It is now based on the Church of Y Tylwth Teg, with its main community situated in the mountains of North Georgia, USA. Here, it has set up the Bangor Institute, which is composed of various schools, including those of Spiritual Consciousness and Natural Healing.

Strands within neo-Paganism

Heathenism

One variation of neo-Paganism is the restoration of the ancient Norse and Germanic religions, or what can be referred to as the 'Northern Tradition'. In fact, those who follow such traditions frequently opt for the term 'heathen' (meaning 'the beliefs of the people of the hearth') rather than pagan. For instance, many who follow the Norse religion prefer the term to distinguish themselves from the more goddess-based Wicca movement. For most adherents to heathenism this may mean little more than using runes (an ancient and mystical alphabet originally associated with Germanic tribes) for divination, meditation, and magic. For others, the rediscovered religion is being revived and reinterpreted for their needs in the contemporary world and has a deeper significance.

In turn, heathenism constitutes perhaps the most diverse of faiths within the range of neo-Paganism. Many gods and goddesses may be evoked from very different polytheistic systems. Thus there are various movements within the broader constituency of heathenism. These include the Ring of Troth, the Odinic Rite, and Odinshof, each of which has its own accentuation. For many of these movements, there are a number of beliefs which appear to be at odds with modern society and are primarily concerned with re-establishing an ancient morality in an alienating world increasingly void of clear moral systems. Hence, it is argued by contemporary heathens, there must be an emphasis on community bonds, family values, and responsibility and respect for elders. This seems to amount to a form of tribalism which frequently displays conservative and patriarchal overtones.

One of the most notable strands of heathenism is Asatru, the North American movement, often known as Odinism in Britain. It is named after the Asa or Aesir, one of the two main families of Norse gods (the other family being the Vanir). Modern-day Asatru is a religion founded on the reconstruction of a belief system as derived from historical sources. It is a polytheistic faith encompassing belief in a multitude of different gods and goddesses and constitutes a more spiritual and ecological form of heathenism. Then, within the broad movement, there are different emphases. For Asatru there is the resurrection of the tradition named Vanatru, centring mainly on the Vanir. This branch takes particular interest in the feminine mysteries and female ancestral networks.

As with most mythologies, Norse beliefs include creation myths and end-of-the-world narratives. The polytheistic system has interrelated families of quarrelsome gods, whom periodically have dealings with humans, and these gods have changed their responsibilities to some extent over the centuries as the mythologies evolved. Such religion has a strong ethical side similar to that of most neo-Pagan movements, and like them the revived Norse religions do not actively recruit new members but rely on people seeking out allegiance with those who are like-minded. Heathenism may also have more sinister overtones and this is evident in the neo-Nazism and predominantly political Odinist Fellowship which endeavours to restore the true bloodline of the Nordic and Germanic people and seeks out like-minded extremist movements in North-West Europe.

Wicca

The old English term for a witch is 'Wicca'. Although it is an integral part of the neo-Pagan world, modern witchcraft is worthy of consideration in its own right since, especially in Europe, it represents the largest strand. The designation Wicca was adopted by practitioners to distinguish their beliefs and practices, which have enjoyed a renewed interest since the second half of the twentieth-century. Wicca is essentially a mystery cult involving initiation and a subsequent path of personal fulfilment along with the development of psychic and magical ability. Advancement requires the passage through various grades of commitment. In nominally Christian cultures witchcraft has been regarded as particularly deviant. Curiously, in Britain it was not until the Fraudulent Mediums Act of 1951 that individuals were legally allowed to practise witchcraft as long as they did not intentionally harm anyone.

To some extent witchcraft has been reinvented. Here much is often attributed to the writings of the retired British civil servant, Gerald Gardner (1884–1964) who, in the late 1940s, developed a mixture of beliefs drawn from ancient religious practices, magic, and the esoteric. He belonged to a Rosicrucian group, and was an initiate of Aleister Crowley's Ordo Templi Orientis. In 1954, Gardner published *Witchcraft Today*, which espoused his re-creation of witchcraft as a blend of folklore, masonic rituals, and magic, and had a strong sexual element. His *Book of Shadows* contained ritual and ceremony borrowed from a number of sources.

Before Gardner, however, and providing at the time the support of respectable academic study, was the work of anthropologist Margaret Murray. In *The Witch-Cult in Western Europe* (1921) and *The God of the Witches* (1931) she wrote that the medieval witches did not worship the Devil, but were followers of an old, pre-Christian Pagan religion (today witchcraft has nothing to do with Satanism; witches do not worship Satan). Other books significant in the development of modern Wicca were Charles Leland's *Aradia*, or the *Gospel of the Witches* (1899), based on the teachings of an Italian hereditary witch called Maddalena – which quite possibly initiated Murray's own research. There was also Robert Graves's *The White Goddess* and, to a much lesser extent, the fictional works of those such as Denis Wheatley, which were actually more to do with the occult than with Paganism, but at least kept esoteric religion viable for a new generation.

Murray called the worship of the goddess 'Dianic', after the goddess Diana. Present-day Dianic Wicca would appear to derive much from Murray's thesis. It is a religion of the goddess, and orientated towards the needs of women. For this reason, so it may be argued, Dianic Wicca and similar religions are historically more of a spiritual expression of the feminist movement than anything else. In this respect, one of the interesting developments of witchcraft and paganism has been the adoption of some of their symbols and practices by expressions of feminism, which stress the deviant heritage that the white witch represents (Neitz 1990). Although most Wicca covens are open to both sexes, the radically feminist Dianic covens, which are largely found in the USA, are exclusively female. Here, the head of the coven is a high priestess and, in rites of witchcraft, the power of the goddess is evoked to possess the priestess. Culpepper (1978) suggests that it is perhaps the most conventionally organized form of neo-Paganism in the sense of having initiation procedures and a hierarchical membership of feminine spiritual interest. Indeed, the common theme uniting most practitioners of the craft is the recognition of matriarchal forms of social organization. Some scholars, however, point out that there is actually no evidence whatsoever for a religion of one goddess: early Pagan religions were pantheist rather than female monotheistic. This is evidence of how pagan myths have been reconstructed, although it has become accepted wisdom for many of today's neo-Pagans, making it possible for them to say that they are re-creating the old religions, not creating something which is solely 'New Age'.

Despite the influence of Gardner, Murray, and others, witchcraft also has roots in both the old pagan religions and the occult revival of the nineteenth and early twentieth-centuries, at least according to their own practitioners (Farrar 1971). These include those of the Celts, to which have been added various elements of Freemasonry and Rosicrucianism, as well as Egyptian and classical mythology. Certainly, many who follow the Wiccan tradition insist on the importance of the ancient origins of their beliefs in Celtic and Nordic cults, and the veneration of Greek female deities such as Athene, as well as Isis and Mithras. Equally, the comparatively few 'hereditary witches' believe that their own family tradition and bloodline are significant. Most however, would suggest that the strength of the Wiccan movement lies in its diversity. Many Wiccan groups hold to *The Charge of the Goddess*, which is the nearest thing that Wiccan circles have to a statement of faith. It was written by Gerald Gardner and Doreen Valienre but elements go back over a century. It largely emphasizes the roots of goddess worship under many different names and the life-affirming nature of Wiccan beliefs.

So significant has Wicca been that it has tended to shape other forms of neo-Paganism in a number of central beliefs and orientations. Typical are attitudes towards sexuality. The main source of pagan beliefs and practices on the subject is the mythology of the goddess. In English Wicca, for example, the high priestess Vivianne Crowley argued that the 'negative attitude to women displayed in Christianity has derived largely from negative attitudes towards sex' (Crowley 1994, 116). Crowley describes pagan sexual morality as knowing no boundaries but has regard for the outcome of sexual activity such as unwanted pregnancy and the spread of sexual diseases.

Much interest has been focused on the Great Rite – ritual sex between the high priest and priestess in pagan rituals – but the evidence suggests that it is more symbolic than actual (witches tend to worship naked because the human body itself is regarded as sacred). Paganism particularly affirms the female body and provides rituals for celebrating 'women's mysteries' such as menstruation, lactation, and childbirth. Pagans tend to be disinterested in marriage as a legal institution, seeing it as a device to protect property and dominate women. However, a loving monogamous relationship is confirmed as a personal contract to be honoured. Various pagan groups have created colourful wedding rituals, which are often celebrated at a seasonal festival and add to the increasing range of alternative wedding ceremonies.

Crowley, in *Wicca: The Old Religion in the New Age*, regards the Wiccan craft as very compatible with the New Age movement and advocates it as a way forward for New Agers. Like New Age, Wicca provides a religious framework by establishing humanity's place in the cosmos. It has similar aims to New Age's spiritualized therapies of human potential – allowing the divine to be found in all humans and bringing the perfection of the self rather than the Christian insistence of contact with the divine outside it. Wicca brings a harmonious integration of human beings, establishing metaphysical and psychological truths, while also rediscovering pagan gods and goddesses that express the needs of men and women.

Many involved in Wicca are likely to be those drawn from more affluent groups. Along with other occultist practices, there may have been something of a change in social profile. Once associated with the poorer and less educated section of society, witchcraft has more recently been discovered to attract a disproportionate number of young and the highly educated (Ben-Yehuda & Goode 1985). Luhrmann (1989) has similarly shown how followers of witchcraft and magic in the London area are, for the most part, educated, well-qualified professionals, many of whom are scientifically trained and employed in such industries as computers and pharmaceutical research. Witchcraft, he suggests, is an opportunity to indulge in the irrational and to seek meaning from a radically different perspective to the world.

Druidry

The traditional derivation of the word 'Druid' is from the Greek *drus*, the Irish *daur* and the Welsh *derw*, each meaning 'oak'. This is combined with the Indo-European word *wid*, which denotes knowing and wisdom. A Druid was one who knew or understood oak – the oak being a generic term for all trees. It was not because the Druids worshipped the oak, or any other tree, but suggests that they had a close relationship with nature. Their worship took place in groves and they seem to have regarded trees as symbolic of wisdom and solidarity.

Present-day Druidry of all types is clearly part of the rediscovery of neo-Paganism but is usually quite distinct from the more Wiccan varieties of the recent revival. The two traditions, however, generally appear to have respect for each other and there is a certain amount of cross-fertilization. There are currently around two dozen different Druid organizations in Britain. As with Wicca and other streams of neo-Paganism, they have very different approaches to their beliefs and practices. Some two-thirds of these distinct groups have come together since 1989 in the Council of British Druid Orders.

The principal difficulty with re-creating the ancient religion of the Druids is that little or nothing was written down by the original Druids, or if it was it is long lost. Present-day Druids have had to re-create the religion from what is known or conjectured about the religious and philosophical beliefs of the Celts. Love and respect for nature were and are clearly central. So is the emphasis on oration and song: many of the original Druids were respected as taletellers and bards. It was this latter aspect which was largely at the heart of the Druid revival of the eighteenth and nineteenth-centuries. Bardic schools existed in the Celtic fringes of the British Isles up to the seventeenth-century, and Pagan 'folk' customs including May Day and Hallowe'en still persist.

The revival of Druidry can be traced to several people in the seventeenth and eighteenth-centuries, and again in the nineteenth and twentieth-centuries. Present-day Druidry includes the Ancient Druid Order, said to have been founded in 1717 by Kohn Tolland, which holds regular ceremonies at Stonehenge in Britain. The order can be seen as a counterpart to the female-dominated Wiccan movement. It has an almost restricted male membership. It rejects the idea of a revealed deity, which constitutes the dominant idea of Christianity. In contrast, the emphasis is on hermetic magic, theosophy and the ritual system of sun worship – the sun being the principal spiritual source – and includes, at its height, the summer solstice rite.

Most other orders are more recent. One of the most respected, the Order of Bards, Ovates and Druids, an offshoot of the Ancient Druid Order, was founded in 1964. It has a fairly eclectic membership, which includes both neo-Pagans and Christians. The British Druid Order was founded in 1979 as a specifically neo-Pagan Druid group whose teachings are based on the *Mabinogion* and other early British/Celtic texts. The Secular Order of Druids, founded in 1986, is heavily orientated towards environmentalism and is organized to support the civil rights of Druids to meet at places such as Stonehenge in the face of police opposition. Many of the Druid orders contain three grades or groupings of members. These focus on different talents and interests, and although they are not necessarily progressive levels, as in the Esoteric Mystery Schools, those at the third level would normally have passed through the first two. The British Druid Order, for example, has the grades of Bard (Poet/Seer), Ofydd (Philosopher) and Derydd (Druid).

It is obvious from our overview of the major groupings that neo-Paganism appears to be both growing and diversifying. Precisely how many people are involved in the broad movement is difficult to quantify. Partly, this is because some practitioners do not belong to any of the above organizations, and partly because some may not admit to being pagans because of fear of persecution or ridicule. However, a rough estimate of numbers in Britain has been calculated by Hutton, and some of his rather speculative figures are presented below (see Table 5).

Table 5 Estimate of pagan numbers in Britain, 1992

Major pagan groupings	Numbers
Members of pagan Druid orders	6,000
Initiated witches	10,000
Heathen, shamanic, and pagan magical orders	4,000
Non-initiated pagans	80,000
Total	100,000

Source: Adapted from Hutton, R. (1993) *The Pagan Religions of the British Isles*, Oxford: Blackwell.

Related neo-Pagan practices

Magic

Magical beliefs and practices are by no means limited to 'primitive' or tribal societies. Indeed, such forms of religiosity, if magic can be described in that way, appear to have become increasingly popular in Western societies in recent years. It can be practised individually or as part of Wiccan and Pagan circles and may be subdivided into 'high' and 'low' forms. The high magic represents the traditional magic developed through the centuries via mystics and secret orders and involves complicated ritual, elaborate robes, and much specialized paraphernalia. Low magic is that which is practised by the traditional healer. It is the magic of nature and of the elements. In a coven or group, witches are principally concerned with low magic or 'raising power', which usually means dancing in a circle chanting in a repetitive fashion. The intention will have been discussed beforehand and agreement reached on the visualization of what everyone wants to happen. This may range from bringing a healing to a successful house move.

Magic may also be divided into its white or right hand variants which attempt to bring good results; and black, left hand magic, which seeks the opposite. By far the greater number of practitioners would be concerned with the right hand variety. At the same time, magic has strong moral foundations and this is evident in the belief that there are various factors that are said to affect magical activity. One is the Law of Three-fold Return, which states that magic which aims at harm can rebound on the practitioner with triple negative force. Another is the cause and effect of *karma*. For example, healing magic will not work on an illness which lies within the patient's karmic pattern. Spells frequently perceived as not working include those which seek money and material possession, influence over others, or revenge. Timing is also deemed to be important. Astrological influences can have a bearing on the most auspicious time to cast a spell, but the most important factor is the phase of the moon.

Shamanism

Shamanism is one of the oldest religious traditions of the human race and includes the animistic perception that sees all things as imbued with an inherent vitality. The shaman, through trance or visions, claims to enter the spirit world and communicate with the beings there, working magic or bringing healing back to those in their care. Common to many of these traditions is 'soul retrieval', which is used in many shamanic cultures. The shaman astrally travels to the spirit world and offers the opportunity for the dead to return to the living, or to bring back part of the soul that may have escaped the psychical body because of trauma or illness. Because it is based on individual experience, there is no single set of beliefs – each shaman finds their own way.

Shamanism is part of many Wiccan and Druidic circles and marks one of the clearest overlaps between neo-Paganism and New Age spiritualities. While it is an individual, even solitary, path, contemporary shamans attempt to adapt ancient practices to personal needs today. In the hands of New Agers, shamanism is more about influencing new dimensions of consciousness rather than believing in and visiting other worlds, hence more related to voyages of self-discovery. Courses or workshops appear frequently among the programmes of alternative religions such as the Wrekin Trust and the Findhorn Foundation. In the USA, the revival of North American shamanism is particularly strong. Shamanism is also practised by some of the more established NRMs. For example, the Unification Church combines Christianity with Korean folk shamanism.

Astral travelling

Astral travelling is embraced by various expressions of the occult. It has also enjoyed a resurgence in popularity with the rise of the New Age. Broadly defined, it constitutes the art of sending forth the consciousness at will to other places, other worlds, other times, and then bringing it back with full knowledge of what has been experienced. The projected consciousness is sometimes referred to as the 'astral body', hence the term 'astral projection'. However, there is some argument among practitioners of the art as to just what the astral body is comprised of, as well as disputing what part of the individual it is (if any) that actually ventures forth on these astral journeys.

If it is the consciousness that embarks on a journey, some suggest that it is part of the mind reaching out from the body by actually going deep within itself. Other exponents often refer to astral projection as 'out-of-body-experience'. They believe that it is only the astral self which leaves and is constituted by an emotional layer of the non-physical self – an ethereal layer that tightly surrounds the body like a second aura and acts as a conduit between consciousness, the higher self, and the outside world. Yet others go so far as to say that it is a part of the soul that willingly parts from its physical home to travel forth, remaining attached to the body by only a silver cord, which, if severed, would cause the projector's death.

There is a general agreement among those who claim to experience astral travelling that the astral plane is a definite geographical point outside oneself and it is said to encompass the entire physical and non-physical universe. Even the coherent thoughts of humanity live on the astral plane in what is called 'thoughtforms', or semi-solid projections of consciousness that have been built up over the years by living beings who need those daydream worlds to balance what is lacking in the physical world.

Thought is believed to be action on the astral plane. Will or coherent desire can take the individual where they want to go. It is believed to be a simple skill that can be mastered by anyone, including viewing past lives, exploring other worlds or planets, healing others, or visiting the home of the elements. Historically, astral travelling has been utilized for various enterprises. For instance, it is believed to provide future life projection, allowing an impression or visions of future incarnations.

Astral travelling is acquired through techniques of relaxation and meditation, chanting, and controlled breathing. Meditation practices, for example, are for enhancing occultist endeavours and psychic capabilities and are related to stimulating the *chakras*, or energy centres of the body, which correspond to different mental, emotional, and physical functions. They work as portals between the physical self and the astral world. Meditation cleanses those such as are found in the 'third eye', the heart, or throat.

These processes are often described by practitioners in the form of scientific language: that astral travelling precipitates an actual physiological change which can be measured by medicine through alternations in brain activity levels, as suggested by McCoy in his book *Astral Projection for Beginners* (1999, 10). This and similar literature is often couched with a rhetoric of concern with reaching individual potential, such as finding out the purpose of one's current incarnation, any past-life issues yet unresolved, the state of spiritual progress, and problems in personal relationships (McCoy 1999, 195). Many of these books amount to a kind of do-it-yourself approach in astral travelling. There is, for example, the *Astral Projection Kit*, that also includes literature and the cassette tape *The Practical Guide to Astral Projection*.

Satanism

Satanism is a far less respectable form of fringe religion. Strictly speaking, while it is occultist in nature it has nothing whatsoever to do with neo-Paganism. Rather, Satanism may be seen as having its roots in Christianity. The link between the two was established by Christianity in the Middle Ages when they were mixed as a result of the Christian Church mercilessly stamping out paganism and labelling pagan activities as satanic.

At the same time that interest in the occult grew in eighteenth-century Europe, so did an interest in Satanism. A group of young noblemen led by Sir Francis Dashwood founded the notorious Hell Fire Club based in London. In 1801, an Englishman, Francis Barret, wrote a book entitled *The Magnus or Celestial Intelligence*, a bringing together of scraps of work on Satanism, which claimed to be 'a complete system of occult philosophy', although it never lived up to this claim. Present-day Satanists, as few as they are, fall into several categories. There have been notable contemporary groups such the Ordo Templi Orientis cult which has long been active in Britain and America – stressing sexual rituals and drug abuse – as well as the more reputable First Church of Satan established by Anton Szandor La Vey in 1966 in San Francisco. During the 1970s and 1980s, his cult spread across America and even to Europe. It attracted a group of disciples who were largely comprised of well-educated men in their thirties and forties.

Women are also known to take a prominent role in satanic activities elsewhere. Until relatively recently, the lissom, often semi-clothed figure of Maddalena Stradivari (film star, popular celebrity, and member of the I Spirit Liberi satanic cult) frequently adorned the pages of the more downmarket Italian newspapers whenever one of the 70 or so occult sects in Italy came into the public spotlight.

Finally, Satanism has become the novel theme which inspires the lyrics and stage trappings of some heavy metal bands and contemporary teenage literature and appears to be almost part of a counter-culture in its own right. The themes of Satanism and dark evil forces are also interwoven into numerous fringe media publications of comics and magazines, and are the common inspiration for computer and board games such as 'Dungeons and Dragons'.

Esoteric movements

In some respects this is a catch-all category. Movements as varied as Subud, theosophy, UFO cults, and a number of strands of the New Age movement could be included under this remit. Many of those discussed below are from a wide range of movements which have grown up over the last century. They are by no means restricted to expressions of neo-Paganism. Several are a synthesis of the Judaeo-Christian tradition; others are inspired by the eastern religions.

Historically, in the West, the originators of esoteric movements were often highly unorthodox in both their thought and their lifestyles. Their beliefs tended to be occultist and to emphasize hidden spiritual powers and include both magic and mysticism. Most present-day esoteric movements tend to be eclectic, borrowing from several traditions. Schisms and offshoots are common and generally result from the unorthodox basis of their beliefs and the nature of mysticism itself, which has allowed considerable innovation. Many adherents believe in secret or Ascended Masters who have tremendous powers and have guarded the true religious teachings, the origins of all world religions, for thousands of years. All tend to emphasize secret knowledge, restricted to a select few. The belief in Ascended Masters, more specifically, is related to the conviction that some enlightened individuals have chosen to step off the wheel of reincarnation and now devote themselves to the guidance of mankind. The idea of Masters has been adapted in turn by some expressions of the New Age and many of the movements now to be considered.

The Theosophical Society was founded in 1875 in New York by Helena Petrovna Blavatsky and Henry S. Olcott. From its beginnings the aims were to create the universal brotherhood of man, irrespective of religion, race, or social division; to study ancient religions, philosophy, and science; and to develop man's psychic power. The term 'theosophy' comes from the Greek word *theos* (God) and *sophia* (wisdom). If it can be pinned down to a belief system, theosophy is one that has developed its own theory of evolution. The human race is evolving and so is each individual – progressing through a circle of reincarnation to a higher state. The mystic Masters had long embraced a secret knowledge, which is now available to all to follow in their footsteps. Much has been based on eastern mysticism, spiritualist manifestations, and the belief that all religions have a common spiritual core, alongside the idea of social reform. Today the society has lost much of its initial impetus. There are still theosophical societies in Western Europe, the USA, and elsewhere, although they often appear to be little more than study groups of man's numerous religions and systems of mysticism. However, many of the esoteric movements thriving today have borrowed from some of theosophy's principal beliefs.

Anthroposophy was established around 1900 by Rudolf Steiner. He was a former member of the Theosophical Society and the Rite of Memphis and Misraim, a quasi-masonic occult order. While theosophy is about wisdom of the divine, anthroposophy can be broadly defined as 'man-wisdom'. Rather than evolving to become god-like Masters, Steiner taught that man used to have powers which are now lost to him. The objective is to regain these. Buried deep within human beings are lost secrets. Through meditation and study, humans can rediscover their lost nature and achieve spiritual growth on the levels of the senses, imagination, inspiration, and intuition. There is also a certain Christian influence. Steiner taught that Christ's death and resurrection were supremely important. Christ can help man ascend to the higher levels that he once knew, but the powers of darkness hold him back through the external material world. This enterprise marks an attempt to merge science and religion and has extended into such areas as education and organic farming. Over 500 Waldorf schools are now believed to teach according to Steiner's principles.

Another offshoot of theosophy is that established by Alice Bailey, who claimed that she was contacted by various Masters and began channelling messages from them. In 1923 she founded the Arcane School to teach her followers. Her teachings were basically theosophical, with an emphasis on the imminent coming of Maitreya Buddha, which could also be interpreted as the Second Coming of Christ, or another reincarnation of Krishna, or the Jewish messiah, or the Muslim Imam Mahdi. The Buddha is all of these. After her death, Bailey's movement splintered into various offshoots. One, led by Benjamin Creme, claimed similar communication with a Master and again foretold of Maitreya's return. Although Creme claims various sightings, they are perceived as but a prelude to the Day of Declaration when Maitreya will contact the entire world.

A further movement with its roots in theosophy is the I Am movement, which was founded by Guy and Edna Ballard in 1931. Both claimed a regular contact with Saint-Germain (an eighteenth-century alchemist and important Master in several esoteric movements) and other renowned Masters. The movement teaches that the all-knowing, ever-present, eternal God ('I Am', Exodus 3:14) is in all with a spark of Divine Flame. Humans can experience this presence, love, power, and light – the power of the Violet Consuming Flame of Divine Love – through quiet meditation and repeating 'affirmations' and 'degrees'. It is a form of metaphysical positive thinking which teaches that by 'affirming' something one desires, one can cause it to happen.

Freemasonry

To the lay person, the Freemasons are a mysterious, even sinister brotherhood. With a membership that has included Winston Churchill, Franklin Roosevelt, and Oscar Wilde, the movement still remains an enigma with few informed commentaries on its beliefs and practices. All members have to swear on the pain of death not to reveal masonic secrets to outsiders. This semi-secret, as well as highly ritualistic, nature of Freemasonry has made it the subject of widespread suspicion and Christian attack for centuries. On both sides of the Atlantic there has been continued concern regarding its political and business influence, as well as its involvement in such institutions as the police force and the judiciary. There is good evidence that masons help each other to obtain employment and promotion, and recognize each other by their secret signs and phrases.

Freemasonry, although with ancient origins (it evolved from the guilds of stonemasons and cathedral builders of the Middle Ages), became particularly popular in the eighteenth-century, and was in keeping with the interest that the middle-classes had with secret societies of all kinds. At that time there was a strong occultist element, which today has largely degenerated into purely ceremonial activity. It amounts to a system of mysticism observed by the lodges of 'free and accepted masons'. The secret signs used by itinerant masons were devised for the purpose of mutual recognition. Aspects of it can be traced back to the Knights Templar – a militaristic monastic order originally associated with the eleventh- and thirteenth-century crusades. In essence, the Templars protected pilgrims who travelled from Europe to Jerusalem. After the Crusades, the Templars returned to their chapters, where many of the secret meetings and rites began. Holy relics were associated with the orders, including the Holy Grail.

Today, the Masons are very different in their practices and orientation. The Grand Lodges control what is known as 'craft' Freemasonry and brethren (since membership is exclusively male) often refer to the Brotherhood as 'the Craft'. Craft Freemasonry covers the three degrees of Entered Apprentice, Fellow of the Craft, and Master Mason. The vast majority of members rise no higher than the latter. Beyond that there are a number of other levels that are extremely secret and of which little was known for a considerable time. However, a good deal about the broad range of rituals, which often involve wearing medieval attire, has been made public as part of a recent policy of openness.

Freemasonry is largely to be found in Anglo-Saxon communities, with over one hundred Lodges (over half in the USA). Each is largely independent and most reflect the character and political complexion of the countries in which they are established. The Brotherhood's stated aims of morality, fraternity, and charity are well known, and it is certainly the case that the Lodges donate considerable money to a wide range of non-Freemasonry charities. The attitude towards women is notorious: the Freemasons do not merely exclude women from their ranks, but disassociate themselves from any other societies that have female members. In terms of social composition, the Lodges are constituted largely by privileged, wealthy, and middle-class people in professional or business positions.

Rosicrucianism

There are many different Rosicrucian organizations across the world. Some are more secretive than others, reserving their membership to Freemasons of the highest grades. Others have an open membership, but are nonetheless difficult to join. Inspired by early seventeenth-century mystical works various movements emerged. They told of the alleged exploits of Christian Rosenkreutz, who was born in 1378, travelled in the Middle East, and died at the age of 106. The story goes that when his tomb was discovered in 1604, his body had not corrupted. Rosenkreutz set up a fraternity, the House of the Holy Spirit, dedicated to the well-being of mankind, social reform, and the healing of the sick. This reformation of the whole world was to be accomplished by men of secret, magical learning. Rosicrucian societies began to emerge around Europe and, in the nineteenth-century, there was a resurgence of interest, especially in Britain and the USA. More recent orders have grown up. Among them is Lectorium Rosicrucianum (1929). Its teachings are a version of Gnostic Christianity, regarded as a heresy by the established church, which teaches of the spiritual core of all world religions and mystical schools. There is also reference to two natural orders having polar opposites of good and bad: the material world and the spiritual world. Salvation is gained through self-mortification and a spiritual rebirth.

Contemporary esoteric movements

The Order of the Golden Dawn is based on a spurious manuscript in the nineteenth-century which contained fragments of 'Golden Dawn' rituals that owed much to Freemasonry, with elements of astrology and alchemy. By 1888, it had become a secret society very much like that of the Freemasons and the Rosicrucians, in that it awarded 'degrees' as members progressed up the ladder, but its principal emphasis was on the study of magical theory and ritual. The main degrees were Neophyte, Zelator, Theoricus, Practicus, and Philosophus. For a few there was an inner circle with the three degrees of Adeptus Minor, Adeptus Major, and Adeptus Exemptus. The outer order studies only the theory of magic; the inner circle teaches practical ritual magic. Over the years, the movement has divided into more magical and Christian mystical wings. In its time it has been one of the most intensive and all-embracing esoteric schools.

Of particular significance in the evolution of esotericism has been the North American order, Builders of the Adytum. As with similar schools, the philosophy has a practical element. The aim is for members to develop through mastery of themselves in order to gain not just a spiritual higher self but health and prosperity. In some respects, the programme followed is not dissimilar to Scientology. After associate members have taken the introductory courses, they may be admitted into a group known as Pronaos, practising ritual magic. Like most esoteric groups, the school teaches both Cabbala and tarot. The Cabbala's *Tree of Life* is used symbolically to represent the relationship between God and man. It is derived from a mystical philosophical system based on the esoteric interpretation of the Jewish scriptures, especially the Torah. The tarot provides a pictorial version of inner knowledge.

The Society of Inner Light was established by Dion Fortune (1890–1946) in 1922. She was once a member of Stella Matutina, an offshoot of the Order of the Golden Dawn. In one vision in her revelation she met Jesus and the Ascended Master Comte de Saint-Germain. She practised magic, a blend of esoteric Christianity, Cabbalism, and tarot, with some strong neo-Pagan elements. The society has changed the emphasis of its teachings over the years. It was once strongly influenced by Alice Bailey's doctrine of the Secret Masters. It also exploited the Alexander Technique for improving physical posture, and even some ideas culled from Scientology. Now it seeks to expand consciousness and to realize the Divine Intention that is concerned with the true purpose and destiny of each human being. Following initial training, the Society teaches three different Paths: the Mystic, the Hermetic, and the Green Ray. The former attempts to cast every aspect of the ego aside that separates it from God. The latter seeks to understand the works of God in nature. The Hermetic Path constitutes a middle way and endeavours to comprehend things spiritual while controlling the impulses of the senses. It also lays great stress on moral living, courteousness, good citizenship, self-control, and responsibility.

The Servants of the Light was founded in 1972 by W.E. Butler, formerly a member of the Society of Inner Light, and an ordained priest in the Liberal Catholic Church. The School is organized on fairly standard lines of progression from Novice upwards through a 50-lesson main course. These divide into three degrees. The first is largely based on the art of healing and a practical guide to mysticism. The second includes a practical workshop after which adherents become a Frater or Soror of the Fraternity of the Servants of the Light and help those studying below them. The third degree is by invitation only and little is known of this except by initiates themselves. A great emphasis is put upon the Cabbala throughout since it is regarded as the foundation of the Western mystical tradition. It also has clear links with Egyptian and Greek thought, the Gnostics, and Neoplatanists. Members are encouraged to become familiar with mythology of all sorts since they are held to have some true spiritual value. There are some 2,000 members worldwide, making the order one of the largest and influential esoteric movements.

The London Group, now with an international influence, was founded in 1975 by a former senior member of the Society of Inner Light. It offers two rudimentary courses, to be taken consecutively: first, basic occult tenets and an introduction to the Cabbala; and second, an introduction into the modern mysteries, particularly the practical use of symbol and ritual. The second part outlines the structure and methods of a modern occultist group. If students progress satisfactorily, they may be invited to take a Threshold course to prepare for entry into the Fraternity. The London Group stresses the practical nature of its work. The primary goal is personal regeneration, with the clear understanding that this will benefit others.

The Inner Light Expansion typifies many esoteric groups. It has no formal organization or membership. To do so would go against its principal teachings. Given that it is based on mystical experiences, there are no rituals and only the briefest of codified beliefs. The movement, if it can be designated as such, was established in 1967 by Hugh Emil de Cruz. It is now based at Santa Brigida, Spain, and adherents are contacted largely through a mailing system. De Cruz preaches against all organized religion since it detracts from the true spiritual path, although his belief system does appear to contain some elements of Islam and Hinduism. He does not condone fortune telling, witchcraft, or tarot cards (although healing cards are used), and denounces gurus and 'masters', although there is the acceptance that higher beings in the divine realm may freely decide to incarnate to spread the divine light.

Human beings are sparks of Allah's divine light. In the 'higher realities', according to de Cruz, we think and receive all we wish for without struggle or the desire to possess the many selves. The sources of true spirituality are within, as is the experience of the language of 'dream symbology' for true guidance from God. Muhammad was a great prophet but the Koran is merely the creation of human scribes who have misled the world as much as the Judaic/Christian scriptures. We construct our own material reality and experiences according to our desires and deeds. According to de Cruz, we are also living between future and past life experiences and simultaneously abide in alternative realities. The 'now' must be used to expand the supreme light of Allah and to trust in God alone as our 'inner partner'. Sex and materialism are not frowned upon. The Inner Light, which is the highest form of meditation, can also help us to expand in all pleasures, joys, and creative capabilities.

Locating neo-Paganism and esotericism

Daniel Harms (1999) has attempted to disentangle the different expressions of neo-Paganism, esotericism and magic. This he does with reference to their possible origins, that is, pre-modern, modern, or post-modern. Essentially, by making these divisions Harms is showing how a range of beliefs and practices over the centuries have legitimized themselves with reference to the cultural idioms of the time.

The 'pre-modern' is characterized by reference to tradition and frequently to lineage. Paganism and magic clearly call upon pre-modern philosophical traditions. Those practising paganism draw inspiration from a pantheistic, pre-modern past. Much is typified by the association with Celtic culture. This association may involve a retraditionalization and commodification of Celtic identity. Other pre-modern beliefs and practices are related to heathenism. Those involved in pre-modern mysticism (also influencing magical practices) are the Cabbala, Gnosticism, and the Hermetic tradition.

For Harms, the 'modern' also involves an emphasis on science, systems of information, and the construction of meta-narratives. The Renaissance, and then the Enlightenment, brought radical changes for magical practices. Increasingly, magic appeared to embrace scientific values. For example, the Cabbala discernibly became subject to scientific influence and was systematized. Much was also evident in Crowley's version of magic, which displayed the Enlightenment values of science, rationalism, democracy, and the transformation of the self.

Harms insists that the 'post-modern' can be identified by an emphasis on fluctuating beliefs, humour, playfulness, and the relativism of personal and local context. As far as magic is concerned, meta-narratives are collapsing, with beliefs and practices often left to the preferences of individual practitioners who perform magic according to their subjective experiences. There is evident a mix and match of beliefs and practices which have little regard for tradition, history, or systems. This involves an open embrace of different systems, symbols, and pantheons – often transformed into a *bricolage* and juxtaposition of pagan and occult worlds.

Within post-modernity, the morality of paganism becomes confused because it is idiosyncratically and syncretically constructed by each practitioner. This results in a retraditionalization that may put an emphasis on a particular strand of paganism on to which other traditions are grafted. For example, Wicca may borrow beliefs and practices from the Druid or Heathen traditions. It is the post-modern variety of neo-Paganism and esotericism which prevails today.

Summary

It is evident that the various forms of neo-Paganism and esotericism considered above offer a vast variety of beliefs and practices. Often such beliefs and practices are difficult to pin down with any great detail. This is not just a reflection of developments in post-modernity working themselves out in contemporary spiritualities. Rather, it is implicit in the degree of mysticism involved. This means that much is put down to interpretation and experience, as well as a dislike for codified teachings and organizational structures synonymous with many of the major world religions. In many respects, this means that the extent of these movements is hard to verify. Indeed, there are many aspects which do not fall within organizational frameworks and may be fairly frequently practised among the general population. This may include superstition, occultism, astrology, and divination. These more hidden forms of religious practice will be considered in the next chapter.

Further reading

Barrett, D. (1998) *Sects, 'Cults' and Alternative Religion. A World Survey and Sourcebook*, London: Cassell.

Graham, H. (1995) 'Satanism in Britain Today', *Journal of Contemporary Religion*, **10** (3), 283–96.

Hole, C. (1977) *Witchcraft in England*, London: Book Club Associates.

Marty, M. (1970) 'The Occult Establishment', *Social Research*, **37**, 212–23.

Rawlinson, A. (1997) *The Book of Enlightened Masters: Western Teachers in Eastern Traditions*, Chicago, IL: Open Court.

Figure 5 Depiction of the fall of Adam and Eve from *The Watchtower* magazine, Jehovah's Witnesses

Source: *The Watchtower*, February 1995

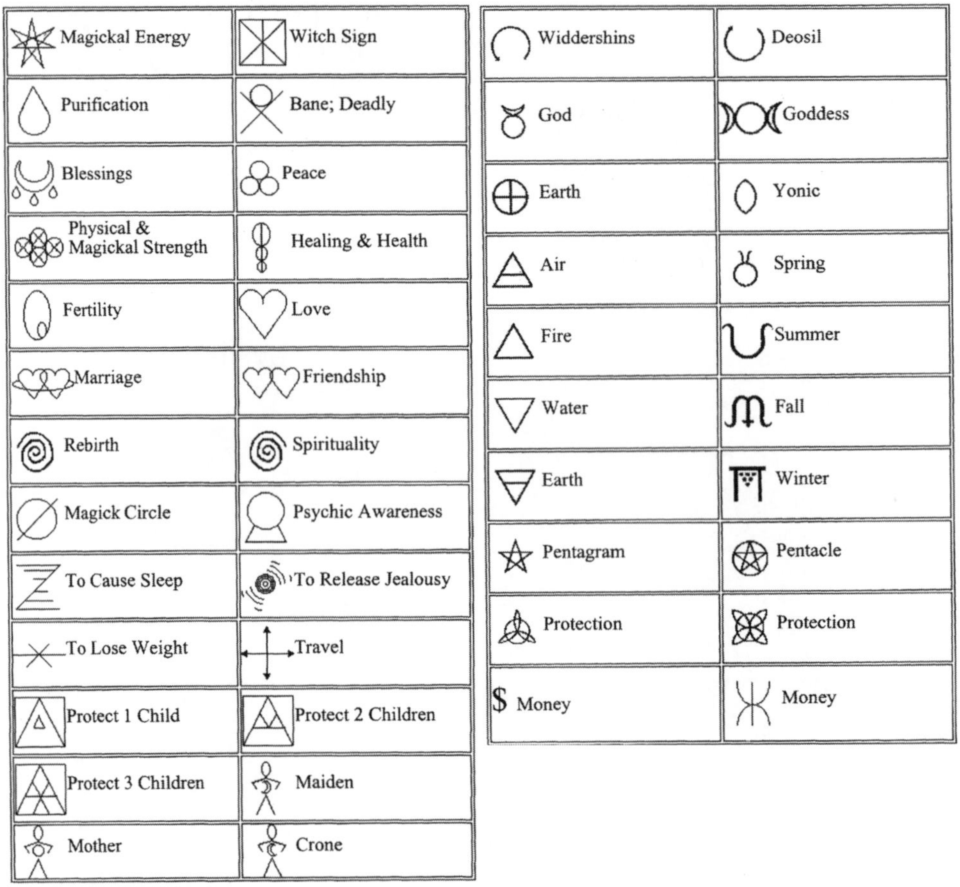

Magickal Energy	Witch Sign	Widdershins	Deosil
Purification	Bane; Deadly	God	Goddess
Blessings	Peace	Earth	Yonic
Physical & Magickal Strength	Healing & Health	Air	Spring
Fertility	Love	Fire	Summer
Marriage	Friendship	Water	Fall
Rebirth	Spirituality	Earth	Winter
Magick Circle	Psychic Awareness	Pentagram	Pentacle
To Cause Sleep	To Release Jealousy	Protection	Protection
To Lose Weight	Travel	Money	Money
Protect 1 Child	Protect 2 Children		
Protect 3 Children	Maiden		
Mother	Crone		

Figure 6 Pagan symbols in use among neo-Pagan groups today

Figure 7 Enoch Adeboye, leader of the Redeemed Christian Church of God,
Nigeria, with seventy churches in the UK

Source: *Renewal*, October 1997

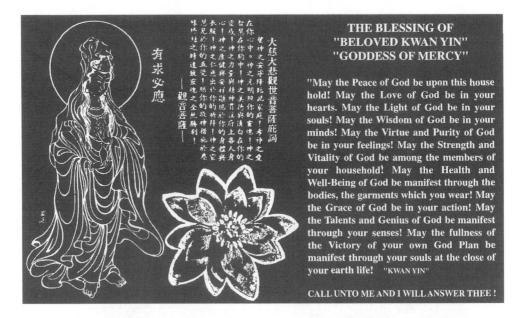

Figure 8 Healing card, Divine Inner Light movement

Figure 9 Image of worship in the Charismatic Renewal Movement

Source: *Alpha Magazine*, May 1995 © Trinity Square Ltd

10 Popular forms of religiosity

Running parallel to organized or 'official' forms of religion are those which might be termed, perhaps rather misleadingly, as 'popular' or 'common', religiosity. These are the more hidden but enduring aspects of alternative religion not considered so far and they vary from popular superstition and mysticism, to a wide variety of occultist practices. Historically, some expressions of superstition and folklore beliefs pre-date Christianity in Europe (Towler 1974). However, for centuries they have been detectable underneath the apparent domination of mainline Roman Catholicism and Protestantism and have competed with them for acceptance, particularly among rural populations (Gretton 1965). Their importance has varied over time and evidence suggests that there has been a general tendency for a range of popular religions to come to the fore at times in which Christianity was weak. Today, it is possible that they are becoming more relevant since mainstream Christianity appears to be on the wane. Hence, far from being a cultural remnant of past times, these aspects of religion may operate much like NRMs in filling some kind of spiritual 'gap' and provide a focus of meaning and significance, if not belonging, to a wide variety of people.

There are a few further observations to be made. Firstly, it must be recognized that there may be no stark distinction between mainline Christianity and popular religion. Numerous superstitions can be detected *within* the history of the Church. For instance, many have long been connected to veneration of the saints, as in the Roman Catholic Church. Frequently, individuals may both practise Christianity and endorse superstitious beliefs simultaneously, while for others the latter are the exclusive focus and held as legitimate and quite normal dimensions of religious life (Campbell & McIver 1987). Secondly, it is also evident that some types of current alternative religion have borrowed from earlier folk beliefs but have given them a new twist. This is perhaps most obviously the case with some strands of New Age spirituality. More broadly, the apparent increasing popularity of folk beliefs gives further substance to the view that contemporary expressions of religiosity are those which allow individuals to select components of their meaning system from a wide assortment of religious representation.

Superstition

'Superstition' is not an easy term to define. As in the case of magic, it may simply be understood as representing an attempt to explain or even manipulate one's environment through various mystical or metaphysical means. In advanced industrial societies, where the primary means of understanding and controlling the world is through rational and scientific techniques, the level of superstition appears to be surprisingly fairly high. For instance, a study in England by Abercrombie *et al* (1970) discovered that around 22 per cent of those sampled believed in lucky numbers and 18 per cent in lucky charms, while over 75 per cent 'touched wood' for good fortune. The study also indicated that those who regarded themselves as 'religious' were far more likely to be superstitious than those who claimed to be 'non-religious'. Individuals who frequently went to church, however, were clearly less likely to be superstitious.

There is at least a measure of evidence here that superstition may fill a spiritual need for those without Christian allegiance. Contrary testimony, nonetheless, suggests that those who indicated some dedication to mainstream Christianity also supplemented their beliefs and practices with non-official beliefs, including extra-sensory perception and psychic teachings (Bibby 1987). Yet, whatever the spiritual mix, it is possible to argue that such expressions of superstition are little more than a cultural artefact from earlier times. Abercrombie *et al* (1970) found that there was no substantial commitment to many beliefs. Only around 6 to 8 per cent of those surveyed expressed a feeling of uneasiness if they did not perform the appropriate actions demanded by superstitious ideas.

A related area to that of popular superstition is belief in the occult. Astrology, hexing, palmistry, numerology, amulets and charms, water divining, and various forms of divination such as tarot or pendulum are included under this remit. Although these may be an integral part of the New Age movement and of a number of the occultist practices already considered, some have nonetheless long enjoyed a wider popular acceptance. Research in recent years seems to indicate their increasing appeal or at least expanding marketability.

If indeed an interest in these 'alternatives' constitutes a growth area, it may be largely a result of social change and cultural trends rather than solely the decline in mainstream Christianity. As we have seen, a number of commentators have argued that the 1960s and 1970s were periods of occult revival in Western societies and were intrinsically linked to aspects of the counter-culture which developed at the time (Marty 1970; Truzzi 1972). On the other hand, since at least some related beliefs are derived from the folk traditions of various ethnic groups (Crapanzano & Garrison 1977), it may be argued that in the fluid culture of contemporary societies occultist activities have spread beyond their ethnic confines to the mainstream. Another discerning observation is made by McGuire (1992, 108) who stresses the link between the occult and the contemporary preoccupation with the themes of health and healing. Hence, occultist activities are to be found as an integral part of alternative medicine and therapy. It may, for example, be an important aspect of divining causes of illness, herbal cures, or seeking a cure for sickness.

At a more general level, what largely amount to occultist beliefs appear wide-spread. The findings of at least one survey suggest that an interest in them may in future be to the detriment of traditional Christianity, if the attitudes of a younger generation are anything to go by (see Table 6).

Table 6 Teenagers involved in occult practices in England, 1992

'Have you ever been involved in any of the following?'	Non-church group	Church group
Ouija	26	8
Astrology	18	10
Tarot	13	6
Hypnosis	5	3
Crystals	3	2
Reflexology	3	2
Channelling	3	1
I Ching	2	1

Source: Adapted from Brierley, P. (1993) *Reaching and Keeping Teenagers*, London: Christian Research Associated, p. 80.

Popular occultist practices and beliefs come in various forms. Those discussed below are some of the more popular and in many respects epitomize the growth of these forms of alternative religion. What is evident in many of these expressions of occultism is how they have frequently been given a new direction and supplied with an appeal, especially through the vast amount of popular literature produced, to human potential, healing, and personal success. There is, by way of illustration, *Mountain Magic*, a book written for the popular North American market on magic, which explores the rich folk-lore of the southern Appalachian Mountains. It is concerned with omens, portents, curses, and cures dealing with issues of family and home, romance and children, health and dying. It claims to focus on the 'magical aspects of the lives of mountain people ... ', and boasts an introduction to 'practicing natural magic' that can be applied to day-to-day life.There are many similar volumes widely on sale today.

Astrology

Astrology involves, through a reading of the zodiac signs, a set of beliefs focusing on the idea that impersonal forces in the universe influence human life. However, under the general category of astrology fall a wide variety of practices ranging from sophisticated, complex speculations about the future, to very crude newspaper horoscope columns. Most people encounter astrology through reading star or sun signs in the latter, which bear little relation to what advocates claim is 'real' astrology as practised and written about by highly skilled, professional astrologers. From a person's date, time, and place of birth, astrology takes into account not only the zodiac signs but many other factors too, building up a sophisticated picture of the total person. Astrology is said, nonetheless, to have far greater significance than the lives of individuals. Thus, in order to prove the validity of their art astrologers will point to their ability to predict significant world events. For instance, leading up to 1989 and the fall of the Berlin Wall, there were said to be major conjunctions of planets that many astrologers saw as heralding great global events that were later interpreted as the beginning of the collapse of world communism.

As the planets orbit the Sun, they also orbit an individual's birthchart and are believed to trigger changes within the individual and his/her life since they control different aspects within it. By being aware of the planetary dynamics operating in our birthchart, it is deemed possible to discover that our lives can be placed within a wider context of patterns and rhythms and that every phase has significance, astrologically speaking. Astrology is forwarded by practitioners as a means for the individual to get a better sense of how their present circumstances came about and what course of action would be to the best advantage. This more serious endeavour concerns mentally ascribing certain 'values' to the planets according to how they are arranged within three cycles or circles. The circle of the *zodiac* informs which sign the planet is in; the *diurnal* circle relates which house the planet is in; and the *aspect* circle tells in which phase the planet is located. Looking at a planet in this way, it is believed to be possible to get a feeling of what it is 'doing' in the individual's chart. A Sun square in Mars, for instance, will immediately indicate on the astrological map that a person will need to express energy in a forceful way.

Most astrologers believe that a horoscope tells us about a person's predisposition and preferences, rather than insisting that events in one's life are predetermined. Knowing one's horoscope is meant to permit more choices as it becomes clear who we are and what we will become. According to one practitioner (Boston 1998, 3), 'We can choose to work with the inherent strengths and weaknesses in our nature and grow towards wholeness as a consequence.' This kind of emphasis ties neatly with today's cultural focus on human potential and personal choice. Moreover, through stressing the importance astrology has in dealing with human relationships, the modern variant comes to have a strong socio-psychological dimension. By using what is known as *synastry*, two people's horoscopes can be compared, and areas of compatibility and conflict assessed. This allows an understanding of the motivations and limitations of friends, partners, family members, and work associates. It is also possible to identify and anticipate career preferences – perhaps by tying individual skills with personal preferences and values. It is clear, then, that contemporary books on astrology stress a practical aspect. Boston (1989, 5) suggests the following to his readership:

Write a list of your ten best qualities (including skills and aptitudes), then five qualities or aspects of your behaviour that you would like to change. When you cast your own birthchart using the techniques described later in this book, look at your list again and see whether the qualities you wrote down are reflected in the birthchart.

More recent books on astrology also stress the link that it has with health and healing. Typical is Dylan Warren-Davies' *Astrology and Health: A Beginner's Guide* (1989). This book maintains that certain star signs and planets are associated with certain diseases and specific parts of the body and observable 'elements'; for instance, the Air Element represents mental processes and mental health. To be sure, this is not a new development since the link with health goes back to the ancient Egyptians. However, it is now given a far greater emphasis and contemporary underpinning. There are also books that deal with another major interest in recent years, hereditary concerns (Peel 1994). The felt need to find out who our ancestors were and how their lives affect us has given way to an interest in assembling family 'trees'. Astrology can help in this endeavour. At the bottom end of the market there are also popular books such as *Sun Signs and Horoscopes*, which take up the broad theme of astrology in enhancing human happiness. Hence, astrology can help with choosing holidays, money, careers, the home, mate selection, and even 'chatting up other star signs' makes compulsive reading for some (King 1993).

Astrology may typify a great deal of the extent and depth of the following of occultist practices. The proportion of the USA population believing in astrology seems to be somewhere between 15 per cent (Gallop & Castelli 1989, 75–6) and 25 per cent (Greil & Robbins 1994, 16). Similar evidence has been produced by a Canadian survey, which found that about 35 per cent of respondents believed in astrology and 75 per cent consulted a horoscope at least occasionally. However, while some people may be committed to astrology to the extent that they could be said to comprise a cultist movement, the great majority of those expressing interest do not embrace it as a central aspect of their lifestyle (Feher 1994). In addition, while a number of elements of common religion, for example herbalism, are kept alive by distinct rural subcultural groups or ethnic groups, it has been discovered that astrology is more prominent in urban, rather than rural contexts (Fischler 1974, 287). In terms of social background, perhaps the most important variable when it comes to astrology is that of age. One study found that although the young were more likely to know more about the subject and be interested in it, a higher percentage of older persons were actually committed (Wuthnow 1976).

Divination

Astrology may be interpreted as a form of divination if it is primarily comprehended in terms of seeking to understand the spiritual patterns that underlie life and in discerning future events. It is by no means alone in such an enterprise since numerous other ancient arts related to divination have gained a popularity and today often include hitherto almost lost practices as explored in such volumes as *The Complete Guide to Coffee Grounds and Tea Leaf Reading* (Zed 1997). Besides these peripheral activities are those occultist forms which are more widely practised and include tarot, dowsing, and numerology.

Tarot

The 78 cards of the tarot have been used in different forms for a good 600 years in Europe and as a card game it was first played by the Italian nobility. Over the centuries, the cards have come to stand for allegories of moral teaching and philosophy, coded systems for magic and esoteric wisdom, and gateways for meditation. Most importantly, however, since the eighteenth-century the tarot has come to be used as a form of divination and the quest for supernatural knowledge of the past, present, and future. Its significance is that it works with pictures rather than with words and it is the pictures which are particularly evocative, mysterious, and suggestive of whole worlds of meaning.

There are various forms of illustrated tarot cards. Some depict Celtic themes or are identified as, for example, Merlin Tarot or Norse Tarot, while there are those used by particular esoteric groups such as the Servants of the Light. Perhaps the most popular, however, are the major and minor Arcanas variations which have fully illustrated pictures that give a clear indication of their meaning. Whatever their precise form, a new deck of cards has to be 'energized', which usually involves asking for a blessing of the cards so that they will bring peace and healing for those who seek help and protection. They are shuffled and dealt off the top of the pack or, alternatively, among other ways of distribution, half the pack is cut and discarded. The cards are frequently 'spread' or laid out to amplify their meaning. In doing so, tarot use can be extraordinarily complex.

The scenes depicted on the tarot cards include popes and jugglers, hermits and fools, alongside kings and queens. Some portray the Last Judgement and are derived from Christian eschatology, while Satan also makes an appearance. According to practitioners, the symbols and colours of the tarot cards are being read by the unconscious. Tarot is believed to help individuals understand the importance of symbols in everyday life. The full moon warns of mysterious happenings. The sun promises hope and joy. Other cards represent allegorical scenes, the meanings of which are more obscure and sometimes almost lost over the centuries. The cards have taken on the meaning of a story, that of the soul's journey, from birth through the various trials and challenges of life, and finally to death and perhaps resurrection. Interwoven with this narrative are found threads of initiation and mystic enlightenment.

Dowsing

The ability to dowse is believed by practitioners to be a natural talent and akin to developing a basic intuition. The tools used, frequently a pendulum, and 'L' or 'Y' rods, are based on a binary readout of 'yes' or 'no' answers to questions posed by the practitioner. L rods are generally used for water divining and are anticipated to respond to the question 'is there any water here?' The search proceeds to more specific questions, which also solicit a yes or no response, for example, 'is there a water pipe beneath this lawn?'

In dowsing an image is conjured up in the mind of the dowser. Hence, when looking for water, perhaps an image of an underground stream will be evoked. The L rod is held in the hands, as if it is two pistols, bent at right angles. On discovering water, it is expected to open outwards. The Y rod is a more traditional instrument and is usually in the form of a forked stick, although modern variants are available. In the search for water, and practically anything else, the rod is expected to move up and down accordingly. A pendulum may also be used for dowsing and is believed to operate in various ways, including turning clockwise or counter-clockwise when it is properly 'tuned' to the dowser's vibrational patterns.

Practitioners of dowsing today tend to play down mystical interpretations of what is an ancient art, although it is still seen as tapping a conscious source of energy. Now they are more likely to advance its 'scientific criteria'. As two authors on the subject put it:

> As you set out to master the preliminary stages of dowsing, think of your brain as being part of a computer, perhaps a supercomputer. The dowsing that you do with the standard dowsing tools is also essentially an on-off process.
>
> (Ross & Wright 1990, 11)

The simple example given above does little justice to the complexities of dowsing, which appears to have no limits in divining capacities. Hence, dowsing may be used for healing, map reading, and even spiritualism. Organized practitioners, such as the American Society of Dowsers, are taught preliminary stages and then four advanced stages after which certificates can be awarded. Like other occult activities, then, dowsing has become increasingly professionalized in order to give it a greater respectability.

Numerology

As with astrology, numerology is believed to make it possible to predict trends which will influence the future. Those who take the art seriously advance it as an earnest science. One of the earliest accounted instances of numerology being used comes from around 10,000 years ago, and later there are accounts from the ancient Babylonians and Egyptians. It is, however, mainly to the Greeks and Hebrews that contemporary numerology traces its roots and first appears to be an attempt to give numbers a spiritual and mystical significance.

Pythagoras, the Greek mathematician, astrologer, and philosopher, is recorded as saying that numbers are the basics of all nature. He held that everything could be reduced to mathematical terms, and if expressed as a numerical value, the universe would be better understood. Besides this Greek influence, the Hebrews, using the Cabbala, formed a different system, but both ultimately translate letters into numbers. Currently, there are several numerological systems, although many opt for the Cabbalistic form. In all of these expressions, different numbers are held to have specific significance. For example, the number 9 is believed to be the number of eternity and, according to some, appeared over and over again in the life of the late John Lennon. He was born on that day of the month, lived at addresses with the number 9 featuring prominently, met Yoko Ono on that day of the month, and died on that date. Such numbers are also supposed to reveal various aspects of an individual's life, including personality traits. Numerology, however, is far more complicated that this short appraisal suggests. Much of it is concerned with adding and multiplying significant numbers to reveal likely outcomes in the future. Numbers also have relevance for star signs. Thus, for example, 9 is the number associated with Scorpio.

Today, like related aspects of the occult, books on numerology abound. As with other specialisms, the art is given a unique interpretation to appeal to a contemporary clientele. While some universal themes may be explored, such as the numerical significance of a name, others are directed to very modern concerns. Hence, the book *Numerology For Beginners* (Arcarti 1998) relates itself to the importance of numbers in choosing a partner, moving house, changing job, or starting a business. How this works out in practical terms, to provide an illustration, is that when moving house one is reminded to be aware that towns and places can be converted into numbers and could be calculated to be a fortuitous omen or otherwise.

Palmistry

The practice of hand analysis is thousands of years old. What is more popularly and specifically known as palmistry is but one element of it that has come to be associated with magic, witchcraft, and frequently dishonesty. However, those who claim to be earnest professional practitioners distance themselves from notoriety and also claim to take into account the entirety of the hand – its overall shape, including the fingers, nails, and joints, because individually and collectively they are surmised as saying something about one's personality and disposition. Together with the shape and size of the palm and the lines marked on it the hand indicates habits, actions, and past, present, and future events. There are Heart Lines and Head Lines and (in addition to the significance of the back of the hand) fingers, thumbs, and fingerprints. These all denote different aspects of human nature and experience. There is the Line of Faith, which is said to be relevant to life expectancy and other future influences. Hands also indicate something about human relationships of the past and anticipated future. They can reveal how an existing or potential love affair is likely to develop. Children or potential children are also shown on the lines of the palm.

Modern practitioners, now claiming a growing popularity for their art, seek a greater respectability, and the tone of their writings is that of a pseudo-science. Typical is Criscuolo and Crisp's *The Hand Book: The Complete Guide to Reading Hands* (1994), which suggests, for example, that mental activity can now be observed in the hands, or the claim that left-handed and right-handed people are 'wired' differently. Much of the literature points out that the art of hand reading was used in civilizations such as China as a means of psychology and health counselling; it later became a superstitious practice more related to palmistry. It is viewed as an ancient and lost practice. Thus modern practitioners attempt to separate themselves from the more recent intuitive fortune-teller. Many stress differences between palmistry and hand analysis. The latter is said to seek an understanding of the emotional, mental, and physical breakdown of the person's character and energy using the hand as an indicator. We are told that it does not attempt to tell the future but sees individuals facing random variables in their life with personal strengths and weaknesses, skills and disabilities. Through understanding one's attributes, more enlightened choices and reactions can be made.

Various aspects of hand reading have always been concerned with health. The hands, particularly the Line of Life, can apparently show when one's health is below par before an actual illness takes hold and manifests in the rest of the body, thus allowing preventative measures to be taken. Besides this emphasis, contemporary hand reading also accentuates numerous contemporary concerns. Much weight is given to the uniqueness of every individual and the fact that this is mirrored in the hand. Such an emphasis is increasingly orientated towards popular themes typically related to potential worldly success, predicting a fruitful career, and fulfilling a variety of ambitions.

Spiritualism

Spiritualism, in one form or another, is as old as human civilization. However, in its present form it emerged as something of a craze in the USA in the mid-nineteenth-century following a story associated with the case of the Fox sisters and their experience of restless spirits in their house in New York State. Their spiritualist endeavours to rid themselves of these unwanted manifestations made national news in the press. The methods they used in contacting the spirit world spread across the USA to England and other European countries. The main tenet of the spiritualism that they developed was that the soul survives physical death and lives on eternally. Moreover, it can be communicated with through the help of spiritual guides. So influential was their work that in very little time spiritualist churches were established and professional mediums emerged in the USA and across Europe.

Today, spiritualist churches often offer services similar to those held in non-conformist churches, in that they are quite informal, and include hymns and prayers. The obvious difference is that every service also includes a demonstration of mediumship, commonly called clairvoyance, at which the medium passes on short 'messages' from spirits of the deceased to members of the congregation. Churches also offer other activities such as lectures, discussion groups, and what are called development circles, which are orientated towards the training of mediums. Increasingly, spiritualist churches are holding healing sessions that are also extended to people's pets. Not all mediums work within the spiritualist movement, although the majority do. The more itinerant ones travel from church to church taking services and many give private sittings in their own home.

There is, in addition, a Christian spiritualist movement which looks at Jesus as the Greatest Master. Today, something of a renaissance is taking place in many spiritualist churches. In 1999, the Spiritualist National Union claimed 20,000 full members in Britain. This revival is also marked by the publication of popular books which call on everyone, not just a gifted minority, to develop their gifts of mediumship. This go-it-alone philosophy is extolled in such aptly named titles as *Contacting the Spiritual World: How to Develop Your Psychic Abilities and Stay in Touch With Loved Ones* (Williamson 1998).

Practices related to oriental occultism

In addition to those leading forms of occultism considered so far, there are a number of oriental practices that have also become more popular in the last few decades. Some have been known in the West for some time. Others, including Feng Shui, are comparatively newly discovered, even though they have been in existence for thousands of years.

I Ching

The I Ching is a three thousand year-old book originally put together in order to communicate with gods and spirits. It offers a way to deal with personal problems by keeping people in touch with the *Tao* or Way, the creative life that is known as the unconscious in the West. Put simply, it has been billed as a system orientated towards helping to 'find your way in life' (Karcher 2000, 7). The I Ching is a set of 64 divinatory figures, each made up of a name, a six-line graph, and a group of oracle phases. These figures are purported to act like mirrors for the unconscious forces shaping any personal problem or situation. Each is associated with events, objects, and direction, and each suggest a way forward in a person's life.

As a form of oracle, the I Ching is asked a question and the answer comes through what the conscious mind sees as chance, but is supposed to reach human spiritual, emotional, and psychological depths. In order to achieve this, six coloured marbles may be picked out of a basket, three coins thrown six times or, alternatively, the dividing and counting of 50 yarrow-stalks may be used. This 'chance' event lets a spirit involved in a personal problem circumvent human conscious control and pick one of the oracle's symbols to provide an answer. The I Ching uses these symbols to give a mirror of what is going on 'behind' the scenes in a person's life. The symbols of the *I* describe the way spirits are moving the imagination: they are the 'seeds' of events in the world. Hence, the *I* is connected with these spirits and invites a dialogue with the Tao.

Feng Shui

The aim of Feng Shui, 'the Art of Living in Harmony', is to enable individuals to find their ideal living environment and through this attain health, prosperity, and happiness. The first reports of its existence appeared just over a century ago from missionaries and consular officials in China. Those who practise Feng Shui boast that it amounts to the profoundest interpretation and observation of the relationship between man and nature. It is meant to alter people's understanding of the world in which they live, as well as radically affecting their lifestyle. It is aimed at improving a person's home environment, his or her relationship with others, and used to draw omens related to the future. The Chinese exponents of the art claim that where people live and how they allocate and arrange the rooms of their home can significantly influence the harmony of their lives and general welfare. By taking advantage of the 'life energy' called *Chi*, which flows everywhere, a person can affect the whole tenor of their well-being. Feng Shui is also concerned with the location of the home, for its position in a neighbourhood may be adversely affected by the 'bad influences' of *Sha*. The essential life-giving forces, on the other hand, can be channelled to the home by the position of adjacent buildings, roads, even hills and waterways. The appeal of this philosophy to a home-centred Western society is perhaps obvious, but it also has the attraction of being concerned with a person's broader well-being. As one of its Western exponents puts it:

> Most people are interested in how to succeed in life … and this is the type of advice in which modern Feng Shui specialises. It offers a code for regulating your life and a plan about where to live so that you can exploit your potential to the full. … I happen to believe that Feng Shui is important for several reasons. It can make where you live special or meaningful, which in turn helps to foster a bond between a person and a place. It gives you an incentive to make a house into a real home, because good living conditions contribute to good health and these can lead to happiness, person success and prosperity. … But what makes Feng Shui so fascinating is the fact that it has a mystical side as well as a practical side.
>
> (Waring 1997)

The social backgrounds of occult practitioners

Precisely who is involved in the broad range of occult activities that exists today, including those discussed above, has been a neglected area of concern with sociologists until relatively recently. In the mid-1970s, Hartman (1976) made the informed guess that every USA city with a population of 100,000 had various types of occult activity involving between 100 to 2,000 persons. Most of the major cities have frequent conventions attracting witches, astrologers, eastern mystics, palmists, serious magicians, spiritualists, parapsychologists, and even Satanists. Hartman found in her study that of those devoted to such beliefs and practices, only one third were affiliated to organized groups. Astrologers, about 9 per cent of this constituency, were the most organized. The majority, then, practised on their own outside official organizations. Nearly two thirds of the sample of her study of the range of occult practitioners were female, and were generally young. Over half were 35 and under. Of this sample, 80 per cent were of Northern and Central European extraction. 44 per cent claimed to believe strongly in God (although mostly not the Christian God), and only 1 per cent definitely did not.

Hartman's sample was hardly representative of the American population as far as educational and occupational background was concerned. Only 13 per cent apparently obtained less than a high school education, while 63 per cent had at least some college background. They also appeared to be notably upwardly mobile. Politically, they were non- or anti-authoritarian and not particularly interested in issues of crime, the protection of traditional morals, and the advancement of civil rights. They were, however, concerned with topics pertinent to the environment, quality of life, and interpersonal relationships. In embracing these interests, then, these individuals appeared to be pre-dating the more coherent themes of the New Age movement.

More recent research suggests that participants of pagan and occultist spiritualities display certain demographic features including age, gender, class, educational background, and ethnicity. Many studies have suggested that they tend to be part of the post-war generation of baby boomers, being born between 1945 and the mid-1960s (Adler 1986; Lynch 1977). However, a new generation of practitioners, aged between 16 and their mid-20s, may be emerging with an interest in these spiritualities through the New Age movement.

Most studies report slightly higher numbers of female than male participants. These range, at the high end, from Lynch (1977), who reports 72 per cent of females and 28 per cent of males, through to a more even ratio of about 50:50 in the studies of Jorgenson and Jorgensen (1982). The significance of social class is inconclusive. Participants in the USA and UK have been shown to be involved in a wide range of employment. McHugh and Swain (1999) found that occupations ranged from skilled workers, to the caring professions, through to the unemployed. Kirkpatrick *et al* (1986) found that pagans tended to be more highly educated than average (66 per cent had college degrees). Interestingly, 80 per cent of this sample, although well educated and in high status jobs, tended to be low earners. This suggests that status frustration might be the reason for becoming a pagan, although it is possible that some pagans work part-time in order to devote more of their lives to spiritual activities. Finally, research tends to suggest that pagans and occultists are overwhelmingly Caucasian in origin, with more of an ethnic mix in the USA than Europe. This might be attributable to a rehabilitation of some indigenous religions such as Santeria (Pavlino 1995), a cult that originated in Cuba among the slaves on the sugar plantations and spread to neighbouring islands and the USA, principally among blacks and Hispanics.

Summary

Many of the studies which consider who is involved in popular occultist activities conclude by suggesting that they should not be viewed as a fad but as a major, long-term trend in contemporary religion. Thirty years after Hartman's study, judging by the literature that is produced by the various occult specialisms, such fringe religion appears to becoming increasingly popular, although it is difficult to conclude to what extent such beliefs and practices can be found among the general population. Nonetheless, they remain important expressions of a hidden dimension of religion and spirituality, albeit increasingly given a practical and this-worldly application.

Further reading

Abercrombie, N., Baker, J., Brett, S. & Foster, J. (1970) 'Superstition and Religion: The God of the Gaps', in D. Martin & M. Hill (eds.), *Sociological Year-book of Religion in Britain*, **3**, London: SCM.

Berry, R. (1999) *Working With Dreams: How to Understand Your Dreams and Use Them For Personal and Creative Development*, London: How To Books.

Campbell, C. & McIver, S. (1987) 'Cultural Sources of Support for Contemporary Occultism', *Social Compass*, **34**, 41–60.

Hartman, P. (1976) 'Social Dimensions of Occult Participation', *British Journal of Sociology*, **27** (2), 199–213.

Peel, R. (1994) *Astrology and Heredity: The Threads of Life*, London: Blandford.

Sadleir, S. (1992) *The Spiritual Seeker's Guide: The Complete Source for Religions and Spiritual Groups in the World*, Costa Mesa, CA: Allwon.

Warren-Davis, D. (1989) *Astrology and Health: A Beginner's Guide*, London: Headway.

11 Human potential and healing movements

This chapter considers the topic of healing and explores the many different and complex ways in which it is addressed through various alternative religions. The theme is included not only because healing is apparently a preoccupation with current expressions of religiosity, but because it is often interpreted in a proactive way and links to the broader yet interconnected areas of life enhancement, human potential, and the attempt to construct the capacity for spiritual enrichment. This concern is by no means restricted to the more obvious realms of the NRMs and New Age. Beliefs and practices emphasizing health and healing, and philosophies of wholeness and naturalness, so long associated with alternative and counter-culture thinking, have found their way into mainstream religion. A measure of this is that some one in five Anglican churches in England now offer public healing services as part of the normal round of parish life. These services are by no means limited to 'the laying on of hands' to cure physical ailments. Many are directed towards dealing with a whole range of emotional and psychological problems which are addressed through numerous techniques of healing.

For many fringe religions, the popular attraction of health and healing may now be articulated through pre-existing beliefs and practices or, alternatively, the adoption of new ones. For others, healing and an emphasis on human potentialities are their core concern and indeed *raison d'être*. Many of these may be regarded as cultist forms of religion which, unlike others, are not in tension with society but are in line with its dominant values. Some may scarcely appear religious at all or may even deny that they are. Nonetheless, they often implicitly display a religiosity in that the preoccupation with health and healing takes on all-embracing holistic philosophies which dominate and provide meaning to a person's life even if they are this-worldly directed. In short, health, healing, and human potential are given 'religious' qualities.

The contemporary concern with health and healing

In today's more affluent society, health, not just healing, has become a central cultural value, one which has influenced numerous expressions of religiosity. Such a core value has been referred to by Crawford (1984) as 'Healthism'. This term suggests not only a near cultural obsession with health as a matter of being free from sickness, but has come to denote a positive and proactive attitude to health. This preoccupation is derived from a number of wide but overlapping social developments, namely, instrumental rationalism, consumerism, materialistic lifestyles, and the advance of medical science. Healthism represents a focus on optimum performance and efficiency in all aspects of life. It is linked to self-control, discipline, and self-denial. Indeed, there is so much cultural emphasis on health that it is now bordering on a form of religiosity – or even a form of fetishism.

The increasing popularity of teachings of healing and human potential in Western society, as reflected in the practices of many alternative religions, must also be understood with reference to taken-for-granted perceptions of the life course and the contemporary rational negotiation of the lifespan. For contemporary man, control of the environment and scientific progress through medical advance allows a confidence in fulfilling the natural lifespan, which limits the arbitrary and unpredictable aspects of human existence. Predictability and calculability allows the possibility of the individual thinking ahead to anticipate future choices and optional courses of action. In the setting of contemporary society, the altered self, throughout the life course, can be explored and constructed as part of a reflexive process of connecting personal and social change. Life becomes a series of events calculated to overcoming actual and potential risks. This assumes that events do not just take their course, but are under human control (Meyer 1987; Giddens 1991).

As we shall see, many of the alternative practices of today's religions emphasize a continued healing and improvement throughout the individual's life course. At the same time, this interest has a particular orientation. It is evident that while religious healing systems in the past were principally involved with physical healing, the primary concern now is with emotional and psychological restoration or improvement. This again reflects developments in the secular sphere where the link between human potential and self-improvement on the one hand, and psychological techniques on the other, is well established. In his book *The Triumph of the Therapeutic*, Reiff (1966) explored the peculiarly modern predilection for psychological explanations and cures for practically all human dilemmas. In turn, this provides evidence of the advance of medicalization which denotes the extension of the ideology of the medical profession, in particular, the thrust of the psychoanalytical industry that constructs the individual's condition in terms of the psychological, rather than social and environmental problems.

At one level there is much of significance in religion per se which lends itself to developing therapeutic techniques. Aspects of psychotherapy have frequently been found in the religious practices of pre-industrial societies, and there are strong similarities between indigenous forms of non-scientific and spiritual healing and psychotherapy (Torrey 1972). However, the latter-day interest in Western societies with all things therapeutic reflects the specifically cultural conviction that each person has a unique character and special potentialities in an individual-orientated society free from collective restraints and obligations. Much of this fulfils Durkheim's prediction at the beginning of the twentieth-century that the modern world would witness the 'cult of man' – an almost 'divine' recognition of human progress and what man was capable of (Durkheim 1915, 336). This is a prophecy which Westley (1978) believes has come true and is encapsulated in the contemporary human potential movement.

There is little doubt that the concern with health and healing in the West is focused on the *individual*. It is the individual who is treated and restored. There is far less emphasis on the effects of the wider natural and social environment, which may be the most important consideration in underlining the causes of ill health. Featherstone (1982) sees this development as partly a result of medicalization since it is the individual who is the subject and orientation of medical science. To be sure, healing among today's fringe religions comes in many forms. Most however, follow the contours of contemporary culture by concentrating on the individual's health, healing, and potential. The link between this focus on the health of the individual and today's religion therefore comes into stark relief: personal health and healing is congruent with the more privatized and instrumental forms of religion, which lends itself so well to enculturation and marketability.

Such forms of healing, with their emphasis on the emotions and psychological dimensions, have proved to be particularly popular with the middle-classes. Various explanations have been advanced as to why this is so. McGuire (1983), for instance, sees the general emphasis on healing as intrinsically linked to the middle-class cultural value of the success and self-advancement of the individual, alongside the belief that good health is ultimately a personal responsibility. She also speculates that the occupational roles of the middle-classes are a decisive factor in the popularity of emotional healing. The key consideration is occupational alienation. The appeal of emotional and indeed psychological healing reflects the internal contradiction of the structure of production in contemporary society where there is a considerable investment of the self, as well as the rationalized management of the body and emotions. According to McGuire, such developments precipitate problems of different appropriations of the self to different tasks and roles. This is exacerbated by the public-private dichotomy which highlights the discrepancies between the seemingly autonomous self in the private sphere and the controlled sphere in the bureaucratic structure of professional life.

Healing of mind, body, and spirit

For many of today's fringe religious groups that have taken on board themes of healing there is invariably a broader framework than merely the individual's physical and psychological well-being. Rather, to some extent at least, they are inheritors of the spiritual and mystical concerns of the counter-culture of the 1960s. Moreover, similar fashions are to be found much earlier than those of the 1960s and 1970s. To some degree, these were continuations and revivals of earlier ones or drew their inspirations from them, including Taoism and other varieties of Chinese philosophy, Japanese Zen Buddhism, paganism, magic, the occult, and meditation. Integral to many were one form or another of psychological, emotional, or spiritual healing.

Today, many of these counter-cultural themes are mixed with more mainline values. This is a theme developed by Beckford (1984), who argues that the variety of spiritual and therapeutic practices in the new religions may vary considerably, but the underlying concerns are the same. They observably focus on notions of growth at the level of the individual, culture, and spirituality. What he calls the New Religious Healing Movements (NRHMs) permit a confluence of religion and dimensions of healing explicit in enhancing personal 'wholeness' by inducing the image of an 'indivisible universe'. This allows the merging of spiritual growth and the Western cultural value of individual personal development and healing. According to Beckford, NRHMs develop concepts of the self in which it is desirable to construct a 'true' self through restoring a wholeness lacking in people's lives, bringing together spiritual and worldly needs. Religious subcultures, dominated by the theme of healing, generally focus on 'transformation', which involves the process of freely choosing personal development and growth. Human beings are perceived as moving towards a cosmic perfection within the context of an unfolding drama, and are frequently the recipients of the attention of supernatural forces or beings.

At the same time that many expressions of alternative religion have embraced themes of healing and potential, there is now the tendency of once secular human potential movements to become increasingly spiritual. There are positive aspects of wholeness expressed by numerous alternative healing and potential groups which have come to place a stress on spiritual considerations. In particular, 'health' and 'salvation' become practically synonymous with the perfection of the mind and body as well as the spirit. Some commentators like Heelas (1988) and McGuire (1983) have argued that the growth of the therapeutic in contemporary religion is not merely reduced to the social preoccupation with positive views of health, but display a concern with the search for 'meaning'. Heelas argues that while this search necessarily involves a quasi-religious quest, the psychoanalytical component especially tends to lend itself impressively to spiritual themes. Modern psychotherapy carries a concern with the perfection of self and the search for meaning which embraces a dialogue with 'the ultimate, the metaphysical, the complete' (Heelas 1988, 69–70).

Healing in the new religions

Today's NRMs, particularly in the form of client and audience cults, have catered for the complex requirements of individuals. Some focus on the demands and problems of living in the modern world. Others satisfy the needs of people to create more dynamically a change in their self-image and self-perception. Numerous NRMs and many popular forms of religiosity allow aspects of the self to be chosen, shaped, and transformed, especially through healing and therapeutic techniques. In doing so they reflect wider social developments and the growing notion that the emotions and the body are not given, but are reflexively malleable parts of one's identity (Dreitzel 1981). In short, many alternative religions can transform life experiences through religious symbols and beliefs in dealing with felt deprivations and in fulfilling aspirations (Strauss 1976).

In a discussion of world-affirming NRMs, Wallis (1984) points out that one of their principal teachings involves the attempt to unlock spiritual powers dormant in the individual, which can be used for his or her potential by way of personal growth and healing. This appears to have been taken to its furthest conclusions by New Age groups, which tend to associate themselves with optimistic philosophies about the body, health, and nature. The human frame is not viewed as essentially degenerate, nor inevitably subject to the natural impulses which lower man. For many strands of the New Age, it is within the body itself that the latent cure lies, especially when mind, body, and spirit are aligned with one another in attempting to reach the higher self. This gives way to particular forms of healing such as 'channelling' which, while often operating like a form of spiritualism (involving external voices of authority from the spiritual realm), can refer to the act of receiving wisdom from one's own inner self regarding the source of sickness, however that is defined. Another variety is 'quantum healing', which is supposed to reduce blockages and activate the immune system, thus freeing the mind, body, and spirit to heal itself.

Heelas (1996, 84) sees such healing as radically detraditionalized, anti-authoritarian, and informed by epistemological individualism. In short, it challenges orthodox forms of medicine while the healing process tends to be highly subjective. However, as he points out, healing means more than the general sense of curing disease and sickness. It also includes healing the earth, healing the damages inflicted by industrial capitalism, restoring creativity, healing the person in a social and cultural context, and past life healing. Many of these expressions of healing attribute a key role to nature, with its supposed vital forces and energies which lie behind healing, renewal, and recovery.

For the New Age movement, the spiritual realm is intrinsically related to healing. Much stress is on the body's power to heal itself but focuses on the belief that this is enhanced on contact with the spiritual. This emphasis tends to undermine the authority of the healer, at least compared to that of the doctor in the realm of professional medicine. Moreover, while some healers may channel spiritual energies of their own or from the spiritual plain, the function of many is to release 'blockages' and to enhance self-healing. This essentially spiritual element of New Age healing draws heavily on eastern or other non-European spiritual traditions and most could be described as rejecting the dualistic mind-body distinction which underlies much Western medical thinking. At the same time that healing activities are primarily focused on the spiritual, guided meditations often contain references to material rewards, prosperity, and abundance, and all this is often interpreted in some New Age circles as related to 'wholeness'.

Healing beliefs and techniques in the New Age are extremely diverse. A few may be considered here. One is crystal healing which, in fact, is a very ancient form of therapy. It advances the use of crystals and gems to promote and restore a harmonious, balanced, and therefore healthy state of being. It works on the principle that when the mind, body, and spirit of the person are in equilibrium then complete wholeness can be achieved. The crystals are said to have hidden mystical healing energies but quite what this amounts to is open to interpretation. Some practitioners regard them as providing physical patterns of perfection that can inspire individuals to reach their own harmony and balance. Alternatively, their power might be derived from the healing vibrations of colour or the belief that by holding them crystals are able to impart tiny amounts of mineral composition to bring balance and health. Other practitioners stress the need to channel 'light' through crystals and thus bring healing vibrations. Although healing is generated from within, for New Age healing the utilization of internal healing is stimulated by external forces, or what is often termed 'Universal Energy'. Crystals are one way of tapping this. Candles, images, fragrances, and colour are others.

As with rival methods used in the modern-day New Age movement, the stress is on providing a means of empowering the patient and allowing his/her natural internal systems of healing to be 'switched on' so that the healing process begins within the individual. This may not be a conscious decision, since the body, mind, or spirit can be driving the patient, but it is s/he who actually undertakes the first healing process. Sickness is often perceived as a result of subjecting the mind, body, and spirit to such harmful things as stress, poor diet, and artificial chemicals. This ignorance is also extended to lack of knowledge of the person's own healing powers which must be unlocked. Those crystals frequently used include obsidian, amber, clear quartz, fluorite and haematite. They are said to contain 'power' and energy that can be utilized. After use they are generally 'cleansed'.

Popular books such as *Teach Yourself Crystal Healing* (Croxon 2000) encourage people to practise alone and provide a detailed programme on how to proceed, including utilizing spiritual guides and meditation. However, although people are encouraged to practise crystal healing themselves, it is often conducted with a professional practitioner. The role of the latter is to ask the nature of the complaint, to require the patient to lie down, and encourage a simple relaxation exercise. Through vision, touch, or a pendulum, the patient's personal energy is 'read'. The therapist will then start to place crystals on and around the client, depending on what they consider is required, what the patient has said, the result of energy scans, plus intuition. The patient is encouraged to talk about personal problems and, thereafter, is invited to visit parts of their body or mind that acquire healing. This is normally achieved with a combination of crystals and visualization.

A second form of New Age healing is through the interpretation of dreams. This is, of course, by no means limited to the movement. However, New Age literature does tend to put a great deal of emphasis on interpretation as linked to healing and human potential. Adherents are encouraged to explore their own dreams in such titles as *Working With Dreams: How to Understand Your Dreams and Use Them For Personal and Creative Development* (Berry 1999). The interpretation of dreams has long been linked with ancient systems of shamanism and indeed today has psychoanalytical validity. For the New Age, dreams provide an opportunity to examine the emotions, find spiritual truths, allow visualization, project the self, identify hidden conflict, give insights into relationships and health problems or potential health problems, and help individuals to be more creative.

Finally, by way of illustration, there is the New Age utilization of hypnosis. Although, again, with an application to spiritualism alongside a certain amount of scientific validity, hypnosis, as brought to bear by the New Age, can be applied to beliefs and practices such as reincarnation, karma, and astral travelling. Self-induced hypnosis and the experience of various metaphysical approaches are encouraged for past life and future life progression, superconscious mind taps, out of body experiences, soul plane travelling, ascension techniques, and encountering angels.

These are just a few examples indicative of a range of techniques available to the New Age. However, healing techniques turn up in numerous expressions of alternative religiosity. UFO cults are a good example, and their concern with healing is perhaps not too surprising given their emphasis on human evolution and spiritual growth. The Aetherius Society, which has no objection to being called New Age, teaches and practises spiritual healing, alternative medicine, yoga, and dowsing. Healing for the Society means the transfer of *prana*, the Universal Life Force, from the healer to the patient. This energy, which flows freely throughout the universe, when channelled into a person suffering from a disease, can bring about a state of balance within that person. According to Aetherius thinking, anyone can heal: it is not a special gift, but the birthright of every human being.

Christian healing

Christians throughout the ages have believed in the intervention of God to heal, or at least that they have the permission to petition him with prayers for healing. At times, the practice has been normative in the life of the Christian Church, but at other periods it has existed on the Church's periphery. Today, many Christian groups throughout the world have come to endorse the importance of the healing ministry, albeit in an enormous diversity of techniques. Nonetheless, some have made the theme of healing central to their beliefs and practices. Two examples considered here are Christian Science, with its origins in the nineteenth-century, and the more recent neo-Pentecostal movement.

Christian Science

Although Christian Science tends to regard itself as a denomination, in many respects it is very different from orthodox Christianity, not least because of its emphasis on spiritual healing and its extra-scriptural literature which renders it sect-like in nature. The movement was founded by Mary Baker Eddy (1821–1910). Eddy was influenced by Phineas Parkhurst Quimby – an established hypnotist and faith healer. In 1882, Quimby, who taught that all disease and illness are caused by wrong thinking on the part of the sufferer, healed Eddy of a crippling spinal disease. Eddy transformed Quimby's idea of healing powers originating in correct thinking to the power of God. Inspired by biblical references to Christ's healing, Eddy claimed to have discovered Christian Science, or the Divine Laws of Life, Truth, and Love. She studied the bible for a further three years and formulated her doctrines, before teaching it to others. In 1857, she published the first edition of *Science and Health, With Key to the Scriptures*, which Christian Scientists read alongside the bible in their Sunday services.

Eddy opened the Massachusetts Metaphysical College in Boston, where she taught around 4,000 students from 1881 to 1889. Over the following few years her churches multiplied rapidly. However, even before this time some individuals broke away from the church and began to establish their own splinter groups. Perhaps the most significant was that of Emma Curtis Hopkins, Charles and Myrtle Fillmore, and Earnest Holmes, who founded the New Thought movement that combined the ideas of Quimby and Eddy.

Christian Science has a number of key teachings, most of which seem to be in line with mainstream Christianity. The stated tenets of the church to be found in Eddy's *Science and Health* claim a sole biblical inspiration as the guide to everlasting life, the atonement, and God's forgiveness of sin. This is all related to the broader assertion that the teachings mark a return to original Christianity and the discovery of lost 'truths'. However, the movement does not believe that it has a monopoly of the core teachings of the faith: true Christians may be found in other churches as well.

What distinguishes Christian Science from mainstream Christianity is not only a tendency to play down the divinity of Christ and denial of the Holy Spirit as a person in the Godhead, but the emphasis on healing. Moreover, while other strands of the Christian Church have such an emphasis, there is an essential difference. Christian Scientists maintain that healing is accomplished not by asking God to heal someone of illness, but in denying that the sickness exists in the first place. Sickness, of whatever kind, is an illusion. To deny it is to heal it. In addition, the church has a wider agenda of healing and it is also given to mean the healing of relationships, social injustice, psychological problems, and intellectual limitations. There is a general emphasis on health and morality. Like Mormons, strict members refrain from smoking, and from drinking tea and coffee. Although healing is of increasing attraction in the spiritual marketplace, Christian Science has not experienced a reversal of fortunes and its once impressive membership continues to dwindle, from one million members in 1910 to some 120,000 today.

Neo-Pentecostal healing

At the beginning of the twentieth-century, classical Pentecostalism placed a great deal of stress on 'divine healing'. For the early Pentecostals, the concern with healing was not only to 'prove' the existence of God in order to win converts and the rediscovery of the charismata, but to offer its impoverished followers an opportunity for healing in the absence of medical services. For contemporary Pentecostals, healing is now frequently taken in various trajectories. From a relatively early stage of neo-Pentecostalism there appeared to be similarities with the secular human potential movement, albeit transformed within spiritual idioms in some ways not dissimilar and in others radically different from other new religions. By the late 1970s, the appeal of human potential strategies, accompanied by unique forms of psychotherapy, had become diffused throughout the movement and seemed to be one of the principal reasons why the middle-classes were attracted into the Pentecostal fold (Logan 1975, 39). It is clear, however, that healing among Pentecostal groups preceded the recent cultural popularity of alternative medicines and therapies. Neither have such themes been limited to the charismatic wing of the Christian Church. Indeed, there has arisen a whole new generation of evangelicals who have come to endorse the ethic of self-improvement and self-fulfilment in terms of a spiritual quest. Nonetheless, it is neo-Pentecostalism which has healing as a core theme and has developed numerous healing techniques.

There are different aspects of neo-Pentecostal healing when compared with other forms such as that offered by the New Age. Doctrines of sin outline man's fundamental condition and the source of his failure to reach spiritual and worldly potential. Another difference regarding the neo-Pentecostals is their understanding of the nature of transforming healing power. The power is seen as transcendental and exterior to the individual. Believers channel the divine source of that power and are merely the vessel of the Holy Spirit. The 'gifts of the Spirit' are conductive to empowerment, but the origins of that power are *outside* the individual. Put another way, the principal means by which the new self is discovered is through the gifts of the Spirit. These gifts are not 'natural' but bestowed upon the 'born-again' believer, who is enhanced with divine power.

The neo-Pentecostal movement has developed teachings of holism that suggest a much more positive attitude towards this world than that held by earlier evangelical groups. There is an emphasis on the improvement of mind, emotions, and body, as well as the spirit, in such a way that there appears to be practically no boundaries between them. Death may mark the transition towards ultimate perfection, but there seems no limit towards that growth and few restrictions as to what might be healed in the here and now. In this respect, along with other alternative religions, neo-Pentecostals place a great deal of emphasis on emotional healing. There are numerous techniques. However, they tend to focus on themes related to relationships with others and past negative experiences and memories. They may also deal with addictions, mental problems such as depression, and phobias. Thus, what appears to be a spiritualization of secular therapy so alienating to classical Pentecostals, has now become an integral part of church life for most modern Pentecostals.

In today's Pentecostalism there is constant reference not just to a spiritual rebirth, but to the 'empowerment' of the Holy Spirit as vital to the process of spiritual growth. Those such as the healing evangelist, the late John Wimber, have frequently organized conferences around the theme of 'healing the saints'. This involves encouraging Christians to experience the whole spectrum of spiritual gifts, including the receiving and transmission of divine healing. There is an emphasis on individual fulfilment, self-worth, and personal growth through developing natural and spiritual abilities and talents.

A popular technique exploited by charismatic Christians is 'prayer counselling' whereby, in a one-to-one healing session, the patient's emotional problems are revealed to the counsellor by the Holy Spirit through 'words of knowledge' or 'pictures' in the mind. The Holy Spirit thus exposes damaging current relationships or emotional traumas of the past, including emotional wounds inflicted by others involving sexual abuse and the repercussions of personal sin. These are also recognized as being manifested in physical complaints of many different kinds. Alternatively, there is the 'Personal Prophetic Ministry', which appears to be a form of shamanism or divination and deals with the way forward for individual Christians at crucial junctures of their lives. Through this kind of counselling, the Holy Spirit is expected to point the way forward when a set of alternatives are presented.

Techniques of visualization are common practice among charismatics. Critics of the movement, particularly within the Church, have drawn parallels with the techniques of the New Age. Certainly, some techniques do seem to be similar despite their Christian gloss. Much has been culled from the work of the Christian healer, Ruth Carter Stapleton, and involves the replacing of negative memories by reconstructing them in a positive way. Those being counselled are encouraged to 'take Jesus back', by visualizing him, to confront past painful emotional experiences. He is seen as touching, healing, and restoring. In some cases, the believer is taken back into the womb, perhaps to deal with feelings of rejection by the mother.

One of the more controversial aspects of Pentecostal healing is what has become known as 'deliverance'. It is not exclusively concerned with emotional and psychological problems, although much of it is (Hunt 1998). It reflects the considerable stress neo-Pentecostals put on the powers of the demonic and the related theme of 'spiritual warfare' with the forces of darkness. Warfare is conducted at different levels. In regard to healing, it is expressed through deliverance, which can be seen as a form of exorcism for Christian believers and amounts to a type of 'inner' healing. While Christians cannot be 'possessed', they can be 'oppressed' by demons that inflict and enforce a whole range of emotional and psychological maladies or sinful habits that are difficult to break. It can also relate to ancestral curses – the demonic repercussions of the activities of generations past – and even to involvement in the occult and New Age. These demonic ailments must be 'cast out' in order to obtain spiritual cleansing and development. This is frequently achieved by 'naming the spirit' as a kind of metaphor for physical illnesses or emotional problems – a practice related to exorcism that is not unknown in other religions across the world. Today, charismatic Christians can enrol on courses to have demons eradicated or learn how to conduct deliverance. Special conferences are sometimes run by healing organizations such as Ellel Ministries, which has several healing centres in Britain, Canada, and elsewhere.

The Faith movement

Success-orientated North America has proved an especially fertile field for different programmes of self-improvement because of its cultural emphasis on wealth and success. Numerous strategies have focused on personal awareness, confidence awaking, and awakening potential. Some have developed a spiritual element. One of the most common themes related to human potential, personal growth, and spiritual life is that of positive thinking. It is by no means a new synthesis and many of its roots can be traced back to the nineteenth-century.

Perhaps of greatest significance in schools of positive thinking have been the writings of Norman Vincent Peale. Peale's legacy was his insistence that good health can only be achieved by permanently banishing self-defeating attitudes. He offered what has been described as 'a guide for confident living' (Yinger 1967, 99). His influence was found primarily among the urban middle classes who were 'tuned' to his message by their cultural orientations. The appeal was to those who felt inferior and strove for material success, and where positive thinking was believed to bring the reduction of fear and feelings of inferiority. Peale taught that all that was needed was contact with God, so that his power could be channelled into the individual. Fear breaks that contact, but faith restores it: 'If you will utilize the principals of faith … you too, can solve the difficult problems of your personality. You too can really learn to live' (Peale 1940, 1).

The distinctive health and wealth gospel of the Faith movement has been explored briefly in Chapter 4. It has various origins. While many of its teachings are rooted in Pentecostalism, others are related to various schools of positive thinking. Some of its roots can be found in the nineteenth-century writings of Ralph Waldo Emerson and the Unity School of Christianity, as well as the writings of Phineas Parkhurst Quimby. In turn, these men were inspired by the work of Norman Peale. Emerson stressed the power of positive thinking not just as a form of assertive consciousness, but by entertaining metaphysical notions of affecting reality, which makes him a forerunner of the Faith movement. Quimby, the inspiration for the New Thought movement, popularized the notion that sickness and suffering ultimately have their origins in 'correct thinking' (Quimby 1969). His followers (including Warren Felt Evans 1817–89) maintained that man could create his own reality through the confession of faith.

Arguably, the Faith movement has filled the gap left by Christian Science, with similar but perhaps more effective teachings related to healing. While, unlike Christian Science, the Faith ministries do not deny the reality of sickness, Faith teachings and practices are underpinned by the assertion that there is a physical and spiritual law – each governing the different spheres of existence. The spiritual laws are useless without the 'force of faith'. Faith is a spiritual energy which makes the laws of the spiritual world function in that positive power (God) is 'activated' and the negative is overcome. The Faith ministries commonly use such terms as 'victory' or 'overcoming' to refer to breaking through the physical and material limitations of this world by utilizing faith or 'positive confession'. This seems to embrace a law of metaphysical causation in that what is spoken in faith becomes a material reality, whether health, wealth, or anything else the Christian believer desires. Arguably this brings the movement close to some of the practices of the new religions and New Age. It may be perceived as a form of magic and is also evident in the Faith ministry's use of visualization. In respect of the core concerns of health and wealth, some exponents of the gospel call upon Christians to imagine money in their bank accounts or to visualize the healthy restoration of sick parts of the body.

Programmes of self-improvement

From the mid-twentieth-century, positive thinking was transformed into a vast range of secular psychologically based self-improvement movements. Proliferating since the 1970s have been those such as Gestalt training, psychosynthesis, rebirthing, and biofeedback, all of which have mixed psychological insights with strategies of positive thinking. Most are largely beyond our consideration here. However, those that display a spiritual element can be briefly overviewed.

Scientology

Scientology is probably the most well known, widespread, and wealthy of all the personal development organizations which focus on positive thinking and human potential and, arguably, it is the most controversial. The stated aim of Scientology is to create 'a civilization without insanity, without criminals and without war, where the able can prosper and honest beings can have rights, and where man is free to rise to greater heights' (*The Church of Scientology: 40th Anniversary*, 1994, 54).

Bruce (1996a, 179) regards Scientology, like Transcendental Meditation and Rajneeshism, as a good example of a world-affirming new religion on several counts. It does not require renunciation of the world. The great evil for the organization is that more people are not able to enjoy the good things of life because their abilities remain hidden or constrained. The movement offers techniques that will free the inner self and its potential. There is a strong internal circle of practitioners who work for the movement and might be described as followers, although most people participate as customers. Scientology does not demand much by way of change of religious belief, despite the claim to be a 'church', and the organization operates more like a corporate commercial enterprise than a religious institution. Members spend occasional weekends at conferences and then return to their conventional lives. Finally, Scientology organizes advertising and employs marketing techniques to promote services.

The founder of scientology, L. Ron Hubbard, first presented his thoughts on what he called 'Dianetics' through an article in *Astounding Science Fiction*. Hubbard believed that the human mind is a very sophisticated computer. Operating perfectly, it would have complete recall of all sense impressions and vastly improved mental agility. This state Hubbard called 'Clear'. His analogy to Clear was that of a mechanical calculating machine that had a number of keys stuck down so that all its calculations went wrong. Hubbard believed that the source of this malfunction was the mind's natural desire to avoid pain. Painful experiences in the past are stored in our subconscious as 'engrams' and prevent full cognitive functioning.

The book *Dianetics* claims that someone who has reached Clear will have better health, eyesight, and hearing, will be able to deal with any psychosomatic illness, and have greatly increased intelligence. The individual thus becomes an optimum functioning human being. To reach Clear normally takes several hundred hours of auditing, which can prove to be very expensive. It is necessary for the auditor to check over the next few months that there are no new engrams in the reactive mind. The Church of Scientology claims that by 1995 over 45,000 people had reached Clear.

The various techniques of Dianetics were designed to discover the origins of engrams and, by encouraging the patient to confront them, clear them away until the mind is free to function at full capacity. To add scientific credibility to what sounded like a diluted version of Freud's theory of the subconscious, Hubbard designed a machine. The 'E' (for engram) Meter is a crude form of lie detector. Holding a tin can wired to a dial, which can be seen only by the Dianetics counsellor, the client is questioned until a swing on the needle suggests that a sensitive topic has been revealed and then probed for evidence of engrams.

The engram may be triggered by association of events and objects. Although the conscious mind will eventually forget an incident, the reactive mind stores every detail. According to Hubbard, some of the most powerful engrams are constructed while still in the womb. The unborn child hears the angry words of parents caught up in marital disputes or perhaps talk of abortion. Through 'editing', engrams may be deleted. The auditor asks the client questions, leading him or her back to the original incident which caused the engram. Once it is identified, its power is dissipated.

The insistence on the stricter adherence to Dianetics largely came through the broad policy of Hubbard. Initially, Dianetics was merely one psychotherapeutic technique among many. It was one that people would dabble in at the same time as they subscribed to others. The movement was also transitory. People joined and, whether as satisfied or dissatisfied customers, moved on. Hubbard wished to ensure their loyalty. At the same time, he became unhappy about his lack of control over the organization. He was especially concerned about how practitioners at the local level modified some of his original techniques.

Hubbard's response was to claim new revelations and insights, which he used to change Dianetics into the sectarian religion of Scientology. The doctrines and practices were codified and presented as a series of stages in a coherent and lengthy programme structure for consumers. Part of Hubbard's new revelation was a belief in rebirth. After completing the first round of courses and eliminating all engrams, there was then the matter of dealing with those of previous lives, until the individual became an 'operating thetan' (an expression of the soul or life energy in the physical universe). An additional advantage of the staged programme was that it could be used to reinforce consumer commitment. Members were given large discounts on their own expensive courses if they recruited and trained others.

There have been a number of criticisms aimed at Scientology. Some have suggested that Hubbard transformed Dianetics, his original psychotherapeutic system, into the Church of Scientology because of the tax advantages of being a religion. Moreover, critics claim that the behaviour of senior Scientologists over the last few decades has been both illegal and immoral. The church says that it has dealt with these difficulties. Many former Scientologists, who have left for various reasons, still believe in the efficacy of Dianetics. Like all forms of psychotherapy, counselling, and confession, it clearly works to some extent and a number of obvious benefits are observable, at the very least, by unburdening guilt and emotional problems.

An alternative to Scientology is the Neuro-Linguistic Programme (NLP), although like others overviewed below it has more of an implied religiosity. It is a technique rather than an organized religion and is used by several different human potential movements. NLP is seen by its advocates as the art and science of personal excellence and a study of the way that people excel in any given field. It was developed in the mid-1970s by John Grinder, a Professor of Linguistics at the University of California, and Richard Bandler, a psychology student at the same institution, with further input from various others. 'Neuro' is based on the assumption that our experiences and behaviour stem from the neurological processes of our senses and thoughts. 'Linguistic' refers to the fact that we use language to think logically and to communicate with others. 'Programming' refers to the way that people order and structure ideas and actions to produce results.

NLP amounts to an innovating way of looking at how people think, communicate, and behave. It examines how they learn, and teaches more efficient ways of learning, and how to improve the memory. Moreover, it shows how very often our reactions to events reinforce negativity, and explores ways in which they can be made positive. NLP thus teaches how to communicate effectively and how to understand and interpret the signals from other people. More broadly, it instructs people to question what they do and what they believe. The courses run tend to aim at executives and career-minded people. Many major companies, banks, and even government departments and public servants have sent their management executives on NLP courses to improve their efficiency and develop their professional potential.

These courses can be very expensive and obviously have an appeal to the most wealthy. Some are specialized courses such as Trainer Training for teachers, lecturers, and others who might wish to improve their presentation skills. Arguably, there are some similarities with schools of eastern mysticism. For example, the brief biographies of NLP trainers always give the names of the people they themselves trained under. While not an alternative religious system per se, the programme could be seen as similar to new religions of eastern origin that trace themselves back through a progression of gurus, and to esoteric movements claiming the authority of authenticity through their descent from previous movements.

Another alternative is Insight, which draws on different approaches to human potential, including Gestalt and NLP, as well as the Dianetics teaching that unpleasant early experiences can have major negative effects on later life. Based around seminars, the technique includes games and processes involving group exercises conducted with a partner. There will be discussion and sharing of feelings, meditation, and visualization. Those involved in the movement believe that we amount to a mixture of what we really are, the person we fear we are, and the person we pretend to be. Like most of its teachings this is not original since this notion is shared by a number of human potential groups.

The aims of the seminars are to help people see who they genuinely are and to become aware of their fears and limiting beliefs, to drop pretence and 'outer behaviours'. The latter is the image that we present to the world, often a false one. Frequently, this is an unconscious act. At the root of Insight's beliefs is the conviction that each person starts life perfect and unlimited in capabilities. By revealing and dealing with fears and anxieties, early negative experiences can be removed. The spiritual dimension of this is only implied and comes through a philosophy which, like other human potential groups, deals with the human spirit rather than the mind, while it insists that the power of loving can heal everything. However, Insight denies that it is religious, although much of its language certainly borders on that associated with religious forms.

Insight was established by the educational psychologist Russell Bishop and a teacher, John-Roger, in California in 1978. However, it is just one aspect of the larger organization called the Church of the Movement of Spiritual Inner Awareness, founded in 1971. The emphasis of the latter is in becoming a Mystical Traveller who is totally aware on all levels of consciousness, which is at least partly reached through theology and holistic health and healing. The movement provides for those who wish to go further than the philosophy advanced by Insight and seek a fuller spiritual development.

A similar organization is Emin (short for the 'Eminent Way'), which was founded by Raymond Armin in 1972. After his own voyage of enlightenment he became part of a group of people seeking the meaning to life – an educated cluster of individuals most of whom had spent several years investigating various philosophies and religion without finding the answers they sought. Emin seemed to provide them with many convincing answers and established how to lead a productive life. There are now up to 500 Emin members in Britain and perhaps 1,500 elsewhere around the world.

Emin teachings are open to constant revision and development. However, the broad philosophical tenets maintain that creation is ordered by natural law and thus it grows towards completion and that man's life is a high point of this growth as part of his own evolution. People are spiritual and thus have a duty to the universe and humanity. Human life is concerned with learning and development and there is life after death, which must be planned for and worked for individually. Hence, man must be lawful, develop his/her natural gifts, retain high standards, strive to support natural freedoms, expand boundaries of understanding, and avoid hypocrisy and deception. The emphasis is primarily on the individual and group to meet these goals. To this end, Emin has developed a number of techniques which take the adherent through various stages of self-development. Methods used also include astrology and tarot cards, in what amounts to a very eclectic approach to enhancing different aspects of man's instinctive, intellectual, emotional, and spiritual life. However, Emin does not consider itself a religion in its own right but upholds the rights of individuals to follow their own faith.

Transcendental Meditation

The organization associated with the technique of Transcendental Meditation (TM) was founded by the Maharishi ('Great Seer') Mahesh Yogi. From 1956, after two years of self-imposed seclusion, he embarked on his mission to bring to the world the ancient mystical Hindu techniques of TM. He established the Spiritual Regeneration movement with representation in the West as early as 1959 and set up the International Meditation Society and other similar organizations in the early 1960s in order to disseminate his teachings.

In 1968, through George Harrison's encouragement, the Beatles went to India to associate themselves with the Maharishi's teachings, which brought him a vast amount of publicity. Four years later, the Maharishi announced his World Plan, to create one teaching centre per million people in the world. Earlier, in 1970, he had begun the TM-Sidhi Programme, which included Yogic Flying and the idea of simultaneous meditation by many people beneficially affecting the world. By 1980, nearly a million people had taken the rudimentary TM course, while the organization claims that today this figure is closer to four million. Other initiatives have followed including the Maharishi's World Plan for Perfect Health in 1985 and the Maharishi's Programme to Create World Peace in 1980. The 1990s saw a move into British politics with the Natural Law Party, which put up candidates in local, parliamentary, and European elections.

TM describes itself as a technology of consciousness. It has the aim of developing the full potential of the individual and involves both a psychological and spiritual process. It fulfils some of the same self-improvement functions as numerous religious or semi-religious movements. After basic training, each individual is given a mantra, which is claimed to be specially chosen. Those who wish to continue can go on to study more advanced techniques such as Yogic Flying and Maharishi Gandharva-Veda – the science of creating balance in individual and collective consciousness through music.

Every morning and evening users of TM meditate for twenty minutes. There are said to be three major differences from most forms of meditation with mantras: the mantra has no meaning, it is the sound itself which is sacred; it is not sounded aloud since the meditator only 'thinks' the sound; it is believed to be completely natural and effortless and involves no concentration. The TM technique is said to bring the individual in touch with the inner-self, increases intelligence, and generally creates a healthier mind and body. There are also more controversial claims. One is that if a large group of people is practising TM at the same time, it will have a peaceful effect on the immediate area such as lowering crime rates. There is also Yogic Flying. This is usually accomplished by sitting cross-legged, and first rocking, then bouncing until one is able to leap several inches into the air. It is assumed to be true levitation at the moment of heightened spiritual awareness and perfect mind-body coordination.

Adherents claim that TM is not a religion but a scientific strategy. Certainly, it aims to help develop the full potential of the individual. Yet, from one point of view it does appear to have spiritual elements. At the *puja* ceremony, for instance, when a new member is initiated and given a mantra, the Maharishi's spiritual lineage is recited, there is a typical offering of fruit and flowers, and a song of gratitude is sung to Guru Dev (under whom he studied spiritual guidance for 13 years).

Fringe religiosity and alternative medicines/therapies

As already observed, a number of alternative medicines and therapies are linked with religious systems, many of which are very ancient. The increasing popularity of alternative medicines has various explanations. Frustration with orthodox medical services, incurable chronic complaints, counter-culture experimentation, as well as a last resort for fatal illness, are all reasons why people turn to alternative medicine (Hunt 1999).

Another explanation put forward by McGuire (1983) to account for the increasing popularity of alternative medicine and practices is that at least some are related to spiritual journeying. The search for meaning in today's world tends to be reflected in the widespread quest for holistic worldviews as expressed by many alternative health movements and fringe religions through various strands of therapy. These include Christian healing, metaphysical practices, eastern meditation and human potential groups, psychic and occultist strands, and the work of manipulation technique practitioners. Above all, holistic perspectives satisfy a desire for integrating every aspect of human existence, gaining a sense of wholeness in social, material, psychic, and spiritual life. Believing oneself to be in touch with a great power, which can direct one's life, solve one's problems, and authoritatively forgive one's mistakes, may literally empower the individual for more effective living. Such alternatives are popular with the middle-class and educated, reversing trends of earlier decades when many appealed to the poor who could not afford medical fees, although they are still the preserve of ethnic minorities. They are marginally more popular with females than males and preferred by some age categories more than others. Although varying across Europe and the USA, many appear more popular with those in their mid-20s to mid-30s.

A Mori opinion poll in Britain in 1998 showed that faith healing was the third most popular form of alternative medicine/therapy at some 5 per cent, after homeopathy at 11 per cent and osteopathy at 10 per cent, with acupuncture in fourth place at 4 per cent. 'Faith healing' is, however, a very broad category, with those such as 'spiritual' or 'paranormal' sometimes being preferred. In other European countries, by contrast, religious healing scarcely makes the top ten favourites. Practitioners of spiritual healing may use the 'laying on of hands' or simply place their hands over the patient's body without touching it in order to channel healing energies, however these are conceived. So-called distance healing does not even require the presence of the recipient and may be achieved through prayer or other kinds of mindful attention.

Some of the best-known healing alternatives have come from outside the Western context. Acupuncture is perhaps the most widely used. It is an ancient Chinese system of medicine, which holds that meridians, or energy channels, link inner organs and external points of the body. The acupuncturist applies fine steel needles at external points along these meridians to stimulate healing. There is, in addition, Shiatsu, which is a Japanese system of treatment with a similar basis to acupuncture and acupressure. Pressure with the finger on the meridian points is used with therapeutic effects. Some techniques can be learnt for self-help or first aid by the lay person.

Another alternative is Ayurveda, which amounts to an ancient Hindu system of medicine, based on a humoral and constitutional conception of the body. Health is conceived as a condition in which the forces within the body are in a state of balance. A range of therapeutic measures may be used such as medication, massage, surgery, and exercise. Medicines are prepared from a variety of largely herbal materials. Then there is Tai Chi, a traditional Chinese system of exercise or movements practised in order to cultivate the coordination of mind, body and soul. Another is Unani Tibb, which amounts to a traditional system of medicine practised mainly among Muslim communities derived from South Asia. It has some affinities with Ayurveda. A variety of medications of herbal and mineral origins are used. A practitioner of this system of medicine is popularly known as a 'hakim'.

There are also a number of Western alternative healing measures. This includes anthroposophical medicine, which was developed by the philosopher Rudolf Steiner (1861–1925) in conjunction with medical associates. It was intended to extend conventional medicine rather than to establish an alternative system and is based in a broad spiritual view of the human individual that embraces a variety of therapeutic techniques including the use of herbal medicines, art therapy, and eurhythmy. A more ancient method is that of dowsing. The dowser uses a pendulum and a 'witness'– a small piece of the patient's nail clippings, for instance. S/he divines the patient's problems by holding the pendulum over the 'witness' and observing how it oscillates in response to questions. Dowsers usual prescribe homeopathic remedies to treat patients.

Also linking healing with spirituality are colour healing, which utilizes the energy found in the colour spectrum to transfer healing energy, and aromatherapy, which is the art of using scent to change a mood, an unwanted condition, or a health concern, and may be used in preparation for astral travelling. Those forms of healing more concerned with channelling include Reiki healers, who heal by directing energy and augmenting it with symbols. Reiki is the vital life energy which flows through all living things and which can be activated for the purposes of healing. It has its roots in ancient Buddhist teachings and has a strong appeal to the New Age movement.

Summary

There are perhaps two main observations to be made about the significance of healing beliefs and practices in the alternative religions. Firstly, there is the increasing popularity of the healing now on offer. This tells us something about contemporary culture and the central concern for all things related to health in not just a reparative, but positive and proactive sense. Secondly, there is the vast range of practices now on offer. This variety has enlarged and embellished the contemporary spiritual marketplace. Today, the attractions of health and healing offer a great deal to the spiritual 'seeker', whether it is in terms of the truly spiritual or much more worldly concerns.

Further reading

Geldard, R. (1995) *The Vision of Emerson*, Shaftsbury: Element.
Lamont, S. (1986) *Religion Inc: The Church of Scientology*, London: Harrap.
Reid, J. (1996) 'The New Age Movement and the Conflation of Religion and Psychology', in B. Ouellet and R. Bergeron (eds.), *Croyances et Sociétiés*, Fides: Montreal.
Warren-Davis, D. (1989) *Astrology and Health: A Beginner's Guide*, London: Headway.

12 World religions and the faiths of ethnic minorities

The religions of ethnic minorities are increasingly making news in Western societies. There are various reasons why this is so although they tend to polarize around a number of key themes. Firstly, there is the perceived clash between these faiths on the one hand and the values of secular Western society on the other. Secondly, there is the link between ethnicity, religion, and the heated political debate as to whether cultural assimilation is a desirable goal or, alternatively, that a truly pluralist society, which allows for the full range of ethnic and religious diversity, should be encouraged. Thirdly, and relatedly, a high profile has been achieved with the growth of different forms of religious fundamentalism that appear to have profound consequences for the West and for the peace and stability of the world generally.

There is little doubt that ethnic religions are often perceived in terms of the clash of values with wider society. Much was epitomized in Britain, in 1989, by the so-called 'Salmon Rushdie Affair'. Rushdie, a liberal intellectual with a Muslim background, outraged world Islam by the publication of his book *Satanic Verses*, which was interpreted as insulting and blasphemous. From one point of view, the clear issue was the freedom of literary expression, and from another, the rights and sensibilities of religious and cultural minorities in a secular society (Modood 1990). More broadly, it had profound implications for the relationship between Western societies and Muslim countries since Rushdie found himself the subject of death threats (*fatwa*) from the more fanatical wing of Islam. It is clear that even in the most seemingly progressive democracy there are sources of conflict which may result from public intolerance and the lack of knowledge of minority religious groups, while it is often the case that children of different religious faiths often grow up with incomplete and confused understanding of each other's religions (Nesbitt 1997). As a result, ethnic religions may be labelled as 'deviant' and perceived as challenging dominant cultural values and political institutions and, therefore, engendering social divisions and potential instability. It is unlikely that today, in a secular society, they are perceived as different, in as much as they are not within the remit of 'official' historical religion, that is, Christianity. Nonetheless, their status is very much tied up with the culture of ethnic minorities, which may be designated as social 'outgroups', while the visibility of their faiths is enhanced in the increasingly secular societies of the West.

Religion and ethnicity

The relationship between ethnicity and religion is an extraordinarily complex one. Ethnic groups bring with them distinct religious beliefs and traditions. They are by no means all of non-Christian form. Ethnic minorities now constitute sizeable groupings within some of the major Christian denominations or, alternatively, have established their own churches. Nonetheless, the sheer number of people practising non-Christian faiths in Western societies is now significant. At the same time, the relationship between religion and ethnicity is compounded by divisions within the major faiths and the communities themselves. Migrants from various parts of the world may belong to different Islamic sects. Those from the Indian subcontinent may be Hindu, Sikh, Muslim, or Buddhist, while Caribbeans may be divided by their loyalties to various Christian denominations. Conversely, black Caribbean Christians may identify more with fellow believers from the white host population, while Islam may unite individuals with different ethnic and national origins.

Despite the complexities of the relationship between religion and ethnicity, it is clear that religious faith remains a core concern of life for many minorities. This is particularly so for those from the Third World where religious belief and practice are a vital ingredient of social existence. Moreover, the importance of religion for ethnic minorities may actually be enhanced by the problems involved in the process of migration and the transition from one society to another. This is obviously so for the first generation of migrants. Religion provides an island of meaning, tradition, and belonging. In short, religion allows an anchorage for those experiencing social upheaval and new, perhaps hostile, environments. Hurh and Kim's (1990) research findings of Korean migrants to the USA are not untypical of a number of studies underlining the importance of religion for new migrants. It was found that those already of the Christian faith often intensify their need for fellowship in exclusively Korean churches in the USA, and even some non-Christians are attracted to such congregations. These churches not only provide meaning to being uprooted from all that is familiar and help overcome a feeling of alienation in a new country, but allow a sense of belonging, largely regardless of gender, age, and socio-economic status. They do this by creating a microcosm of both formal and informal aspects of Korean society. At the same time, they also seem to play an important role in satisfying the needs of social prestige, power, and recognition within the immigration community. This appears to be especially so for male immigrants. It is they who are primarily expected to 'succeed' in the new country. However, they cannot easily penetrate the economic structures of the USA in order to do so. The Korean church, therefore, offers a substitute in allowing some of these aspirations to be fulfilled through positions of authority and status within church hierarchies.

Part of the link between ethnicity and religion is the matter of boundary maintenance. Such maintenance is aimed at confirming the integrity and solidarity of the ethnic group by firmly establishing the cultural differences with wider society. Indeed, its role for the early generations of migrants is vital: the strengthening of boundaries is frequently why ethnic groups survive in the face of even the most overwhelming adversity. The importance of religion is that it brings a clearer delineation of the culture of a community and promotes internal solidarity even where it was not especially strong beforehand. This sense of solidarity is likely to be enhanced by discrimination, persecution, or even perceived persecution by the host society.

As regards the attitude of Western states towards ethnic religion, it is evident that policies range considerably. They vary from state neutrality in religious affairs, as in Belgium and Holland, to the overt secularism of Sweden and the upholding of a state religion in Denmark. More widely, most Western nations at least pay lip service to the idea of a multicultural society, although others such as France have strong assimilation policies. Additionally, there are varying attitudes regarding citizenship, which may encourage different levels of political activity by the religio-ethnic group. It certainly seems that political activity by Muslims has tended to emerge more quickly in those countries where immigrants could acquire citizenship relatively easily, notably Britain and France.

Hammond and Warner (1995) believe that assimilation is advanced by the transformation of religion into more private expressions. They argue that the evidence suggests, at least in the USA, that the relationship between religion and ethnicity may be on the decline (although this noticeably varies from one ethnic group to another) – even at a time when communities in the USA are claiming their ethnic distinctiveness. Hammond and Warner speculate that neither religion nor ethnicity will disappear in the near future but the linkage between the two is almost certain to be weakened. Religion becomes increasingly a matter of individual choice for members of ethnic minorities, as it does for the host population. This can largely be regarded as assimilation. Hammond and Warner also maintain that ethnicity, along with other social background characteristics, will have a declining effect in determining religious identity because of the incursions made by other religions into ethnic enclaves. A sign of this is that Pentecostal Protestantism has made considerable inroads into Hispanic Catholicism, as has black Islam into African American Protestantism. Such a weakening of the relationship between ethnicity and religion does not mean that religion fades in importance for expressing ethnic concerns. Neither does it suggest that because religion is becoming a matter of individual choice it is of lesser importance. Indeed, it may actually be of greater psychological significance even as its social and ethnic consequence diminishes. Nonetheless, the declining link between religion and ethnicity continues as a long-term trend.

The implications of global fundamentalism

The relationship between ethnic minorities and the host nations in the West has recently been impacted by the rise of global fundamentalism. The global structure prior to 1980 largely rested on the balance of power between the USA and the Soviet empire. With the collapse of Communism, the emerging world order is now based mainly on the hegemony of the free market alongside a commitment to liberal democracy. In the post-Cold War world, many Western nations have come to see religion as a source of global division and disruption. It is the perceived threat of global religious fundamentalism which has drawn the greatest attention (Esposito & Watson 2000).

Although fundamentalist movements have emerged among the major world religions, including Judaism, Hinduism, and Sikhism, to Westerners the forces of Islamic revival seem the most alarming and potentially dangerous expression. This is because, firstly, Islam is believed to reject and resist many of the premises of Westernization and so-called 'progress' and, secondly, because it is the world's fastest growing religion, with well over one billion adherents. There are, of course, the dangers of overestimating Islam as some kind of 'peril' to the West. Much of the Islamic world remains largely untouched by fundamentalist developments. However, there are many currents within the faith that have moved towards fundamentalism, such as the Shi'ites in Iran, who attract a great deal of attention because they have previously dared to challenge the West in socio-political conflicts in the Middle East.

As with Christian fundamentalism in the West, Islam and other faiths appear to constitute the forces of reaction and tradition against an ever-changing world. Indeed, some commentators have come to see fundamentalism as one of two developing global camps, one representing the spreading modernizing impulse from the West, and the other the forces of tradition and a cultural tribalism that calls on religious resources. Hence, there is now a global conflict between radically different cultures, epitomized by world Westernizing tendencies, and its resistance by a rapidly expanding reactionary expression of religion, epitomized by Islamic fundamentalism impacting as far afield as Iran, the Sudan, and Afghanistan. This image of conflict has been cogently described as 'McWorld versus Jihad' (Barber 1995). Referring to the Muslim community, Kepel (1994) suggests that the aim of the fundamentalists is to Islamize modernity rather than to modernize Islam. For reactionary versions of the faith, the task is to spread Islam to the whole of humanity while defending the Muslim identity that is currently being undermined.

The rise of fundamentalist movements is to some degree due to Western world dominance. In the nineteenth and early twentieth-centuries, the Middle East had been subject to the aggression of Western expansion and colonialism, which still colours the attitudes of the Muslim countries in the region today. The Iranian Revolution of 1979 might be therefore interpreted as primarily a response to Western dependency (Gerami 1989) and as an effort to give a marginalized Third World region greater access, through a revitalization of Islamic cultural differences, to perceived global material and cultural resources monopolized by the West (Beyer 1994, 174–5). The Gulf War in the early 1990s, between the nations of the West and Iraq, once more showed that the former still had considerable global economic and political interests in the region.

The global expansion of fundamentalist non-Christian religion has also influenced ethnic minorities in the West and there are direct implications for the nations of Europe and North America. This is not just simply a result of clashes of culture, as with the Rushdie affair, or global conflicts such as the Gulf War. Rather, these events feed into structures of discrimination and deprivation experienced by ethnic minorities in the West. Kepel (1997) notes the number of poor and alienated young blacks in the USA, Indian and Pakistanis in Britain, and North Africans in France, who seek to construct a community identity and are thereby making a deliberate cultural break

with the dominant values in societies they believe exclude them. Religious movements satisfy many of their needs. In the USA, the Black Muslim movement founded
by Elijah Muhammad, previously made famous by Malcolm X and Louis Farrakham,
was a model for many groups in Europe from the 1990s. They sought to construct a
new morality which fought against drug dealers and addiction, and to break with
dominant Western norms in order to mark out a strong community identity and
protect those living in ghettoes.

Once, the Black Muslim movement was profoundly intolerant of other non-black
races and religions. Their beliefs and Koranic references were interpreted as forming a
protest against the values and attitudes of the dominant white American culture,
where a dualist ideology of some black Muslims identified the 'evil' nature of Western
materialistic societies and the white oppressors (Lincoln 1989). It was also relatively
unconnected with Islam as a world religion. The spread of global fundamentalism
began to change all that. In turn, some strands of the movement have embraced a
wider vision and embarked on an intense study of world Islam, becoming part of the
Sunni branch of the international faith and linking with Muslims of other countries.

In France, there has been the influence of the Islamic Salvation Front (ISF).
Following the collapse of the FLN (National Liberation Front) regime in Algeria, the
support of the ISF rocketed and gave rise to a mass Islamic party, which quickly
reached the fringes of power. The Gulf War of 1991 intensified the conflict and there
was at least some support for Saddam Hussein's war effort among France's population of Arab or Muslim origin. At the same time, in Britain, Rushdie's work alienated
a great number of ordinary Muslims outside the inner circles of mullahs and Islamic
community leaders. The controversy surrounding the book brought together those
who felt that their closest beliefs had been attacked, reinforcing many Muslims' sense
of community and making them even more receptive to the mullahs and the more
militant Islamic leaders.

World religions in the Western context

The rest of this chapter is concerned with discussing the complex situation of world
religions other than Christianity within Western societies. It will consider the link
between these faiths and ethnicity where applicable, address the broader issue of
levels of adaptation and assimilation, and identify those variables most likely to
enhance or bring about a rejection of Western culture. These major world religions
are firstly introduced with a brief overview of the basic beliefs and practices.

Islam

Beliefs

Islamic history narrates how, in AD 611, the Prophet Muhammad began to have intercession with the angel Gabriel who related to him the will and purpose of God, Allah.
The teachings Muhammad received were written down in the Koran, which is by far

the greatest sacred word for Muslims. Although the book may be 'interpreted' in other languages, it can never adequately be translated because its expression in Arabic is an integral part of its sacredness. It was originally written in Arabic and is still read in the language by all Muslims, thus simultaneously maintaining the purity of that language and identifying Islam with Arabic-speaking peoples.

'Islam' means 'submission' or 'surrender' to the will of God. The essence of the Muslim 'creed' is that 'There is no God but God, and Muhammad is His Prophet'. There is only one God, but there have been several prophets, including Abraham and Jesus. Muhammad was the last and greatest of the prophets, with the final revelation of Allah. Because of the Middle Eastern origins, Allah is the same God as the Jewish Yahweh and God the Father of the Christians. In AD 622, Muhammad, encountering religious opposition to his teachings of the unity of God and his denunciation of idolatry, moved north from his birthplace Mecca to Medina, both in Saudi Arabia. This *hejira* (flight, emigration) now marks the start of the Muslim calendar. All Muslims must attempt to make a pilgrimage to Mecca and Medina at least once in their lives. This is one of the five Pillars of Islam, the others being belief, prayer, fasting, and alms giving.

Just as Christianity has its Roman Catholic, Orthodox, and Protestant wings, most global religions display major divisions which, today, complicate their link with ethnicity and nationality. This is why it is difficult to make generalizations regarding the Islamic community in the West. The history of Islam has resulted in the formation of numerous different strands and traditions. The earliest division was that which occurred in the late seventh-century, originating in the political dispute over the leadership of the Islamic world between the Sunni, who now constitute approximately 90 per cent of all Muslims in the Middle East and the Indian subcontinent. The remaining 10 per cent are of the Shi'a variety. Some countries such as Britain do have sizeable Shi'a populations centred on often impressive mosques funded by the wealthy Ismaili 'Sevener' community. These stem from the migration from ex-colonial East African countries. However, the Sunni, particularly those subscribing to the Hanafi school of Islamic law, predominate among Muslim communities in most Western societies. Divisions have also occurred among Sunni Muslims between the traditionalists and more radical factions. This has at least some implications for the West. The traditionalists include the Deobandis sect that seeks to justify its teachings by reference to the Koran, the Hadith, and the Hanafi law school. The Deobandis sect tends not to be involved with political questions in the West but solely with what it perceives as the purity of Islam. Even more traditionalist is the Jamiat Ahl E Hadith sect (based originally on the Wahabi movement in Saudi Arabia), which attempts to go back beyond the teachings of the Law Schools and to base itself principally on the Koran and the Hadith. This faction is often concerned with the immediate social conditions of Muslims living in Europe and North America. In contrast, the Jamaat-i-Islami has a wider and more radical agenda. Here, the focus is not so much on local circumstances in the West, but in seeking to win the modern world for Islam and to persuade such states as Pakistan to eschew Western influences and uncompromisingly adopt Islamic ordinances into their constitutional system.

An alternative to these factions are the Barelwi who are led by Sufis. The Barelwi are a sizeable grouping in some Western countries with teachings and practices ranging from sophisticated philosophical doctrines to simple popular magical practices. Sufism is the mystical side of Islam, dating as far back as possibly the first century of the faith. 'Sufi' is Arabic for 'wool clad', referring to the traditional coarse robe of the mystic. Sufism is rich with poetic literature, music, and ecstatic dance – particularly the famous whirling dervishes of some Sufic orders (or *tariqas*, meaning 'way'). Perhaps because it puts the believer's personal relationship with God before the strict outward observance of religious practice, Sufism has been regarded with suspicion by Islam itself, while at the same time being highly respected for its spiritual and intellectual qualities. The emphasis is on dance, chanting the names of God, and healing, the aim being to achieve a loving union with God. Among recent Sufi writers who have been influential in the West are Hazrat Inayat Khan, who initially introduced Sufism, and Idris Shah. Sufism has influenced several of the more esoteric and mystical strands of the New Age movement in the West where it is less strongly linked with its Muslim origins.

Adaptation in the West

Islamic communities offer good examples of the principal developments of a world religion and its significance for ethnicity in the Western environment. The relevance of boundary maintenance, as well as the effects of discrimination by the host society, state policies, and levels of assimilation, must be taken into account.

Muslims have not always found it easy to respond to the challenges of living within Western cultures. The broad picture can be said to be a paradoxical mixture of achievement and frustration, acceptance and alienation, polarities of assimilation and isolation. In many respects, these communities have been more stringent in sustaining religious beliefs and practices than other faiths. For Muslims, the institution of *purdah* (the regulations concerned with behaviour and dress, which reinforce the separation of male and female spheres) is particularly important. Several surveys have noted many differences between Muslim and non-Muslim Asians in supporting their religion. Attitudes towards female dress and gender roles are frequently virtually unchanged between Muslim parents and their children, while Sikh and Hindu children are sometimes observably more flexible than their parents in adapting to Western conventions. Muslim parents also appear to be a good deal more stringent in their parental control of their children into the teenage years (Anwar 1981; Joly 1984). Similarly, Muslim children have been discovered to be more endeared to traditional arranged marriages than their Sikh and Hindu counterparts (Nielson 1989).

Not only have such Islamic cultural codes been retained, but in fact they have also been strengthened in response to the insecurities and threats in the new surroundings of the West. Mandel's study (1996) of Turkish Muslims in Germany shows how they understood themselves to be in the land of the 'infidel', surrounded by a world that is profane and *haram*. In this situation they managed to create a realm for themselves – establishing frontiers of distinctiveness ranging from dietary habits to language, from dress to domestic arrangements, which provide meaningful expressions of Turkish Muslim identity abroad. More widely in the West, problems have often manifested themselves in a clash of cultures particularly in the hostility to liberal attitudes towards sexuality and in the desire for the education of children in accordance with Islamic principles. Other difficulties have included Muslim dietary requirements and specific needs related to death and burial.

Such markers of cultural identity may be internally imposed, yet they are frequently fostered by experiences of discrimination or perceived discrimination. In Britain, the government's tightening of immigration controls, especially since the 1960s, precipitated the creation of Asian community support groups and enhanced cultural bonds, which encouraged the dedication to the Islamic faith and the stepping up of the construction of mosques as centres of community life (Barton 1986). Bloul (1996), in much the same way, has shown how in France local conflict over the right of Muslim schoolgirls to wear hair covering in class became a contentious topic. The controversy was utilized by hostile local native French to arouse fears of the Muslim population as an 'internal Islamic threat' while, in response, the migrants used it as part of the construct of a contrary worldview, or what Bloul terms an 'alternative universalism'.

It would be wrong to produce a one-sided view of the Islamic community. Volt (1991) argues that while there are undoubtedly problems in fulfilling Islamic obligations in the midst of a secular society, these are not unresolvable. In fact, in a variety of respects Muslims are not essentially different from other minority groups. Historically, Islam has always adapted itself to local conditions and has frequently proved to be tolerant of other faiths. There are also signs of assimilation. As Abdullah points out in the case of Germany, only slightly over half of the 1.7 million Muslims living there actually practise Islam (Abdullah 1995, 77). Evidence in Britain shows that the younger generation of Muslims with a Western education are inquisitive about their roots and seek an earnest understanding of their cultural identity. At the same time, however, they have come to question some of the cultural and religious postulates of their parents. While this may create certain dilemmas for the young, a challenge of traditional values may ultimately herald a greater assimilation (Ali 1992, 113).

Considerable overlap may exist in the cultural values of Western host society and those of ethnic minorities. Certainly, some factions of the Islamic community have always been more endeared to Westernizing influences. For instance, Pakistani Muslims in Britain have frequently been divided along regional and social class lines. Earlier settlers were drawn from rural areas with strong kinship ties and a greater religious commitment. Later immigrants have been derived from Western-orientated elites who find themselves more at home within the British environment. A predominantly middle-class representation of Asian Muslims has also been evident among those who have immigrated to the USA in recent years and they are reputed to show a greater affinity with Western culture.

Judaism

Beliefs

Judaism was the first of the great monotheistic religions and it is at least partly from the faith that both Christianity and Islam stem. What is unusual about Judaism is that it does not actively seek to recruit converts from other religions. This is largely

because it is associated with one people, the Jews. According to Jewish law, it is sufficient for someone to have been born of a Jewish mother for them to be regarded as a
Jew. However, a person born of a Jewish father and a non-Jewish mother is not Jewish
but a Gentile.

The history of the Jewish people began in Mesopotamia where successive empires
of the ancient world came and went before the Jews could be identified as a separate
people – emerging as a distinct nation somewhere between the nineteenth and
sixteenth-centuries BC. The Covenant between the one God and his people was first
formulated by Moses and is central to understanding Judaism today. Judaism should
not be regarded as a religion like the other major world faiths. It is the religion of a
distinct nation that brings no clear dichotomy between the religious and secular
aspects of the Jewish faith. Historical awareness, cultural consciousness, and Jewish
identity are all bound together within a religious framework. Hence the Torah (the
first five books of the Old Testament) and expected modes of behaviour that it insists
on are intrinsically bound up with the Jewish way of life. This foundation has been
built upon by the wisdom of prophets, rabbis, and a huge body of commentary to the
Torah. Through these the Jewish faith teaches basic beliefs about God, revelation, and
humanity and expresses these doctrines in ceremonies, rituals, and laws, which are
enshrined in various institutions and unique Jewish cultural attributes. The distinctiveness and unity of the Jewish nation has ensured a tortured history. Since the sixth-
century, the Jews have been a largely diasporic people scattered across the world.
Persecution has often followed, ranging from that in Poland in the Middle Ages to the
Nazi holocaust in the twentieth-century. Persecution, however, has frequently
strengthened the nation and its survival is truly remarkable. This was proved when, in
1948, the state of Israel was restored.

Although Judaism is the religion of the codified Laws, like other world religions it
has its mystical expression. This is the Cabbala, which, in essence, is an esoteric philosophical system based on a unique interpretation of the Jewish scriptures, especially
the Torah. Its deepest roots are unknown but it developed into a formulated system in
eighth-century Spain, and was further elaborated by *Zohar*, a mystical work written in
the late thirteenth-century. The Cabbala is often interpreted as the foundation of the
Western mystical tradition, including esoteric Christianity. As suggested earlier
(Chapter 11), it has also inspired more recent expressions of mysticism.

Adaptation in the West

Today, the largest communities of Jews outside Israel and the former Soviet Union
are to be found in the USA, Britain, and France. In such countries Judaism also
constitutes the longest established religio-ethnic constituency and for that reason it
may be conjectured that it provides a useful case study for measuring levels of assimilation. The difficulty is that it is virtually impossible to draw conclusions given the
variety of social and political contexts in which the Jewish community is located.
Secondly, there have been different 'waves' of Jewish immigration into Western
countries. In Britain, for example, there are Jews whose ancestors have had a presence

for centuries. However, since the end of the Second World War successive influxes of migrants from different parts of the world have ensured that it is possible to speak of both 'native' and 'immigrant' Jews.

There is good evidence that Jewish communities exposed for a considerable length of time to the processes of social and geographical mobility have found their sense of identity slowly eroded. Social mobility, through occupation and wealth, brings ascribed status as defined by wider secular society, not by the religious community. Different lifestyles and life experiences, determined by income and social prestige, appear to undermine the cohesion of a distinct ethnic-religious group which had previously been united by the same historical and collective experience. Simultaneously, the relevance of geographical dispersion for the Jewish community may be appreciated in terms of Wade Roof's argument that the maintenance of religious commitment in highly differentiated Western societies depends, above all, on a localized traditional perspective shared by persons who interact frequently, thus providing mutual support for belief and practice (Roof 1976). Largely congruent with this analysis, subsequent research on Jewish communities in the USA has found a relationship between community size and formal participation in the Jewish faith. Locality is, therefore, imperative in strengthening bonds, uniform religious practices, and the sense of parochial community among Jews (Rabinowitz 1992).

Evidence in Western Europe and the USA suggests that Jews are generally well integrated into economic and political life. Mobility has ensured that religion is the only thing which distinguishes Jews from non-Jews. Indeed, we may conclude that, at least in the USA, Jews can no longer be regarded as a distinct ethnic group in any meaningful sense. Rather, they are only separated from the rest of the nation by their religious differences. In short, they are so well integrated into social and economic life that religion becomes the only factor for most Jews in differentiating themselves from the non-Jewish population. In the USA the Jewish community constitutes a powerful political lobby that has enjoyed considerable influence on successive governments' international policy in respect of Israel and the Middle East. However, this is not merely to be interpreted as the successful mobilization of an ethnic community, but also as the willingness to participate within established political structures as part of the desire to be accepted as conforming to mainstream society. This can primarily be viewed as a response to the long-standing institutionalization of anti-Semitism and considerable apprehension about being labelled as 'deviant' or 'other'. Hence, Jews have tended to strive towards conventional values through normative agreement with conventional morality, aspiring towards middle-class status and material success. Moreover, the decline of the Orthodox religion may reflect the feeling of the great majority of Jews who, unlike Protestant fundamentalists, believe that their traditional faith does not preclude conforming to mainstream values. This assessment of contemporary Judaism is, however, one which can be contended. Older forms of culture and identity may die out as a result of occupational location, residential patterns, and institutional affiliation. However, new ones may develop which are equally viable. In the USA, socio-economic success does not necessarily equate with ethnic assimilation. Rather, social mobility has not undermined a feeling of religious and ethnic identity. Data from the 1970s and 1990 National Jewish Population Surveys suggests that for over four hundred years the Jews' exceptional social and economic mobility has made them the most successful religious and ethnic group. The unique level of mobility has bound them together as a community even if, at the same time, it has eroded more intensive and devotional ritual aspects of religious life.

There is more to consider. Western culture is undoubtedly increasingly secular. Hence, it can be argued that the same secularizing forces that have undermined traditional Christianity have also eaten away at the religious faith of well-established ethnic communities and plausibly enhanced assimilation. As far as Judaism is concerned, evidence in Britain indicates a decline in attendance at synagogues, especially by the young, a greater incidence of intermarriage with non-Jews, and an increase in the divorce rate of Jewish marriages. If the young can be regarded as providing indices for the strength of Judaism, the future does not appear promising. In the 1980s, up to two-thirds of young Jews in Britain did not marry in a synagogue, preferring instead the simple ceremony of a secular registry office. Another indication is the findings of Kosmin and Levy's (1983) study of religious ritual practice in Jewish schools compared to non-Jewish schools in Britain. Although the former scored higher, once home background was taken into account there was virtually no difference between the two groups in terms of the religious socialization of young people. According to this study then, the next generation is not being rigorously inculcated with traditional religious values.

The fact that Jews have survived widespread dispersion and persecution can, to a great degree, be put down to a sense of historical mission and its accompanying religious beliefs and core cultural values. However, to some extent the religious unity of the Jews has been weakened over time since Judaism has no one spiritual head, no equivalent to a Papal leader. Furthermore, in the West far-reaching transformations have taken place in the faith which do more than hint at ongoing assimilation and point to the increasing effects of secularizing processes. In most countries in the West the majority of Jews are still affiliated to one or other variety of Orthodox Judaism. Even so, evidence points to the evolution of the faith, including profound changes within the Orthodoxy as the pressures of modern society take their toll. It is clear that Orthodox Jews have had to find strategies of survival largely by transforming and reinterpreting beliefs. In the USA especially, there has been something of a resurgence of expressions of religious Orthodoxy, or even Ultra-Orthodoxy. However, this sizeable revival can be interpreted as a form of fundamentalism that has emerged as a response to events in the Middle East and, more importantly, the liberalization of the faith in the West within the boundaries of an increasingly secular society. It is the 'progressive' sector of Judaism, divided into Reform and Liberal varieties, which provides the most explicit indication of change. Reformed Judaism, beginning in the nineteenth-century, attempted to evolve a living faith created in line with modern conditions. It brought certain liturgical changes and revisions in ritual designed to make the service of the synagogue more intelligible to the laity. Liberal Judaism is more radical in its theological formation and practice. Here, Sabbath observance and ritual circumcision are abandoned and interpreted as archaic traditions while other 'outdated' ritual is seen as crushing the spiritual element of the faith. In their more progressive form synagogues are so unconcerned with ritual that, for example, females attend services with their heads uncovered and not even rabbis eat kosher foods. Although the emergence of Reform and Liberal Judaism has inevitably brought conflict with the Orthodoxy, their attraction is conceivably to those Jews alienated by what they feel is its suffocating tradition and who might otherwise give up the faith altogether. In other words, it sustains a kind of safety net that enhances the viability of the Jewish community. The overall result, at least in the contemporary context of the USA, is that Judaism is increasingly developing denominational characteristics based not so much upon social and economic divisions but on Orthodoxy, Conservatism, and Reform.

Hinduism

Beliefs

Hinduism is the oldest of the major established religions, although it is extremely diverse and fragmented in its beliefs, practices, and traditions. The term 'Hindu' literally refers to the people and culture of the Indus Valley region, on the borders of Pakistan and India. The earliest of the beliefs now incorporated into Hinduism date back as long ago as 3,000 BC, though the sacred book of 1,028 hymns, the *Rig-Veda*, was composed around 1400–1200 BC.

Hinduism believes in a vast polytheistic system of gods and goddesses and an equally wide range of ways of worship. As Hinduism spread geographically, its flexibility by way of beliefs allowed it to absorb and to adapt to local religious ideas. Of the literally millions of gods and demi-gods, most of them are unique to particular regions. However, the best known are the 'trinity' of Brahma the creator, Vishnu the Sustainer, and Shina the destroyer. Given the number of gods and the age of the religion, it is hardly surprising that there are many quite different varieties of Hinduism.

A common belief of all expressions of Hinduism, however, is that of reincarnation, the idea that after death the soul is reborn in another body. The quality of the next existence lived depends on what is learnt in the current life. Above all, Hindus strive to attain *moksha*, or liberation from the cycle of death and rebirth. There are various paths to *moksha*, including those listed in the *Bhagavad Gita*: *jnana merga* – the path of wisdom, by which one lives a life of meditation; *karma marga* – the path of action regarding one's allotted duty; and *bhakti marga* – the path of devotion and dedication to God. Each path requires letting go of the self, senses, and this world.

Adaptation in the West

The broad range of teachings associated with Hinduism, the variables of different waves of immigration from India and East Africa, and internal divisions by castes have encouraged a fascinating combination of conservatism and innovation in the Western situation. In the transplantation of Hinduism the demands of new locations, links with India, and the length of residence away, as well as particular geographical traditions, have all influenced the significance of the faith at a local level in the West.

While it may be true that traditional ritual demands are not easy for the Hindus in another social context, most have adapted, to one degree or another, to the Western environment (Thomas 1993). At times there has been a simple cultural divergence expressed in religious terms. For instance, Hindus have traditions related to gender and sexuality which are at odds with the value-orientations of mainstream society. However, perhaps above all, there is the significance of caste. In India, the ancient Hindu myth of the four varnas legitimated the division of labour and, subsequently, a rigid social caste system which developed in the thirteenth-century and has continued in rural areas until today. In the West, communities and temples may be divided by linguistic and caste lines, not so much out of an ideological commitment to the caste system, but because they provide, amongst Indians, a 'natural' source of identification. This does not mean, however, that the relevance of caste may not be declining. Adjustments are frequently made in the practices related to the issues of social and spiritual purity that are very much tied up with the central role of caste and there have sometimes been adaptations enabling the family and wider community to assimilate into the Western structure.

Evidence from Holland has shown that migration has brought the gradual erosion of the caste system alongside the decline of sectarianism and other-worldly expressions of Hinduism. Indeed, Hinduism appears to be developing more universal aspects and is gradually being transformed into a broad faith for the Indian community as a whole (Burg 1993). Change in the caste system for the Hindu constituency is, however, an uneven process. In some instances, especially in the case of a sect like the Swaminarayan, caste divisions and distinctions of gender, as traditionally understood, are strictly maintained. Certainly, caste divisions are also fairly stringently upheld universally when they apply to the choice of marital partners and are probably linked to the matter of ensuring the family line.

Sikhism

Beliefs

'Sikh' means 'disciple'. The founder of Sikhism, Guru Nanak (1469–1539), regarded himself as a disciple who followed the teachings of the mystic Kabir (1440–1518), some of whose words are contained, along with Nanak's and several other Sikh gurus, in the holy scriptures, the *Adi Granth* ('the Book'). Because of its geographical origins and the beliefs of its founders, Sikhism contains elements of Islam and Hinduism, especially Bhakti Hinduism (devotion to God rather than religious ceremony and idol worship) and aspects of Sufism. Sikhism is monotheistic, with God seen as the supreme guru. The ten gurus from Nanak to Gobind Singh (1666–1708) are deeply revered. Sikhism is a faith that stresses the individual's relationship with God and follows the gurus who have revealed him. The *Adi Granth* is also described as a guru, as is the Sikh community, the *Guru Panth*. Sikhs therefore pursue unity with God through worship, through reading the *Guru Granth Sahib*, and by providing service to the community.

There are over six million Sikhs worldwide. They largely originate from the Punjab, on the borders of India and Pakistan, where they have often been caught between Hindus and Muslims. The Mongols in particular were hostile towards them and the Sikhs developed into a warlike people. The devout Sikh wears not just a turban but a sword (*kirpan*) at all times. These are part of the five *Khalsa* symbols or five 'Ks', which also include the *kesh* (unshorn hair), *kangha* (comb), *kara* (steel bracelet), and *kachch* (short trousers for ease in fighting).

In various respects Sikhism may not appear, at least at first sight, to lend itself well to the Western environment of secularism. Yet some aspects have yielded to assimilation, even while others refuse to compromise. Although for historical reasons Sikhism is often seen as a militant religion, at heart it is profoundly democratic and egalitarian, with keen social awareness and a spirit of reconciliation. Sikh revivalist movements have taken hold in North America throughout the twentieth-century but these have not always been in tension with Western culture. One in particular, Sikh Dharma, as we have seen (Chapter 7), is better known as the Healthy, Happy, Holy Organization. The practice of Kundalini Yoga, which focuses on breathing regulation and on the meditation on God's name, is also taught by Western Sikhs.

Adaptation in the West

For many of the ethnic minorities in the West political developments in certain regions of the world remain of great significance. Sikhism is a prime example since it is very much concerned with nationalist aspirations, that is, the independence movement in the Punjab from Indian rule. Thus, religious and nationalist sentiment was raised when, in 1984, the Indian army invaded the Golden Temple in Amritsa – the Sikhs' most holy site. There have been implications for the West. The more militant pro-Khalistani groups regard countries with large Sikh communities, such as Britain and Canada, as bases from which the national struggle could be mobilized. Moreover, in European countries the contest for control of the Sikh temples has at times seen a struggle between 'moderates' and 'militants' with different attitudes to an independent state of Khalistan. The origins of Sikhism in the Punjab and its adherence to the Punjab language in worship will ensure that, for the foreseeable future, it remains the religion of a particular linguistic and cultural grouping. Nonetheless, Sikhism retains a great diversity of the culture from which it originates, so that it is not constructive to embrace terms like 'popular Sikhism'. That acknowledged, the practice of arranged marriages and the rigorous division of the sexes are generally still upheld, while co-education is reluctantly accepted, and inter-caste marriages discouraged. The matter of caste is also particularly significant. In a fascinating study, Nesbitt (1997) examined the religious lives and attitudes of British-born children from two Punjab communities, the Valmikis and the Ravidasis. These are two castes traditionally associated with impure work (formerly known as 'untouchables'). Their stigmatization and marginalization is, to some extent at least, carried over into the British setting within the Sikh community and has proved to have far-reaching implications for individuals and family life. At times, migration to the West has strengthened the core values of Sikhism. However, practical and economic needs have eroded boundary maintenance (Jeffery 1992, 89–94). While the visible *Khalsa* symbols of the faith are central to the beliefs of Sikhism, how they have been maintained (or otherwise) provides both a measure of assimilation on the one hand, and the reaction of the secular state to ethnic religions on the other. In the early 1970s, the British government was forced to alter its laws regarding the compulsory wearing of helmet protection for motorcycle riders, which would have excluded Sikhs from wearing turbans. At the same time, the general discarding of *Khalsa* symbols demonstrates a wish to assimilate to Western norms of dress and behaviour and, in practical terms, to give a more 'favourable' impression when seeking employment (Helweg 1991). Sikhs have discarded the *kirpan* largely because they are conscious of the British laws against carrying arms and have also frequently done away with the knee breeches usually worn as an undergarment. They have thus effectively departed from their *Khalsa* vows. Of the five symbols it is usually the steel bracelet (*kara*) which is retained since it is regarded as the least obtrusive.

Some commentators have noted that Sikhs frequently display an entrepreneurial spirit and high level of professional skills, which are conducive to successful integration into Western social and economic structures. Certain aspects of the Sikh faith have similarly lent themselves to assimilation. Sikhism is looked upon by its adherents as a progressive, reforming religion. Sometimes its radicalism and popularism have spilled over into the political arena. Hence, Sikhs have been very active in political campaigns and are frequently well represented in labour organizations. Moreover, unlike some other religions, or division of religions in which ancient traditions must be maintained, Sikhism, because of its reforming character, has not experienced as many difficulties as other faiths in being transplanted to an alien soil (Thomas 1993). For instance, Bhacha (1985) has shown that migrants to Britain predominantly belong to the Ramgarhia caste that arrived from East Africa during the 1960s and 1970s. They are highly educated, urbanized, and motivated in terms of material and status aspirations. As a consequence, adults have achieved a high degree of occupational success, while their children repeatedly perform well at all levels of education. While there is the danger of over-exaggeration, evidence suggests that increasingly Sikhs are successful business people and are moving more rapidly into the professional occupations than many other ethnic groups.

Jainism

Beliefs

The Sanskrit word *Jaina* derives from *jina* ('conqueror') an epithet given to a line of human teachers who, having overcome the human passions, obtained enlightenment. They taught the doctrine of non-violence and subsequently attained the freedom from rebirth, which constitutes spiritual deliverance. The Jains are broadly those who credit these spiritual conquerors with total authority and act according to their teachings. Jinas, also called Tirthankaras, show their followers how to achieve liberation from the cycle of reincarnation by attaining the Three Jewels – right knowledge, faith, and conduct. Correct conduct means abandoning violence, greed, and deceit, being chaste, and taking a series of vows.

The Jain way of life is dominated by the need to achieve a favourable rebirth or, better still, to obtain liberation from the cycle of birth and rebirth altogether. For some this means becoming a member of a monastic order. Lay people also attempt to follow as closely as possible the austere lifestyle of the monk, chiefly by avoiding violence and pursuing a career, such as trade or banking, which does not involve doing direct harm to life. As in Buddhism, lay people can develop their own spirituality by providing the monks with their daily physical needs.

The Jain religion emerged in India between the seventh and fifth-centuries BC, although Jains consider their faith to be eternal, and periodically renewed. They believe that time is infinite, made up of many cosmic cycles stretching back millions of years. Each cycle contains periods of advancement and of decline, when faith and human behaviour reach a low point. During times of decline, a Tirthankara – a pathmaker or maker of a ford across the ocean of rebirth – appears. He will revive the religion and show people how to morally behave and achieve liberation.

Adaptation in the West

It is estimated that some 80,000 of the total of four million Jains now live outside India, including roughly 25,000 in Europe and over 20,000 in the USA (Cort 1990). Those who are now second and third generation immigrants may have little or no direct contact with the land of their origin but nonetheless perceive themselves as Jains. It is among them that the most obvious signs of change and adaptation can be found. While an important festival such as *Paryushan* (a *Shvetambara* (monastic) festival held during *caturmas*, the four-month ascetic monsoon retreat) maintains its importance, Jainism cannot be practised in the same manner in the West as in India.

Dunas (1992) has suggested that the attitude of Jains in the West manifests itself in two different modes of belief, which he describes as neo-orthodoxy and 'heterodoxy'. The former is a type of Jainism which would be recognizable to traditional followers. It includes ritual, recitation of prayers and mantras, full acceptance of the authority of Mahavira (the 24th and perhaps most important Tirthankara) and his teachings, and a concern with correct practices and sectarian exclusivity, all typically associated with women and older people.

Heterodoxy involves an interpretation of Jainism as theistic and free from the mysticism which many feel to be a feature of the religion, with the fordmakers being viewed as in some ways the manifestation of God intervening directly in human affairs. Here, God-focused devotion plays an important part and the Jains who have espoused this heterodoxy see no contradictions in worshipping in Hindu or Sikh temples. Heterodoxy presents itself as modern and progressive, with an emphasis on those aspects of Jainism which can be interpreted as scientific and rational and may therefore be accommodated to encompass Western modes of thought. This includes the strong advocacy of vegetarianism and the advantages of a balanced and healthy diet, non-violence, the value of meditation, a rejection of ritual and sectarianism, and a belief in the possibility of unaided self-perfection.

Buddhism

Beliefs

The word 'Buddha' means the 'Enlightened One', and there have been a number of Buddhas over the centuries, the best known (and founder of Buddhism) being Siddhartha Gautama (*c*.560–480). Siddhartha was born into a high-ranking Indian family. Giving up his status in order to live a spiritual life, he sought 'enlightenment' in order to free himself from the cycle of death and rebirth. The Buddhist religion is based on his life and teachings.

By practising morality and meditation and gaining wisdom, Buddhists aim to escape from the cycle of reincarnation and attain *nirvana* (translated as 'no-being'), the ultimate, peaceful, transformed consciousness. Each and every religious act of Buddhists begins with 'taking refuge' in the Three Jewels (*triratna*): the Enlightened One (the Buddha), the Teaching (the Dhamma), and the Community (the Sangha). The most important goal for the Buddhist is to follow the Eightfold Path, which involves full understanding of the Buddhist truths, living well, and avoiding work that might be harmful to others. In this way, Buddhists hope to achieve a favourable rebirth after death, or even to reach enlightenment, a state of spiritual purity which is completely free from worldly concerns.

Early on in the history of the faith, Buddhism branched out into a great diversity of orders and schools of thought, ordination, and teaching lineages. Some have developed mutually incompatible positions on matters of discipline and doctrine; others have retained a large number of common teachings and practices. The two main strands of the traditional faith are Theravada and Mahayana Buddhism, which split from each other at a very early stage. The former lays great stress on an individual's own self-improvement and salvation, though this can be attained only by living a strict monastic life. The latter has a lifestyle that is less strictly ascetic, depending more on faith and devotion. It lays greater emphasis on the possibility of anyone becoming a *bodhisattva* (someone destined for enlightenment) who then delays his passage, or nirvana, until he has helped others along the same path. Tibetan, Chinese, and Japanese Buddhism all stem from Mahayana Buddhism. A third strand, Tantric Buddhism, is more text-based and ritualistic, with much emphasis on the recital of mantras.

Adaptation in the West

The general pattern of the world religions being spread to the West by the migration of ethnic minorities does not stand in all cases. On occasion, evangelizing endeavours have been embarked upon by exponents of eastern mysticism as a result of the deliberate exportation of some faiths. This may not always have been with quite the zeal of Christian missionaries spreading their gospel across the globe, especially during times of Western colonial rule. Nonetheless, Hindu teachings, for instance, along with religions from Japan and Korea, have penetrated the West for over a century through missionary initiatives. None of these have impacted in this way quite as impressively as the various schools that constitute the Buddhist faith. While obviously appealing particularly to people from India and the Far East, Buddhism has very often proved popular to, and indeed been spread by, sections of the white population, namely those within the middle-classes, mostly the intelligentsia, academics, and a range of professional occupations (Tipton 1982). The various traditions of Buddhism have impacted in different ways on Western countries. The Theravada tradition of Sri Lanka, once part of the British Empire, became the predominant orientation of the Buddhist Society (founded 1907) and Buddhism generally throughout Britain. Nonetheless, Zen Buddhism and the Tibetan Vajrayana are two other popular alternatives (Somers 1990). The latter has grown since 1959, following the Chinese invasion of Tibet, when many leading lamas succeeded in fleeing to the West. The historical development in the USA, however, took a different root. The predominant tradition there has always been Zen, which continues to have a strong influence today (Ellwood 1979). Indeed, Zen Buddhism has proved very fashionable in the Western world since the 1960s, and amounts to a fusion of Mahayana and Chinese Taoism. Its aim is the direct experience of enlightenment (*satori*). In the USA, its popularity stemmed from the influx of Chinese immigrants into California in the nineteenth-century, followed by Japanese immigration. Increasing divisions within the Buddhist faith are common in the West. In Germany, for example, it is expressed in up to sixteen principal schools, which have often found it difficult to establish common ground as Buddhists.

Although Buddhism seems remote from Western traditions, certain aspects of it do appear to be congruent with Western values. Buddhism and other forms of eastern mysticism seem to lend themselves well to the emphasis on self-improvement and the desire for experience and enlightenment, or as part of a contemporary search for identity. In the West, there are Buddhists active in religious ceremonies, presenting lectures, holding meditation classes, advancing cultural activities such as handicrafts, calligraphy, vegetarian cooking, and various community services (Somers 1990). However, Buddhist groups display a range of responses and strategies to the challenge of adapting to the modern West, some remaining firmly traditional. Yet, in the Western context, Buddhism is often transformed. In the case of the USA, even groups that have kept organizational continuity with the old sects in Asia have adapted to American conditions. Buddhist groups generally see themselves as part of the Buddhist ecumenical movement and maintain contacts with other faiths, although they do not always show much enthusiasm for dialogue. There is some interfaith discussion. For example, the Samye Lingh order that holds annual interfaith conferences and has set up a retreat centre at Holy Island in Scotland, is primarily Buddhist, but open to other faiths.

New Buddhist movements

In the form of NRMs, Buddhism is represented (although not in its best light) by the Rajneesh organization that has been discussed earlier (in Chapter 7) largely within the context of cult controversies. The movement, however, is not just inspired by Buddhism, but by Christianity, Taoism, Hinduism, and Sufism. These have been moulded together in a this-worldly orientated philosophy. According to Rajneesh's teachings, we are all buddhas, identical with God ('brahma'). All of creation is divine. Thus, the world should be affirmed, not denounced. The mind tends to work with a set of taboos and prohibitions that run counter to man's inner nature, often created by the social order in which we live. Man must be liberated from these prohibitions which restrict spiritual, emotional, psychological, and material development. Given this kind of philosophy, it is not surprising that the Rajneesh movement has appealed to an affluent constituency. Heelas and Thompson's survey (1986, 91) of its followers indicated that over 60 per cent had university degrees, 80 per cent were professional white-collar workers, while 90 per cent considered themselves 'successful'.

Soka Gakkai International is a quite different form of Buddhism from the Rajneesh movement. According to its founder, Nichiren (1222–82), the teachings of Buddha himself were 'provisional'. They did not contain the whole truth of Buddhism, but merely what was relevant to mankind at the time. Nichiren had concluded that the Lotus Sutra was the one true form of Buddhism for the age in which he lived. Today, however, adherents believe that Nichiren's teachings are now of greater significance than that of Gautama.

The modern Soka Gakkai movement can be traced back to the 1930s in Japan, the home of Nichiren himself. In the post-war years there was a drive to extend the movement globally and under Daisa Ikeda, the organization's president at present, there are now tens of thousands of followers, including 5,000 in Britain. It is a movement which appears to be missing many of the trappings of traditional Buddhism. There are no monasteries, monks, or distinctive robes, and no breathing meditation or images of Buddha. There are hardly any references to the teachings of Buddha, including the Four Noble Truths or the Eightfold Path.

Because of the utmost significance of the mantra *nam myoho renge kyo* (Salutation to the Lotus Sutra), the basic practice of the Soka Gakkai members is to chant the mantra in the morning and afternoon for twenty minutes at a time. Mantras are held to have power and, as Nichiren originally taught it, this is believed to bring practical results. Hence, members usually chant with some specific purpose in mind. There are numerous benefits to be acquired, both spiritual and material. Here, there is a common overlap with the Rajneesh movement. If one requires a spiritual possession, the power to chant can help provide it, although this is not guaranteed.

In 1991, the Soka Gakkai movement underwent a serious schism. Of central importance to the movement is the Dai-Gohonzon (holy writings said to be inscribed by Nichiren). These are in the possession of the Nichiren Shosu high priests at the temple at Taiseki-ji, at the foot of Mount Fuji. This priesthood regards itself as having a unique position within the movement. As the movement spread globally, the priesthood and laity found themselves taking their brand of Buddhism in different directions and a measure of conflict has ensued. The main contention was that the laity felt a compulsion to adapt and to grow, while the priesthood clung to their traditions. Matters came to a head in the early 1990s, when the priesthood inaugurated a new movement. A number of European members became adhered to this, while some priests joined the opposition's camp. In 1992, the Nichiren Shoshu in the UK changed its name to Soka Gakkai International.

Summary

Perhaps of all the 'alternative' religions in the West, it is those of the ethnic minorities that constantly make news. This is obviously because they are related to complex political issues that are not limited by the confines of nation states but have global repercussions, especially within the context of fundamentalism. At the very least, the significance of such religions is bound up with issues of rights and pluralism, and their significance for ethnic minorities. It follows that such religions are not 'alternatives' at all in the sense that, while they do win converts outside of their ethnic confines, subscribing to them is more related to being socialized into a culture rather than chosen freely in the spiritual marketplace. In that sense, the religions of the ethnic minorities raise a set of issues that do not relate to many of the others we have considered so far.

Further reading

Cohen-Sherbok, D. (1991) 'Jews and Europe', *Religion Today*, **6** (2), 3–5.
Parsons, G. (ed.) (1993) *The Growth of Religious Diversity: Britain from 1945. Volume 1, Traditions*, London: Routledge.
Snow, D. (1976) *The Nichiren Shoshu Buddhist Movement in America*, Unpublished PhD Thesis, University of California: Los Angeles.

13 Quasi-religions

Quasi-religions or, as they are sometimes called, 'implicit religions' appear to be another growth area of the religious fringe. As we have already seen (Chapter 11), perhaps the most obvious range of quasi-religions are the emerging therapeutic and healing cults. However, the category quasi-religion includes such a wide scope of religious life that practically anything can be termed 'religious' according to some criteria. Put succinctly, quasi-religions amount to a range of social phenomena which appear to be religious when certain criteria are applied. At the very least these expressions of religiosity seem to have some qualities in common with more traditional forms, although much depends on how religion is defined. Among the social phenomena which have been designated as quasi-religions by sociological studies are sporting activities, Alcoholics Anonymous, environmentalism, rock music, television, and UFO cults. Some of these expressions, alongside a discussion as to why quasi-religions appear to be proliferating, will be discussed below.

Defining quasi-religions

What do the quasi-religions have in common with more traditional forms? Greil and Robbins (1994, 4) identify two principal characteristics. Firstly, quasi-religions display organizational dynamics similar to those of religious institutions, narrowly defined, whether expressed by way of cults, sects or churches. Secondly, quasi-religions, in line with more orthodox forms, focus on expressions of what might be termed the 'ultimate concerns' of human existence, but possibly without the belief in the supernatural. While, as we shall see, some social phenomena have one or both of these qualities, there are, however, a number of problems involved with definitions of implicit or quasi-religions.

On the first count, social phenomena defined as 'quasi' religions may primarily be designated as such because they do not fall within either popular or common sense views of what a religion is and/or what is officially defined as such by governments and other influential agencies, including anti-cultist groups. Barker (1994) points out that the Unification Church and the Church of Scientology both vehemently describe themselves as religions. However they are often viewed very differently by governments, anti-cultist groups, and popular opinion. Frequently, they are not perceived as 'real' or genuine religion as a result of preconceived ideas about what constitutes religion, as well as implicit assumptions regarding their activities or alleged notorieties (Barker 1994, 102–9).

Conversely, forms of social life designated quasi-religion may refute any suggestion that they are indeed a religion. Greil (1993) maintains that what might or might not be referred to as 'quasi-religions' should largely depend on the basis of the actor's *own* definition and not what others consider as implicitly 'religious' about it. This may mean that the pool of true quasi-religions is relatively small. We may cite two examples. One is the Fourth Wall Community, which was based in New York from the 1950s to the late 1980s. As a psychotherapy group it was dedicated to experimenting in transpersonal therapy and self-realization in a number of innovating ways. Siskind (1990) believes that the group displayed many of the characteristics of a religion. It had a self-designated 'elect' or 'chosen people' dedicated to creating perfect human beings in order to establish a new society; it held apocalyptic beliefs and feared nuclear annihilation and the peril of AIDS; it displayed an unquestioning faith in an authoritarian leadership and threatened the expulsion of 'heretics' from membership; it embraced a belief in absolute good and evil, the saved and unsaved; and there was an emphasis on 'confession' in the form of revelation made to one's therapist. Despite all these attributes of a religion, Siskind maintains that the community would have rebutted the idea that it was a religion. A second and perhaps less obvious example is Alcoholics Anonymous. This, and similar organizations, could be interpreted as a kind of sectarian movement. There are a strict set of beliefs, a strong moral code, and a higher, if vague, 'transcendental' goal. Alcoholics Anonymous, however, would vehemently deny any religious overtones for various reasons, including the need to avoid alienating any one who might consider joining.

Finally, there is the conceptual problem of establishing the boundaries between implicit or quasi-religions on the one hand, and supernaturalist aspects of more traditional forms of religion (with their belief in God, gods, and spirits) on the other. The problem is what to place under the heading of 'quasi' since many groups, particularly 'holistic' movements with their emphasis on spirituality, health, personal growth, and ecology, are difficult to classify clearly as either sacred or secular. It has also been suggested that many groups associated with the occult or astrology could be classified as quasi-religions (Campbell & McIver 1987) and possibly this goes for many strands of the New Age movement as well. At the same time, as Bailey (1997, 7) argues, explicit or traditional forms of religion may themselves display aspects of implicit religion. We may cite the increasing interest that many strands of traditional Christianity have with healing and human potential. This preoccupation is to such a degree as to plausibly make a 'religion' out of largely this-worldly concerns.

The rise of quasi-religions

Various explanations have been advanced for the apparent rise in quasi-religions. One of the most common is that they are fulfilling a spiritual requirement for some people. Traditional religion may be declining but the need remains. Hence, there is the necessity to sustain one form or another of religious belief and to have meaning in the world. The expressions of spirituality, however, are slowly being transformed. Luckmann puts this succinctly when he argues that contemporary societies are witnessing a profound change in the location of religion away from the 'great transcendences' concerned with other-worldly matters, life, and death, and towards the 'little transcendences' of earthly life, especially those which are concerned with self-realization, self-expression, and this-worldly interests (Luckmann 1990). Quasi-religions then, much like the NRMs, should not be viewed as a curiosity or somehow 'outside' society. In fact, they follow its cultural contours and embrace the core values of secularity.

Greil and Robbins (1994) believe that, at least in the USA, quasi-religions are advancing in the space left by the decline of more traditional forms. They maintain that American 'folk' religion with its emphasis on the one God is losing its appeal. Primarily expressed through Christianity, folk religion is no longer satisfying or meaningful to large sections of the population. Simultaneously, the link between the religious and non-religious is more difficult to discern as profound cultural changes continue to take place which blur the distinction between the two in an increasingly secular and materialist world (Greil & Robbins 1994, 16).

In discussing the proliferation of quasi-religions, other commentators have embraced a post-modernist approach. Nesti, for instance, sees quasi-religion arising from the inability of the contemporary Western world to provide a unified system of meaning. Today, people are fragmented into their own life experiences. There is a weakening of social identity and an ignorance of history, which means that the past loses its significance (Nesti 1990, 424–5). Implicit religion includes the search for meaning and identity in a world which finds it increasingly difficult to provide them. This search originates in the individual's life experience, expressing itself by means of a complex system of symbols and practices. These religions allow the unconditional relevance of a person's existence in the here and now. Hence, social forms and experience are translated into spiritual metaphors – giving secular phenomenon spiritual powers. It may also entail notions of a personal voyage or articulate itself in the form of escapism, hence freeing individuals from social and psychological restrictions.

Some examples of quasi-religions

The 'religious' nature of secular organizations

A fertile ground for the study of implicit religiosity is that of secular institutions. Among the less obvious are large-scale business enterprises. In this area, Bromley and Shupe (1990) have described a number of large USA corporations as having sectarian elements including their insistence that employees are strictly committed to a set of beliefs and demonstrate their allegiance. Peven (1968) has also analysed the use by business enterprises of what she calls 'religious revival techniques' to indoctrinate sales personnel into the business ethic and to integrate them into the culture of the corporate.

While secular institutions do not exhibit a specific supernatural dimension, some appear to be linked to what Greil and Rudy (1984) refer to as expressions of 'ultimate concern'. This is because they establish a foundation of meaning and significance to life. One of the most obvious parallels are political organizations, particularly the parties of the extreme left and right of the political spectrum with their strict ideological commitment, most notably those of Marxist and fascist orientation. O'Toole's (1977) study, for instance, has described the process of 'conversion' and commitment in several left-wing political groups in Canada, including the Internationalists and the Socialist Labour Party. Here there are to be observed the sectarian characteristics of a political organization, along with the cult surrounding the leadership and accompanying uncompromising beliefs that border on a kind of dualist worldview which divides the world into the forces of good and evil.

Sport

Sociologically speaking, it is functional rather than substantive definitions of religion which are utilized in categorizing quasi-religions. As we have seen (in Chapter 1), substantive definitions of religion tend to focus on a belief in spiritual beings or the supernatural. Functionalist definitions centre upon what religion does, particularly in terms of reference to sacred practices. It is this latter approach which allows a far broader range of activities and beliefs to be described as religion. Here, Emile Durkheim's functional definition of religion has proved an inspiration to some present-day sociologists since it involves a common set of beliefs and practices which unite a shared collective system of morality. There is, in Durkheim's definition, no mention of the supernatural. It is hardly surprising, therefore, that it has often been utilized in order to discuss such secular concerns as sporting activities to the extent that there is said to be a clear parallel between religion and sport because they have beliefs, symbols, and rituals in common (Prebish 1984, 312).

Soccer has proved a popular theme for discussion. For example, Percy and Taylor (1997) argue that there is much about the sport that appears 'religious' such as rituals, performance and expectations of soccer crowds, expressions of tribalism, a worship of masculinity, and even divination in predicting match results. Similarly, in North America, the theme of sport as a quasi- or secular religion has drawn a great deal of attention. Loy et al (1978) conclude that sport in the USA has helped fill the gap left by the declining civil religion and has reinforced the American way of life. It does this by restructuring myths and values and brings a sense of history and tradition that subsequently enhances social integration. Alternatively, sport may provide forms of 'folk' religion for certain sections of society and constitutes, especially for males, a distinct way of life and subculture (Demerath & Williams 1985, 166). Some sports even appear to display aspects of religiosity which make reference to superhuman or even supernatural entities and elevate personalities to almost divine status. Famous soccer stars frequently assume a demi-god image, while the opposing team becomes designated as the forces of evil.

Television and rock stars

Lemert (1975) suggests that attributes of religion may be applied to social phenomena when what is held as 'sacred' comes to reifying a way of life or culture.

This is particularly so when people begin to apply a 'spirituality' and seek significant meaning and sometimes a moral dimension to their existence and concerns in this world, beyond a mere material aspect. This may be so for some people in their fanatic following of movie or rock stars. In his book *Elvis People. The Cult of the King*, Ted Harrison describes the cult which built up around Elvis Presley, and its growth, following the singer's death in 1977, into what borders on a variety of new religious movement. There is now a flourishing market for Presley 'relics', while his former home at Graceland has become a site of pilgrimage for thousands of people. A 'priest-hood' of impersonators preach the 'gospel' of Elvis throughout the USA and across the world. Presley today has 'disciples' who claim to feel his presence, especially in times of personal tribulation. There is also a range of myths about the alleged supernatural events that attended his birth and his lifelong quest for enlightenment, which are not uncommonly taken as evidence that he was 'chosen' by a higher divine power.

Although Durkheim believed that religion would continue to be pervasive in modern society he could not have anticipated all the forms that it has taken. This is evident in Deena Weinstein's (1992) discussion of the religious dimensions of television as seen in terms of Durkheim's theory. A key feature of contemporary society is its mode of integration: its cohesion is at least partly due to the technological and organizational innovations of the mass media. Hence, one of the core functions of the national media such as television is in depicting society 'to itself and to celebrate it'. Television, then, is more than entertainment. For Weinstein, it functions as the collective consciousness of the social order by manifesting a common set of beliefs and morality. Television personalities become 'church leaders' and may even be conferred a sacred status as they are symbolic expressions of modern collective sentiments. This obviously takes quasi-religions beyond mere functional definitions in making overt references to the supernatural, to gods, spirits, or any such supernatural force or some superempirical realm. Particularly through television, some personalities even appear to have god-like qualities on a par with sports stars, while a number of television shows such as *Friends* and *Star Trek* have become something of a cult, with almost a divine status given to their leading actors. Indeed, it is sometimes these expressions of quasi-religion that perhaps stretch the definition of religion to its furthest point, since they appear to make references to supernatural entities.

Consumerism

Consumerism is the dominant mode of cultural life in the West. The consumption of goods has moved beyond the economic sphere so that it now constitutes core values and lifestyles and permeates most aspects of social existence. So central is consumerism to Western cultural expression that it can be described as a form of religiosity (Douglas & Isherwood 1980). Consumption involves a dedication to a shared set of values; it dominates social life and the life of the individual. Moreover, it constitutes an all-embracing belief system to which Western man pays homage to the exclusion of practically all else. Consumer goods are objects that can be worshipped and venerated – they shape every aspect of our lives. All this is enhanced by media advertising and is essentially linked to aspects of self-improvement. Consumption has come to dominate our views of self-identity and how we give shape to the very meaning of our existence (Munro 1996). This cultural obsession is reflected in many different ways. One is in the act of shopping. It may be said that Sunday shopping has now replaced churchgoing on the Sabbath. Shopping itself becomes a ritual, a 'religious' practice performed for its intrinsic value rather than an end in itself. Much is exemplified by the hypermarkets that often dominate the urban landscape. These have become the new 'churches' of contemporary society.

Environmentalism

The importance of environmentalism to contemporary religion has already been considered within the context of the New Age. However, there is more to be said regarding its implicit religiosity. One enlightening study is that of Bartkowski and Swearingen (1997), which focused on environmental activists and how they sacrilized a natural land mark (Barton Springs, Austin, Texas) that was under the threat of commercial development. Their research raised questions as to whether quasi-religions are always expressed through individualistic channels. The site became a geographical area that was believed to provide a direct access to a supernatural realm and brought activists together with a sense of common identity in opposition to the perceived powers of evil – the commercial speculators. Bartkowski and Swearingen see this as an indication of the reversal of secularity through the reinvention of spirituality, albeit via implicit religious forms and those which display a strong sense of belonging to a movement with a definitive purpose rather than a stringent set of beliefs.

UFO cults

One form of quasi-religion that perhaps borders on a more orthodox form of religiosity is that of the flying saucer cults. The most renowned include the Aetherius Society and the Raelian movement. Among the few informative works in the area of such cults is James Lewis's *The Gods Have Landed*. Several contributors to this edited volume highlight the 'spiritual' aspects of these cults. UFO groups, which have become particularly popular since the 1950s, typically focus on communication with extra-terrestrial life forms who are believed to send messages to human beings through astral travelling or telepathy, as well as physical contact.

These alien beings often seem to be almost supernatural entities since they are far superior in every respect to mankind. The redemption of humanity is expected to come when benevolent aliens show human beings the error of their ways. They may even take 'believers' away to some better place. The messages said to be sent by these extra-terrestrial beings often appear to be of a moral or 'spiritual' kind. Frequently the aliens seem to be imploring the human race to reconstruct the world it threatens to destroy through its ignorance and greed. Other contributors to Lewis's volume cover such topics as those who claim a kind of 'religious' experience after being abducted by aliens, the cultist dimension of UFO groups in their conversion processes to a new worldview, and theological questions raised by the possible existence of extra-terrestrials.

The Aetherius Society is probably the first and certainly the most enduring UFO cult. It was established by George King in 1955. In constant contact with extra-terrestrials through 'cosmic transmissions', King first received communication via a so-called Cosmic Master. Most of the messages appear to give interplanetary news or warn of impending troubles on earth but they also bring messages of hope and encouragement. The beliefs of the Aetherius Society include aspects of Christianity and Buddhism, among other faiths. Members also believe in reincarnation based on the Law of Karma. It is conceived that human beings progress, through various lives, towards perfection. Everyone will eventually become a Master and will continue to evolve from that status. In common with many other mystical movements, the Society believes in a living spiritual hierarchy of Masters, the Great White Brother-hood, including Jesus, Buddha, Krishna, and other monumental religious teachers. They all taught the same principles or the Laws of God.

The Great White Brotherhood is engaged in a battle with evil forces and the Aetherius Society is part of that struggle. It regularly engages in 'Spiritual Pushes' in which, by praying and meditating, members are able to draw 'Parna' (the Universal Life Force) down to earth from a gigantic spaceship, Satellite Three, which is in close orbit around the planet. Among the evils which the Aetherius Society campaigns against are pollution and nuclear power. Members of the society took part in Opera-tion Starlight between 1958 and 1961 so that the Cosmic Masters could charge them with spiritual powers. Members now make regular pilgrimages to the peaks of specially designated mountains, where the movement's symbol is painted.

Specific to the Aetherius Society is the belief that each planet in our solar system is akin to a classroom, where we learn certain life lessons before progressing to the next planet. A person may live on the same planet for thousands of years before graduating to the next planet depending on how much effort he/she puts into living God's laws. The solar system is ruled by a Cosmic Hierarchy, or Interplanetary Parliament, made up of highly venerated Masters, and is based on the planet Saturn. This hierarchy, in turn, is responsible to the Lords of the Sun for the evolution of every form of life in the solar system.

A second significant UFO cult is the Raelian movement. Its leader, Claude Vorilhon (known as Rael), claims that in 1973 he was contacted by beings from another planet. Since that time he has been channelled with messages to pass on to mankind. In 1975, he was allegedly taken in their spacecraft to another planet. Since its formation, the Raelian movement has spread into over fifty countries and claims to have 40,000 members. Rael's own unique message is that the human race is now sufficiently evolved as to understand that man was created by a race called the Elohim who are some 25,000 years more advanced than humans. This creation was through a manipulation of DNA, in the image of the Elohim.

In the past, the Elohim have contacted humanity via the great prophets, including Moses, Jesus, and Muhammad, but through the cultural idiom of the time so that the message was relevant to a particular context. Today, so it is stated (*The Raelian Move-ment: Information*, undated leaflet), humans have advanced with their scientific knowl-edge to the point that they can comprehend the Elohim as their creators. Rael is the prophet of our age and is sent to announce that the Elohim will shortly return to earth to contact all nations. The Elohim bid humans to recognize their role in creation, referred to in ancient religious texts and by their own scientific development. There is also the call to build a new society for the future. This will be achieved through courses of Sensual Mediation held all over the world, enabling individuals to regain control over their lives by questioning all assumed beliefs and behaviour. As each individual becomes more happy and fulfilled, so humanity as a whole becomes more advanced and the society of the future begins to develop. This philosophy applies to all areas of life, including education, love, sexuality, work, leisure, and self-development.

The Raelian movement holds major 'Courses of Awakening' in Europe, the USA, Australia, and Korea. The aim is to create a world of leisure, love, and fulfilment, and to bring about an end to moralistic social restrictions, especially sexual inhibitions. Everyone is encouraged to act as they wish, as long as they do not harm others. It is, then, a hedonistic philosophy. To this, Rael proposes a political system which is to be run by the most intelligent for the benefit of all. It may be concluded that the aims of the movement are similar to many mystical cults. The difference is that their revelation comes from extra-terrestrials rather than from Ascended Masters or God.

What may be seen from this overview of quasi-religions is that many display characteristics of the contemporary world and it is undoubtedly the case that what were once irrelevant to Western society are now more mainstream and related to aspects of social and cultural transformation. We may be entertained by UFO cults; however, they tell us something of significance, not least of all the central place of science and technology in the West. A Gallop poll conducted in the USA in 1987 indicated that 50 per cent of those sampled believed that UFOs existed and that 9 per cent claimed that they might have actually seen one. The key observation is that it was not until the years after the Second World War, with the advance of science and technology, especially when it opened up the possibility of space travel, that stories of UFO sightings began to make news.

At the same time, so it might be argued, UFO cults display aspects of much more primitive forms of human religion. For example, Whitemore (1995) draws parallels between reports of encounters with UFO entities and traditional folklore related to meeting fairy folk. These include the round saucer traces on the ground reminiscent of fairy rings; the elfin appearance of the alien 'little folk'; the abductions during which ordinary time dissolves as it did for those countrymen of yore taken into a fairy mound; the rumours of changeling children and peculiar half-human pregnancies. Likewise, the small circles or tiny implants left by the aliens are very reminiscent of the devil's marks that the witchfinders sought to locate on their victims. In some respects, perhaps, little has changed.

Ethical eating

It is evident that many of the quasi-religions considered above stretch definitions of religion to their furthest extent. However, perhaps none go so far as sociological works which relate diet and dietary regimes to forms of religiosity. How might this be justified? It is clear that the consumption of food has considerable social significance, while dietary practices figure prominently in many religions and forms of religious practice. Food is a key component in numerous religious rituals, such as sacrifice, bringing a symbolic expression to a variety of social sentiments. Alternatively, the ascetic tradition of many major religions emphasize fasting, food avoidance, or taboos. In the West today, however, dietary practices may be said to have developed a form of religiosity all of their own. This can be illustrated by a commercial for 'Crystal Light' low fat food on American television which included the slogan 'I believe in being the best I can be, I believe in watching every calorie'.

The tendency of dietary regimes to express an implicit religiosity is perhaps most notable with the increasing popularity of wholefoods, health food, and organically produced food consumption and vegetarianism. Consumers of these foods, according to some commentators, perceive them as having magical and mystical orientations, even if dressed up in scientific discourse (Delamont 1984). More broadly, there appears to be a deeper dimension, which goes beyond the desire for good health or, in fact, for any clear material goal. It may then be understood, in a consumerist way, as to some extent expressing a desire for a spiritual dimension in daily existence.

In the discussion of what he refers to as 'ethical eating' and the link with alternative lifestyles and values, Sellerberg (1991) suggests that there is an implied religiosity. Concerns about processing, adulteration, denutrification, and contamination of food often go hand in hand with opposition to nuclear power, and even science and technology, and this frequently links with New Age philosophy. It might be concluded that ethical eating is an ethos one would expect to find in an affluent, scientifically and technologically based society – one in which it is no longer credible to seek a meaningful life through traditional spiritual and religious expressions and, above all, supernaturalist ideas.

Summary

In the claim that eating and dieting has an implied religiosity it may appear that the definition of religion has now been stretched just about as far as it will go. However, it does stress the more 'hidden' aspects of alternative religiosity. This raises an important issue related to the sociology of religion as a sub-discipline. By focusing upon these aspects of religion, the concern moves away from substantive definitions of religion and departs from the significance of God, gods, spirits, and the supernatural. This may be an indication of an increasingly secular society and the difficulty that sociology has in locating traditional forms of religion. It may thus mean that implied forms of religiosity have always existed, but that sociologists of religion are willing to identify more and more forms in order to keep the sub-discipline alive in an increasingly secular world.

Further reading

Bailey, E. (1997) *Implicit Religion*, Kampen, The Netherlands: Kok Pharos Publishing House.

Greil, A. (1993) 'Explorations Along the Sacred Frontier: Notes on Para-Religions, Quasi-Religions, and Other Boundary Phenomenon', in D. Bromley & J. Hadden (eds.) *Religion and the Social Order*, **3**, part A, Greenwich, CT: JAI Press.

Greil, A. & Robbins, T. (1994) (eds.) *Between Sacred and Secular: Research and Theory on Quasi-Religion*, Religion and the Social Order, **4**, Greenwich, CT: JAI Press.

Harrison, T. (1992) *Elvis People. The Cult of the King*, London: HarperCollins.

Lewis, J. (1995) *The Gods Have Landed. New Religions from Other Worlds*, Albany, NY: State University Press.

14 The 'rise' of the alternatives: some implications

An overview of alternative religiosn in Western societies suggests that they come in an infinite variety of forms, from quasi-Christian sects, to imported ancient world religions, to entirely new religious movements and quasi-religions. If, collectively, they are replacing mainstream Christianity, it might be argued that a reversal in the decline of religion is taking place and that long-held sociological views regarding the inevitability of the process of secularization (as defined as the 'decline of religion') are being brought into question. In short, the expression may have changed, but it could well be that a demand for religiosity is still to be observed. This final chapter explores these themes.

The alternatives: a revival of religion?

The possibility of a religious revival invariably relates to the question of the true social significance of the alternative religions and their real relevance, if any, beyond offering something positive for those who are directly involved. Hence, it might be conjectured that they are not just marginal forms of religion but are also very peripheral aspects of social life, and that from a historical and long-term perspective the evidence still points towards an overall demise of religion in Western societies. Some commentators such as Steve Bruce (1996b) would suggest that the so-called 'new religiosity' implicit in the rise of many of the 'alternatives' does not make up for the decline of traditional Christianity. The alleged revival of religion appears not to correspond, in any meaningful way, with the commitment that previous generations expressed towards the Christian faith. Furthermore, on the evidence of the last few decades, Bruce argues, there is not really a great deal of religion to be observed and what does exist scarcely constitutes religion at all.

According to Bruce, the number of people who have shown any interest in alternative religions is minute. He maintains that, outside sectarian and fundamentalist forms of religion and those of the ethnic minorities, the commitment to most is slight. The more popular of the newer religions flaunt 'products' which are essentially secular and deal with the here and now rather than being concerned with salvation in the next world. They also fail to offer all-embracing systems of morality. Rather scathingly, Bruce suggests that of the newer alternative religions 'most are consumed by people as a slight flavouring to their mundane lives' (Bruce 1996b, 272–3). Moreover, they are limited to particular social groups. These are overwhelmingly the educated and wealthier members of the middle-classes, who are sufficiently affluent to subscribe to a range of client and audience cults.

There is another related issue that must be taken into account when considering the social significance of the 'alternatives'. Quasi-religions, holistic religions, and what are frequently known as self-spiritualities, appear in many respects to depart from traditionally accepted definitions of religion. This arguably highlights the fact that practically anything can be regarded as religion by using broad criteria and this may even include social phenomena which categorically deny being religious in nature. It may be, then, that any claim to the resurgence of religion ultimately depends on what is meant by the term. Sociologically speaking, this raises both epistemological and ideological issues, so that what constitutes religion is ultimately in the eye of the beholder.

It is beyond the scope of this book to speculate upon the 'true' level of religiosity among the range of alternatives on offer. Indeed, this would be a thankless and impossible task. However, there is another criterion by which to gauge their wider social impact and this may be interpreted as evidence of the relentless growth of secularity. In the early twenty-first-century, religion appears to be increasingly controversial. Whereas, in the 1950s and the 1960s, religion was generally seen as a relatively benign force in society, by the 1980s it had become more and more a politicized topic. Most of the controversies were related to the religious fringe, although mainstream Christianity by no means escaped. There were several principal reasons why this was so. Firstly, NRMs engendered debates as to what is or is not a religion. This was particularly in relation to legal litigations including the alleged abuse of members. Secondly, the state appears to increasingly touch upon some of the traditional rights of religion of all types, such as the freedom to have independent schools for the children of religious minorities. Thirdly, some religions have sought to advance and extend their interests in an increasingly pluralist society. Where there is now no longer one accepted religious truth, religions of all kinds struggle to be recognized and to win over converts in a world where there is the choice not to believe. It is this matter of choice, however, that has perhaps impacted most negatively on mainstream Christianity as the decline in religious socialization of younger generations begins to take its toll. In short, young people are increasingly choosing not to attend church or subscribe to the major tenets of the faith.

The demise of mainstream Christianity revisited

Evidence produced by the European Values Survey over a number of years shows that in Europe there is at least an apparent decline of Christianity in terms of its core doctrines (see Table 7). There is also an indication that some of those which do remain have been significantly transformed. The survey shows that in Europe belief in traditional Christianity has been undermined over a number of decades. Partly, this is because of the rise of competing forms of religiosity such as the new religions and the faiths of ethnic minorities, while levels of disbelief, or at least unconventional interpretations of Christian teachings, have also increased.

Table 7 Erosion of the Christian tradition: international patterns

% who say they believe in	Patterns of belief in God and in life after death				
	Britain	Ireland	France	Denmark	European average
God	76%	95%	62%	58%	75%
A personal God	31%	n.a.	n.a.	n.a.	32%
Absolute guidelines for telling good and evil	28%	n.a.	n.a.	n.a.	26%
Life after death	24%	76%	35%	26%	43%
Heaven	57%	83%	27%	17%	40%
Hell	27%	54%	15%	8%	23%
Reincarnation	27%	26%	22%	11%	21%
% who are definite atheists	9%	2%	19%	21%	11%

Source: Based on the European Values Survey data collected in 1981 (Harding, Phillips & Fogarty 1986, pp. 46–7; Gerard 1985, pp. 60–1).
Note: n.a. = not available

Undoubtedly, there are problems with interpreting such statistics. However, certain trends are clear (Davies 1999). Above all, there no longer remains the comprehensive worldview of some two thousand years that brought together Christian dogma regarding creation, moral behaviour, and afterlife beliefs. In fact, in the secular Europe of today the connections between these aspects of the faith have undergone fragmentation. Whereas the past was epitomized by one form or another of a strongly integrated system of afterlife, morality, and creation belief, in which death was followed by rewards or punishment, for most European people today there is little connection between them. Beyond this appraisal, there are a number of other important conclusions to be made. Firstly, there is a low proportion of the general European population who believe in a personal God. This is particularly so in view of the high proportion of believers in some kind of God that has only a few attributes of the Christian God, as well as the low number of convinced atheists. Secondly, there is a low proportion who believe in an absolute morality of right and wrong. Thirdly, there is a low proportion of believers in the existence of hell, which is well below the proportions of the same populations who believe in some form of afterlife (Catholicism in Ireland nonetheless remains closely attached to the doctrine of hell).

More detailed studies have shown a complicated picture. A more recent survey in Sweden (arguably one of the most secular of societies there is) shows that a high percentage (79 per cent) of the population believe in a 'personal God' but only 7 per cent of these were confessing Christians (Table 8). The research also indicated that the younger generation subscribes to a wide variety of beliefs concerning the paranormal and astrology (Table 9). Again, these statistics are open to interpretation and may be given to suggest that a belief in alternative forms of religion may prevail in the future at the expense of Christianity. The author of the research, Ulf Sjodin (2002), concludes that while a belief in the paranormal and the occult constitute ideologies for a large part of the Swedish population, they are not visible in organized forms. Swedes continue to uphold beliefs in the afterlife and supernatural powers but these are not considered to be associated with inherited religious dogmas. There is thus a kind of private or invisible religion which is founded on many of the doctrines of alternative religions. Sjodin notes, however, that further research needs to be conducted on how important, or central, these values are in the individual's outlook on life. They may turn out to be, he suggests, peripheral and thus fairly harmless and tolerable in a democratic, pluralist society.

Table 8 Beliefs in Sweden

Belief in	Those agreeing to items versus religious self-assessment			
	Confessing Christianity	Religious my own way	I can't say	Not religious
	(7%)	(44%)	(27%)	(22%)
Personal God	79	20	5	1
Lifeforce	18	58	39	24
Life after death	88	57	33	15
Spiritualism	32	42	22	17
Prelimonitory signs	88	88	78	77
UFOs	9	28	26	20

Source: Adapted from Sjodin, U. (2002) 'The Swedes and the Paranormal', *Journal of Contemporary Religion*, **17** (1), 75–85.

One notable feature of these statistics is the high percentage of believers in reincarnation, given that it is not part of and indeed is repugnant to the European Christian tradition. It is now apparent that nearly half the people of Europe believe in some kind of life after death, although they do not know exactly what. About a quarter of those surveyed believed in reincarnation. This development is not new. In 1955, some 25 per cent of English people held such a view – a quarter of all those who believed in any kind of afterlife (Davies 1999). The Western believers, however, are not following Hindu teachings of *karma* in that they do not see themselves having been or likely to return as some other species, but specifically human.

Table 9 Swedish youth's belief in the paranormal

		Girls	Boys
Generally paranormal	Low	31	61
	High	69	39
Astrology	Low	56	78
	High	44	22
UFOs	Low	68	61
	High	32	39
Reincarnation	Low	65	80
	High	35	20

Source: Adapted from Sjodin, U. (2002) 'The Swedes and the Paranormal', *Journal of Contemporary Religion*, **17** (1), 75–85.

Note: Low = Agrees to under 50% of the items
    High = Agrees to over 50% of the items

Neither does reincarnation appear to be attached to any moral code of behaviour (Hanegraaff 1996, 283).

While these figures show a clear change in adherence to Christianity in Europe, the USA is often held to be different in many respects, in that its peoples adhere more rigidly to Christian beliefs and that the Christian fundamentalist revival is indicative of this. However, as we have seen, the impact of the movement is not considerable, while the country remains the home of many NRMs. Moreover, a poll conducted by Gallop in the USA indicated that 79 per cent of the American population feel that there is a distinction between religion and spirituality. Only 40 per cent admit to being religious, while 94 per cent consider themselves to be spiritual. 95 per cent believe in God, but only 57 per cent believe in heaven and 24 per cent in hell.

The evidence, then, suggests that some of the doctrines essential to Christianity do not now hold a central place in the belief systems of Western societies. Rather, they have become part of the mix 'n' match of contemporary religiosity, where traditional Christianity is integrated with a whole variety of non-Christian beliefs. Again, this is not a fresh development since the fragmentation of coherent Christian beliefs extends back into the nineteenth-century. Other forms of religiosity, would also seem to erode the monolithic Christian culture of the West. This is true of many other global religions. The debate about the incongruity of ethnic world faiths and Western culture has disguised the fact that in many respects the faiths of ethnic minorities have influenced Western society in discernible (and sometimes indiscernible) ways. This includes alternative medicines and therapies and meditation techniques derived from non-Christian religions. At the same time, more broadly, such world religions as Buddhism have also clearly influenced a number of the NRMs and, more recently, the New Age.

The decline of Christianity: does it matter?

A number of politicians, church leaders, and church pressure groups have all lamented the decline of the so-called Christian society. For instance, the archbishop of Canterbury announced in 2000 that Britain had become 'an atheist society'. Certainly, it is evident that millions of people have been lost to the churches in the West. It is unlikely that these will be regained. Moreover, the separation of Church and state continues even in those European countries where it has traditionally been strong, and the Church's political power is now minimal. It is obvious that its influence cannot be compared with that of previous centuries. However, even this is open to interpretation. It may well be that the significance of the Church's previous political and state influence could be viewed as either a measurement of its impact on society, or a thorough-going compromise with this world.

It could be argued that Christianity may still provide the foundation of civil religion in Western societies. Evidence suggests that the faith continues to offer the trimmings for state occasions and affords some vague solace for large-scale natural and man-made disasters. In other words, it provides some indistinct ultimate reference point to aid individual and collective psychological restoration. However, it is increasingly difficult to suggest that Christianity provides a common and everyday basis of morality and a unified set of abstract beliefs. Some sociologists, such as Anthony and Robbins (1990), maintain that this may not be for the best – at least as far as American society is concerned. They believe that the decline in Christianity as expressed in civil religion has precipitated a moral malaise in American society which is evident in terms of sexual permissiveness, the increase in the divorce rate and family disintegration, rising crime, and the declining public support of established political institutions. These issues obviously provide fodder for conservative Christian groups ranging from traditional Roman Catholics to Protestant evangelicals who wish to reverse such changes.

Yet, all may not be lost. The plurality of religions in Western societies may have come to replace a civic religion based at least upon a nominal Christianity. This is evidenced in a more recent tentative assessment of religion in the USA by David Martin (1998), a long time observer of contemporary religion, who suggests that while religious belief in America is becoming increasingly diverse, the great majority of faiths carry the core cultural values of the USA. Writing in the *Independent* newspaper, Martin observed religion in Dallas, Texas. He found an infinite variety: Baptists, Korean churches, Armeanian churches, voodooism, Pentecostalism, Sikhism, Islam, Hinduism, and Judaism. Despite this diversity and the far-ranging traditions displayed, many of these faiths, in their own way, encapsulated American values of success, opportunity, freedom, responsibility, individual potential, and the historical celebration of all that is American. Hence, aspects of civic religion, it would seem, can be seen in many of the 'alternatives' since they constitute an integrative, rather than a diversive, force.

Summary and future prospects

This volume has sought to describe, account for, and analyse a whole variety of expression of alternative religions. Like other aspects of cultural life in the West, such religions are extremely diverse and even categorizing them in the way that we have done so here scarcely does them justice. Similarly, it is difficult to draw conclusions and make speculations concerning future developments. It might be stated glibly that there will be both sectors of decline and of growth. For instance, some of the NRMs may have reached their apogee. Those that emerged in the 1960s and 1970s, including the Unification Church or the Jesus movement, are now dwindling and it is unlikely that they will stand the test of time. Indeed, Eileen Barker (1999, 15), a seasoned researcher of NRMs, suggests that despite the large number of new religions and the present sizeable membership of a number of them, there is no indication that any one movement is likely to become a major religious tradition in the future. Those that do remain are also undergoing significant transformations. As Martin (1991) notes, those of a more world-rejecting type are increasingly inclined to accommodate them-selves with the world in order to survive and sustain their membership. It is a recogni-tion that few people seek a full commitment and immersion in a radically different and totally religious way of life.

Despite the concerns of some, it is possible to suggest that in a largely secular society, religion, of whatever kind, is so insignificant as to have few major repercus-sions for its social environment as either a stabilizing force or a disruptive one. What appears to be the case, however, is that the new religions, much like the old, reflect prevailing culture. As the Western way of life has undergone considerable transfor-mation, so has religion. This should not surprise or alarm. New forms are increasingly approximating what Heelas (1996) calls the 'de-traditionalized spiritualities of life', where ancient religions are reinvented for the various and complex needs of individ-uals in contemporary society, but in doing so may engender a form of social integra-tion. There is a preoccupation with all aspects of human potential and perfection, identity construction, and even worship of the self. Much is exemplified by the New Age. In many respects, it is that form of religiosity most removed from traditional Christianity which historically presented a codified doctrinal system and abstract morality. Nonetheless, such new expressions of religion may still provide significance and meaning and, in their holistic approach and emphasis on the environment, present a morality for future generations.

For many sociologists of religion, the areas of expansion are largely accepted to be the cultic religions and various strands of the New Age movement, the religions of various ethnic minorities, and expressions of world faiths of a fundamentalist nature. Simultaneously, a relatively new type of liberal and tolerant spirituality appears to be spreading in radically different dimensions – typically in the form of 'holistic' spiritu-ality or self-spirituality. To these growth areas can be added, so it may be argued, the more hidden aspects of religiosity – particularly the emergence of infinite varieties of quasi-religions, which satisfy the needs of some people for spirituality and meaning. It might also be conjectured that, in the future, many of these religions will prove to be transitory. Movements may tend to rise, grow, and disintegrate quickly. On the other hand, they may be rapidly transformed in line with contemporary Western culture changes. In this respect, their future remains unpredictable. Much will be linked to the fortunes of religion per se, alternative or otherwise. It is likely that in a pluralist society there will be no such designations as 'mainstream' and 'alternatives', but just a myriad of faiths and spiritualities that are reduced to a lifestyle choice for those who seek to indulge.

Bibliography

Abdullah, M. (1995) *Muslim Minorities in the West*, London: Grey Seal.

Abercrombie, N., Baker, J., Brett, S. & Foster, J. (1970) 'Superstition and Religion: The God of the Gaps', in D. Martin & M. Hill (eds.) *Sociological Year-book of Religion in Britain*, **3**, London: SCM.

Abrams, A., Gerard, D. & Timms, N. (eds.) (1985) *Values and Social Change in Britain*, Basingstoke: Macmillan.

Adams, R. & Fox, R. (1972) 'Mainlining Jesus: The New Trip', *Society*, February, 50–6.

Adler, M. (1986) *Drawing Down the Moon: Witches, Druids, Goddess-Worshippers, and Other Pagans in America Today*, Boston: Beacon Press.

Akers, K. (1977) *Deviant Behaviour: A Social Learning Approach*, Belmot, CA: Wadsworth.

Alfred, H. (1976) 'The Church of Satan', in C. Glock & R. Bellah (eds.) *The New Religious Consciousness*, Berkeley, CA: University of California Press.

Ali, Y. (1992) 'Muslim Women and the Politics of Ethnicity and Culture in Northern England', in J. Sahgal & N. Yuval-Davies (eds.) *Refusing Holy Orders*, London: Virago Press.

Ammerman, N.T. (1990) *Bible Believers: Fundamentalists in the Modern World*, New Brunswick, NJ: Rutgers University Press.

Anderson, R. (1980) 'Visions of the Disinherited: The Making of American Pentecostalism', *American Historical Review*, **87**, 1–48.

Anthony, D. & Robbins, A. (1982) 'Spiritual Innovation and the Crisis of American Civic Religion', in M. Douglas & S. Tipton (eds.) *Religion and America: Spirituality in a Secular Age*, Boston: Beacon Press.

Anthony, D. & Robbins, A. (1990) 'Civil Religion and Recent American Religious Ferment', in T. Robbins & D. Anthony (eds.) *In Gods We Trust: New Patterns of Religious Pluralism in America*, New Brunswick, NJ: Transaction Publishers.

Anthony, D. & Robbins, A. (1997) 'Religious Totalism, Exemplary Dualism, and the Waco Tragedy', in A. Robbins & S. Palmer (eds.) *Millenium, Messiahs, and Mayhem: Contemporary Apocalyptic Movements*, New York: Routledge.

Anthony, D., Needleman, J. & Robbins, T. (eds.) (1978) *Conversion, Coercion and Commitment in New Religious Movements*, New York: Seabury.

Anwar, M. (1995) *Young Muslims in a Multicultural Society*, Leicester: The Islamic Foundation.

Arcarti, K. (1998) *Numerology For Beginners*, London: Hodder & Stoughton.

Babbie, E. & Stone, D. (1977) 'An Evaluation of the ESP Experience by a National Sample of Graduates', *Bioscience Communication*, **3**, 123–40.

Badman, P. (ed.) (1989) *Religion, State, and Society in Modern Britain*, Lampeter: The Edwin Mellen Press.

Bailey, E. (1997) *Implicit Religion*, Kampen, The Netherlands: Kok Pharos Publishing House.

Bainbridge, W. (1997) *The Sociology of Religious Movements*, New York: Routledge.

Barber, B. (1995) *McWorld Versus Jihad*, New York: Times Books.

Barker, E. (1983) 'With Enemies Like That: Some Functions of Deprogramming as an Aid to Sectarian Membership', in J. Richardson (ed.) *Conversion Careers: In and Out of the New Religious Movements*, London: Sage.

Barker, E. (1984) *The Making of a Moonie*, Oxford: Blackwell.

Barker, E. (1985) 'New Religious Movements: Yet Another Great Awakening', in P. Hammond (ed.) *The Sacred in a Secular Age*, Berkeley, CA: University of California Press.

Barker, E. (1992) *New Religious Movements: A Practical Introduction*, London: HMSO.

Barker, E. (1994) 'But is it a Genuine Religion?', in A. Greil & T. Robbins (eds.) *Between Sacred and Secular: Research and Theory on Quasi-Religion*, Religion and the Social Order, **4**, Greenwich, CT: JAI Press.

Barker, E. (1999) 'New Religious Movements: Their Incidence and Significance', in B. Wilson & J. Cresswell (eds.) *New Religious Movements: Challenge and Response*, London: Routledge.

Barkun, M. (1986) *Crucible of the Millenium*, Syracuse, NY: Syracuse University Press.

Barr, J. (1978) *Fundamentalism*, London: SCM Press.

Barrett, D. (1988) 'The Twentieth-Century Pentecostal/ Charismatic Renewal in the Holy Spirit, With its Goal of World Evangelism', *International Bulletin of Missionary Research*, **12**, July, 119–29.

Barrett, D. (1998) *Sects, 'Cults' and Alternative Religion. A World Survey and Sourcebook*, London: Cassell.

Barrett, L. (1977) *The Rastifarians: The Dreadlocks of Jamaica*, Jamaica: Sangster's Book Stores.

Bartkowski, J. & Swearingen, W. (1997) 'God meets Gaia in Austin, Texas: A Case Study of Environmentalism as Implicit Religion', *Review of Religious Research*, **38** (4), 308–24.

Barton, J. (1986) 'Religion and Cultural Change in Czech Immigrant Communities, 1850–1920', in R. Miller & T. Marzik (eds.) *Immigrants and Religion in Urban America*, Philadelphia: Temple University Press.

Bastian, J. (1983) 'The Metamorphosis of Latin American Protestant Groups: A Sociological Perspective', *Latin American Research Review*, **28** (2), 33–61.

Bauman, Z. (1990) 'Postmodern Religion', in P. Heelas (ed.) *Religion, Modernity and Post-Modernity*, Oxford: Blackwell.

Beckford, J. (1975) *The Trumpet of Prophecy: A Sociological Study of Jehovah's Witnesses*, Oxford: Blackwell.

Beckford, J. (1978) 'Conversion and Apostasy', in D. Anthony, J. Needleman & T. Robbins (eds.) *Conversion, Coercion and Commitment in New Religious Movements*, New York: Seabury.

Beckford, J. (1983) 'The Public Response to the New Religious Movements in Britain,' *Social Compass*, **30** (1), 49–68.

Beckford, J. (1984) 'Holistic Imagery and Ethics in New Religious Healing Movements', *Social Compass*, **31** (2/3), 259–73.

Beckford, J. (1990) *Religion and Advanced Industrial Society*, London: Unwin Hyman.

Beckford, J. (1992) 'Religion, Modernity and Post-Modernity', in B. Wilson (ed.) *Religion: Contemporary Issues*, London: Bellew Publishing.

Bell, D. (ed.) (1963) *The Radical Right*, Garden City, NY: Doubleday.

Bellah, R. (1967) 'Civic Religion in America', in R. Richey & D. Jones (eds.) *American Civic Religion*, New York: Harper & Row.

Bellah, R. (1975) *The Broken Covenant: American Civil Religion in a Time of Trial*, New York: Seabury Press.

Bellah, R. (1976) 'New Religious Consciousness and the Crisis of Modernity', in C. Glock & R. Bellah (eds.) *The New Religious Consciousness*, Berkeley, CA: University of California Press.

Ben-Yehuda, N. & Goode, E. (1994) *Moral Panics: The Social Construction of Deviance*, Oxford: Blackwell.

Berger, P. (1967) *The Sacred Canopy*, Garden City, NY: Doubleday.

Berger, P. (1979) *The Heretical Imperative*, London: Penguin.

Berry, R. (1999) *Working With Dreams: How to Understand Your Dreams and Use Them For Personal and Creative Development*, London: How To Books.

Beyer, P. (1994) *Religion and Globalization*, London: Tavistock.

Bhacha, P. (1985) *Twice Migrants*, London: Tavistock.

Bibby, R. (1978) 'Why Conservative Churches are Really Growing, Kelley Revisited', *Journal for the Scientific Study of Religion*, **17** (2), 127–38.

Bibby, R. (1987) *Fragmented Gods: The Poverty and Potential of Religion in Canada*, Toronto: Irwin.

Bird, F. (1978) 'The Pursuit of Innocence: New Religious Movements and Moral Accountability', *Sociological Analysis*, **40** (4), 35–46.

Bloul, R. (1996) 'Engendering Muslim Identities: Deterritorialization and the Ethnicization Process in France', in B. Metcalf (ed.) *Making Muslim Space in North America and Europe*, Berkeley, CA: University of California Press.

Boston, G. (1998) *Astrology: A Beginners Guide*, London: Hodder & Stoughton.

Bowman, M. (1993) 'Reinventing the Celts', *Religion*, **23**, 147–56.

Bozeman, J.M. (1997)'Technological Millenarianism in the United States', in A. Robbins & S. Palmer (eds.) *Millenium, Messiahs, and Mayhem: Contemporary Apocalyptic Movements*, New York: Routledge.

Brierley, P. (1989) *A Century of British Christianity: Historical Statistics 1900–1985*, London: Research Monograph, MARC Europe.

Brierley, P. (1991a) *'Christian' England*, London: Marc Europe.

Brierley, P. (1991b) 'The New Age is Coming', *Research Monograph*, **35**, London: Marc Europe.

Brierley, P. (1993) *Reaching and Keeping Teenagers*, London: Christian Research Associated.

Brierley, P. (2000) *Religious Trends*, London: Marc Europe.

Bromley, D. (ed.) (1988) *Falling from the Faith*, Newbury Park, CA: Sage.

Bromley, D. & Hadden, J. (eds.) (1993) *Religion and the Social Order*, **3**, part A, Greenwich, CT: JAI Press.

Bromley, D. & Hammond, P. (eds.) (1987) *The Future of the New Religious Movements*, Macon, GA: Mercer University Press.

Bromley, D. & Shupe, A. (1979) 'The Tnevnoc Cult', *Sociological Analysis*, **40** (4), 361–6.

Bromley, D. & Shupe, A. (1981) *Strange Gods: The Great American Cult Scare*, Boston: Beacon Press.

Bromley, D. & Shupe, A. (1990) 'Rebottling the Elixir: The Gospel of Prosperity in America's Religio-economic Corporations', in T. Robbins & D. Anthony (eds.) *In Gods We Trust: New Patterns of Religious Pluralism in America*, New Brunswick, NJ: Transaction Publishers.

Brouwer, S., Gifford, P. & Rose, S. (1996) *Exporting the American Gospel*, Routledge: New York.

Bruce, S. (1988) *Rise and Fall of the New Christian Right in America*, Oxford: Clarendon Press.

Bruce, S. (1996a) *Cathedrals to Cults*, Oxford: Oxford University Press.

Bruce, S. (1996b) 'Religion in Britain at the Close of the Twentieth Century', *Journal of Contemporary Religion*, **11** (3), 261–74.

Budd, S. (ed.) (1993) *The Sociology of Religion*, London: Penguin.

Burg van de, C. (1993) 'Surinam Hinduism in the Netherlands and Social Change', in S. Budd (ed.) *The Sociology of Religion*, London: Penguin.

Burghart, R. (ed.) (1987) *Hinduism in Great Britain*, London: Tavistock.

Calley, M. (1965) *God's People*, Oxford: Oxford University Press.

Campbell, C. (1972) 'The Cult, the Cultic Milieu and Secularization', in M. Hill (ed.) *A Sociological Yearbook of Religion in Britain*, **5**, London: SCM.

Campbell, C. (1999) 'The Easternization of the West', in B. Wilson & J. Cresswell (eds.) *New Religious Movements: Challenge and Response*, London: Routledge.

Campbell, C. & McIver, S. (1987) 'Cultural Sources of Support for Contemporary Occultism', *Social Compass*, **34**, 41–60.

Campbell, H. (1980) 'Rastifarianism: Culture of Resistance, *Race and Class*, **22** (1), 1–22.

Carey, S. (1987) 'The Indianization of the Hare Krishna Movement', in R. Burghart (ed.) *Hinduism in Great Britain*, London: Tavistock.

Cashmore, E. (1979) *Rastaman: The Rastifarian Movement in England*. London: Unwin.

Caulfield, M. (1975) *Mary Whitehouse*, London: Mowbray.

Chalfont, H., Beckley, E. & Palmer, C. (1987) *Religion in Contemporary Society*, Palo Alto, CA: Marxfield Publishing.

Coleman, S. (1991) 'Faith Which Conquers the World. Swedish Fundamentalism and the Globalization of Culture', *Ethnos*, **56** (1/2), 6–18.

Collins, R. (ed.) (1983) *Sociological Theory*, San Francisco: Jossey Bass.

Conway, F. & Siegelman, J. (1982) 'Information Disease: Have Cults Created a New Mental Illness?', *Science Digest*, **60** (1), 86–92.

Cort, J. (1990) 'Models Of and For the Study of Jains', *Methods and Theory in the Study of Religion*, **2**, 42–71.

Cox, H. (1994) *Fire from Heaven*, Reading, Mass: Addison.

Crapanzano, V. & Garrison, V. (1977) *Case Studies in Spirit Possession*, New York: Wiley.

Crawford, R. (1984) 'A Cultural Account of Health: Control, Release and the Social Body', in J. McKinley (ed.) *Issues in the Political Economy of Health Care*, New York: Tavistock.

Criscuolo, N. & Crisp, T. (1994) *The Hand Book: The Complete Guide to Reading Hands*, London: Optima.

Crowley, V. (1994) *The Phoenix from the Flame*, London: Aquarian.

Croxon, R. (2000) *Teach Yourself Crystal Healing*, London: Hodder & Stoughton.

Culpepper, E. (1978) 'The Spiritual Movement in Radical Feminist Consciousness', in J. Needleman & G. Baker (eds.) *Understanding the New Religions*, New York: Seabury Press.

Cupitt, D. (1998) *Post-Christianity*, in P. Heelas (ed.) *Religion, Modernity and Post-Modernity*, Oxford: Blackwell.

Davies, C. (1999) 'The Fragmentation of the Religious Tradition of the Creation, After-life and Morality: Modernity Not Post-Modernity', *Journal of Contemporary Religion*, **14** (3), 333–60.

Davies, R. & Richardson, J. (1976) 'The Organization and Functioning of the Children of God', *Sociological Analysis*, **37** (4), 321–39.

Delamont, S. (1984) *Appetites and Identities: An Introduction to the Social Anthropology of Western Europe*, London: Routledge.

Demerath, N. & Williams, R. (1985) 'Civic Religion in an Uncivil Society', *Annals of the American Academy of Political and Social Science*, **480**, 154–66.

Derks, F. (1983) *Uittreding Uit Nieuwe Religieuze Bewegingen*, Unpublished research report in Psychology of Religion: Katholieke Universieit Nijmegen.

Dobbelaere, K. (1992) 'Roman Catholicism: Function Versus Performance', in B. Wilson (ed.) *Contemporary Religious Issues*, London: Bellew Publishing.

Douglas, M. & Isherwood, B. (1980) *The World of Goods: An Anthropology of Consumption*, Harmondsworth: Penguin.

Douglas, M. & Tipton, S. (eds.) (1982) *Religion and America: Spirituality in a Secular Age*, Boston: Beacon Press.

Downton, J. (1979) *Sacred Journeys*, New York: Columbia University Press.

Dreitzel, K. (1981) 'The Socialization of Nature: Western Attitudes Towards Body and Emotions', in P. Heelas & A. Lock (eds.) *Indigenous Psychologies: The Anthropology of the Self*, New York: Academic Press.

Dunas, P. (1992) *The Jains*, London: Routledge.

Durkheim, E. (1915) *The Elementary Forms of the Religious Life*, London: Allen & Unwin.

Ebaugh, H. (1988) 'Leaving Catholic Convents: Towards a Theory of Disengagement', in D. Bromley (ed.) *Falling from the Faith*, Newbury Park, CA: Sage.

Edgell, S. & Hetherington, K. (eds.) (1996) *Consumption Matters*, Oxford: Blackwell.

Ellwood, R. (1973) *One Way: The Jesus Movement and Its Meaning*, Engelwood Cliffs, NY: Prentice Hall.

Ellwood, R. (1979) *Alternative Altars: Unconventional and Eastern Spirituality in America*, Chicago: University of Chicago Press.

Ellwood, R. (1996) 'New Religions and the Reinvention of Polytheism: Alienation and the Reinvention of Polytheism: Alienation, Postmodernism and UFOs', in B. Ouellet & R. Bergeron (eds.) *Croyances et Sociétiés*, Montreal: Fides.

Esposito, J. & Watson, M. (eds.) (2000) *Religion and the Global Order*, Lampeter: University of Wales Press.

Farrar, S. (1971) *What Witches Do*, London: Hale.

Featherstone, M. (1982) 'The Body in Consumer Culture', *Theory, Culture and Society*, **1** (2), 18–31.

Featherstone, M. (1990) 'Introduction' of *The Global Culture*, London: Sage.

Featherstone, M., Hepworth, M. & Turner, B. (eds.) (1991) *The Body: Social Process and Cultural Theory*, London: Sage.

Feher, S. (1994) 'The Hidden Truth: Astrology as Worldview', in A. Greil & T. Robbins (eds.) *Between Sacred and Secular: Research and Theory on Quasi-Religion*, Religion and the Social Order, **4**, Greenwich, CT: JAI Press.

Fenn, R. (1990) 'Pre-Modern Religion in the Postmodern World: A Response to Professor Zylerber', *Social Compass*, **37** (1), 96–105.

Festinger, L., Riecken, H. & Schachter, S. (1965) *When Prophecy Fails*, Minneapolis: University of Minnesota Press.

Finke, R. (1977) 'The Consequences of Religious Competition: Supply-Side Explanations for Religious Change', in L. Young (ed.) *Rational Choice Theory and Religion: Summary and Assessment*, New York: Routledge.

Fischler, C. (1974) 'Astrology and French Society: The Dialectic of Archaism and Modernity', in E. Tiryakian (ed.) *On the Margins of the Visible*, New York: Wiley.

Flanagan, K. & Jupp, P. (eds.) (1996) *Post-Modernity, Sociology and Religion*, Basingstoke: Macmillan.

Friedrich, O. (1995) 'New Age Harmonies', in A. Lehman & J. Meyers (eds.) *Magic, Witchcraft, and Religion: An Anthropological Study of the Supernatural*, California State University: Chico.

Fursr, E. (ed.) (1991) *Palatable Worlds. Sociocultural Food Studies*, Oslo: Solum.

Gallagher, J. (2001) '"All I am is Religion": David Koresh's Christian Millenarianism', in S. Hunt (ed.) *Christian Millenarianism: From the Early Church to Waco*, London: Hurst & Co.

Gallop, G. & Castelli, J. (1989) *The People's Religion: American Faith in the 1990s*, New York: Macmillan.

Gee, P. (1992) 'The Demise of Liberal Christianity?', in B. Wilson (ed.) *Religion: Contemporary Issues*, London: Bellew Publishing.

Gerami, S. (1989) 'Religious Fundamentalism as a Response to Foreign Dependency: The Case of the Iranian Revolution', *Social Compass*, **36** (4), 45–80.

Gerard, D. (1985) 'Religious Attitudes and Values', in A. Abrams, D. Gerard & N. Timms (eds.) *Values and Social Change in Britain*, Basingstoke: Macmillan.

Gerlach, L. & Hine, V. (1970) *People, Power and Change: Movements of Social Transformation*, Indianapolis, IND: Bobs-Merril.

Giddens, A. (1991) *The Consequences of Modernity*, Cambridge: Polity Press.

Gill, R., Hadaway, C. & Marler, P. (1989) 'Is Religious Belief Declining in Britain?', *Journal for the Scientific Study of Religion*, **37** (3), 507–16.

Gilley, S. & Sheils, W. (1994) *A History of Religion in Britain*, Oxford: Blackwell.

Glock, C. (1958) *The Role of Deprivation in the Origin and Evolution of Religious Groups*, Survey Research Centre, A–15, Berkeley, CA: University of California Press.

Glock, C. & Bellah R. (eds.) (1976) *The New Religious Consciousness*, Berkeley, CA: University of California Press.

Goddijn, W. (1983) 'Some Religious Developments in the Netherlands (1947–1979)', *Social Compass*, **XXX** (4), 409–24.

Gordon, M. (1974) *Assimilation in American Life: The Role of Race, Religion and National Origins*, Oxford: Oxford University Press.

Gould, J. (1965) (ed.) *Penguin Survey of the Social Sciences*, Harmondsworth: Penguin.

Greeley, A. (1990) 'Religion and Musical Chairs', in T. Robbins & D. Anthony (eds.) *In Gods We Trust: New Patterns of Religious Pluralism in America*, New Brunswick, NJ: Transaction Publishers.

Greil, A. (1993) 'Explorations Along the Sacred Frontier: Notes on Para-Religions, Quasi-Religions, and Other Boundary Phenomenon', in D. Bromley & J. Hadden (eds.) *Religion and the Social Order*, **3**, part A, Greenwich, CT: JAI Press.

Greil, A. & Robbins, T. (1994) 'Introduction: Exploring the Boundaries of the Sacred', in A. Greil & T. Robbins (eds.) *Between Sacred and Secular: Research and Theory on Quasi-Religion*, Religion and the Social Order, **4**, Greenwich, CT: JAI Press.

Greil, A. & Robbins, T. (eds.) (1994) *Between Sacred and Secular: Research and Theory on Quasi-Religion*, Religion and the Social Order, **4**, Greenwich, CT: JAI Press.

Greil, A. & Rudy, D. (1984) 'What Have We Learned From Process Models of Conversion? An Examination of Ten Case Studies', *Sociological Focus*, **17** (4), 305–21.

Gretton, J. (1965) 'Denmark's Garden of Sex', *New Society*, 30th October.

Gusfield, R. (1963) *Symbolic Crusades: Status Politics and the American Temperance Movement*, Urbana, IL: University of Illinois Press.

Hadaway, C., Marler, P. & Chaves, M. (1993) 'What the Polls Don't Show', *American Sociological Review*, **58**, December, 741–52.

Hadden, J. & Shupe, A. (1987) 'Televangelism in America', *Social Compass*, **34** (1), 61–75.

Hamilton, M. (ed.) (1975) *The Charismatic Movement*, Erdmans, CA: University of California Press.

Hammond, P. (ed.) (1985) *The Sacred in a Secular Age*, Berkeley, CA: University of California Press.

Hammond, P. & Warner, K. (1995) 'Religion and Ethnicity in Late-Twentieth-Century America', in W. Roof (special ed.) *The Annals of the American Academy of Political and Social Sciences*, **572**, May, 55–66.

Hanegraaff, W. (1996) *New Age Religion and Western Culture: Esotericism in the Mirror of Secular Thought*, New York, Leiden: E.J. Brill.

Harding, S., Phillips. D. & Fogarty, K. (1986) *Contrasting Values in Western Europe*, London: Macmillan.

Harms, D. (1999) *Power Without and Within: A History of Legitimization and Subversion in Western Magical Tradition*, Unpublished MA, Department of Anthropology, University of New York at Buffalo.

Harper, C. (1974) 'Spirit-Filled Catholics. Some Biographical Comparisons', *Social Compass*, **XXI**, 311–24.

Harrison, M. (1974) 'Sources of Recruitment to Catholic Pentecostalism', *Journal for the Scientific Study of Religion*, **13** (3), 49–64.

Hartman, P. (1976) 'Social Dimensions of Occult Participation', *British Journal of Sociology*, **27** (2), 199–213.

Heelas, P. (1988) 'Western Europe: Self-Religions', in S. Sutherland & P. Clarke (eds.) *The World's Religions*, London: Routledge.

Heelas, P. (ed.) (1990) *Religion, Modernity and Post-Modernity*, Oxford: Blackwell.

Heelas, P. (1996) *The New Age Movement*, Oxford: Blackwell.

Heelas, P. (ed.) (1998) *Religion, Modernity and Post-Modernity*, Oxford: Blackwell.

Heelas, P. & Lock, A. (eds.) (1981) *Indigenous Psychologies: The Anthropology of the Self*, New York: Academic Press.

Heelas, P. & Thompson J. (1986) *The Way of the Heart*, Wellingborough: Aquarian.

Helweg, A. (1991) *Sikhs in England: The Development of a Migrant Community*, Delhi: Oxford University Press.

Hill, M. (1971) 'Typologie Sociologique de L'ordre Religieux', *Social Compass*, **XVIII**, 45–64.

Hill, M. (ed.) (1972) *A Sociological Yearbook of Religion in Britain*, **5**, London: SCM.

Himmelstein, J. (1986) 'The Social Basis of Anti-Feminism: Religious Networks and Culture', *Journal for the Scientific Study of Religion*, **25** (1), 1–15.

Holt, J. (1940) 'Holiness Religion: Culture Shock and Social Reorganization', *American Sociological Review*, **5**, 740–7.

Hornsby-Smith, M. (1987) *Roman Catholics in England*, Cambridge: Cambridge University Press.

Hunt, S. (1995) 'The "Toronto Blessing". A Rumour of Angels', *The Journal of Contemporary Religion*, **10** (3), 257–72.

Hunt, S. (1997) '"Doing the Stuff". The Vineyard Connection', in S. Hunt, M. Hamilton & T. Walter (eds.) *Charismatic Christianity: Sociological Perspectives*, Basingstoke: Macmillan.

Hunt, S. (1998) 'The Radical Kingdom of the Jesus Fellowship', *Pneuma*, **20** (1), 21–42.

Hunt, S. (1999) 'Considering the Alternatives', *Sociology Review*, **8** (3), 9–14.

Hunt, S. (2000) ' "Winning Ways": Globalisation and the Impact of the Health and Wealth Ministries', *Journal of Contemporary Religion*, **15** (3), 215–30.

Hunt, S. (ed.) (2001) *Christian Millenarianism: From the Early Church to Waco*, London: Hurst & Co.

Hunt, S. (2001a) *Anyone for Alpha?: Evangelism in a Post-Christian Society*, London: Darton, Longman & Todd.

Hunt (2001b) ' "At the Cutting Edge of What God is Doing": Millenarianism Aspects of British Neo-Pentecostalism', in S. Porter (ed.) *Faith in the Millenium*, Sheffield Academic Press: Sheffield.

Hunt, S. (2001c) 'The British Black Pentecostal "Revival": Identity and Belief in the "New" Nigerian Churches', *Ethnic and Racial Studies*, **24** (1), 104–24.

Hunt, S., Hamilton, M. & Walter, T. (1997) 'Introduction' to S. Hunt, M. Hamilton & T. Walter (eds.) *Charismatic Christianity: Sociological Perspectives*, Basingstoke: Macmillan.

Hunt, S., Hamilton, M. & Walter, T. (eds.) (1997) *Charismatic Christianity: Sociological Perspectives*, Basingstoke: Macmillan.

Hunter, J. (1987) *Evangelicalism: The Coming Generations*, Chicago: Chicago University Press.

Hurh, W.M. & Kim, K.C. (1990) 'Religious Participation of Korean Immigrants in the United States', *Journal for the Scientific Study of Religion*, **29**, 19–34.

Hutton, R. (1993) *The Pagan Religions of the British Isles*, Oxford: Blackwell.

Jeffery, P. (1992) *Migrants and Refugees. Muslim and Christian Pakistani Families in Bristol*, Cambridge: Cambridge University Press.

Johnson, B. (1961) 'Do Holiness Sects Socialize in Dominant Values?', *Social Forces*, **39**, 301–16.

Johnson, S. & Tamney, J. (1984) 'Support for the Moral Majority', *Journal for the Scientific Study of Religion*, **23** (2), 183–96.

Johnson, L. (1996) 'Speaking of Mother Earth: Native American Spirituality and the New Age Movement', in B. Ouellet & R. Bergeron (eds.) *Croyances et Sociétiés*, Fides: Montreal.

Joly, D. (1984) 'The Opinions of Mirupi Parents in Saltley, Birmingham, About Their Children's Schooling', *Research Papers: Muslims in Europe*, **24**, December.

Jorgenson, D. & Jorgensen, L. (1982) 'Social Meanings of the Occult', *Sociological Quarterly*, **23**, 273–89.

Judah, J. (1974) *Hare Krishna and the Counter Culture*, New York: John Wiley.

Karcher, S. (2000) *I Ching: An Introduction to Working With The Chinese Oracle of Change*, Dorset: Element Books.

Kelley, D. (1978) 'Why Conservative Churches are Still Growing', *Journal for the Scientific Study of Religion*, **17** (2), 165–72.

Kemp, A. (1993) *Witchcraft and Paganism Today*, London: Michael O'Mara Books.

Kepel, G. (1994) *The Revenge of God: The Resurgence of Islam, Christ and Judaism in the Modern World*, Cambridge: Polity Press.

Kepel, G. (1997) *Allah in the West: Islamic Movements in America and Europe*, Cambridge: Polity Press.

Khasala, K. (1986) 'New Religious Movements Turn to Worldly Success', *Journal for the Scientific Study of Religion*, **25** (2), 233–47.

King, T. (1993) *Sun Signs and Horoscopes*, Leicester: Blitz Editions.

Kirkpatrick, R., Rainey, R. & Rubi, K. (1986) 'An Empirical Study of Wiccan Religion in Post-Industrial Society', *Free Inquiry in Creative Sociology*, **14** (1), 33–8.

Kosmin, B. & Levy, C. (1983) *Jewish Identity in an Anglo-Jewish Community*, London: Board of Jews.

Kranenborg, R. (1996) 'Sects: A Danger to the Mental Health of the Population?', in B. Ouellet & R. Bergeron (eds.) *Croyances et Sociétiés*, Fides: Montreal.

Lang, K. & Lang, G. (1960) 'Decisions for Christ: Billy Graham in NYC', in A. Vidich & D. White (eds.) *Identity and Anxiety*, New York: The Free Press.

Larkin, G. (1974) 'Isolation, Integration and Secularization: A Case Study of the Netherlands', *Sociology Review*, **22** (1), 401–18.

Lehman, A. & Meyers, J. (eds.) (1995) *Magic, Witchcraft, and Religion: An Anthropological Study of the Supernatural*, California State University: Chico.

Lemert, C. (1975) 'Defining Non-Church Religion', *Review of Religious Research*, **16** (3) Spring, 186–97.

Levine, E. (1980) 'Rural Communes and Religious Cults', *Adolescent Psychiatry*, **8**, 138–53.

Lewis, R. & Bromley, G. (1987) 'The Cult Withdrawal Syndrome', *Journal for the Scientific Study of Religion*, **26** (4), 508–22.

Liebman, R. (1983) 'Mobilizing the Moral Majority', in R. Liebman & R. Wuthnow (eds.) *The New Christian Right*, New York: Aldine.

Liebman, R. & Wuthnow, R. (eds.) (1983) *The New Christian Right*, New York: Aldine.

Lincoln, C. (1989) 'The Muslim Mission in the Context of American Social History', in G. Wilmore (ed.) *African American Religious Studies*, Durham, NC: Duke University Press.

Lipset, S. (1963) 'Three Decades of the Radical Right', in D. Bell (ed.) *The Radical Right*, Garden City, NY: Doubleday.

Loftland, J. (ed.) (1976) *Doing Social Life*, New York: Wiley & Sons.

Loftland, J. (1979) 'White Hot Mobilization: Strategies of Millenarian Movements', in M. Zald & J. McCarthy (eds.) *The Dynamics of Social Movements: Resource Mobilization, Social Control, and Tactics*, Cambridge, Mass: Winthrop Publishers, 156-66.

Loftland, J. & Stark, R. (1965) 'Becoming a World Saver: A Theory of Conversion to a Deviant Perspective', *American Sociological Review*, **30**, 862–75.

Logan, J. (1975) 'Controversial Aspects of the Movement', in M. Hamilton (ed.) *The Charismatic Movement*, Erdmans, CA: University of California Press.

Loy, M., McPherson, B. & Kenyon, G. (1978) *Sport and Social Systems*, Reading, MA: Addison-Wesley.

Luckmann, T. (1967) *The Invisible Religion*, New York: Macmillan.

Luckmann, T. (1990) 'Shrinking Transcendence, Expanding Religion', *Sociological Analysis*, **50** (2), 127–38.

Luhrmann, T. (1989) *Persuasions of the Witch's Craft: Ritual Magic and Witchcraft in Present Day England*, Oxford: Blackwell.

Lynch, F. (1977) 'Towards a Theory of Conversion and Commitment to the Occult', *American Behavioral Scientist*, **20**, 887–909.

Lyotard, J. (1984) *The Post-Modern Condition*, Manchester: Manchester University Press.

Mandel, R. (1996) 'A Place of Their Own. Contesting Spaces and Defining Places in Berlin's Migrant Community', in B. Metcalf (ed.) *Making Muslim Space in North America and Europe*, Berkeley, CA: University of California Press.

Martin, D. (1965) 'Towards Eliminating the Concept of Secularization', in J. Gould (ed.) *Penguin Survey of the Social Sciences*, Harmondsworth: Penguin.

Martin, D. (1978) *A General Theory of Secularisation*, Oxford: Blackwell.

Martin, D. (1990) *Tongues of Fire: The Explosion of Pentecostalism in Latin America*, Oxford: Blackwell.

Martin, D. (1991) 'The Secularization Issue: Prospects and Retrospects', *British Journal of Sociology*, **42**, 465–74.

Martin, D. (1998) *Independent* newspaper, 11th July 1998.

Martin, D. & Hill, M. (eds.) (1970) *Sociological Year-book of Religion in Britain*, **3**, London: SCM.

Marty, M. (1970) 'The Occult Establishment', *Social Research*, **37**, 212–23.

Marty, M. (1978) *Fundamentalism*, Boston: Beacon Press.

Marx, J. & Ellison, D. (1975) 'Sensitivity Training and Communes: Contemporary Quests for Community', *Pacific Sociological Review*, **18** (4), 442–62.

Mauss, A. & Perrin, R. (1992) 'Saints and Seriousness', *Review of Religious Research*, **34**, 176–8.

McBain, D. (1992) *Discerning the Spirits. Checking the Truth in Signs and Wonders*, London: Marshall Pickering.

McBain, D. (1997) *Fire Over the Waters. Renewal Among the Baptists and Others From the 1960s to the 1990s*, London: Darton, Longman & Todd.

McCoy, E. (1999) *Astral Projection for Beginners*, Saint Paul, MIN: Llewellyn Publications.

McDonald, M. (1994) 'Celestine Prophet', *Mclean's*, October 10, 54.

McGuire, M. (1983) *Healing in Suburban America*, New Brunswick, NJ: Rutgers University Press.

McGuire, M. (1992) *Religion: The Social Context*, Belmont, CA: Wadsworth.

McHugh, N. & Swain, G. (1999) *The Mirror*, 7th September, 23–5.

McKinley, J. (ed.) (1984) *Issues in the Political Economy of Health Care*, New York: Tavistock.

McLuhan, M. (1962) *The Guttenberg Galaxy*, Toronto: Toronto University Press.

Melton, G. (1987) 'How New is New? The Flowering of the "New" Religious Consciousness Since 1965', in D. Bromley & P. Hammond (eds.) *The Future of the New Religious Movements*, Macon, GA: Mercer University Press.

Metcalf, B. (ed.) (1996) *Making Muslim Space in North America and Europe*, Berkeley, CA: University of California Press.

Meyer, J. (1987) 'Self and Life Course: Institutionalization and its Effects', in G. Thomas, F. Meyer & J. Boli (eds.) *Institutional Structure: Constituting State, Society and the Individual*, Newbury Park, LA: Sage.

Miller, D. (1997) *Reinventing American Protestantism*, Los Angeles: University of California Press.

Miller, R. & Marzik, T. (eds.) (1986) *Immigrants and Religion in Urban America*, Philadelphia: Temple University Press.

Modood, T. (1990) 'British Asian Muslims and the Rushdie Affair', *British Political Quarterly*, **61**, 143–60.

Munro, R. (1996) 'The Consumption View of Self: Extension, Exchange and Identity', in S. Edgell & K. Hetherington (eds.) *Consumption Matters*, Oxford: Blackwell.

Needleman, J. & Baker, G. (eds.) (1978) *Understanding the New Religions*, New York: Seabury Press.

Neitz, M. (1990) 'Quasi-Religions and Cultural Movements: Contemporary Witchcraft as a Churchless Religion', in A. Greil & T. Robbins (eds.) *Between Sacred and Secular: Research and Theory on Quasi-Religion*, Religion and the Social Order, **4**, Greenwich, CT: JAI Press.

Nelson, G. (1968) 'The Concept of Cult', *Sociological Review*, **16** (3), 351–62.

Nesbitt, E. (1997) ' "Splashed with Goodness", The Many Meanings of Amrit for Young British Sikhs', *Journal of Contemporary Religion*, **12** (1) January, 17–34.

Nesti, A. (1990) 'Implicit Religion: The Issues and Dynamics of a Phenomenon', *Social Compass*, **37** (4), 423–38.

Niebuhr, H. (1957) *The Social Sources of Denominationalism*, New York: World Publishing.

Nielson, S. (1989) 'Islamic Communities in Britain', in P. Badman (ed.) *Religion, State, and Society in Modern Britain*, Lampeter: The Edwin Mellen Press.

Oegema, D. (1987) 'Potentials, Networks, Motivations, and Barriers and Steps Towards Participation in Social Movements', *American Sociological Review*, **52**, 519–31.

O'Toole, R. (1977) *The Precipitous Path: Studies in Political Sects*, Toronto: Peter Martin.

Ouellet, B. & Bergeron, R. (eds.) (1996) *Croyances et Sociétiés*, Montreal: Fides.

Palmer, S. (1994) *Moon Sisters, Krishna Mothers, Rajneesh Lovers*, Syracuse, NY: Syracuse University Press.

Parsons, G. (ed.) (1993) *The Growth of Religious Diversity. Britain Since 1945*, 1, London: Routledge.

Pavlino, A. (1995) 'Spiritualism, Santeria, Brujeria and Voodooism', *Journal of Teaching in Social Work*, **12**, 105–24.

Peale, N. (1940) *A Guide to Confident Living*, New York: Prentice Hall.

Peel, R. (1994) *Astrology and Heredity: The Threads of Life*, London: Blandford.

Percy, M. (1995) 'Fundamentalism. A Problem for Phenomenology', *Journal of Contemporary Religion*, **10** (1), 83–91.

Percy, M. & Taylor, R. (1997) 'Something for the Weekends, Sir? Leisure, Ecstasy and Identity in Football and Contemporary Religion', *Leisure Studies*, **16**, 37–49.

Peven, D. (1968) 'The Use of Religious Revival Techniques to Indoctrinate Personnel: The Home Party Sales Organization', *Sociological Quarterly*, **20**, 97–106.

Porter, S. (ed.) (2001) *Faith in the Millennium*, Sheffield Academic Press: Sheffield.

Porter, S. & Richter, P. (eds.) (1995) *The Toronto Blessing Or Is It?*, London: Darton, Longman & Todd.

Porter, T. (1992) 'Some Recent Developments in Seventh-day Adventism', in B. Wilson (ed.) *Religion: Contemporary Issues*, London: Bellew Publishing.

Prebish, C. (1984) 'Heavenly Father, Divine Goalie: Sport and Religion', *The Antioch Review*, **42** (3), 306–18.

Puttick, E. (1999) 'Women in New Religious Movements', in B. Wilson & J. Cresswell (eds.) *New Religious Movements: Challenge and Response*, London: Routledge.

Quimby, R. (1969) *The Quimby Manuscript*, New York: Thomas Lowell.

Rabinowitz, J. (1992) 'The Effects of Demographic Dynamics on Jewish Communal Participation in the United States', *Sociological Analysis*, **53** (3), 39–54.

Reader, I. (2001) 'Violent Millenarianism with a Christian Touch: Syncretic Themes in the Millennial Perspective of Aum Shinrikyo', in S. Hunt (ed.) *Christian Millenarianism*, London: Hurst & Co.

Redford, H. (1995) *The Celestine Prophecy: An Experiential Guide*, New York: Warner Books.

Reid, J. (1996) 'The New Age Movement and the Conflation of Religion and Psychology', in B. Ouellet & R. Bergeron (eds.) *Croyances et Sociétiés*, Montreal: Fides.

Reiff, D. (1966) *The Triumph of the Therapeutic*, New York: Harper Row.

Richardson, J. (ed.) (1983) *Conversion Careers: In and Out of the New Religious Movements*, London: Sage.

Richey, R. & Jones, D. (eds.) (1967) *American Civic Religion*, New York: Harper & Row.

Richter, P. (1995) 'God is Not a Gentleman', in S. Porter & P. Richter (eds.) *The Toronto Blessing Or Is It?*, London: Darton, Longman & Todd.

Richter, P. & Francis, L. (1998) *Gone But Not Forgotten: Church Leaving and Returning*, London: Darton, Longman & Todd.

Robbins, A. & Palmer, S. (eds.) (1997) *Millenium, Messiahs, and Mayhem: Contemporary Apocalyptic Movements*, New York: Routledge.

Robbins, T. & Anthony, D. (1990) (eds.) *In Gods We Trust: New Patterns of Religious Pluralism in America*, New Brunswick, NJ: Transaction Publishers.

Robbins, T. & Palmer, S. (1997) 'Patterns of Contemporary Apocalypticism in North America', in A. Robbins & S. Palmer (eds.) *Millenium, Messiahs, and Mayhem: Contemporary Apocalyptic Movements*, New York: Routledge.

Roberts, R. (1994) 'Power and Empowerment', *Religion Today*, 9 (3), 3–13.

Robertson, R. (1970) *The Sociological Interpretation of Religion*, Oxford: Blackwell.

Robertson, R. (1992) *Globalization: Social Theory and Global Culture*, London: Sage.

Rochford, E. (1985) *Hare Krishna*, New Brunswick, NJ: Rutgers University Press.

Roof, W. (1976) 'Traditional Religion in Contemporary Society: A Theory of Local-Cosmopolitan Plausibility', *American Sociological Review*, 41, 195–208.

Roof, W. (special ed.) (1995) *The Annals of the American Academy of Political and Social Sciences*, 572, May, 55–66.

Roof, W. & McKinney, W. (1985) 'Denominational America and the New Religious Pluralism', *Annals*, 480, 24–38.

Roof, W. & McKinney, W. (1987) *American Mainline Religion: Its Changing Shape and Future*, New Brunswick, NJ: Rutgers University Press.

Ross, E. & Wright, R. (1990) *The Diving Mind. A Guide to Dowsing and Self Awareness*, Rochester, VER: Destiny Books.

Sahgal, J. & Yuval-Davies, N. (eds.) (1992) *Refusing Holy Orders*, London: Virago Press.

Sargant, W . (1957) *Battle for the Mind*, London: Heinemann.

Schlsinger, A. (1932) 'A Critical Period in American Religion, 1875–1890', *Massachusetts Historical Society Proceedings*, LXIV.

Sellerberg, M. (1991) 'In Food We Trust: Virtually Necessary Confidence and Unfamiliar Ways of Attaining It', in E. Fursr (ed.) *Palatable Worlds. Sociocultural Food Studies*, Oslo: Solum.

Sharot, S. (1992) 'Religious Fundamentalism: Neo-Traditionalism in Modern Societies', in B. Wilson (ed.) *Religion: Contemporary Issues*, London: Bellew Publishing.

Shupe, A. (1997) 'Christian Reconstructionism and the Angry Rhetoric of Neo-Pentecostalism in T. Robbins & S. Palmer (eds.) *Millenium, Messiahs, and Mayhem: Contemporary Apocalyptic Movements*, New York: Routledge.

Shupe, A. & Bromley, D. (1979) *The 'Moonies' in America*, Beverly Hills, CA: Sage.

Sihvo, J. (1988) 'Religion and Secularization in Finland', *Social Compass*, XXXV/1, 67–90.

Simpson, J. (1983) 'Moral Issues and Status Politics', in R. Liebman & R. Wuthnow (eds.) *The New Christian Right*, New York: Aldine.

Siskind, A. (1990) 'The Sullivan Institute/ Fourth Wall Community: "Radical" Psychotherapy as Quasi-Religion', in A. Greil & T. Robbins (eds.) *Between Sacred and Secular: Research and Theory on Quasi-Religion*, Religion and the Social Order, **4**, Greenwich, CT: JAI Press.

Sjodin, U. (2002) 'The Swedes and the Paranormal', *Journal of Contemporary Religion*, **17** (1), 75–85.

Smart, N. (1971) *The Religious Experience of Mankind*, London: Fontana.

Smart, N. (1995) *Worldviews: Crosscultural Explorations of Human Beliefs*, Engelwood Cliffs, NJ: Prentice Hall.

Smith, T. (1992) 'Are Conservative Churches Really Growing?', *Review of Religious Research*, **33**, 305–59.

Snow, D. (1976) *The Nichiren Shoshu Buddhist Movement in America*, Unpublished PhD Thesis, Los Angeles: University of California.

Snow, D. & Machalek, R. (1983) 'The Convert as a Social Type', in R. Collins (ed.) *Sociological Theory*, San Francisco: Jossey Bass.

Snow, D. & Phillips, C. (1980) 'The Loftland-Stark Conversion Model: A Critical Reassessment', *Social Problems*, **27**, 430–47.

Somers, J. (1990) 'Tibetan Buddhism in Britain', *Religion Today*, **6** (2), 1–3.

Stacey, W. & Shupe, A. (1982) 'Correlates of Support for the Electronic Church', *Journal for the Scientific Study of Religion*, **21** (4), 291–303.

Staples, C. & Mauss, A. (1987) 'Conversion and Commitment', *Journal for the Scientific Study of Religion*, **26** (2), 83–147.

Stark, R. & Bainbridge, W. (1980) 'Secularization, Revival and Cult Formation', *Annual Review of the Social Sciences of Religion*, **4**, 85–119.

Stark, R. & Bainbridge, W. (1985) *The Future of Religion*, Berkeley, CA: University of California Press.

Stark, R. & Bainbridge, W. (1987) *A Theory of Religion*, Berkeley, CA: University of California Press.

Stoeltzel, J. (1983) *Europe at the Crossroads*, Paris: Presse Universitaire de France.

Strauss, R. (1976) 'Changing Oneself: Seekers and the Creative Transformations of Life Experience', in J. Loftland (ed.) *Doing Social Life*, New York: Wiley & Sons.

Sutherland, S. & Clarke, P. (eds.) (1988) *The World's Religions*, London: Routledge.

Tabor, J. & Gallagher, E. (1995) *Why Waco?*, Berkeley, CA: University of California Press.

Thomas, G., Meyer, F. & Boli, J. (eds.) (1987) *Institutional Structure: Constituting State, Society and the Individual*, Newbury Park, LA: Sage.

Thomas, K. (1974) *Religion and the Decline of Magic*, London: Weidenfeld & Nicolson.

Thomas, T. (1993) 'Hindu Dharma in Dispersion', in G. Parsons (ed.) *The Growth of Religious Diversity: Britain from 1945. Volume 1, Traditions*, London: Routledge.

Thompson, J. (1974) 'La Participation Catholique dans Le Mouvement du Renouveau Charismatic', *Social Compass*, **XXI** (2), 325–44.

Thompson, W. (1997) 'Charismatic Politics: The Social and Political Impact of Renewal', in S. Hunt, M. Hamilton & T. Walter (eds.) *Charismatic Christianity: Sociological Perspectives*, London: Macmillan.

Tinney, J. (1971) 'The Black Origins of the Pentecostal Movement', *Christianity Today*, 8th November, 4–6.

Tipton, S. (1982) *Getting Saved From the Sixties*, Berkeley, CA: University of California Press.

Tiryakian, E. (1974) 'Towards the Sociology of Esoteric Culture', in E. Tiryakian (ed.) *On the Margins of the Visible*, New York: Wiley.

Tiryakian, E. (ed.) (1974) *On the Margins of the Visible*, New York: Wiley.

Torrey, E. (1972) 'What Western Psychiatrists Can Learn from Witch Doctors', *American Journal of Orthopsychology*, **42**, 69–76.

Towler, R. (1974) *Homo Religiosus: Sociological Problems in the Study of Religion*, London: Constable.

Troeltsch, E. (1931) *The Social Teachings of the Christian Churches*, London: Allen & Unwin.

Truzzi, M. (1972) 'Definitions and Dimensions of the Occult: Towards a Sociological Perspective', *Journal of Popular Culture*, 5, 635–46.

Turner, B. (1991) 'Recent Developments in the Theory of the Body', in M. Featherstone, M. Hepworth & B. Turner (eds.) *The Body: Social Process and Cultural Theory*, London: Sage.

Tylor, E. (1903) *Primitive Culture*, London: Mowbray.

Victor, J.(1992) *Satanic Panic*, Chicago: Open Court Publishing.

Vidich, A. & White, D. (eds.) (1960) *Identity and Anxiety*, New York: The Free Press.

Volt, J. (1991) *The Muslims of America*, New York: Oxford University Press.

Wagner, P. (1988) *The Third Wave of the Holy Spirit*, Ann Arbor, MI: Servant Press.

Wagner, P. (1992) *Warfare Prayer*, Venturer, CA: Regal Books

Wald, K., Owen, D. & Hill, S. (1989) 'Evangelical Politics and Status Issues', *Journal for the Scientific Study of Religion*, **18** (1), 1–16.

Walker, A. (1985) 'From Revival to Restoration. The Emergence of Britains New Classical Pentecostalism', *Social Compass*, **32** (2–3), 261–71.

Walker, A. (1997) 'Thoroughly Modern: Sociological Reflections on the Charismatic Movement from the End of the Twentieth Century', in S. Hunt, M. Hamilton & T. Walter (eds.) *Charismatic Christianity: Sociological Perspectives*, Basingstoke: Macmillan.

Wallis, R. (1976a) *The Road to Total Freedom: A Sociological Analysis of Scientology*, London: Heinemann.

Wallis, R. (1976b) 'Observations on the Children of God', *Sociological Review*, **24** (4), 807.

Wallis, R. (1982) 'Charisma, Commitment and Control in a New Religious Movement', in R. Wallis (ed.) *Millennialism and Charisma*, Belfast: Queen's University Press.

Wallis, R. (ed.) (1982) *Millennialism and Charisma*, Belfast: Queen's University Press.

Wallis, R. (1984) *The Elementary Forms of New Religious Life*, London: Routledge & Kegan Paul.

Walter, T. (1990) 'Why Are Most Church-goers Women?', *Vox Evangelica*, **95**, 599–625.

Waring, P. (1997) *The Way of Feng Shui: Harmony, Health, Wealth and Happiness*, London: Souvenir Press.

Warner, R. (1993) 'Work in Progress Towards a New Paradigm for the Sociological Study of Religion in the United States', *American Journal of Sociology*, **98** (5), 1044–93.

Warren-Davis, D. (1989) *Astrology and Health: A Beginner's Guide*, London: Headway.

Waugh, E., Abu-Laban, B. & Qureshi, R. (1983) *The Muslim Community in North America*, New York: Free Press.

Weber, M. (1965) *The Sociology of Religion*, London: Methuen.

Weinstein, D. (1992) 'Television as Religion: The Reemergence of the Conscience-Collective', *Listening: Journal of Religion and Culture*, **20** (1), 6–16.

Westly, F. (1978) 'The Cult of Man: Durkheim's Predictions and Religious Movements', *Sociological Analysis*, **39**, 135–45.

Whitemore, J. (1995) 'Religious Dimensions of the UFO Abductee Experience', in J. Lewis (ed.) *The Gods Have Landed: New Religions from Other Worlds*, Albany, NY: New York State University Press.

Williamson, L. (1998) *Contacting the Spiritual World: How to Develop Your Psychic Abilities and Stay in Touch With Loved Ones*, London: Piatkus.

Willoughby, W. (1981) *Does American Need a Moral Majority?*, Plainfield: Haven Books.

Wilmore, G. (ed.) (1989) *African American Religious Studies*, Durham, NC: Duke University Press.

Wilson, B. (1966) *Religion in a Secular Society*, London: Weidenfeld & Nicolson.

Wilson, B. (1970) *Religious Sects*, London: Heinemann.

Wilson, B. (1976) *Contemporary Transformations of Religion*, London: Oxford University Press.

Wilson, B. (1979) *Contemporary Transformations of Religion*, Oxford: Clarendon Press.

Wilson, B. (1982) *Religion in Sociological Perspectives*, Oxford: Oxford University Press.

Wilson, B. (ed.) (1992) *Contemporary Religious Issues*, London: Bellew Publishing.

Wilson, B. & Cresswell, J. (eds.) (1999) *New Religious Movements: Challenge and Response*, Routledge: Sage.

Woodhead, L.& Heelas, P. (eds.) (2000) *Religion in Modern Times*, Oxford: Blackwell.

Wright, N. (1997) 'The Nature and Variety of Restorationism and the "House Church" Movement', in S. Hunt, M. Hamilton & T. Walter (eds.) *Charismatic Christianity: Sociological Perspectives*, Basingstoke: Macmillan.

Wright, S. (1987) *Leaving Cults: The Dynamics of Defection*, Washington, DC: Society for the Scientific Study of Religion.

Wright, S. (1988) 'Leaving New Religious Movements', in D. Bromley (ed.) *Falling From the Faith*, Newbury Park, CA: Sage.

Wuthnow, R. (1976) *The Consciousness Reformation*, Berkeley, CA: University of California Press.

Wuthnow, R. (1978) *Experimentation in American World Religion*, Berkeley, CA: University of California Press.

Wuthnow, R. (1988) *The Restructuring of American Religion: Society and Faith Since World War II*, Princeton: University of Princeton Press.

Wuthnow, R. (1993) *Christianity in the Twenty-First Century*, Oxford: Oxford University Press.

Yinger, T. (1967) *The Invisible Religion*, New York: Macmillan.

York, M. (1995) 'The Church Universal and Triumphant', *Journal of Contemporary Religion*, **10** (1), 62–71.

York, M. (1996) 'Post-Modernity, Architecture, Society and Religion: 'A Heap of Broken Images', or 'A Change of Heart', in K. Flanagan & P. Jupp (eds.) *Post-Modernity, Sociology and Religion*, Basingstoke: Macmillan.

York, M. (2001) 'New Age Millenarianism and Its Christian Influences', in S. Hunt (ed.) *Christian Millenarianism: From the Early Church to Waco*, London: Hurst Publishers.

Young, L. (ed.) (1977) *Rational Choice Theory and Religion: Summary and Assessment*, New York: Routledge.

Zald, M. & McCarthy, J. (eds.) (1979) *The Dynamics of Social Movements. Resource Mobilization, Social Control, and Tactics*, Cambridge, MA: Winthrop Publishers, 156-66.

Zed, S. (1997) *The Complete Guide to Coffee Grounds and Tea Leaf Reading*, Israel: Astrology.

Zurcher, L. & Kirkpatrick, R. (1976) *Citizens for Decency: Anti-Pornography Crusades as Status Defence*, Austin: Texas University Press.

Glossary of terms

alternative medicine	a generic term designating a vast range of medical systems and therapies not generally used in orthodox scientific medicine.
alternative religion	a generic term designating a vast range of religions that do not constitute mainstream Christianity.
animism	the belief that all living objects, places, natural phenomena are imbued with a soul or spirit.
anthropology	the study of man, in particular in pre-industrial societies. Cultural anthropology is concerned with the belief system and religious beliefs and practices of such societies.
boundary maintenance	the attempt by subcultural groups to differentiate themselves from other social groups.
brainwashing	a term suggesting that the mind has been cleared of established ideas by persistent suggestion and indoctrination.
Buddhism	world religion based upon the original teachings of the Buddha and subsequent enlightened teachers.
conservative religion	that wing of any given faith which tends towards a maintenance of tradition and a belief in the literalism of all scripture and holy writings.
conversion	a much-debated term related to a change in a person's worldview to one that is overwhelmingly religious in orientation.
cult	a term used in sociology to categorize innovating forms of religion, which may range from those espousing aspects of human potential to expressions of mysticism.
cult controversies	disputes concerning the beliefs, practices, and strategies of conversion associated with unconventional religious groups.

denomination	a form of church organization that is separate from the state and stresses voluntary association and freedom of conscience in matters of belief and practice.
disengagement	the process by which members of religious organizations come to give up their allegiance.
divination	techniques for providing insight into or discovery of the unknown or the future by supernatural means.
doomsday cults	a negative term used to describe religious movements that believe in the imminent end of the world.
easternization	the growing impact of eastern culture, including belief systems, on Western societies.
ethnic minorities	a term pertaining to cultural or ethnic groupings other than the dominant socio-cultural majority.
faith movement	branch of Pentecostalism which puts an emphasis on the belief that 'divine' health and prosperity is the guaranteed right of every believer.
feminist spiritualities	forms of religion which venerate female deities and/or accentuate female qualities.
functional definitions of religion	definitions of religion based upon the normative functioning of religion for society as a whole, social groups, or for the benefit of the individual.
fundamentalism	expressions of religion that claim the true interpretation of the faith by a return to the 'fundamentals'. This often includes a form of elitism and literal interpretation of holy writings.
globalization	a term which suggests that national, political, and cultural boundaries are breaking down. Countries across the world are increasingly influenced by other cultures and traditions as the economic and power structures of these societies become interrelated and interdependent at a global level.
glocalization	the accommodation of global cultural, political, and economic influences to localized conditions.
goddess worship	a veneration of the female deity(ies), especially the Earth Mother (Gaia).
heathen	one who venerates ancient gods and embraces a non-monotheistic form of religion.
Hinduism	the polytheistic religion of the Hindus which stresses the necessity of a better rebirth.

holistic	that pertaining to the unity and wholeness of all things.
human potential movement	a movement, becoming increasingly popular since the 1960s, which puts an emphasis upon human physical, intellectual, and sometimes spiritual development.
Islam	a world faith based on the belief in the one God (Allah), the 'truth' of the holy scriptures of the Koran, and the teachings of the Prophet Muhammad.
Jesus movement	generic term used to denote a number of groups broadly espousing a Pentecostal form of Christianity. It largely emerged on the West Coast of the USA in the late 1960s.
Judaism	the religion of the Jewish people based in the belief of the one God, the scriptures of the Old Testament, and the faith in the coming messiah.
liberal Christianity	that wing of Christianity which seeks to make the faith relevant to contemporary conditions. It is identified by a concern for social issues and a non-literate interpretation of the miraculous in Judaic-Christian scripture.
magic	the art of influencing the course of events by the attempted occult control of nature or spirits.
mainstream religion	a term generally denoting the historical dominance of various strands of Christianity as organized into churches and denominations.
marginalization	a term denoting the stigmatization of individuals and groups as a result of their actual or perceived negative attributes.
medicalization	a term which denotes the increasing spread of the medical profession and its ideology into various dimensions of social life.
millenarianism	literally the belief in the thousand year reign of Christ to come. Sociologically speaking, the term denotes expectations of the end of the world and establishment of a supernatural order.
modernization	the process of social development identified by such features as the growth of rationalism and science and the decline of religion, industrialization, a division of labour, high standards of living and public education, and a capitalist economy.
monotheism	the belief in the one God, typified by Christianity, Islam, and Judaism.
morality	an abstract system of beliefs pertaining to what is perceived as desirably good and what is intrinsically evil.

moral panic	a sudden and widespread exaggerated fear that the morality of society is being undermined.
mysticism	a term that refers to the spiritually allegorical; occultist, esoteric, or of hidden spiritual knowledge. It is often identified with eastern religion but can be found in many expressions of religiosity.
Neo-Pentecostalism	a term that originally referred to the Pentecostal movement within mainline churches from the mid-twentieth-century. It now denotes various new expressions of Pentecostalism (see below).
New Age	a generic term referring to a movement emerging since the 1970s that has various strands including occultism, paganism, animism, polytheistic beliefs, magic, and witchcraft.
New Christian Right	a movement associated with Christian fundamentalism in the USA that is directed towards bringing moral and political change.
New Religious Movements	a generic term referring to numerous alternative religions arising from the mid-1960s including those derived from the major world faiths, the human potential movement, or syncretic in belief and practice.
objectivity	an unbiased approach to understanding the world, including the social world.
occult	spiritual knowledge regarded as secret, esoteric, and mysterious beyond the range of ordinary knowledge; involving the supernatural, mystical, and magical.
pagan	a reference to forms of religion that are non-monotheistic, based upon occultism and animism. The term is closely associated with that of heathenism, hence that which is not Christian.
patriarchy	societies or social structures established on the rule and dominance of the male sex.
Pentecostalism	movement of Christian renewal emerging outside the established churches at the beginning of the twentieth-century in the form of 'classical' Pentecostalism. Pentecostalism places great emphasis on the charismata, healing, prophecy, speaking in tongues, etc.
phenomenological approach	a sociological approach concerned with how human beings make sense of the natural and social world.
polytheism	a belief system pertaining to the existence of more than one god.
post-modernity	a form of social life which comes after modernity. It is a result of a period of intensified change that creates uncertainty, ambiguity, cultural fragmentation, and diversity.

Protestantism	a reference to any of the Christian bodies that separated from the Roman communion during the Reformation. It now refers specifically to all non-Catholic churches and denominations.
quasi-Christianity	expressions of religiosity that cull some beliefs and practices from traditional Christianity, but in other respects diverge considerably from the mainstream faith.
quasi-religions	organizations or phenomena in social life that express some dimensions of religiosity, whether described in terms of functional or substantive definitions of religion.
rationalism	the way of understanding the world with reference to reason and scientific procedures.
reincarnation	the belief in the transmigration of the soul, that the soul is reborn after death into another human or animal form.
religious socialization	the social pressures and conventions by which people may come to accept the legitimacy of the beliefs and practice of a particular religious faith.
renewal movement	movements which seek to reinvigorate a particular religious faith, often by attempting to seek the initial spiritual experiences that began it.
Roman Catholicism	that part of the Latin church that remained under Roman obedience after the Reformation and accepts the jurisdiction of the Pope as supreme head of that church.
Satanism	veneration of the personification of evil.
sects	a term designating breakaway factions from established religious traditions. They are identified by exclusivism, elitism, and disassociation from the world.
secularization	although sociological definitions differ, the term usually denotes the decline of religion and/or the shift of religiosity from the public to private sphere of belief or practice.
shamanism	the attempt to contact the spirit world through various forms of divination.
Sikhism	a monotheistic sect derived from Hinduism.
spiritual marketplace	a sociological term implying that, literally or metaphorically, religion has become subject to the dynamics of consumerism and economic production.
stigmatization	negative labels applied to those who are perceived to have negative attributes.

substantive definitions of religions	definitions of religion that focus upon the importance of beliefs systems related to the supernatural.
supply-side religion	term denoting the organizational and productive element of contemporary religion that satisfies the consumer 'demand' of religion.
survivalist cults	USA-based movements which stockpile food and weapons in anticipation of a global apocalypse that they believe will come through nuclear war, environmental disaster and racial conflict.
syncretic movements	religious movements which bring together the beliefs and practices of different faiths into one framework of doctrine and practice.
UFO cults	forms of spirituality focusing on a veneration of extra-terrestrial beings.
visualization	strategies utilized in healing and other practices to bring about metaphysical change by use of the imagination.
witchcraft	the attempt to utilize powers through non-scientific and metaphysical means, often including spells and incantations.

Index